W9-CMP-967

TEACHING PHYSICAL EDUCATION IN SECONDARY SCHOOLS

A Textbook on Instructional Methods

McGraw-Hill Series in Education

HAROLD BENJAMIN, *Consulting Editor-in-Chief*

ARNO A. BELLACK *Teachers College, Columbia University*
CONSULTING EDITOR, SUPERVISION CURRICULUM AND METHODS IN EDUCATION

HAROLD BENJAMIN *Emeritus Professor of Education*
George Peabody College for Teachers
CONSULTING EDITOR, FOUNDATIONS IN EDUCATION

WALTER F. JOHNSON *Michigan State University*
CONSULTING EDITOR, GUIDANCE, COUNSELING, AND
STUDENT PERSONNEL IN EDUCATION

McGraw-Hill Series in Health Education, Physical Education, and Recreation

DEOBOLD B. VAN DALEN, *Consulting Editor*

EVANS, BACON, BACON, AND STAPLETON · Physical Education for Elementary Schools
KENNEY AND LAW · Wrestling
KNAPP AND LEONHARD · Teaching Physical Education in Secondary Schools: A Textbook on Instructional Methods
KRAUS · Recreation Leader's Handbook
METHENY · Body Dynamics
METHENY · Movement and Meaning
TORNEY · Swimming
WILLGOOSE · Evaluation in Health Education and Physical Education

TEACHING PHYSICAL EDUCATION IN SECONDARY SCHOOLS

A Textbook on Instructional Methods

Clyde Knapp

Professor of Education and Physical Education
University of Illinois

Patricia Hagman Leonhard

Lecturer in Educational Psychology, College of Education
University of Illinois

68928

McGraw-Hill Book Company

New York, St. Louis, San Francisco, Toronto, London, Sydney

TEACHING PHYSICAL EDUCATION IN SECONDARY SCHOOLS:
A Textbook on Instructional Methods
Copyright © 1968 by McGraw-Hill, Inc. All Rights Reserved.

TEACHING METHODS FOR PHYSICAL EDUCATION:
A Textbook for Secondary School Teachers
Copyright 1953 by McGraw-Hill, Inc. All Rights Reserved.
Printed in the United States of America. No part of this publication may be reproduced, stored in a retrieval system, or transmitted, in any form or by any means, electronic, mechanical, photocopying, recording, or otherwise, without the prior written permission of the publisher.

Library of Congress Catalog Card Number: 68–13518
35075
34567890 MAMM 754321069

GV363
K58
1968

PREFACE

The central purpose of *Teaching Physical Education in Secondary Schools* is essentially the same as its first edition, *Teaching Methods for Physical Education:* to present material which will help both in-service and preservice teachers of physical education gain an in-depth understanding of the teaching process. It focuses on instructional methods. It deals with the underlying factors and principles related to the selection and use of teaching methods, and presents a wide variety of basic styles, patterns, techniques, and procedures appropriate for use in teaching secondary school physical education.

The text is organized to cast the role of methods in the context of the accepted structure of the total work of the school. This design recognizes the areas of *curriculum, instruction, supervision, administration,* and *evaluation* as interrelated processes. By maintaining a sharp focus on the instruction process within this broader framework, a more meaningful and realistic view of teaching methods can be presented.

Prepared as a text for methods, or teaching-techniques courses during the junior, senior, or fifth year of teacher-education programs, this book assumes that previous or parallel experiences serve to assist students in developing personal and professional competencies. Individual competence in teaching rests upon personal qualities, expertise in subject matter, understanding of the function of physical education in the total education program, understanding of adolescents and how they learn, and ability to utilize apt methods, techniques, and procedures for organizing and guiding the physical education learning experiences of secondary school youth.

This volume assumes that the subject matter of physical education, the contribution of physical education to the total educational program, and curriculum planning have already been studied in other parts of the professional curriculum. It also recognizes that most teacher-education programs expose students to introductory learnings in adolescent psychology, evaluation, and administration of physical education. This textbook, which views instructional methods as the heart of the teaching strategy—the work of the teacher—serves to reinforce a student's learning in all these areas of the teaching process.

This revised edition has been reorganized to strengthen this central purpose. Also, in light of significant changes which have occurred since the first edition was published, new material has been added and much of the original material has been recast. Among recent advances reflected throughout the book are the increased national attention to education on all levels; the changing societal function of secondary schools; the increased enrollment in secondary schools; the changes in the socioeconomic climate for today's adolescents; the national attention to physical fitness; and the research explosion in education, psychology, and technology which has caused the methods, materials, and functions of teachers to be closely reexamined.

The authors' basic philosophy of physical education and teaching remains the same. Emphasis is placed upon physical education which, as an important means for personal and social development, integrates with other phases of the school curriculum in achieving the broad social objectives of education. Teaching is considered an act of inquiry in which the teacher thinks and acts creatively, ever evaluating, ever changing his methods and procedures.

Methods, therefore, are to be studied, understood, and tried rather than learned, remembered, and applied. Since teaching represents an interwoven human enterprise, teachers cannot rely upon a collection of mechanical techniques. Underlying facts and principles indicate the desirable procedures to be followed in given situations; these situations involve a variety of circumstances concerning learners, school and community characteristics, facilities, supplies, time, and teachers. Accordingly, this volume serves to show prospective and beginning teachers how to choose effective and efficient methods based upon analysis of learners and of learning situations.

Theory and practice meet in the consideration of methods. Those who attempt to teach methods are frequently confronted with student frustration caused by gaps beween theory and practice. Theory and philosophy point the way for practice. But it is necessary for the beginning teacher to translate theory which he accepts as ideal into practice which may fall short of expectations. Hence, a purpose of studying methods is to assist the prospective and inexperienced teacher to bridge gaps which are real to him. This volume aims to provide such assistance.

Part I, Orientation, consists of an introductory chapter which defines the meaning and scope of method, indicating the role of method in relation to the total work of the school. It also presents a brief analysis of the work of the secondary school physical education teacher, describes the scope of his professional task, and casts the role of method in that perspective.

Part II, Bases to Method, deals with understandings and educational processes which are preliminary to the selection of instructional methods. Before methods can be selected there must be (1) an understanding of how students learn and (2) an analysis of the nature and needs of the students to be taught. From this basis (3) a selection of physical education objectives can be made which recognizes both the nature of the learner and the contemporary social purposes of education. In light of the objectives (4) physical education curricula or programs can be designed. These four major areas are discussed in separate chapters.

Part III, Instructional Patterns and Media, consists of five chapters. The first outlines both traditional and modern modes of describing basic types of methods. The second deals with procedures which apply to teaching specific kinds of learning in physical education, i.e., knowledge and understanding, attitudes and appreciation, and motor skills. The third and fourth chapters consider techniques for teaching the various types of activities which make up the physical education program. The fifth chapter reviews audio-visual instructional methods and techniques.

Part IV, Planning and Guiding Learning Experiences, devotes its first chapter primarily to planning the lesson and unit. It also considers means of selecting effective methods and discusses the involvement of students in the planning process as a worthwhile learning experience for them. The other three chapters treat organization and management of the class, intramural, and recreational, and interscholastic programs.

Part V, Relation of Instruction to Other School Functions, explains the scope of supervision, administration, and evaluation in the work of the school. The relationship of *instruction* to these three major areas is clarified. Special reference is made to student participation in these functions as a type of instructional method.

The authors are indebted to the many individuals who have made both direct and indirect contributions to the substance of this volume; not the least of these are Miss Ruth Gorrell and Mrs. Nancy Magnuson, who gave invaluable assistance in preparing the manuscript. We are also grateful to Jonathan C. Hill of Kalamazoo, Michigan, who provided us with illustrations for the text.

Clyde Knapp
Patricia Hagman Leonhard

CONTENTS

part 1
ORIENTATION

INTRODUCTION

A text on teaching, on methods, must focus upon teacher acts and strategies, and upon what the teacher may do to provide optimum conditions for learning. Focusing upon methods is complicated by the fact that instructional methods, necessarily, are interrelated and integrated with all other aspects of school organization and operation. Curriculum, evaluation, supervision, and administration all affect selection of instructional methods and, indeed, at times become a part of method.

Part I clarifies the role of method in educational programs and indicates the frame of reference for the text. The single chapter of this orienting part discusses meaning and scope of method, defines the various areas or categories of school organization and operation, clarifies interrelationship of method to these areas, shows how patterns of method tend to be either teacher-centered or student-centered, indicates a philosophy of method as well as a central thesis of the text, and introduces the foundations or sources of method. It also describes, generally, the work of a physical education teacher to help the reader propel himself, vicariously, into a teaching situation, and better understand the effect all aspects of school organization have upon instructional methods. It further discusses a relatively new trend in education, the use of symbolic models to describe more accurately and analytically various educational processes.

chapter 1

THE ROLE OF INSTRUCTIONAL METHODS IN EDUCATION

MEANING AND SCOPE OF TEACHING METHODS

Teaching refers precisely to the organization and conduct of learning experiences. The purpose of teaching is to induce change or growth in the learner. Technically speaking, there can be no teaching unless learning takes place, although individuals can and frequently do learn when not under the direction, guidance, or influence of another person. This implies, then, that teaching involves action on the part of a person; that this person, or teacher, stimulates learning by organizing, guiding, and directing experiences of students. It is important to bear in mind that a teacher arranges the environment and stimulates and guides the learner's activities in that environment. It is the student who learns; each individual student must do his own learning. Teaching brings the student a learning environment for the purpose of enhancing the efficiency of learning. The means the teacher uses to organize and guide experiences, to induce learning, are called *teaching methods.*

The above paragraph may suggest that teaching methods relate only to procedures and techniques used in a teacher's direct relationship with students. Not so, because students learn from all contacts with their environment. All decisions made and actions taken by teachers which affect the learning environment for students represent teaching methods. Thus, a teacher might arrange for early class members to practice or play as soon as they arrive at the teaching station. Such a procedure involves having the gymnasium, or other class locale, ready for use, arranging for distribution and care of equipment and supplies; it might involve student leaders or committees who accept responsibility for practice or other activity as well as for safety and for equipment or supplies. Providing for experiences such as these represents methods of teaching as much as those means used to promote learning in situations where a teacher directly leads a class.

It proves difficult, if not impossible, to draw a precise and distinct line between various kinds of duties a teacher performs, to say which represent teaching methods and which something else. All teaching duties relate to student learning. Whether he is discussing a student's progress with a parent, serving on a curriculum committee, assisting with a health examination, caring for equipment, or planning or conducting a class meeting, the ultimate goal of the teacher is student learning and growth. In dealing specifically, as this text does, with the techniques and procedures of conducting learning experiences for students, the importance of all a teacher's duties and every aspect of the school environment is never minimized. Rather the text approaches the problems of teaching from the standpoint of instructional methods, indicating the related effects of other facets of the school environment upon the learning of students.

OPERATIONAL FUNCTIONS OF THE SCHOOL

The meaning and scope of teaching methods are best understood in their full implications when discussed in light of a precise definition of the total work of the school. The work of the modern school consists of a sequential but interrelated series of processes. Terms generally applied to these processes include *curriculum, instruction, supervision, administration,* and *evaluation.* Curriculum deals with the selection of desired educational outcomes and learning experiences to achieve these outcomes. Instruction relates to the conduct of the learning experiences. Supervision aims to improve both the design and process of instruction. Administration provides the setting for learning. Evaluation, an overlapping function, appraises the outcomes and methods of all the areas of work of the school.

Subsequent chapters explain more fully the relation of each of these areas to the central subject of this book, instructional or teaching method in physical education, but the reader must understand at the outset that instruction is but one though the focal point in the work of the school. Instruction never becomes effective unless based upon acceptable goals and a sound selection of learning experiences and unless, further, schools make provisions for an adequate setting for learning. Supervision and evaluation serve concurrently to assure the approximation of desired outcomes. In other words, the contents of this book focus upon the instructional aspects of the work of the school which have to do with the interaction of students with planned learning experiences in physical education. The experiences selected through curriculum planning, the type of curriculum planning itself, the administrative structure surrounding physical education, the means of supervision employed, and the methods used to evaluate—all affect students and what they learn.

This text discusses primarily the instructional methods used in physical education, assuming that other texts available to students similarly focus upon the processes of curriculum planning, administration, supervision, and evaluation. The five areas become basically inseparable in function, however. The text, therefore, maintains the larger setting though viewed from the standpoint of the problems of instruction.

STYLES OR PATTERNS OF METHODS

Methods for the classroom have been variously categorized in the years since scientific thought has been focused on the process of teaching. The emerging types of instructional methods for classroom use, labeled in various ways, include the lecture method, the recitation method, the project method, the laboratory method, the dramatic method, the socialized-recitation method, the group-discussion method, the problem-solving method, and the discovery method.

Fundamentally these types represent two basic styles or patterns of instruction. The lecture method and the recitation method typify a *teacher-centered approach;* the others listed, a *student-centered approach.* The teacher-centered approach is characterized by teacher domination in planning instruction, conducting classroom activities, and evaluating results. It should be pointed out that a person using a teacher-centered approach may include elements of a student-centered approach, He does this if he makes decisions primarily on the basis of his expectation of what may be best for the student involved. With a student-centered approach, students may become involved in the selection of goals, subject matter, methods to be used, and control of their own activities.

Types of methods for physical education have not been so neatly categorized as those for general classroom use. Whereas each of the methods listed for classroom use has implications for physical education, neither singly nor as a whole do they translate directly for teaching physical education although they probably apply to physical education as much as they do to the teaching of art, industrial arts, music, typing, or sewing. No one pattern or style provides a solution for all teaching situations. There is no one best type; each learning situation dictates its own special approach. The text emphasizes a student-centered pattern of instruction, at least one in which the student is held paramount. It presents, within a broad framework of student-centered methods, both the principles and concepts which underlie method, and a wide variety of appropriate procedures, techniques, and methods pointed toward successful teaching in physical education.

PHILOSOPHY OF METHOD

Suggestions made throughout reflect a democratic philosophy as applied to method. Use of democratic procedures in education appears basic. The primary purpose of education in the United States centers on preparing individuals for living in a democratic society. Research, as well as philosophy, supports the principle that the best way to assist individuals to acquire the skills, knowledges, attitudes, and appreciations to live effectively in a democratic society is through school practices which epitomize democratic procedures. Democratic method constitutes an all-pervasive force which can permeate the entire social climate of the school. It is not readily expressed in a pat list of procedures and techniques. It does require persistent cooperation among all members of the school family in determining school purposes, selecting learning experiences, carrying on instruction, and evaluating outcomes. It implies shared responsibilities among students, teachers, school personnel other than teachers, parents, and other patrons for the success of the school program.

CENTRAL THESIS OF TEXT

Adherence to a student-centered approach to method means that students as maturing organisms with their complex problems of social, physical, intellectual, and ethical maturation are held paramount in all the considerations. Students as a center of reference receive primary consideration in all matters of school organization, with efforts directed toward determining the individual and group needs of boys and girls and organizing, managing, and conducting all experiences of the school to meet these needs.

In addition to this student-centered approach, the text also rests upon the thesis that instructional method must be compatible with the goals sought, that means determine ends. Thus, if one wishes to emphasize as a purpose of education the producing of persons who will obey commands, he emphasizes giving commands and insisting upon continual exact response; if the central purpose of education lies in preparing students to live in a democratic society, then the methods used to teach desired skills, attitudes, habits, appreciations, and understandings give students practice in democratic behavior. The principle that methods should be compatible with goals sought, or that processes involved basically influence outcomes, will receive more specific treatment later. At this point it may help to establish the principle that methods and the total environment affect learning; each reader probably knows of one or more instances in which persons learned undesirable things, such as breaking rules without detection while playing a game or cheating on one's income taxes, while they were participating in learning situations which were planned with only desirable outcomes in mind. Chapter 4, The Objectives of Physical Education, explains the concept that a game itself does not serve as a means to some goal. Unsocial outcomes, outweighing possible values, are likely to accrue, indeed may accrue, if organization and conduct do not provide favorable student interaction with the environment.

When considering methods, then, three factors appear paramount: (1) It is the student who learns, and he must be the center of consideration; (2) a student learns from all conditions in the environment surrounding his learning experiences; and (3) the methods used must be compatible with the goals sought.

FOUNDATIONS OF METHODS

In answering the crucial question, "What is the best way to organize and conduct specific learning activities so the best possible results accrue for students?" where can the teacher turn for assistance? No simple formula exists for selecting the best methods. The variable factors in any one learning situation would not be likely to be duplicated in a second instance. In any one circumstance a teacher must be concerned with such factors as the status and needs of each student, the character of the group, the available time for learning, the available facilities and equipment, the unique characteristics of the activities used, and the strengths and weaknesses of the teacher himself. Variation of any one of these factors materially affects the methods used. For example, assume all factors mentioned above are constant for two swimming groups, with the exception that one teacher uses an indoor pool and the other an outdoor pool. The teacher leading students in an indoor pool with optimum water temperature uses a quite different approach to his lesson from the teacher handling a group in an outdoor pool with exceptionally cold water. Extent and type of land drills, length of drill periods in the water, intervals at which verbal directions are given, and types of recreational activities used—all would vary for the two groups.

The very complexity of conditions which exist in any learning situation prevents reliance on a set of stereotyped techniques. Rather the effective teacher must rely on an understanding of and ability to create and utilize procedures unique to the circumstances at hand. Certain guides and a vast store of workable techniques are available to teachers. The basic principles and guides to teaching come from three sources—*the psychology of learning, the nature and needs of students,* and *an analysis of successful practice.* A primary foundation emerges from the psychology of learning. Knowledge of the principles of learning assists teachers to select a sound method of teaching. Chapter 2 deals with the nature of learning and considers those foundations which underlie physical education teaching methods.

One example may serve to illustrate how an understanding of the principles of the psychology of learning contributes to effective teaching. An inexperienced assistant coach, working with high jumpers of a varsity track and field squad, noticed at the end of the third week of the season that the jumpers' improvement had fallen off and that five of the six candidates had made no progress at all during the past week. He called the group together, showed them their records, with biting sarcasm accused them of loafing, poor attitude, and lack of school spirit, and made it quite clear what he thought of their chances for success in coming meets. He concluded his berating by announcing that the group would put in an extra practice session on Saturday morning before the remainder of the squad reported and that they would also report before school and during the noon hour on Monday. An elemental knowledge of the psychology of learning would have revealed to this coach that the high jumpers probably had reached a perfectly natural plateau in their learning and needed relaxation or a change of pace in their training routine, not more of the same. Further, his unjustified attitude of scorn may well have so undermined student-teacher rapport as to affect materially his future teaching success with the boys. Learning curves and the effect of student-teacher rapport on learning comprise but two of the many factors about learning which give direction to the selection of appropriate teaching methods.

The nature and needs of students are a fundamental guide to teaching. Educational programs exist to prepare individuals to live effectively, to be worthwhile to themselves and to society. Students learn only to the extent that they become motivated and then only within the limits of their capacities. Knowledge of the general characteristics of growth and development, of physical, social, and emotional maturation, as well as understanding the particular abilities, interests, and needs of his own students, helps the teacher to select appropriate and effective methods in various situations.

Teachers must consider not only general principles of how learning takes place but also the specific ways in which individuals learn. Learning itself is a highly individualized procedure, and what works effectively for one individual or group may prove ineffective for another. For instance, criticism which might stir a bold and poorly motivated boy toward effective learning might make a timid boy more fearful. Or a strongly motivated group of college physical education majors may respond favorably to a method of teaching swimming which finds them in deep water the first lesson, whereas some members of a group of Cub Scouts, taught by the same method, may become paralyzed with fear to the extent that their learning to swim is indefinitely delayed. To select the best method a teacher must understand the nature and needs of his students. Chapter 3 discusses the nature of adolescents with special reference to physical education.

A third source of guides to teachers in the selection of method lies in an analysis of successful practices, the empirical discovery of procedures and techniques which work. It must be emphasized, however, that teachers must avoid deciding to use a method just because it has been used successfully by others. Rather, one must analyze a workable method and the probable causes for its success and compare it with alternative methods before deciding it is the way for him to proceed. One example may help. Recently one of the authors observed a veteran teacher trying to help a quiet, soft-spoken, new teacher get off to a good start by advising the young man to copy the style he had found successful. The veteran's style, which included loud talk, a good deal of kidding, some "ham" acting, joking, and needling, seemed consistent with his personality. For many years he has been a colorful and popular faculty member in a small- to medium-sized high school. After the principal asked the veteran how he expected the reserved new man to use a teaching style appropriate for a rather flamboyant person, the veteran laughed heartily and said, "That is stupid, isn't it?" and to the new teacher said, "I won't try to help you again unless you ask for it." Later chapters describe methods which have been used successfully and the principles which underlie them. Teachers and students will find many practical suggestions.

Research concerning teaching methods for physical education is helpful, although it is limited as a basis for widespread use in the selection of method. Some current practices spring from such research although most are derived either empirically or from implications of research in the psychology of learning, some of which applies quite directly to physical education since psychomotor learning is involved. Among the most helpful learning research applied to physical education as a discrete field have been studies relating to the relative worth of a "whole" method, a "whole-part-whole" method, or a "part" method, and those concerning length and distribution of practice sessions. More research is needed; therefore the pace is likely to increase. Researchers of physical education teaching methods need to spend more time in classrooms, gymnasiums, and playgrounds and depend less upon research within the confines of laboratories which facilitate rigid control of some variables but do not produce classroom situations.

There are also some corollary bases to method. These include the nature of the desired educational objectives and the nature of the activities selected to reach those goals. An illustrative example can best describe the effect the nature of objectives has on methods used. Assuming that the objectives are acceptable in the total circumstances of the school, one group of twelfth-grade students volunteers to assist with the supervision and conduct of the noon-hour physical recreation program. A second group, in connection with a project in the photography unit of a physics course, wishes to make a motion picture of basic techniques in a typical high school sport. For their different purposes, both groups select for a given unit in their physical education program the game of volleyball. How does the difference in objectives affect the methods used? Group A, the recreation group, decide that they must know how to score and referee if they are to do a good job of leading the noon-hour program. They know that they must be able to organize the groups quickly and give help on basic techniques to those less familiar with the game. The methods used in their class, then, place emphasis on such factors as permitting students to organize their own teams, having the entire group call the score each time a play is made, having students referee and explain pointers and rotating techniques, and providing take-home written quizzes on scoring and rules for study.

Group B, the photography-minded group, is chiefly interested in securing good pictures of separate game skills. They divide into small groups of four or five, each practicing a different basic skill. The teacher works with each group in turn, and later groups are paired to analyze and criticize each other's techniques. All boys are to be included in the movies, and efforts are made to discover each boy's major competency. Toward the end of each period the separate groups are combined into teams, and a spirited game is played, with major emphasis placed upon perfection of technique.

Different activities, as well as different objectives, affect the selection of an appropriate method. Each different activity in the program of physical education presents different teaching problems. A complex team sport requires a different sequence to its whole than a single skill activity such as discus throwing. Teaching a group the game of tennis, with all individuals doing approximately the same thing, presents different problems from a team sport in which each individual has a different role to play. The informality which contributes to a beginning square dance class may be quite unacceptable in a beginning archery class with younger boys and girls who lack the awareness of the potential danger of bows and arrows. To teach physical education effectively, one must understand the nature of the objectives of physical education and the unique problems of each activity within the program. Chapters 4 and 5 discuss the objectives of education, both mental and physical, and the scope of physical education programs, the understanding of which is preliminary to a discussion of specific methods of teaching.

OTHER FACTORS AFFECTING METHODS

Previous references to factors which affect the selection of methods indicated ideal ways to organize learning. Many times, however, factors in the environment necessitate selection of what is best, rather than ideal, for the situation. For example, during the spring term it might be regarded as worthwhile to teach water safety as approaching summer increases the likelihood of swimming and boating accidents. Obviously techniques for doing this in a school which has no swimming pool would differ substantially from those in a neighboring school with a pool.

Other factors which similarly affect methods include grouping and scheduling practices, the time and the kinds of equipment available, indoor and outdoor facilities, community mores, and teacher competency. Teacher responsibility in relation to such factors is twofold: (1) Optimum conditions for learning should be ascertained and efforts made to provide the best possible setting for learning; (2) recognizing that conditions often fall short of ideals, the next task is to use ingenuity and extra effort to adjust methods so that good results will be achieved despite existing conditions.

Too often teachers accept the handicap of less than ideal conditions and do too little to make the best of them while planning for improvements. For example, new teachers A and B both discover that they have only two soccer balls to begin the unit of soccer. Teacher A accepts this fact, divides his class into four teams, and permits students to play full games for the entire period, coaching incidentally the best he can and trying to divide his attention equally between the two groups of novices. He rationalizes his position by saying that he is teaching by the "whole" method. Teacher B sets down his objectives, which include for a beginning class knowledges, skills, and attitudes toward the game as a whole with emphasis on mastery of certain fundamental techniques. He determines that equipment necessary to do this requires at least one soccer ball for each four students in the maximum-sized class. He writes a minimum order for soccer balls and armed with his objectives and proposed methods, discusses the problem with the school principal. A case like this may take persistent long-range planning to achieve adequate budgetary procedures to produce suitable equipment. The important factor is that teacher A who accepted the equipment as he found it and settled for less apt methods did not begin the process to improve conditions.

Chapter 16, Method and Administration, explains more fully the relation of administration to method and gives practical suggestions for adapting methods to existing conditions.

Teacher competency also has a major influence on methods used. A teacher inexpert in or unfamiliar with his subject matter or a variety of teaching procedures cannot employ the same methods used successfully by a highly skilled teacher. Each teacher must learn how to compensate for his deficiencies and continually improve his ability to conduct learning experiences. Chapter 15, Method and Supervision, approaches this problem and explains ways in which teachers in service may improve their competency in instructional methods.

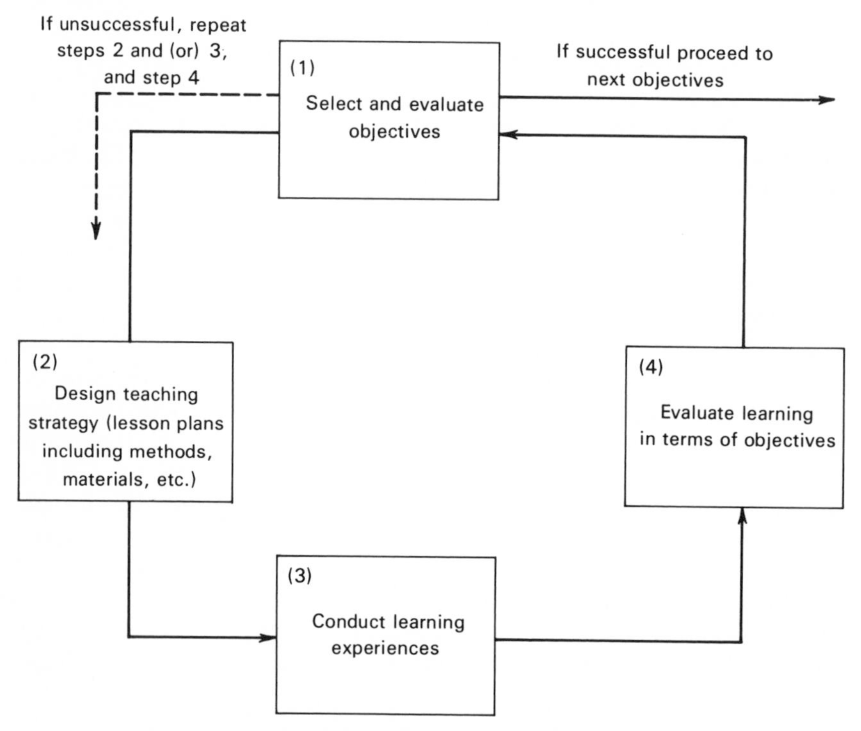

Figure 1 A diagrammatic model of the teaching process

THE USE OF MODELS IN TEACHING

The preceding discussion describing the many variables which affect the selection of methods implies the extreme complexity of teaching-learning processes. One current trend in education is toward the use of paradigms or models to aid in more precisely analyzing the elements in any educational effort. This system is a direct outgrowth of accelerated research efforts in teaching and learning which require the elements under study to be accurately and precisely defined.

The symbolic models used for this purpose are analogous to the replica models described in Chapter 10, Use of Audio-Visual Materials. *Replica models* are a physical reconstruction of the real object. Typical examples include contour maps, models of the human body, and tabletop made-to-scale athletic fields on which various game layouts and equipment can be arranged to preplan safe and efficient deployment of teaching stations. Similarly one can construct *symbolic models* to describe more intangible elements of teaching-learning situations. A symbolic model can be presented diagrammatically or verbally. A simple diagrammatic model of the teaching process is illustrated in Figure 1.

This diagrammatic model can be presented as a verbal model as follows:

1. Define, select, and evaluate objectives.
2. Design the teaching strategy to achieve step 1.
3. Conduct the learning experience.
4. Evaluate to ascertain if the learner has achieved the objectives.
5. If successful, advance to the next learning objectives.
6. If unsuccessful, evaluate the design of the teaching strategy and redesign if necessary.
7. Repeat step 3 (with original or redesigned teaching strategy) and step 4. Then proceed to step 5 or through 6 and 7 again.

Within the scope of this model additional models of any element of the process can be constructed. Muska Moston,[1] for example, has developed definitive and highly descriptive models of physical education teaching-learning. He gives particular emphasis to teaching styles and the way in which each affects the types of goals achieved. He has applied models of four different styles of teaching to a wide variety of activities. He draws implications about the use of each style for effective achievement of the overall objectives of physical education.

The concept of the model approach is basically one of logic and or-

[1] Muska Moston, *Teaching Physical Education*, Charles E. Merrill Books, Inc., Columbus, Ohio, 1967.

ganization. The researcher tries to define accurately what his problems are and to make assumptions about what he should do about them. He tries to analyze and describe all possible variables in the situation under study. The teacher pursues exactly the same course, but his problem is often much more difficult when he attempts to design a model. The researcher, to be successful, must control the climate and variables in his situation. The teacher is most often faced with an ever-changing and relatively uncontrolled situation. Just as learning theories developed in the laboratory are difficult to translate to the classroom (a topic discussed in Chapter 3), so is it difficult to apply a teaching theory and make it work in every classroom. This means that a symbolic model of a teaching method has value for a given teacher only if it applies to the specific conditions of the individual classroom, or if it is general enough to provide him with background understanding which he can in turn adapt to his own circumstances.

Certain precautions must also be taken even in using models designed for a specific situation. A model of a football field is only an approximation of the real thing. It is generally scaled down to usable size, and many fine points such as movable equipment, density of the grass, intensity of lights, and wind patterns might be omitted. These very factors may materially affect certain uses under real conditions. So, too, with symbolic models. It is never possible to anticipate and describe all possible variables. Usually just major factors or structures are presented. Minor variables may require adjustment in terms of the real situation as the teaching-learning experience progresses. As long as the teacher uses his model as a guide and not as a completely charted course he can make the kind of flexible adjustments which teaching as a creative art demands.

Models are valuable tools for the teacher because they provide a system to help him carefully think through the logic of the problem he has to solve or the operation he must carry out. They serve their best purposes when they require the teacher to think analytically about what he is trying to do, how he is trying to do it, and what the effects both his selected goals and the methods he uses to achieve them will have on the learner.

Models, like objectives, can be general or specific, simple or complex. A number of examples of models will be found throughout this volume. The book's chief purpose, however, is to give the reader a sufficient background of knowledge and understanding so that he will be able to efficiently design his own teaching models and consistently apply the highest professional competency to designing and carrying out basically sound teaching-learning practices.

THE IMPORTANCE OF THE TEACHER

The modern secondary school requires many workers—teachers, administrators, supervisors, custodians, and other types of staff personnel. All other personnel serve in the last analysis to assist teachers to do the best possible work in guiding the learning of boys and girls. Important as each person's role may be, teachers are the key in educational programs. Administrators, supervisors, and other staff workers achieve their goals only as they succeed in assisting teachers to do their jobs in the best possible way.

VERSATILITY: A PROFESSIONAL REQUISITE

Teaching physical education has many ramifications. It requires an understanding of growth and development, of the needs and drives of the individuals, and of the educative process. It also demands knowledge of a wide variety of activities through which physical, mental, social, and emotional needs may be satisfied. A specialist in the dance or in one or two sports may make significant contributions in specific areas, but the person who would lead all the citizens of a school through developmental physical education must appreciate and know how to teach many activities. Physical education classes, intramurals, recreation, sport clubs, and, in many instances, especially for beginners, teaching in other subject-matter fields—all command attention of the teacher or director of physical education.

The extent to which specialization is desirable is not fully understood. In small high schools it may be necessary for one or two teachers to teach everything that is to be taught in physical education and in sports. However, in large high schools specialization may be quite possible though opinion concerning its desirability varies. Those in favor of specialization argue that an expert in an activity can teach better than one who has only ordinary ability and background in that activity; those who argue for one person teaching his class all of their physical education point out that while activities are important the students are more important, that the resourceful teacher knows enough about a variety of activities to be able to teach reasonably well, and that being with his students continually permits him to know them much better.

Whatever one thinks about the desirability of specialists' doing the major portion of the teaching or whatever one thinks of team teaching, it seems apparent that in physical education some activities lend themselves to specialization better than others. Among activities which seem most appropriate for specialization are the dance, swimming, and gymnastics. These three activities require more expertise than others for successful teaching, and they represent activities in which some physical educators are not very well skilled or prepared.

Generally speaking a secondary school physical education teacher should be able to teach games and relays; tumbling and stunts; conditioning; some adaptive or corrective physical education; rhythms and dancing; a variety of team games such as touch football, soccer, speedball, field hockey, basketball, volleyball, and softball; a variety of individual and dual games such as tennis, golf, handball, badminton, table tennis, shuffleboard, horseshoe and quoits, track and field, aquatics, and winter sports.

The work of a physical education teacher extends far beyond the activities undertaken during class and extraclass instruction periods. A teacher must do a great deal of planning, organizing, administering, supervising, studying, counseling, reading, and recording at times when the groups are not in session to assure good results for students from every learning experience.

Does the job seem impossible? Certainly it is not possible for any one person to develop a high degree of specialization in each activity. But one person can effectively lead students in many activities. Unmistakably any one teacher will have more ability in some activities than in others. It is important that the teacher appreciate the potentialities of each activity. Too frequently teachers with strong likings tend to narrow a program. The woman who is tremendously enthusiastic about the dance may slight sports, and the sports-minded teacher may neglect the dance. The man who personally loves rugged team games may give little attention to individual and dual games, and so on. Teachers enthusiastic and intense about particular activities fulfill an important function. They are likely to do a creative and superior job of teaching. It should be understood, however, that a good program of physical education includes variety sufficient to provide each student with an opportunity to learn and participate in several team games, several individual and dual games, selected rhythmic activities, basic swimming skills, and a number of other individual and group physical activities. Versatility, then, appears to be an essential characteristic of a successful physical education teacher. In addition, he must take a scholarly attitude toward his work.

TEACHING AS AN ART AND A SCIENCE

The successful teacher makes optimum use of scientific procedures whenever they are known. He utilizes to the fullest extent all known facts about the nature of the learner and the learning process. He has a thorough grasp of his subject matter field and understands the unique contribution of physical education to the social purposes of education. He realizes the complexity of the teaching process. He knows that teaching cannot be reduced to a formula of procedures and techniques to meet all situations. He knows that he must be an artist in the true sense of the word, consistently showing sensitivity to the multiplicity of factors which affect both the learner and the teaching environment. His instructional procedures are characterized by experimentalism and creativity. He fully recognizes the potential worth of the dynamic and socially positive environment he can create for boys and girls through physical education activities. The mature teacher recognizes that teaching is both an art and a science; the successful teacher has the ability to put his belief into practice.

SUMMARY

Teaching may be defined as the organization and conduct of learning experiences. It serves to bring the student into a learning environment and enhance the efficiency of the learning process. The means the teacher uses to organize and guide learning experiences are called teaching methods.

The total work of the school consists of the sequential but interrelated processes of curriculum, instruction, supervision, administration, and evaluation. Competence in instructional methods necessitates understanding the relationship of each of these areas to teaching methods and the optimum use that may be made of all school activities for instructional purposes.

A student-centered approach to instruction represents the most desirable pattern of instruction in the light of accepted principles of the psychology of learning and the purpose of education in a democratic society. Adherence to a student-centered approach to method means that students as maturing organisms with their complex problems of social, physical, intellectual, and ethical maturation are held paramount in all considerations.

The basic principles and guides for teaching, the foundations, come from the psychology of learning, the nature and needs of students, and an analysis of successful practice.

The nature of educational objectives and the type of activities used in the program also dictate choice of methods. In addition, a variety of factors in the environment affect choice of methods. Teachers should always strive to provide ideal settings for learning, but where conditions fall short of ideals, teachers should exercise skill and ingenuity to utilize methods which will achieve good results despite conditions as they exist.

Teachers are the key personnel in any school organization. Administrators, supervisors, counselors, and other members of school staffs fulfill their functions by assisting teachers to do the most effective work possible with boys and girls.

The work of the physical education teacher includes the leading of students in a wide variety of satisfying motor activities, as well as the essential planning, supervising, administering, managing, counseling, and evaluating which result in good learning experiences for students.

Teaching is both an art and a science. Teaching cannot be reduced to a formula, but each teacher must be aware of the many factors which affect both the learner and the environment for learning. His instructional procedures must be characterized by experimentalism and creativity.

Questions and problems for discussion

1. Give several examples of learnings acquired by typical high school students which result from experiences that are neither planned nor adult-directed. Include a number of negative as well as positive learnings.

2. List other social institutions through which students receive adult-directed and planned instruction in physical education. Compare their relative influence with that of schools.

3. List factors in a typical school environment which influence students in addition to those in the classroom or in directed extraclass activities. Evaluate the importance of these influences.

4. Indicate some of the effects which organization of the school day has on student learning in physical education. Which practices aid learning? Which hinder it?

5. Briefly describe any simple learning experience such as one meeting of a tenth-grade girls' folk dance class. List in turn factors of curriculum, instruction, administration, supervision, and evaluation essential to effective conduct of the learning experience. Consider possible effects of omitting attention to any one of these areas.

6. By analyzing current texts and other literature, make a checklist of all possible duties of men or women physical education teachers. Ask several teachers in service to check your list for completeness.

7. Select any period of history or type of social institution. Show how the purposes or objectives of the society or institution determine the way in which physical activities are organized.

8. Considering the hundreds of years society has been concerned with some kind of organized education, how do you account for the lack of highly standardized and precise teaching methods which could be readily taught to prospective teachers?

Selected references

Abraham, Willard: *A Time for Teaching*, Harper & Row Publishers, Incorporated, New York, 1964.

Alcorn, Marvin D., James S. Kinder, and Jim R. Shunent: *Better Teaching in Secondary Schools,* Holt, Rinehart and Winston, Inc., New York, 1964.

Brownell, Clifford Lee, and E. Patricia Hagman: *Physical Education—Foundations and Principles,* McGraw-Hill Book Company, New York, 1951.

Bruner, Jerome S.: *The Process of Education,* Harvard University Press, Cambridge, Mass., 1961.

Bucher, Charles A.: *Foundations of Physical Education,* The C. V. Mosby Company, St. Louis, 1964.

Burton, W. H.: *The Guidance of Learning Activities,* 3d ed., Appleton-Century-Crofts, Inc., New York, 1962.

Callahan, Sterling Grundy: *Successful Teaching in Secondary Schools,* Scott, Foresman and Company, Chicago, 1966.

Collins, William M.: *Methods of Teaching in the Elementary and Secondary Schools,* Pageant Press, New York, 1965.

Cowell, Charles C., and Hilda M. Schwehn: *Modern Principles and Methods in Secondary School Physical Education,* 2d ed., Allyn and Bacon, Inc., Englewood Cliffs, N.J., 1964.

Davis, Elwood Craig, and Earl L. Wallis: *Toward Better Teaching in Physical Education,* Prentice-Hall, Inc., Englewood Cliffs, N.J., 1961.

Gassett, Henry Edward: *The Art of Good Teaching,* David McKay Company, Inc., New York, 1964.

Grambs, Jean D., and L. Morris McClure: *Foundations of Teaching,* Holt, Rinehart and Winston, Inc., New York, 1964.

Oberteuffer, Delbert, and Celeste Uhlrich: *Physical Education,* 3d ed., Harper & Row, Publishers, Incorporated, New York, 1962.

Williams, Jesse F.: *The Principles of Physical Education,* W. B. Saunders Company, Philadelphia, 1964.

part 2
BASES TO METHOD

INTRODUCTION

Instructional methods have been defined as ways in which learning experiences are organized and conducted. Before methods are selected something should be known about the nature of students, how they learn, and the kinds of learning experiences which contemporary education should provide. Part 2 deals with these prerequisites to method selection.

Chapter 2 explains the distinction between teaching and learning. It describes recent findings from the psychology of learning and indicates their relevance for physical education. Chapter 3 discusses general principles of growth and development defining such terms as needs, interests, abilities, and behavior. Specific characteristics of the adolescent age group are presented including treatment of the changing sociological problems of today's youth. Suggestions of ways in which physical education uniquely contributes to the growth and development of adolescents and a discussion of its function in the school guidance program conclude the chapter. Chapter 4 offers an overview of the general objectives of physical education and their relationship to the general objectives of education, and discusses some of the current trends in selecting and describing objectives for today's secondary schools. Chapter 5 treats the physical education curriculum, suggesting both content and procedures for program development.

It is logical to assume that most students of physical education will have given some attention to each of these areas of study before taking a course in methods. Thus, this part serves as a review of those major factors and current trends in these areas which are especially pertinent to selecting physical education instructional methods.

chapter 2

TEACHING AND LEARNING

INTRODUCTION

In this chapter the reader should keep in mind the distinction between teaching and learning. Teaching centers about the organization of learning experiences. Its purpose is to make learning more efficient. Teaching is the process of helping other individuals to learn. A teacher plans the learning experiences of his students in order that the learning process becomes as efficient as possible. He encourages learning by providing means of motivation which promote initial interest in learning and maintain a necessary level of interest until the student achieves the learning outcome. He also guides the learner through the learning experience, reducing to a minimum the amount of random or trial-and-error effort. He further serves as diagnostician, noting where progress toward goals has been misdirected; and he assists the learner to recognize acceptable progress and accomplishment of desired goals.

The very nature of learning as described in this chapter presupposes that the student be the center of teaching. Activity on the part of the teacher, no matter how satisfying to the teacher as an individual, proves of little worth unless his efforts result in student activity leading to student growth. A teacher cannot merely show or tell what he desires; he must lead the student in actually experiencing the desired learning. The showing or telling is merely one step in the teaching process.

Unless the teacher understands how students learn, apt selection of teaching methods cannot be made. This chapter reviews some of the underlying principles of learning, principles which form a basis for the selection of teaching methods. While examples are drawn from physical education in illustrating principles of learning, the detailed applications of these principles to the teaching of physical education are made in later chapters.

THE LEARNING PRODUCTS OF PHYSICAL EDUCATION

Chapter 4, The Objectives of Physical Education, describes four basic areas common to various statements of physical education objectives. The four include health, social ends, emotional development, and recreation. If one accepts these four as areas to which physical education should contribute, it follows that the acquiring of motor skills and the development of strength and endurance are in the nature of media through which social, emotional, and recreative ends are achieved, rather than ends in themselves. Development of satisfying social characteristics, emotional adjustments, as well as physical development, are part and parcel of learning through physical activities.

Some teachers may consider it unnecessary to plan for social and emotional learning because of a belief that desirable social and emotional adjustments naturally and automatically accrue from a base of motor skills and strength and endurance. Such a belief is naïve. Every teacher can recall individuals who possess superior motor ability but who could improve their social and emotional adjustment. The star athlete who refuses to cooperate with his teammates is an example. So, too, is the weight lifter, so satisfied with his prowess that he withdraws from participation in group activities. The physical education teacher must be concerned with the development of behaviors which mark an educated person, as well as with the acquisition of motor skills and the development of strength and endurance. The learning products of physical education, then, are skills, knowledges and understandings, habits, attitudes, and appreciations, which lead to total social, emotional, and physical development, not just the acquisition of motor skills and the development of motor fitness for their own sake.

NEED FOR LEARNING ECONOMY IN PHYSICAL EDUCATION

Considerations of effectiveness and economy of learning procedures are central, basic, and pervasive for physical education teachers. They strive to achieve interesting ways to guide learning which result in purposeful activity because effective learning requires activity that has aim and meaning for the learner. They work for pleasant and strain-free surroundings that produce desirable social and emotional development as well as adequate motor skills. They work and plan to achieve programs that permit optimum development of each individual within a framework of group activity. The scope of the activities, or subject matter, is broad indeed. A whole host of potentially worthwhile learning experiences are available.

Teaching of physical education and coaching of teams are, to a large extent, a fight against time. A wide range of outcomes is desired; available time is short. A cry in physical education is, "Teach a variety of activities." It is a sound cry. All young people, extreme deviates excepted, can profit by experience in several team games, several individual and dual sports, rhythmic activities, tumbling, gymnastics, swimming, use of the great outdoors, activities designed to develop strength, endurance, and good body mechanics, training in muscular relaxation, and test activities. But in the great majority of schools the time is all too limited. Motor skills, particularly, require practice and repetition. Management of time for economy and efficiency is a central and basic issue facing the secondary school physical education teacher.

High school coaches are faced with complicated skills and games that must be taught in a limited amount of time. Consider the game of football. It calls for highly skilled individual fundamentals and for complicated team procedures in attack and defense. Compare the high school coach with the college coach. The high school man works with relatively inexperienced players, and the season is less than three months. The college man not only deals with experienced players, but also has more time for teaching because of spring practice sessions which seldom are available to high school coaches. Success depends upon the effective use of time. Economical learning procedures are a must.

LEARNING DEFINED

Learning is growth, learning is development, learning is experience, learning is the something new that is added. Not all psychologists agree with this broad view of learning. When one says learning is growth, one must use the word "growth" in the broad sense of growth in knowledges, skills, attitudes, habits, and appreciation akin to development, rather than in a purely maturation sense. Growth as maturation refers to change in behavior which accrues by the mere passage of time, without respect to practice. If intervening practice fails to affect the behavior, the changes are not classified as learning. Most development is a complex combination of maturation and learning. A child cannot learn to walk until he has reached a certain stage of maturation, but the conditions in his environment may determine the sequence and progress of his ability to walk.

Premature education, instruction before the proper maturation level has been reached, not only is useless but also may be harmful because of the production of unnecessary tensions. Attempts to teach children to read before they are mature enough for it are ineffective and confusing to children. Long ago Arnold Gesell and Helen Thompson [1] found that instruction and practice in stair climbing produced little result. One of a pair of identical twins was given instruction and practice over a period of time, but at the end of the practice period the other one could climb the stairs about as well as the one who had practiced.

Although premature education is useless and may be harmful, it should be made clear that growth and development are affected by experiences and environment as well as by factors which cannot be hurried. Giving young children developmental experiences, involving them with activities or programs designed to promote readiness, actually will affect maturation and enhance learning at a later date. For example, a child who has been confined to a playpen or crib and not allowed to creep and crawl freely may be unduly delayed in walking. The readiness of the Gesell twins for stair climbing was, of course, affected by inherent limitations on the possible rapidity of physical maturation; it may also have been affected by early encouragement of skill development through physical activity, by absence of such encouragement, or by an environment which discouraged or made impossible physical activity and exploration which would hasten development. A young child who is read to from a very early age and given books with pictures to feel, handle, and look at is much more likely to learn to read when sufficiently matured physically than is a child deprived of these advantages.

Too frequently, learning is thought of as only the acquisition of knowledge or skill. Such acquisition, of course, is a part of learning. But more is involved. Both the process and the result of learning bring about a changed individual who behaves and reacts differently from the way he did before the learning experience. Changed attitudes, interests, understandings, outlooks, and behaviors result from learning. The aim of education involves more than helping learners secure information and develop skills; it involves the guiding of purposes, attitudes, and interests which affect living, which help or hinder the individual in laying foundations that lead toward a life productive of personal satisfactions and usefulness to society.

[1] Arnold Gesell and Helen Thompson, "Learning and Growth of Identical Infant Twins: An Experimental Study by the Method of Co-twin Control," *Genetic Psychological Monograph*, vol. 6, no. 1, 1929.

Learning, in a broad sense, is the adjustment of the whole organism to a new situation. Learning consists of progressive changes in behavior which accrue as the result of exposure to a problem situation that motivates the organism to interact meaningfully with it. Learning can be interpreted as problem solving, the attainment of goals, or the satisfaction of motives.

BASIC CONCEPTS AND PRINCIPLES OF LEARNING

A great deal is known about conditions which facilitate learning and circumstances that hinder it. It would be delightful to be able to say that we know precisely how learning takes place. This is not possible even though theories concerning learning have been presented for hundreds of years and the subject has been studied experimentally since the start of the twentieth century.

Why do multiple theories of learning exist? Why do not new ones replace older ones instead of being added? Because men have had varying experiences and different ways of thinking. It is a complete answer when applied to theories developed prior to the twentieth century, when philosophers formulated explanations of learning. It is only a partial answer when the theories involved are those which have developed from scientific investigations which appeared on the scene about 1900.

A tabular presentation below of representative theories by Morris L. Bigge gives a panoramic view of some important characteristics and implications of theories as arranged by him. He labels numbers one through four in the table as the "mind substance family." This family is made up of theories developed philosophically before the twentieth century. His other two categories represent development based upon experiments. Numbers five, six, and seven he labels "associationistic family," and eight, nine, and ten he calls "gestalt-field family."

Readers interested in studying more about theories of learning may read the book by Bigge and other books dealing with comparative theories.[2]

A reason for the existence of many theories of learning is that systems are built upon interpretations of and extrapolation from experimental evidence. Thus, differences in experimental design as well as differences in viewpoint may lead to differing explanations of learning. The theorist

[2] Ernest R. Hilgard and Gordon H. Bower, *Theories of Learning*, 3d ed., Appleton-Century-Crofts, Inc., New York, 1966; Winfred F. Hill, *Learning: A Survey of Psychological Interpretations*, Chandler Publishing Company, San Francisco, 1963; S. Koch (ed.), *Psychology: A Study of Science*, McGraw-Hill Book Company, New York, 1959; Ernest R. Hilgard (ed.), *Theories of Learning and Instruction, The Sixty-third Yearbook of the National Society for the Study of Education*, Part I, The University of Chicago Press, Chicago, 1964.

TABLE 1 Representative theories of learning

Theory of learning	*Assumption concerning the basic nature of man*	*Psychological system or outlook*
1. Mental discipline	bad-active (mind substance)	faculty psychology
2. Mental discipline	neutral-active (mind substance)	classicism
3. Natural unfoldment	good-active (natural)	romantic naturalism
4. Apperception	neutral-passive (mental)	structuralism
5: S–R bond	neutral-passive (physical or mental)	connectionism
6. Conditioning (with no reinforcement)	neutral-passive (physical)	behaviorism
7. Reinforcement and conditioning	neutral-passive (organism)	reinforcement
8. Insight	active (natural)	gestalt psychology
9. Goal insight	neutral-interactive	configurationalism
10. Cognitive-field	neutral-interactive (psychological)	field psychology or relativism

Source: Morris L. Bigge, *Learning Theories for Teachers,* Harper & Row, Publishers,

who wants to find precise laws that can predict the behavior of people in general is likely to design experiments which will produce observable responses to precise stimuli, that is, which show what subjects do. One whose dominant interest is in what is understood, rather than what is done, is likely to design experiments that may provide information concerning insightful learning or, in other words, how subjects come to understand.

Research in learning has emphasized laboratory studies of limited, fragmented learning tasks. Why? Because learning variables can be rigorously controlled in laboratories, whereas controls which provide assurance of cause-effect relationship are difficult to apply to classes or groups in schools. As psychologists seek to explain learning behavior in general on the basis of results of laboratory experiences they may be

Basis of transfer	*Key persons*	*Contemporary exponents*
exercised faculties, transfer automatic	St. Augustine John Calvin J. Edwards	many Hebraic-Christian fundamentalists
cultivated mind or intellect	Plato Aristotle	M. J. Adler St. John's College
recapitulation, no transfer	J. J. Rousseau F. Froebel	extreme progressivists
apperceptive mass	J. F. Herbart E. B. Titchener	many teachers and administrators
identical elements	E. L. Thorndike	J. M. Stephens A. I. Gates
conditioned responses	J. B. Watson	E. R. Guthrie
reinforced, or conditioned, responses	C. L. Hull	B. F. Skinner K. W. Spence
transposition of insights	M. Wertheimer K. Koffka	W. Köhler
tested insights	B. H. Bode	E. E. Bayles
continuity of life spaces, experience, or insights	Kurt Lewin E. C. Tolman J. S. Bruner	R. G. Barker A. W. Combs H. F. Wright

Incorporated, New York, 1964, pp. 12–13.

overextended. Discussing this, David P. Ausubel[3] has said, "Extrapolation of rote-learning theory and evidence to school-learning problems has therefore had many disastrous consequences. It perpetuated erroneous conceptons about the nature and conditions of classroom learning, led educational psychologists to neglect research on factors influencing meaningful learning, and hence delayed the discovery of more effective technics. . . ."

Is it necessary to learn a great deal about details of various theories of learning in order to teach effectively, in order to manage teaching-learning situations adroitly? Fortunately, it is not. Some principles of learning, some conditions which facilitate acquisition of knowledge and skill, are

[3] David P. Ausubel, "Some New Directions for Research in Classroom Learning," *College of Education Record,* University of Washington, 30:3, March, 1964, p. 33–39.

compatible with all theories of learning and can be manipulated to establish favorable teaching-learning environments whether or not the instructor is a sophisticated scholar of learning theory.

It seems necessary, however, for a teacher to know the general characteristics of contrasting groups of theories. Persons or groups who attempt to find precise laws for prediction of behavior can be classified roughly as "associationists," whereas those who explain learning as largely a function of insightful understanding can be called "gestalt-field theorists." Other terms used to identify association-group ideology include stimulus-response, conditioning, and connectionist; terms which apply to explanations belonging to the gestalt-field group include cognitive, gestalt, and gestalt-derived.

A teacher whose inclination, consciously or unconsciously, is to favor an association-group explanation of learning will tend to break learning tasks into logically arranged segments or parts and progress with the idea of building one segment upon another until all are learned and add up to a whole. One whose tendency is to favor a gestalt-field, or understanding, rationale of how we learn will assign larger chunks for learners to attack, will incline toward the use of a whole-part-whole approach to learning, and will seek clusters of related items or parts whose relationships to each other add unity and meaning.

Wolfgang Köhler lectured in the United States in 1925.[4] However, concepts of learning through insight, through understanding of a a gestalt, a whole, came to the fore in the United States only after the translation from German to English of Köhler's *The Mentality of Apes*[5] and K. Koffka's *The Growth of the Mind*.[6] Köhler's reporting of experimental evidence that apes could use sticks and boxes as tools brought the knowledge that apes can learn insightfully, that they can solve a problem by figuring things out. Since the experiments were designed so that the apes could not reach the goal (food) with any one stick or any one box, and since the apes did place sticks together and placed box upon box to reach desired goals, the conclusion that even apes can learn insightfully seems inescapable. Nevertheless association-group theories in the conditioning tradition persist and have important contributions to make whether or not they provide universal explanations of learning.

Some things may be learned best through attempts to understand, to see relationships, to see sense, while others may require frequent repeti-

[4] Wolfgang Köhler, "Intelligence in Apes," in Carl Murchison (ed.), *Psychologies of 1925: Powell Lectures in Psychological Theory*. Published by Clark University, Worcester, Mass., 1927.

[5] Wolfgang Köhler, *The Meaning of Apes*, trans. by E. Winter, Harcourt, Brace & World, Inc., New York, 1935.

[6] K. Koffka, *The Growth of the Mind*, trans. by R. M. Ogden, Routledge & Kegan Paul, Ltd., London, 1942.

tion of correct response. In other words, teachers do well to organize some learning tasks on a basis consistent with an insightful-gestalt-cognitive type of explanation of the learning experience and handle others according to a theory in the conditioning tradition. According to an experimental study, juggling three balls is learned with less practice when only the whole act is practiced than it is when component parts are practiced and later combined; the whole act is a cluster of parts whose relationship to each other add unity and meaning.[7] The results of this study support a gestalt-type theory.

Now let us think of a task which seems to be learned most effectively if the teacher depends upon conditions which are supported by an association-group theory. Assume that you wish to teach a sprinter to respond more quickly to a starting signal; you wish to lessen the lapse of time between a starting signal (sound of a gun) and a reacting movement on the part of the learner. Repetition of practice is needed; the learner needs to respond to the stimulus repeatedly to decrease his reaction time; he needs conditioning in the psychological sense.

Gagné delineates eight classes of learning. In his preface he says:

> Although many people, including me, have tried for years to account for actual instances of learning in terms of a small number of principles, I am currently convinced that it cannot be done. To the person who is interested in knowing what principles of learning apply to education my reply is: The question must be asked and answered with consideration of what capability is being learned. The answer is different depending on the particular class of performance change that is the focus of interest.[8]

He then describes eight classes of learning, thus using an approach different from that used by the association group and the gestalt-insight group of theorists. Since Gagné's work has been mentioned, it should be pointed out that when learning theorists write textbooks designed for use in basic courses dealing with learning or educational psychology they do not present their theories as such but rather treat teaching and learning on a more pragmatic basis. Gagné, however, proposes the theory that theory must be divided into at least eight categories according to types of learning to account for "laws" or explanations of learning. The categories are (1) signal learning, (2) stimulus-response, (3) chaining, (4) verbal association, (5) multiple discrimination, (6) concept learning, (7) principle learning, and (8) problem solving.

[7] Clyde Knapp and W. Robert Dixon, "Learning to Juggle: II. A Study of Whole and Part Methods," *Research Quarterly of the American Association for Health, Physical Education and Recreation*, 23:398–401, December, 1952.

[8] Robert M. Gagné, *The Conditions of Learning*, Holt, Rinehart and Winston, Inc., New York, 1965, pp. v–vi.

SOME BASIC PRINCIPLES COMPATIBLE WITH ALL THEORIES OF LEARNING

Much of the disagreement between the varying learning theories lies on the theoretical level. Through past experiment and through empirical analysis of practical learning experiences, certain basic understandings and common agreements about the nature of learning are available as guides to teachers. A selection of these are summarized as follows:

1. Learning results in progressive changes in behavior.
2. Motivation is central to learning; it is the heart of the process. Incentives, interests, tensions, pressures, urges, drives, and purposes represent various aspects of motivation.
3. The learner must perceive, "get the idea," know what he must do, get a concept, and proceed to develop, smooth, and perfect his concept.
4. Learning depends upon impressions received by the sensory receptors. Sight, hearing, touch, taste, and smell represent the avenues of learning. Kinesthetic feel, which might be thought of as an extension of touch, is of primary importance in the learning of motor skills.
5. Attempts, approaches, trials, or provisional tries must be made. Drill or practice is essential to motor learning, which seldom takes place by pure insight.
6. Learning is an active process, it comes from acts of the learner, be they mental or physical or both. There must be a release of energy directed at the learning problem.
7. Learning is brought about through the interaction of the organism with the environment. Establishment of surroundings that are physically, socially, and emotionally favorable is important.
8. Perfection of motor skills requires repetition of correct forms of movement.
9. Social development depends upon experiences with others in socialized situations. Practice is necessary as is teacher guidance.
10. Emotional development, adjustment, and personal integration depend upon the complex interaction of the individual with his environment. Adequate adjustment to conflicting feelings is basic to desirable emotional development. Among the many things involved in the determination of the direction of emotional development are development of attitudes and controls concerning anger, love, hate, and fear; interpersonal relationships; self-expression; degree of satisfaction, or lack of satisfaction, of the needs for security, inde-

pendence, recognition, belonging, and feelings of competence and worthwhileness; facing of reality and ability to withstand frustration; adjustments to conflicts caused by sex drives and by desires for independence in a society that establishes many controls; and the use of adjustment mechanisms. Experiences judged by the individual to be satisfactory and successful, or unsatisfactory and unsuccessful, are the cornerstones of emotional development. Successful experiences are required for adequate development.

11. Learning is highly individualized. Ability to learn depends upon innate ability and previous experiences that make the individual what he is. There is wide variation not only in knowledges and skills but also in attitudes and emotions, making the effectiveness of any learning experience variable for each individual.

MOTIVATION

Central to all learning, motivation is a key condition that determines effectiveness in any learning experience. Desires, incentives, pressures, tensions, urges, interests, abilities, and anxieties all affect motivation. Intrinsic motivation (learning carries its own reward) is superior to extrinsic (external to or apart from the basic essence of the learning activity itself). Extrinsic motivation is a necessary starting point for much learning. It may be divided into motivation through such factors as rewards and punishment, compulsion and fear of punishment, on the one hand, and through such elements as drives for recognition, approval, and excellence, on the other. The boy who studies Latin because he is driven to it operates under compulsion, perhaps under fear, and probably for the reward of securing a respectable grade in the course and being accepted at a college. This represents a relatively ineffective form of extrinsic motivation. The boy who plays football because of a desire to gain recognition is motivated by a better form of extrinsic motivation. In a sense such motivation is intrinsic because it is a real drive based upon a real desire. The boy who plays football because he likes to play the game has achieved intrinsic moving power, the most desirable form of motivation.

Intrinsic motivation is most desirable and should be sought and worked for. However, physical education teachers usually find it necessary to use extrinsic devices (outside the activity itself) especially during the early stages of learning; extrinsic motivation can serve well as a pump-primer.

Rewards, such as teacher approval, prizes, and good grades, may set the stage for more real interests in the activity. Fear of punishment and desire to avoid criticism, manipulated as incentives by some teachers, are not very good motives. They tend to say "don't" instead of "do," thus directing attention to the undesirable. Also they are likely to result in poor relationships and emotional tensions.

Emphasis upon success provides motivation of high quality and intensity. It leads toward strong interests and real internalization of motivation. Psychologically, success depends upon how the individual himself regards success. Some pupils formulate goals that allow little chance for success; others, too easily satisfied, set their sights too low. A most important function of the teacher is to help learners set goals that are both achievable and challenging. Student goals that are too high to be realistic lead to discouragement; those set too low impede progress by leading to inertia.

The stimulation of new interests, new curiosities, and new motives is a primary requisite for effective learning. Incentives should be used for the purpose of helping the learner to create internalized interests in desirable activities. Instruction should be welcomed from within rather than forced from without. Purposeful self-activity is a requirement for learning; mechanical repetitions made at the demand of someone else and without interest and attention are of little avail.

Learners' acceptance of school activities as projects of their own motivates effectively. A group who feel that they must perform distasteful tasks under compulsion learn ineffectively. When a group or an individual feels a proprietary interest, motivation is likely to be high. A class which accepts the challenge of responsibility for the success of a venture releases energy and sets the stage for inspired creative work. For these reasons, teachers who bring students into the planning and managing of activities deal with one of the strongest of motivation techniques.

Motivation has dynamic and complex qualities. It is given force by the needs of the learner and the needs of the situation. An incentive or a teacher technique that moves one pupil to purposeful self-activity may have little effect on others. The able teacher notices signs of poor motivations such as inertia, aggressive behavior, and reluctance to make attempts. Further study of individuals, reexamination of methods, and reconsideration of the appropriateness of subject matter are indicated when motivation and morale are not at a high level.

Confidence affects success. Feelings of confidence and competence affect performance favorably. Conversely, feelings of doubt and incompetence lead to poor performance. Persons who believe that they can succeed approach a task with more vigor and better emotional tone than do those who fear failure. The football coach who advises his players to believe in themselves, to be a bit cocky, and to take possession of the field and dominate the proceedings is attempting to capture the power that comes with confidence, with belief in one's ability. The coach who sees to it that his players have multiple success experiences, be they the winning of games or the achievement of other goals and subgoals, builds confidence on sound and effective foundations.

TRANSFER OF LEARNING

Problems of transfer are of tremendous importance. Since education is for the purpose of helping people to live with satisfaction and usefulness, the outcomes are to be judged according to the manner in which educated people live. Considerable experimental evidence concerning transfer in school is available, and the picture is reasonably clear. Concerning the more important problems of transfer to out-of-school living and to adult life, it is necessary, unfortunately, to depend largely upon observation, opinion, logic, and hypotheses.

Thorndike's theory of transfer according to *identical elements* states that specific things learned in one situation become useful in other situations. Some psychologists regard this as repetition of something already learned rather than as transfer. The child who learns to balance his body while hopping on one foot in playing hopscotch will be able to balance his body while hopping on one foot in a relay race. The boy who learns to catch a basketball while running may be able to utilize many of the same movements in catching a football on the run.

The theory of *generalization of experience*, advanced by Judd, holds that education is training in how to think, how to generalize, and how to be scientific. Although Judd spoke of generalization of intellectual activity, it is reasonable to believe that motor, social, and emotional learning follow a similar pattern. According to this theory, transfer is determined by method of teaching and learning; subject matter has relatively little effect. School experiences affect subsequent thinking and acting if the student has been taught to generalize. Thus, if education helps one to attack a problem by defining it, marshaling pertinent information, formulating and testing hypotheses, and arriving at sound conclusions, such a generalized procedure is likely to be used when similar problems are met.

Bagley has theorized that *ideals of procedure* such as neatness and orderliness transfer when consciously worked for and when they are emotionalized and given value by the learner. This may be thought of as an extension of the generalization theory. Generalization transfers if it becomes an ideal.

Gestalt psychologists believe that transfer occurs through *insight into the whole of a perceived situation*, and that *cues* which release previously formed patterns are important. They deny the identical elements transfer theory. It is the configuration, or mosaic, that counts. The whole may give meaning to some of the parts that are quite different from what they would be if the part stood by itself. Pressey and Robinson have proposed a theory of transfer by *common elements.* They reason, on the basis of their interpretation of experimental evidence, that there may be transfer of fact, skill, or method if there is a common element and if the common element is perceived.

Social and emotional experiences may transfer. It is believed that the best training for living in the future is to live fully today. An education that emphasizes development of desirable social qualities through experiences in social situations is based upon the assumption that qualities developed through school experiences will become a part of one's pattern of living. Similarly, emotional behaviors developed in school help to lay a foundation for continuing emotional behavior and adjustment. How do social and emotional learnings transfer from school to out-of-school and adult situations?

If school experiences duplicate out-of-school situations, school behavior may be repeated elsewhere. This might be thought of as transfer of identical elements, or it might well be regarded as simply repetition. There may be transfer through generalization of concepts of how to behave in socialized situations, how to get along with people, and how to adjust to emotional tendencies and pressures in conformity with Judd's theory.

Ideals, attitudes, dispositions, self-reliance, perseverance, feelings of confidence, and the like may transfer. If Bagley's theory—that attitudes must be elevated into ideals and given emotional tone in order for transfer to be effective—is correct, then strong attitudes and emotionalized responses not only transfer as such but become the bases for transfer of associated factors. Attention to attitudes and to emotional aspects of education thus represents the backbone of teaching for transfer. Social and emotional sets may transfer according to the gestalt theory of insights and cues which bring forth previously formed patterns.

Whichever theory or theories of transfer may be closest to truth, it seems apparent that social and emotional behaviors learned in school affect desirable transfer a great deal more than any subject matter in and of itself. In the area of health, for instance, it is generally accepted that knowledge alone proves insufficient. Desirable interests, attitudes, dispositions, and feelings toward healthful behavior are a requirement for the most effective health behavior, a requirement for effective transfer in terms of action. Whether or not a person incorporates physical activity into his living over a long period of years depends largely upon interests and attitudes.

LENGTH AND DISTRIBUTION OF PRACTICE PERIODS

Too many physical education teachers, perhaps especially coaches, arrange time so that single periods of practice on isolated skills and segments of games are too long for optimum results. Reviewing research in a supplement to the regular issues of the *Research Quarterly* of the American Association for Health, Physical Education, and Recreation which was a project of the Research Council presented to commemorate the seventy-fifth anniversary of the association, Dorothy R. Mohr [9] points out that of 45 studies concerning distributed and massed practice found in psychology 40 favored distributed practice, three favored massed practice, and two found no significant differences. She noted that while the many experiments conducted by psychologists favored distributed practice in about 90 percent of the cases, results of studies within physical education present a picture of less agreement, and more research will be needed before strong claims concerning distributed and massed practice can be based upon studies reported in physical education literature.

A considerable amount of research indicates that, generally speaking, short and spaced practice periods prove more economical than longer ones. Nevertheless optimum length depends upon the nature of the learning task. Short and distributed practices should be used for isolated or fatiguing or relatively uninteresting skills, longer periods for skills which have a broad scope. Some reasons for the effectiveness of short periods are maintenance of a higher interest, a greater concentration of attention, less fatigue, and less boredom. Most of the experimental evidence in motor learning concerns the development of skills such as typewriting, handwriting, learning mazes, speed of tapping, target striking, and juggling. There is little evidence concerning the most economical distribution of practice time for learning combinations of motor skills such as one finds in the total process of playing basketball. In addition, much of the boredom accompanying drill in physical education skills often results from standing in line waiting a turn rather than from actual practice of a skill.

In an early and highly regarded study Frederick W. Cozens [10] found that distributed practice periods were superior to massed or concentrated periods for learning to hurdle, run the half mile, broad-jump, put the shot, and throw the discus. Clyde Knapp and W. Robert Dixon,[11] using university male seniors as subjects, reported that daily five-minute practice

[9] Dorothy R. Mohr, "The Contribution of Physical Activity to Skill Learning," *Research Quarterly of the American Association for Health, Physical Education, and Recreation*, vol. 31, no. 2, pp. 321–350, May, 1960.

[10] Frederick W. Cozens, "A Comparative Study of Two Methods of Teaching Class Work in Track and Field Events," *Research Quarterly of the American Association for Health and Physical Education*, 2:75–79, December, 1931.

[11] Clyde Knapp and W. Robert Dixon, "Learning to Juggle: I. A Study to Determine the Effect of Two Different Distributions of Practice in Learning Efficiency," *Research Quarterly of the American Association for Health, Physical Education, and Recreation*, 21:331–336, October, 1950.

periods were more economical of practice time than fifteen-minute periods every other day in learning to juggle three balls. The study showed that one minute of practice time during daily five-minute periods produced as much learning as 1.8 minutes of practice during fifteen-minute periods every other day.

The same authors, working with Murney Lazier [12] and the Evanston, Illinois, Township High School freshman boys, found that daily five-minute periods produced learning in less practice time than did fifteen-minute practices every other day, and found that relative effectiveness of these two time distributions was about the same for high school freshman boys as for university male seniors.

Franklin Henry and Jim Brozek,[13] working with conscientious objectors who had volunteered for physiological and nutritional experiments, found no significant differences in learning progress between groups who practiced gross body-reaction time and pattern tracing with the following practice distributions: (1) three trials a day, (2) two trials a day, (3) one trial a day, (4) three trials a week, (5) irregular, i.e., at choice of subject, and (6) irregular but within a six-week period. Each practice session consisted of the same routine, 75 reactions to a gross body movement signal and one turn at pattern tracing which took seven to eight minutes.

Joseph B. Oxendine [14] experimented with progressive changes in length of practice using mirror tracing as the skill. Three practice schedules were arranged; for one group the length of each succeeding practice period increased, for another each succeeding period decreased, and for the third every practice was of the same duration. The group using equal length practice learned best, and the increasing-practice group learned better than did the decreasing-practice group.

Olive Young [15] compared the rates of learning archery and badminton. Some college classes met and practiced four times per week, others two times per week, with the total amount of time equal. Archery was learned

[12] Clyde Knapp, W. Robert Dixon, and Murney Lazier, "Learning to Juggle: III. A Study of Performance by Two Different Age Groups," *Research Quarterly of the American Association for Health, Physical Education, and Recreation,* 29:32–36, March, 1958.

[13] Franklin Henry and Jim Brozek, "Relation between Distribution of Practice and Learning Efficiency in Psychomotor Performance," *Journal of Experimental Psychology,* 37:16–24, February, 1947.

[14] Joseph B. Oxendine, "Effect of Progressively Changing Practice Schedules on the Learning of a Motor Skill," *Research Quarterly of the American Association for Health, Physical Education, and Recreation,* 36:307–315, October, 1965.

[15] Olive Young, "The Rate of Learning in Relation to Spacing of Practice Periods in Archery and Badminton," *Research Quarterly of the American Association for Health, Physical Education, and Recreation,* 25:231–243, May, 1954.

more rapidly by the four-day group; badminton players progressed more rapidly with the two-per-week schedule.

John M. Harmon and Arthur G. Miller,[16] using billiards as the learning task, compared the effectiveness of (1) additive practice, i.e., gradually lengthening periods, (2) practice three days per week for three weeks, (3) daily practice, and (4) practice once a week. Additive allotment of time proved somewhat superior to the others. Robert N. Singer[17] used the novel skill of bouncing a basketball off the floor and into the basket. Each of three groups took 80 shots: the massed practice required 80 consecutive shots; a relatively massed time allotment gave five-minute pauses between several 20-attempt trials; and distributed practice gave twenty-four hours between sets of 20-shot practices. Distributed practice (twenty-four-hour intervals) was more effective than the other two for immediate acquisition but retention, as measured one month later, was better for the massed and relatively massed groups.

Experimental evidence concerning length and distribution of practice periods would be more helpful to physical education teachers if more information relative to team and individual games was available. However, the general hypothesis that relatively short and distributed periods produce superior results may be stated with confidence. Appropriate distributions depend upon interests and abilities of the learner and upon the type of skill being practiced. A coach who, dissatisfied with learning progress when things are going badly, announces, "We'll stick with this until we get it," is wasting time. He might better direct practice to another skill or segment and return later to the one causing difficulty.

LEARNING BY WHOLES AND PARTS

As indicated above, gestalt-field explanations of learning hold that behavior depends upon unified patterns and upon an insight into and understanding of relationships, combinations, patterns, configurations, and syntheses to facilitate learning. Hence, according to theories in this tradition, people learn best when confronted with unified thoughts or tasks rather than with a situation which calls for one response to one stimulus.

Theories in the associationistic-conditioning family hold that one learns as he is conditioned or habituated to one bit of information or skill, then to another and another. He will achieve mastery as each of several seg-

[16] John M. Harmon and Arthur G. Miller, "Time Patterns in Motor Learning," *Research Quarterly of the American Association for Health, Physical Education, and Recreation,* 21:182–187, October, 1950.

[17] Robert N. Singer, "Massed and Distributed Practice Effects on the Acquisition and Retention of a Novel Basketball Skill," *Research Quarterly of the American Association for Health, Physical Education, and Recreation,* 36:68–77, March, 1965.

ments are perfected, and when each component has been mastered the learner will have full knowledge or will have the ability to perform a skill as he adds the various parts.

It may seem logical for a teacher to expect that if he requires his students to learn each part of a gross movement they will have the ability to do the whole as soon as each of the parts is mastered. On the surface this seems logical enough but it may prove to be unsound psychologically. As an illustration think of two contrasting approaches to teaching a golf swing.

Let us assume that a grip and a stance would be taught in essentially the same way regardless of beliefs about what conditions favor efficient learning. Gestalt-field–oriented teachers likely will agree that each of these skills represents a unified pattern, hence a large enough whole to provide a pattern or synthesis in itself. Associationistic-oriented teachers would view each as a small enough part to segregate for practice.

Now consider the rest of a golf swing. A gestalt-oriented director of learning probably would show and briefly explain the key points of the swing and ask the learner to try. Between trials this teacher would encourage the learner to repeat in further trials what he did reasonably well previously, explain or show correct performance of parts which the learner did poorly, prescribe more trials, and repeat this process.

An associationistic-oriented teacher might break the swing into parts and ask the learner to practice each part until he could do it right before proceeding to another part. Thus one might start with the first half of the backswing, then proceed to the second half of the backswing, the pivot, the first half of a downswing, the eye movements, and the follow-through, and permit trying the whole swing only after each of the above six parts has been learned. A difficulty is that the relationship between the parts, as well as the parts themselves, needs to be learned. The person who perfects numbers one and two and three and each part through number six, is faced with another learning problem as he attempts to put them together. In figure 2, Illustration A shows a theory which might underlie a part-by-part approach. The parts of the circle add up to a good circle. Illustration A_1 shows what the actual result of a part-by-part approach may be. The parts add up to a broken circle. Illustration B shows a gestalt-insight approach. The single line between parts shows that instead of each triangle being an independent part, each is dependent upon the others. Using such a method the teacher first sees how the learner can comprehend and perform the whole swing. Then he helps the pupil smooth and improve and perfect his swing by giving encouragement and advice and information between practice swings. The teacher may indeed prescribe specific practice on one or more of the steps, but only if a diagnosis of complete swings shows need.

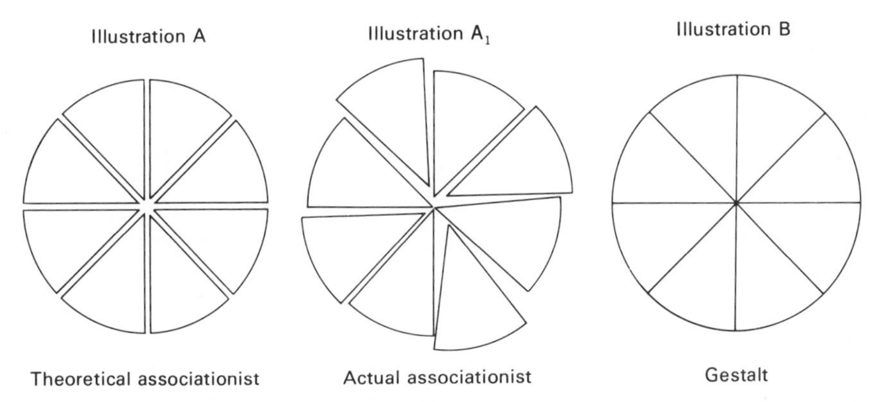

Figure 2 According to Associationist theory, the sum of the parts equals the whole (Illustration A); but in reality (Illustration A_1), learning the component parts does not assure mastery of the whole. In gestalt theory, however, the parts intertwine to make a whole (Illustration B).

According to gestalt-field family theories, all mental phenomena have structure or pattern. Ideas, events, and impressions have meaning because of their relationships to a context or pattern. Learning is creative, and discovery is the essence of it. Failure to learn is failure to construct a satisfactory configuration or structure or pattern or gestalt. New ideas have meaning only as they fit into a whole. A whole is more than the sum of its parts because each part has significance only as it fits with other parts and with a whole. An experience has one meaning to one person, another meaning to another person, because meaning depends upon experiences within and without the present experience. What makes a gestalt a configuration, a pattern, for one may be too complicated for another.

If gestalt-field theories are correct, it would seem that learning by wholes would be greatly superior to learning by parts. What is the situation in motor learning? Experimental evidence is not conclusive. The difficulty probably is more with semantics and with a concept or definition of a whole than it is with a real learning process.

Using infantry trainees as subjects, S. S. McGuigan and Eugene F. MacCaslin [18] studied the effect of part and whole methods of learning rifle marksmanship. They found the whole method superior to the part both for slow and sustained firing at targets. Ralph L. Wickstrom [19] experi-

[18] Eugene F. MacCaslin, "Whole and Part Methods in Learning a Perceptual Motor Skill," *American Journal of Psychology*, 68:658–661, December, 1955.

[19] Ralph L. Wickstrom, "Comparative Study of Methodologies for Teaching Gymnastics and Tumbling Stunts," *Research Quarterly of the American Association for Health, Physical Education, and Recreation*, 29:109–115, March, 1958.

mented with teaching several basic tumbling and gymnastic stunts to college men. One group learned by a whole method, another by a direct repetitive method. Subjects using the whole method learned with fewer trials. Clyde Knapp and W. Robert Dixon [20] reported a two-part study of whole and part methods, using juggling three balls as the task. The first part of the study compared learning by working with not less than three balls during all practices (whole) to learning by working with either one ball or with two (part). It took the part group 20 percent longer to learn. The second part of the study, using two different groups of subjects, compared learning by using the same whole method described above to learning by using any part or whole method or combination the subjects cared to use. It took the free-choice part group 30 percent longer than the whole-method group to reach the learning criterion.

What constitutes a whole? Using basketball for an analogy, is playing the full game necessary for a whole experience? Does two-against-two qualify as a whole experience? Does shooting a free throw constitute a whole? What makes a gestalt? The question cannot be answered in absolute terms. The import for the selection of teaching method may be stated as follows: A whole method is always superior to a part method when a whole is defined as the largest whole, or unified whole-part, which the learner can grasp without undue confusion. Ineffectiveness of a part or drill method springs principally from an inability to relate the part to a whole and from lack of interest. The whole-part-whole method helps the learner to relate parts to wholes, and it makes part practice more interesting. Generally speaking, teachers may be quite sure that a whole-part-whole-part-whole, etc., method will produce superior learning of complicated motor skills.

The question of appropriate speed during the early stages of practice relates to whole and part methods. Slow-motion performance, frequently used when a learner approaches a complicated skill, may be unrealistic because the slow movement will not be used in the total act. Research on this point seems to show that full-speed movements should be practiced from the start. Ruth E. Fulton [21] found that a group emphasizing speed from the start, in striking a moving ball, developed a greater accuracy than the group which made accuracy of stroke the primary aim from the start of the experiment.

[20] Clyde Knapp and W. Robert Dixon, "Learning to Juggle: II. A Study of Whole and Part Methods," *Research Quarterly of the American Association for Health, Physical Education, and Recreation,* 23:398–401, December, 1952.

[21] Ruth E. Fulton, "Speed and Accuracy in Learning a Ballistic Movement," *Research Quarterly of the American Association for Health, Physical Education, and Recreation,* 13:30–36, March, 1942.

W. H. Solley[22] experimented with three groups learning a thrust at a target. The group which emphasized speed developed greater speed and as much accuracy as the group which emphasized accuracy; the groups which emphasized both speed and accuracy became the most accurate. In another study Solley[23] found that initial emphasis upon speed was readily transferred into speed and accuracy but that accuracy learned at low rates of speed was lost when speed was increased.

KINESTHETIC PERCEPTION

Empirical evidence has led most physical education teachers and coaches to the conclusion that kinesthetic perception, muscular feeling, is highly important for learning skills. "Feel it," "groove it," and "remember how it felt" represent advice frequently given. Scientific support can be found in the literature of biology and physiology. Physical education literature also indicates that kinesthetic perception is important. Louise L. Roloff[24] found eight tests of kinesthesis that have merit and concluded that there was a positive relationship between motor ability and kinesthesis among the college women subjects. However, no statistically significant evidence showing the superiority of experimental teaching emphasizing a kinesthetic approach was found.

The idea of blindfolded practice has been used as a means of encouraging kinesthetic perception, especially by basketball coaches teaching free throwing. Research concerning kinesthesis within physical education has tended to emphasize the use of blindfolds in its experiments. Describing a pioneer effort, Coleman R. Griffith[25] reported an experiment in learning to drive a golf ball in which one group practiced blindfolded for four weeks, then without blindfolds for two weeks. The other group practiced for six weeks but, of course, without blindfolds. During the early part of the experiment the performance of the blindfolded group was inferior. But by the end of the fourth week, the blindfolded group actually did a little better than the other group. At the conclusion of the experiment the blindfolded group were superior.

[22] W. H. Solley, "Speed, Accuracy, and Speed and Accuracy as an Initial Directive in Motor Learning," *Motor Skills Research Exchange*, 3:76–77, March, 1951.

[23] W. H. Solley, "The Effects of Verbal Instruction of Speed and Accuracy upon the Learning of a Motor Skill," *Research Quarterly of the American Association for Health, Physical Education, and Recreation*, 23:231–240, May, 1950.

[24] Louise L. Roloff, "Kinesthesis in Relation to the Learning of Selected Motor Skills," *Research Quarterly of the American Association for Health, Physical Education, and Recreation*, 24:210–217, May, 1953.

[25] Coleman R. Griffith, "An Experiment in Learning to Drive a Golf Ball," *The Athletic Journal*, vol. 11, no. 10:11–13, June, 1931.

The indication that spatial performance based upon kinesthetic cues may be a specific ability, rather than one which applies to dissimilar situations, is given by Bryant J. Cratty [26] who found little or no ability to transfer learning from a gross motor task to a fine motor task among blindfolded subjects learning to traverse a large locomotor maze (111 feet long) and a small stylus maze (44 inches long). Kinesthetic cues provided the learning since neither visual nor auditory information was available. In another study Cratty [27] found that prior practice on a similar stylus maze caused initial positive transfer to a locomotor maze, and that prior practice on a dissimilar, a reversed mirror, pattern caused initial negative transfer. Cratty indicated that since subjects did not report awareness of pattern relationships he regarded the transfer as largely unconscious. Reporting another study Cratty [28] described an experiment in which one group of male university students moved blindfolded through curved half-circle pathways 8 times, another group 12 times, another group 16 times. Immediately afterward each group traversed a straight pathway. In response to the experimenter's query about feelings of opposite curvature in the straight pathway, subjects with 12 trials in a curved pathway reported more opposite curvature; i.e., they reported more after-effects than did either of the other two groups. Cratty hypothesized that 12 trials resulted in an optimum attention level and that more trials may have caused reduced attention or concentration.

MENTAL ASPECTS OF MOTOR LEARNING

In addition to having the kinesthetic qualities described above, motor learning is perceptual, cognitive, rational, and thoughtful. The learner forms his first concept of movement by observing, listening, feeling, or reading, or through some combination of these avenues, and by thinking about information and feelings coming from these sources. As he progresses the learner expands his concept by analyzing his trials, his attempts, and his practice, and by receiving advice from the teacher. Muscles, kinesthetic sensations, eyes, ears, and speech are called upon to learn

[26] Bryant J. Cratty, "Comparison of Learning a Fine Motor Task with Learning a Similar Gross Motor Task Using Kinesthetic Cues," *Research Quarterly of the American Association for Health, Physical Education, and Recreation,* 33:212–221, May, 1962.

[27] Bryant J. Cratty, "Transfer of Small-pattern Practice to Large-pattern Learning," *Research Quarterly of the American Association for Health, Physical Education, and Recreation,* 33:523–535, December, 1962.

[28] Bryant J. Cratty, "Figural After-effects Resulting from Gross Action Patterns: The Amount of Exposure to the Inspection Task and the Duration of the After-effects," *Research Quarterly of the American Association for Health, Physical Education, and Recreation,* 36:237–242, October, 1965.

motor skills. Learning to play games involves judgments of distance, direction, and moving objects in space; analysis of performance; decisions concerning when and where to execute certain maneuvers; information concerning rules and etiquette; appropriate relations with teammates, opponents, and officials; control of emotions; care and protection of the body; and many other things which require information and reflective thinking.

"A good picture is worth a thousand words" is as true in physical education as in any field of learning and more true of physical movements than of most other areas. Some individuals have intellectual and observational abilities which permit them to grasp a movement or even a rather complicated series of movements in short order. Others require repeated observations, explanation, and practice. A good deal of practice always is needed to achieve higher levels of performance.

MENTAL PRACTICE

A division between mental aspects and kinesthetic sensations proves difficult and perhaps unwise to make. The following review of selected research on mental practice could have been presented under Kinesthetic Perception above since muscular sensation is involved. It is placed here because it deals directly with mental practice.

Robert T. Kretchmar, Hoyt Sherman, and Ross Mooney [29] considered the problem of learning by watching and by feeling. They concluded that some students have the ability to learn about a motor skill by watching a performance. They believe that while learning varies considerably among individuals, ability to *catch by empathy* does exist. It involves the capacity to feel as if one were doing himself what he sees performed. To learn effectively by watching requires keen observation. However, in addition to observation there needs to be a transfer of the movement idea to muscular feel.

What effect does mental practice, i.e., thinking through a task, have upon motor learning. Some experiments indicate that such practice facilitates motor learning substantially. R. A. Vandall, R. A. Davis, and H. A. Clayton [30] reported that mental practice daily over a period of eighteen days was helpful in learning to hit a target with darts and about as effective as daily physical practice in learning to shoot free throws. A group of boys who practiced free throws (physical practice) for twenty

[29] Robert T. Kretchmar, Hoyt Sherman, and Ross Mooney, "A Survey of Research in the Teaching of Sports," *Research Quarterly of the American Association for Health, Physical Education, and Recreation,* 20:238–249, October, 1949.

[30] H. A. Clayton, "The Function of Mental Practice in the Acquisition of Motor Skills," *Journal of General Psychology,* 29:243–250, October, 1943.

days improved 41 percent; a group who shot free throws on the first day, engaged in mental but not physical practice on the second through nineteenth days, then shot again on the twentieth day improved 43 percent. Another group shot on the first day and again on the twentieth day with no intervening practice either physical or mental; they improved 2 percent.

Wilbur E. Twining,[31] wishing to find the results of an experiment similar to the one by Vandall, Davis, and Clayton, conducted a ring-toss study in which groups tossed rings as follows: (1) 12 subjects threw 210 rings on the first and twenty-second days; (2) 12 subjects threw 210 rings on the first day, 70 rings each day on the second through twenty-first days and 210 on the twenty-second day; (3) 12 subjects threw 210 rings on the first day, mentally rehearsed their first day's activity for fifteen minutes daily on the second through the twenty-first days, and threw 210 rings on the twenty-second day. Group 1 (first and twenty-second days only) improved 4.3 percent, a chance gain; group 2 (daily physical practice) improved 137 percent; group 3 (mental practice) improved 36 percent. Twining concluded that mental practice was effective.

Undirected mental practice is superior to directed according to John Gerald Jones.[32] In his study 73.33 percent of his college male subjects who engaged in undirected mental practice passed the gymnastic skill hock-swing upstart on the first trial whereas, 40 percent of those who engaged in directed mental practice did so. Learning is more effective when the learner builds the image, the cognitive pattern, himself. If the teacher attempts to direct his thinking, the completion of the image may never occur. Similarly if a teacher of a skill provides external stimuli to the learner through spoken direction while the learner is trying to perform a movement, there may be interference with the learner's concentration and with his building of his own cognitive pattern and his own kinesthetic image. L. Verdelle Clark [33] found mental practice to be nearly as effective as physical practice of one-handed basketball shooting. Subjects were given instruction and then took 25 shots to secure initial scores. The physical-practice group took 25 shots a day for fourteen days; the mental-practice subjects met daily for sessions of reading, thinking, and imagining themselves taking 25 shots. Subjects were subdivided by ability: superior, middle and low. Superior subjects improved 16 percent with

[31] Wilbur E. Twining, "Mental Practice and Physical Practice in Learning a Motor Skill," *Research Quarterly of the American Association for Health, Physical Education, and Recreation,* 20:432–435, December, 1949.

[32] John Gerald Jones, "Motor Learning without Demonstration of Physical Practice," *Research Quarterly of the American Association for Health, Physical Education, and Recreation,* 36:270–276, October, 1965.

[33] L. Verdelle Clark, "Effect of Mental Practice on the Development of a Certain Motor Skill," *Research Quarterly of the American Association for Health, Physical Education, and Recreation,* 31:560–569, December, 1960.

physical practice and 15 percent with mental practice; middle subjects, 28 percent with physical practice and 23 percent with mental practice; and low subjects, 44 percent with physical practice and 28 percent with mental practice.

Mental practice, no doubt, helps one to learn motor skills. While the effectiveness of mental rehearsal of game-condition situations is universally accepted, the idea of mental practice for movements regarded as purely physical has far less than unanimous approval. Teachers should encourage mental rehearsal. Outside-of-class practice and reading assignments should be considered.

LEARNING CURVES

Learning seldom, if ever, shows smooth progress. Learning curves, graphical representations of progress at intervals during the learning process, may show rapid gains at some points, slow progress at others, and no learning or even retrogressions at other times. Periods of little progress and losses are believed to be caused by such things as lapses in motivation, boredom, ill health, emotional disturbances, dullness resulting from fatigue, changes in the nature of the skill, difficulties in integration of combinations of movement, psychological limits, and physiological limits. Avoidance and modification of plateaus rest upon finding the causes and eliminating them. Periods of rapid progress are related to strong determination resulting from high interest and motivation.

SUMMARY

Students of methods should maintain a clear distinction between teaching and learning. Teaching centers about the organization of learning experiences, its purpose being to make learning more efficient. A teacher plans a learning experience to make the learning process as efficient as possible. A teacher cannot merely show or tell a student what he desires him to learn but must lead him in actually experiencing the desired learning. The showing or telling is merely one step in the teaching process.

Learning can be interpreted as problem solving, the attainment of goals, or the satisfaction of motives. Learning in a broad sense is the adjustment of the whole organism to a new situation.

Gestalt-field theories hold that each person's behavior depends upon a unified pattern. A whole becomes more than the sum of its parts because parts act upon each other to make a whole what it is. Associationistic-family theories hold that learning is a result of building block upon block, learning one part, then another, until all parts add up to a whole.

Some learning tasks require different types of procedure from others.

Methods consistent with a theory in the gestalt-field tradition may be highly effective in most situations while approaches consistent with an associationistic explanation of learning may prove more useful when there is a need for establishing a fixed response to a given situation.

Motivation is central to all learning. It is a key which determines effectiveness in any learning experience. Intrinsic motivation (learning which carries its own reward) is superior to extrinsic (motivation external to or apart from the basic essence of the learning activity itself).

Transfer of learning of a fact, skill, or method may occur if there are common elements and the utility of the common element is perceived.

For the learning of skills, short practice periods distributed over rather long periods prove more economical than long practice periods over a short time span. The nature of the skill determines the optimum length for practice periods. Short lengths of time prove best for isolated, fatiguing, and uninteresting skills; longer periods should be used for practice of skills having broad scope.

According to field theories, learning by wholes is superior to learning by parts. For motor learning a whole method is superior to a part method when a whole is defined as the largest whole, or unified whole-part, which the learner can grasp without undue confusion.

Kinesthetic perception is important to motor learning. One must translate ideas into muscular action and get the feel to learn a motor skill. Motor learning is perceptual, cognitive, rational, and thoughtful, and involves mental as well as physical aspects of learning.

Mental practice helps in the learning of motor skills. Outside-of-class practice and reading assignments are in order.

Learning rarely progresses at a steady pace. It may be rapid at some points and slow at others. It may retrogress at points and be static at others. Periods of rapid progress are usually related to strong determination resulting from high interest and motivation.

Questions and problems for discussion

1. List means by which students are motivated to learn in physical education in secondary schools. Place them in order of their overall educational value, and discuss the reasons for your placement.

2. What specific suggestions would you offer to a teacher who is having difficulty motivating a conditioning class of ninth-grade boys or girls, composed of youngsters who scored exceptionally low on motor-fitness tests and retests?

3. How would one determine what constitutes satisfactory units of learning (meaningful wholes) in physical education activities? Give several examples.

4. From your own experience in physical education activities indicate instances where transfer of learning apparently occurred. Describe other instances where transfer might have been expected but did not occur.

5. Are some motor skills learned more effectively when taught by conditioning, i.e., in a manner consistent with an associationistic theory of learning, while others are learned better if taught in ways consistent with a gestalt-field explanation of how learning takes place? If yes, give examples.

6. State ten topics or problems which reveal areas of needed research in teaching methods for physical education.

7. Distinguish between growth as learning and growth as maturation. Discuss some of the implications of maturation for teaching physical education.

8. Describe some of the present-day school practices in both physical education and other areas of the secondary school curriculum which seem to deny the learning principle that learning is an active process and takes place only through activity on the part of the learner. Describe some of the good practices.

Selected references

Bernard, Harold W., and Wesley C. Huckins (eds.): *Readings in Educational Psychology,* World Book Company, Tarrytown-on-Hudson, N.Y., 1967.

Blair, Glenn Myers, R. Stewart Jones, and Ray H. Simpson: *Educational Psychology,* 3d ed., The Macmillan Company, New York, 1968.

Bugelski, M. R.: *The Psychology of Learning Applied to Teaching,* The Bobbs-Merrill Company, Inc., Indianapolis, 1964.

Combs, A. W.: *The Professional Education of Teachers,* Allyn and Bacon, Inc., Englewood Cliffs, N.J., 1965.

Cratty, Bryant J.: *Movement Behavior and Motor Learning,* Lea & Febiger, Philadelphia, 1964.

———: *Social Dimensions of Physical Activity,* Prentice-Hall, Inc., Englewood Cliffs, N.J., 1967.

Cronbach, Lee J.: *Educational Psychology,* 2d ed., Harcourt, Brace & World, Inc., New York, 1963.

Crow, Lester D.: *Psychology of Human Development,* Alfred A. Knopf, Inc., New York, 1967.

DeCecco, John P. (ed.): *Human Learning in the School,* Holt, Rinehart and Winston, Inc., New York, 1963.

Klausmeier, Herbert J., and William Goodwin: *Learning and Human Abilities: Educational Psychology,* 2d ed., Harper & Row, Publishers, Incorporated, New York, 1966.

McDonald, Frederick J.: *Educational Psychology,* 2d ed., Wadsworth Publishing Company, Belmont, Calif., 1965.

chapter 3

UNDERSTANDING AND GUIDING TODAY'S ADOLESCENTS

INTRODUCTION

Secondary school educational effort must, in the last analysis, derive operational direction from the nature and needs of students. Learning, which in Chapter 2 is defined as a change in behavior as the result of experience, can take place only if it is within the capacity of the individual to learn. Further, the effectiveness of the learning experience will be enhanced if it is meaningful to the learner. It follows, then, that to be most effective, secondary school physical education programs must be based upon an understanding of the general nature of the needs, interests, abilities, behavior, and characteristics of the adolescent age group which the school serves. They must also be based on an understanding of the social milieu of today's youth. The ways in which physical education and its teachers uniquely contribute to the growth and development of adolescents and to the guidance function of schools provide added insight into teaching methodology. This chapter presents an overview of these topics, serves as a general review for students who already have been introduced to adolescent psychology, and summarizes the implications of this area for teaching physical education in secondary schools.

Before one begins a study of any age group, certain fundamental terms associated with growth and development need clarification. The terms growth and development themselves, often used synonymously, actually connote shades of separate meanings. *Growth* refers to an increase in the bulk, size, complexity, efficiency, or value of any physical or mental aspect of the organism. *Development* refers to an unfolding of abilities as the organism moves to optimum maturity. Growth and (or) development are usually judged by how satisfactorily the individual approximates general traits within the limits imposed by his heredity and environment. Growth and development are continuous and unified processes although not necessarily always in the direction best for the individual and society. Optimum maturation of the individual depends upon the compatible balancing of the capacities of the individual and the requirements of his environment. A review of the meanings of such commonly used terms as needs, interests, abilities, and behavior serves to clarify aspects of this complex interrelationship.

NEEDS

Needs, as used in understanding human behavior, concern a complex system of motives whose roots lie in the biological and psycho-social nature of man. They represent consistent tendencies of the human organism in goal-seeking behavior. A basic need can be thought of as a state of tension which drives a person to action in an attempt to relieve tension. Needs spring from original endowment (heredity) and from environmental conditions (experiences). It seems trite to say that one is what he is because of heredity and environment, but it does somewhat clarify issues to call attention to the fact that human behavior can seldom, if ever, be ascribed to one or the other. Behavior results from influences of both—from the interactions between what one is born with and what has happened to him. These needs, these states of tension, are desirable not only for the survival of the species biologically, but also for the accomplishment of man's unique social purpose. Drive to activity is both a biological and social prerequisite. The human body needs to provide itself with food and water to survive and with sexual activity to reproduce its kind. Satisfaction of the hunger, thirst, and sexual drives is necessary for human survival. Activity drive is a requirement for social progress and satisfaction. A complacent and easily satisfied person who is not driven to action by tension-producing needs lacks motivation for accomplishment. Weakly motivated individuals often seem colorless and dull. Strong motivation which stirs action comprises a prime requisite for effective learning, whether the learning be rote memory, problem solving, or motor skill. Motivation rests upon felt needs; it is highly individualistic and complicated, yet it is possible to ascribe it to the categories of basic needs of the individual.

CLASSIFICATION OF NEEDS

Most psychologists who deal with the issue of needs classify them as organic (biological and physiological), on the one hand, and psychological (social or personality), on the other hand. Any system of classification of human needs, however, provides only a summary for convenience.

Psychological needs modify organic needs, and the organism affects psychological needs. They are interdependent, and the complex interaction among the various needs compels humans to action or inaction. The fact that the lists presented by many authors vary greatly does not mean that little is known about basic human needs. It simply means that writers present a classification as one means of providing a frame of reference. Classifications may help to integrate thinking, to contribute to orderly overall thinking, to constitute valuable starting points, but they do not present a complete picture of human needs. Rather, they form a basis for analysis, useful in identifying the needs of an individual or group, just as a statement of general objectives of physical education forms a base helpful to the teacher who sets about formulating objectives for an individual or group. It must be remembered, however, that each individual develops unique needs which are not the same as the needs of others even though they have the same foundation in basic needs.

Many authors have attempted to list the fundamental human needs; some have presented short lists, others long. Not all psychologists agree that such lists serve useful purposes because they feel that too many items become meaningless and that too few may result in oversimplification of the complexity of human behavior. If the limitations of lists are recognized, they can have value in helping people to understand the needs and behavior of themselves and others. Experienced psychologists do not need to refer to a list for the purpose of helping to determine what may be the cause of given behaviors; they are well aware of the basic drives that impel men to action. But prospective teachers and teachers inclined to treat symptoms instead of causes may find that a list helps to direct their attention to causes for the behavior of their students. Little danger lies in such lists other than two dangers which are common to any insufficient knowledge of psychology: (1) the tendency to believe that a small amount of study prepares one to give competent advice, and (2) the erroneous tendency to diagnose as abnormal behavior that which is just different rather than truly deviant.

The bibliography at the end of the chapter gives resources for a study of the various ways in which today's psychologists are classifying needs.

A summary of the kinds of needs which are generally recognized as basic include:

Orangic needs	*Psychological needs*
Hunger	Status
Thirst	Achievement
Sex	Approval
Elimination	Security
Prevention of pain	Love or affection
Balanced activity-rest periods	Independence
Maintenance of body temperature	Affiliation
Maintenance of air supply	

TABLE 2 Developmental tasks from infancy through later life

Infancy and early childhood (birth to 6 years)	
Learning to walk	Achieving physiological stability
Learning to take solid foods	Forming simple concepts of social and physical reality
Learning to talk	Learning to relate oneself emotionally to parents, siblings, and other people
Learning to control the elimination of body wastes	Learning to distinguish right and wrong and developing a conscience
Learning sex differences and sexual modesty	
Middle childhood (6–12 years)	
Learning physical skills necessary for ordinary games	Developing concepts necessary for everyday living
Building wholesome attitudes toward oneself as a growing organism	Developing conscience, morality, and a scale of values
Learning to get along with age-mates	Achieving personal independence
Learning an appropriate masculine or feminine social role	Developing attitudes toward social groups and institutions
Developing fundamental skills in reading, writing, and calculating	
Preadolescence and adolescence (12–18 years)	
Achieving new and more mature relations with age-mates of both sexes	Achieving emotional independence of parents and other adults
Achieving a masculine or feminine social role	Achieving assurance of economic independence
Accepting one's physique and using the body effectively	Selecting and preparing for an occupation
	Preparing for marriage and family life

DEVELOPMENTAL TASKS

Closely akin to needs are *developmental tasks,* which have particular value because of their easy translation into the specific work of the school. They are valuable for purposes of understanding the learner and formulating objectives that are meaningful to both the learner and society. Developmental tasks have been described by staff members of the University of Chicago's Committee on Human Development as midpoints between an individual need and a societal demand, partaking of the nature of both. The Havighurst [1] concept of developmental tasks divides

[1] Robert J. Havighurst, *Human Development and Education,* used by permission of David McKay Company, Inc., New York, 1953.

Preadolescence and adolescence (continued)

Developing intellectual skills and concepts necessary for civic competence

Desiring and achieving socially responsible behavior

Acquiring a set of values and an ethical system as a guide to behavior

Early adulthood (18–35 years)

Selecting a mate

Learning to live with a marriage partner

Starting a family

Rearing children

Managing a home

Getting started in an occupation

Taking on civic responsibility

Finding a congenial social group

Middle age (35–60 years)

Achieving adult, civic, and social responsibility

Establishing and maintaining an economic standard of living

Assisting teen-age children to become responsible and happy adults

Developing adult leisure-time activities

Relating oneself to one's spouse as a person

Learning to accept and adjust to the physiological changes of middle age

Adjusting to aging parents

Later life (60–)

Adjusting to decreasing physical strength

Adjusting to retirement and reduced income

Adjusting to death of spouse

Establishing an explicit affiliation with one's age group

Meeting social and civic obligations

Establishing satisfactory living arrangements

---

the life-span into six periods and defines tasks for each age group that are based upon skills, attitudes, and understandings that the individual has need to achieve. The tasks and the need to achieve them arise out of the physical and mental characteristics of the individual and the unique cultural forces which surround his particular life cycle. Learning to talk, for example, depends on basic biological abilities and maturational characteristics. What the child learns to say and how he develops his verbal ability is culturally determined. A list of Havighurst's developmental tasks will help the reader understand the total concept of growth and development and serve to put in perspective the role of the adolescent, the age group under consideration in this text.

INTERESTS

In using or defining the term *interests,* the educator need not struggle with the usual semantic differences between the lay and professional use of a word. Interests simply refer to the individual's personal preferences. It is frequently difficult to account for interests of individuals. In general, interests and abilities go together although it is difficult to separate internalized interests from those pressed upon one by his environment. Thus the boy who turns out for basketball and engulfs his total energies and aspirations into making the team may be motivated by his desire to please his former basketball star parent, gain the status of team membership, succeed in something he knows he can do well, or any one of many different motives. Whatever the motive for the preference it must take secondary consideration in analyzing interests. If the interest is there, it is likely to result, barring subtle subconscious conflicts, in a realistic means of motivating and communicating with the learner. It is in this frame of reference that interests are discussed.

The professional as well as the popular use of the word "interests" does refer to what the individual says he wants or likes to do; the really basic need, direct or indirect to the activity, that he wants to satisfy has secondary importance as long as emotional conflicts do not intercede.

A teacher has the dual responsibility of helping students have worthwhile experiences based upon existing interests and stimulating the development of new interests. In addition, teachers need to curb unwholesome interests and to check those that lead to unwarranted and unrewarding expenditures of time and energy. Since the existing interests of children have grown out of their past experiences, new interests are created in much the same way. By enlarging the breadth of experience of the individual, by exposing him to a variety of activities, by surrounding the new activities with social approval of various kinds, especially peer approval, and by properly guiding the individual's interaction with them, teachers can help the individual form new interests of use to him in his adjustment to adult life.

ABILITIES

What is ability? What is meant by the statement, "He is an able person"? Is ability a general characteristic, or is it specific? Is it possible for a person to be equally able at any pursuit he might undertake? What ingredients determine ability? Is heredity or constitutional capacity the most fundamental determinant, or are experiences and circumstances the most important factors in the development of abilities?

According to the *Comprehensive Dictionary of Psychological and Psychoanalytical Terms*, an *ability* is the "actual power to perform an act, physical or mental whether or not the power is attained by training and education. Ability implies that the task can be performed *now*, if the necessary external circumstances are present; no further training is needed." [2]

Authorities consider constitutional capacity the most important and relatively constant determinant of potential ability. Capacity places ceilings over developmental possibilities. But most individuals fail to develop the upper limits of their potentialities. The everlasting intertwining of the sum total of experiences and circumstances, of course, determines the extent to which an individual realizes the possibilities with which he is endowed by nature.

Existence of specialized abilities seems apparent. Do they result from fundamental endowment, or do they emerge from interests that have been developed through experiences? Both factors play a part, and it is difficult to determine which operates more powerfully in individual cases. A person who pursues a specialty for which he is ill fitted may achieve little success. But a person with gifted innate ability may be stifled by the lack or misdirection of favorable experiences and circumstances. Real masters have high inherited ability plus adequate developmental experiences.

Motor ability consists of specialized abilities and coordination between various specialized movements. Although the phenomenon of many excellent all-around athletes would seem to indicate the presence of some unitary general motor ability, none has been isolated by well-known research. It is likely that such all-around ability results from such basic factors as strength, speed, reaction time, visual acuity, competitive determination, freedom from inhibiting emotional characteristics, and perhaps some unidentified factor of general coordination. While it is true that there are

[2] H. B. English and Ava C. English, *Comprehensive Dictionary of Psychological and Psychoanalytical Terms*, Longmans, Green & Co., Inc., New York, 1958.

good all-around athletes, it is equally true that certain performers excel in some sports and exemplify mediocrity in others.

DISPERSION OF ABILITIES

The existence and distribution of inherited biological abilities among human beings, whether general or specific, largely follow a chance arrangement or the so-called normal curve of distribution. Learned abilities do not necessarily follow this smooth curve but are likely to be represented by an accumulation of cases anywhere along the curve, high, low, or middle, depending upon the sampling and the extent of experience of the individuals concerned. In any event, most school populations include students of both high and low abilities, and though these are fewer in number than those who might be about average, they are of great educational importance. The school has a responsibility to help students of high ability to develop the upper limits of their capacities in order to promote individual self-realization and, more important, to fully utilize their potential for society. Equally, the school has the important responsibility of helping low-ability students become satisfied and useful members of society. And it is of paramount importance not to overlook giving equal attention to the average student who may be neglected while the exceptional child monopolizes the school's attention.

BEHAVIOR

Behavior refers to the organism's mode of response to stimuli. Everything the individual does can in a nonrestricted sense be termed behavior. One's actions result from needs that exist as tensions. Tensions are normal and desirable; they are entirely necessary to progress. The extremely placid person who has few needs that express themselves as tensions accomplishes little. Tensions result in abnormal behavior only when they become extreme and unsatisfied over long periods of time. Everyone has problems, but the number of real problem children is relatively small and would be much smaller if parents and teachers better understood the reasons why boys and girls behave as they do—like human beings. It is important to face reality, to face problems and attack them intelligently. Teachers should help students analyze their real problems and plan solutions.

Aggression in various forms represents common and normal behavior. Direct aggression, when possible and socially approved, provides a rapid means of relieving tension. But direct aggression frequently is not possible, and still more frequently overt aggression is disapproved in American culture. Although there are times when hitting an interferer on the nose would make a person feel much better, such action almost always proves unwise. If the other fellow is bigger and stronger, discretion becomes greater than valor. But fear of failure is a mild deterrent when compared to social approval. American culture and civilization respect the rights of others; they, of course, are not based upon the law of the jungle—survival of the fittest. Punishment is approved only after due process.

Aggression may result from frustration. It takes various forms. If not aimed directly at those responsible for the frustration, aggression may be directed toward substitutes or may be turned inward. A frustrated worker may be unusually aggressive toward his wife and children; a frustrated teacher may take it out on his students. Habitual internalizing of aggression causes real trouble. Undue self-blame causes a tremendous amount of unhappiness both for the person who does it and for those close to him.

Adjustment mechanisms are behavior responses to problems difficult or impossible to attack directly. They are tension reducers and maintainers of self-respect. Everyone uses some of them as compromises. While excessive use of any adjustment mechanism leads to maladjustment, moderate usage is normal and valuable.

GENERAL CHARACTERISTICS OF ADOLESCENTS

The tremendous emphasis given to adolescence by educational and psychological writers leads some readers erroneously to think that it is a period entirely different from any other. True, it is a period during which tensions and difficulties often are heightened because of rapid growth and changes in urges. But it is a part of growing up that starts at birth and continues throughout life.

The adolescent period does present problems of a unique nature. Rapid and uneven growth sometimes makes for poor body control. Sexual maturation causes boys and girls to regard each other in new ways. A late childhood period during which boys like to be with boys and girls with girls precedes desires for heterosexual social contacts. Anxieties appear about body changes. Boys wonder about a seeming inability to handle their bodies after spurts of growth. They may become concerned over the appearance of new pubic, underarm, chest, and facial hair, or, more likely, over the lack of these characteristics in themselves as they note development in age-mates. They feel reticent and insecure about expressing newly felt desires to be with girls. Those who mature later than others often lose confidence in old friends who show tendencies to like girls. They may become overly impressed by temporary skin blemishes which are due to imbalances of glandular secretions. Girls may become concerned about changes in body contours, increased size of breasts, and widened hips. From the standpoint of vigorous physical activity, temporary lessening of ability to handle their bodies is more serious with boys than with girls because of greater interests in sports among boys and because boys' status in their peer culture depends to a greater extent upon competence in physical activity.

During adolescence the individual prepares for adulthood. He wrestles with his need for independence, revolting from dependence upon parents and other adults with considerable frequency but returning to lean upon them from time to time. He must learn to accept responsibility and to manage his own affairs. Difficulties arise when the adolescent wants to proceed to independence too rapidly and when parents, teachers, and others put on too many brakes. If adult controls are removed, the adolescent achieves independence before he is likely to be able to use it wisely. But if parents, teachers, and others dominate, the individual may grow to a mature age without achieving the independence necessary to maturity.

The need for independence, coupled with the need for assuring dependence, leads to ambivalent behavior in the adolescent. Mature behavior is common; so, too, is regression to childish behavior. Consequently, alternating patterns of revolt against authority on the one hand and leaning upon adults on the other hand become the devious path of adolescent behavior. Parents and teachers who permit and encourage the individual to accept as much responsibility as he can shoulder and who also graciously and willingly hold themselves ready to serve as pillars upon which the youngsters can lean are the ones who are of real aid to the development of the adolescent.

Another common characteristic of adolescence centers about the achievement of appropriate and satisfactory association with the opposite sex. Physical appearance and clothing take on aspects of tremendous import to the young person who wants to make himself or herself attractive to the opposite sex. Boys are driven hard by desires to be strong, virile, manly, and handsome; desires to be attractive and good-looking provide powerful motivation for girls. Homes and schools that provide rich opportunities for boys and girls to engage in wholesome activities together help adolescents to achieve feelings of adequacy and naturalness in the presence of each other.

Adolescence is a period during which the individual does a good deal toward the formation of value concepts for living. Conflicting desires need to be integrated and balanced; points of view toward self, others, and the world are tentatively formed; problems of religion confront the individual as he considers conduct, origin, and destiny. High ideals are characteristic of adolescents, fortunately so because of the need for settling life goals and the necessity of restraints, particularly those of sex urges.

SOCIAL MILIEU

Social forces are an important contribution to adolescent development. Peer-group influence may be so strong that at times youngsters are more affected by desires for peer approval than by advice from parents, teachers, or other adults. A teen-age subculture may express value systems and typify modes of response.

INFLUENCE OF PEER GROUPS DURING ADOLESCENCE

The influence of his peer group is more important during adolescence than at any other period during life. Peer opinion pervades the typical adolescent's thinking and acting. Even though he is seeking independence from the adult members of his family and community, he retains a strong need for support. This he often finds within his peer group by submitting to the safety of thinking, dressing, acting, and conforming to the values of other youth. By surrounding himself with a like-behaving group he not only finds security in response to his dependency needs, but can reinforce his needs to achieve family independence by identifying with nonadult persons.

The adolescent peer groups which are most likely to be influential with the individual, the ones with which he is most likely to identify, are usually members of a relatively small and select clique. Cliques are usually composed of individuals from similar socioeconomic backgrounds who tend to become a group because of already existing interests, experiences, and values. They survive because of mutually existing ties of compatibility, goals, and friendships. Plans for the future play a particularly important role. In early adolescence commonness of interests is important, but in later adolescence, particularly in regard to pairing with members of the opposite sex, acceptability of the chosen individual by his own group plays an important role.

Because peer groups tend to be formed by already existing factors, they have less influence on adolescent values than is sometimes thought. On the basis of extensive studies on the subject, R. F. Peck and R. J. Havighurst concluded that adolescent peer groups are reinforcers, rather than originators, of values which have been acquired from their parents (good or bad) and approved by their social class. As a whole, adolescents do respect, accept, and in turn reward the same moral behavior as their parents.[3]

The adolescent peer groups who are delinquent gangs do not negate this theory since basic research on juvenile delinquency tends to show that many of the delinquents come from areas in which such behavior is

[3] R. F. Peck and R. J. Havighurst, *The Psychology of Character Development*, John Wiley & Sons, Inc., New York, 1960, p. 139.

socially accepted and approved. In addition studies have shown that much delinquency stems from disturbed family relationships and personal maladjustment, including or caused by ambivalent and often destructive child-parent relationships.

EMERGENCE OF A DISTINCTIVE TEEN-AGE SUBCULTURE

Adolescence is a transitional period from childhood to adulthood. It varies in length from culture to culture and varies within cultures with different families and different socioeconomic levels. The physical and psychological characteristics of adolescence have been described in the preceding section, but actually adolescence is both a social and a physiological phenomenon. In some cultures the onset of puberty marks the end of childhood and the beginning of adulthood. In our culture a girl may be fully matured sexually by twelve years old, but may remain within the protective bosom of her family for many more years. The beginning of adolescence is clearly marked by basic physiological changes. The end of adolescence is determined by such social factors as the child leaving home, getting a job, becoming self-supporting, or otherwise assuming the tasks of adulthood. The problems faced by boys and girls during this period have both biological and sociological aspects, and the teacher who would understand his secondary school students must be keenly aware of the multiplicity of social problems facing the modern adolescent.

Among the important developments of the sixties is the peaking of a longtime trend toward a clearer delineation of an adolescent culture unique unto itself. There are those who disagree about what characterizes a subculture, and those who scoff at the notion that the term is used accurately in regard to teen-agers. Those concerned with the problems of adolescents, however, are more frequently using this terminology because of the startling cohesiveness which characterizes the present generation of adolescents. The subculture tag has been applied because increasingly the modern teen-ager is developing his own value system, his own mode of response, and is more than ever isolating himself from adult society. A number of factors have served to bring this about.

The adolescent in our present culture is mature biologically in a society in which he is economically and sociologically immature. In the following brief summary of some of the current trends and major problems in dealing with adolescents, one pervading point of view must be kept in mind. There are normative patterns of development, and there are definitive trends; but *there is no typical teen-ager.* There are underachievers and overachievers; there are culturally deprived, culturally disadvantaged, and culturally favored; there are those who have wealthy, economically secure, or poor parents, or just one or none at all; there are emotionally deprived who can be rich or poor; there are those who are neglected and (or) abused and those who are overindulged—some of these at the same time; there are those who are socially conscious and those who are socially indifferent; there are the dull and the brilliant, the well-adjusted and the maladjusted, the physically ill and the vibrantly healthy, the handicapped and the nonhandicapped. Each is an individual with a different set of adjustment and developmental problems which he will deal with in varying degrees of success.

In addition to perceiving a teen-ager as an individual the reader must never underestimate the complexity and swiftness of changing forces in our current society. No definitive or in-depth sociological analysis of the teen-age culture is intended in this brief discussion of several of the current trends. Selected issues are pointed out to call attention to the fact that the student with whom the secondary teacher will work lives in a complex and ever-changing world. His society is never static nor does the particular milieu ever affect two students quite the same way. The many diverse factors which influence the social patterns of modern teen-agers and the development of their subculture include those related to industrialization, population trends, and economic affluency, and various by-products of these basic ones.

Factors related to industrialization The change from an agrarian to an industrial society was the first step in breaking the unity of the home as the major educative force in the life of the child. On the farm the child's education, other than for varying levels of intellectual skills, was centered about the home. Parents shaped their children in their own image. At the present time, not only is the father's skill likely to be extremely specialized, but with the rapidly changing character of industrial expansion it is estimated that the average worker of tomorrow who is in school today may have to change his vocation—not his job—as many as three times during his lifetime. Obsolescence, due to our incredible technical advances, seems to be the major by-product of industry today. Parents, then, can no longer serve as the vocational model for their children.

Technological advances demand more skilled and adaptable workers. This requires a higher level of education, which means that the schools must hold the adolescent age group for longer and longer periods. Not only is more education needed, but the lack of unskilled jobs in our present society has put emphasis on programs to keep as many students as possible in high school for as long as possible. It is hard to believe that in 1900 only 11 percent of high school–age students were in school and in 1930 only 51 percent. This means, then, that we are isolating more of our teen-agers for longer periods into the institution of the schools. At an age period when they are seeking their own identity, we have, through such institutions as the schools, youth corps, and other programs, pressed them into a more confined world of their own. (See also Changing Purposes of Secondary Schools, page 85.)

The attempts to extend the secondary school education of all youth has been one force resulting in the current concern with social class differences. Even though the United States as a whole is ever expanding its middle classes, educational attention has been focused on severely handicapped children from lower socioeconomic strata. Often these children suffer from inadequate development of preschool skills, and their value systems, aspirations, and comprehensions mitigate against their competing successfully with more culturally favored children in schools that are invariably oriented to middle-class values.

Factors related to population trends Current population trends have served to magnify the degree and kinds of problems or issues associated with the emergence of a distinctive teen-age subculture. In the 1965–1975 decade there will be major shifts in the population balance. By 1975 approximately 65 million people will be 45 or older, and 160 million people will be under 45. By 1970 half of the population of the United States will be under 27. In 1965 there were approximately 15 million people aged 14–17 and 12 million aged 18–21, and by 1975 there will be approximately 33 million in these age groups, an increase of approximately 33 percent. By the last half of the sixties one-half the population was under 25, and one-third of the population was under 20. The ratio of this age group to the total population is steadily rising.

The ramifications of these figures are manyfold. Some alarmists fear a youth takeover, which in the last analysis is naïve in terms of the simple truth that the adult population controls the economic and political system. On the optimistic side it is well to remember that inherent in our American democratic system is the cultural and intellectual appreciation of the new, and that when the Declaration of Independence was signed, more than half the population was under 18 years of age.

The true challenge for education, where population trends and economic factors are concerned, rests upon understanding and providing for the fullest development and utilization of the nation's greatest asset: the vigor, the idealism, the strength, and the creativity of its youth. America is uniquely blessed in this regard. It behooves the educator to nurture this great resource.

Factors related to economic affluency The significance of the increasing number of persons in the teen-age population takes on specific coloration as a result of the affluency of the contemporary economic system. The amount of money the teen-age group has to spend in our economy has aided them in the trend to identify themselves as a particular subculture. The external trappings of this identification, which has tended to alarm many adults, are much more numerous in the present era. Economic affluency has given the teen-ager the ability to increase peer identification in many visible ways.

By the late 1960s it was estimated that the teen-age population had approximately 15 billion dollars in ready cash to spend each year. This figure is expected to reach 25 billion dollars early in the 1970s barring unforeseen economic reverses. This amount does not include basic costs of room, board, clothing, and medical and educational expense, but rather, funds to spend on so-called nonessentials.

Lest one jump to the conclusion that this money is solely the handout of indulgent parents, it is important to point out a paradox in our culture. The high school–age youth who drops out of school may find extreme difficulty in finding unskilled employment sufficient to support himself, let alone a family. The part-time worker who wishes to pick up spending money at a minimum wage has more, although perhaps still not enough, opportunity. Even so, it is estimated that approximately 60 per cent of the teen-age group has some form of part-time work to supplement their family-derived contributions.

What has this ready cash in such total significant amounts to do with encouraging more distinctive teen-age subculture characteristics? It means that various commercial interests are catering specifically to the tastes and fads of this group. Many examples can be given. Needless to say, when 80 percent of all single music records are purchased by teen-agers, record manufacturers will publish records in music styles that appeal to this market. The same principle holds true in regard to the facts that over half of the movie attendance is made up of teen-agers; 20 percent of all hosiery is bought by this group; one out of nine automobiles sold, 4 percent of new and 7 percent of used, are purchased by teen-agers. Until the late fifties the only magazines aimed directly at this group were a few classic types. By the middle of the sixties approximately 75 magazines designed exclusively for the teen market commanded a total sale of over 21 million copies a month.

The teen magazines, coupled with radio, movie, and television programs aimed at the teen market, have fostered the spread of teen fads of all kinds. A fad which begins on the West Coast is quickly picked up and displayed in other parts of the country and is soon nationwide in existence. Most teen fads tend to start on the craft or local level, and if an item seems to have commercial possibilities it is quickly marketed. For example, a few teen-agers bought Navy surplus pea jackets, and within a few months fashion-crafted pea jackets hit the market. The leather clothing worn by the motorcycling set for protective reasons subsequently reached the haute couture level in the form of many articles of clothing including slacks, skirts, and even evening dresses. Teens have always had fads of one kind or another, but unique to this era is the number, and the rapidity, in which they are passing. Most such fads last about six months, although some do result in longtime trends, such as in clothing and automobile styles.

National communications media directed toward teen-agers have caused language also to take on a marked change. Slang has always been widely used in American language, but the present teen-ager makes much greater use of a private language. Sociologists feel that the private language of the teen-ager is another manifestation of his desire to shut himself off from the adult world. As soon as a word becomes too common it tends to be changed. Magazines and the radio and television disc jockeys have implemented the more widespread use of this second language and the rapidity of its change. In the space of a little over a year, something that was "really super" ran the gamut of such words as "sharp," "cool," "boss," "spiffy," "tough," and "groovy." "Real cool" passed on to "dead instant" or "out of sight."

The function of a private language (as opposed to the formal language) is to give the user a sense of privacy and identification. It is interesting to note that major users of private languages, barring the intellectual factor per se, have tended to be deprived, isolated, or other "out" social groups. Thus, a private language can be found in prisons, ghettos of all kinds, or in any other situation where one feels defiant, helpless, or afraid. It is significant to note that many of the terms used by the socially affluent teen-ager of today have found their origin among the less privileged socioeconomic groups both here and abroad. Of educational significance is the fact that many inner city children bring this private language to school, and for many this is, in truth, their primary (and not their secondary) language. Whereas the affluent student tends to leave the teen-agers' private language out of the classroom and quickly outgrows its use, for many it becomes the language of the home. It passes on to their children who develop the same handicap in adjusting to our middle class–oriented school systems.

Other social factors related to the teen subculture The automobile has, without question, fundamentally influenced teen-age society. It provides a sense of freedom and an actual physical means to escape from the adult world. Psychologically it gives to some a projection of power and a peer status symbol second to none. Studies have shown that a student's grades tend to drop once he has an automobile. Part of this drop results not because he is necessarily oversocializing, but rather because he is taking on part-time work to support his automobile or is working long hours on its upkeep and repair.

The rise in illegitimacy among teen-agers is another crucial social problem. Among the many factors which have contributed to this problem are less home supervision, the automobile, a general cultural prepossession with sex, the advent of the birth control pill. In 1940 there were 40,000 illegitimate births per 4,000,000 births. By the mid-sixties this had risen to 101,000. This factor, coupled with figures that show the American girl is maturing at an earlier age, would suggest that the junior and senior years of high school are much too late to introduce sex education into the schools. In addition, to support this contention, there has been a marked rise in venereal disease rates since 1957. The vigorous education programs during World War II and after and the introduction of the miracle drugs decreased the incidence of venereal disease to an all-time low in 1957, but since that time it has been gradually rising. Disregarding moral considerations the rise is related to at least two basic factors. First, drug-resistant strains of organisms which cause venereal diseases have developed making quick cure less effective in many cases. Second, the major increase in the disease has been in the fourteen- to eighteen-year-old group, many of whom, because of the slacking off of public concern and education in this regard, were little aware of the existence of this hazard. Often they were not alert to recognizing and seeking help for early symptoms.

Other health hazards have impinged on the teen-age society. Suicide has risen to the fifth major cause of death among teen-agers, and these figures do not include the possible subtle relationship of the automobile death rate to deliberate or subconscious suicide attempts. The number one cause of teen-age death is accidents, a majority of these involving the automobile. Disregarding the automobile, the suicide rate itself testifies to the fact that the teen-ager in our society is faced with innumerable pressures.

Narcotic pushers have not overlooked the teen-age market. The very restlessness and rebellion of this age group make them easy victims to the initial adventure of this experience. The Federal Dangerous Drug Act of February 1, 1966, hit particularly at the pep pill and barbiturate traffic, which plagues many segments of the population. But even as the well-enforced effects of this law made traffic in these drugs less profitable, and therefore less pursued, others sprang up to take their place. Glue sniffing and the use of marijuana, LSD, and other psychedelic drugs began to capture the headlines as increasing teen-centered social problems. Despite the fact that a small percentage of youth is involved, the very existence of the problem makes it essential for the leader of secondary school youth to be aware of it as one aspect of the sociological climate of youth.

GUIDANCE AND PHYSICAL EDUCATION

The preceding section has described some of the basic physical, psychological, and sociological characteristics and problems of today's adolescents. How can physical education contribute to meeting the needs of this age group? How does physical education uniquely contribute to the guidance function of the schools?

CONTRIBUTIONS OF PHYSICAL EDUCATION TO NEEDS OF ADOLESCENTS

Needs are involved, complicated, and individualized. What are some of the ways physical education can meet real needs? Physical educators must not be presumptuous; neither physical education nor any single curriculum area can stand by itself. Physical education does have important contributions to make toward the satisfaction of physical, social, and emotional needs and toward the growth and personal adjustment of adolescents.

The reader should note that the following discussion draws its examples from both the program and methods levels. That is, certain types of activities in the program contribute to satisfying the needs of adolescents; how those activities are organized and conducted is also equally important.

Physical education and physical needs Among young people the need for activity is almost as universal as the needs for food, fluid, elimination, and shelter. Fundamental laws of biology—food, activity, and rest—demand that the organism be used. Most of school life tends to be sedentary; physical education satisfies needs for physical activity to a greater extent than does any other curriculum area. Physical activities have excellent therapeutic value in providing for release from tensions and for self-expression. Modern civilization tends toward sedentary living; physical education helps to equip people with abilities and interests that cause them to make healthful physical activity a part of their living over a long period of years.

Physical education and social needs Social influences mold interests, personalities, and characters. They pervade living and behavior to such an extent that they are likely to be the number one factor in the development of most persons. They are so important to the growing youngster that they become a basic concern of the school as well as of the home. Desires for social approval, for recognition, and for status motivate so powerfully that they will not, let alone should not, be submerged.

The big social questions as they concern most individuals are, "Do I belong?" and "What is my status?" What can physical education do to make boys and girls feel that they belong and that they have status? Physical skills are important in peer acceptance or rejection. Successful performance in sports is highly regarded by adolescents. Acceptance and rejection of girls is affected by physical abilities, though to a lesser extent than with boys.

Since performance in sportlike activities is an important factor in social adjustment, the physical educator can help the youngster to adjust by helping him to improve his motor ability. Emphasis should be placed upon helping those whose abilities are low, whereas teachers and coaches, understandably thrilled with outstanding performances, frequently bend their best efforts toward work with those who already possess good ability and give insufficient attention to those most in need of help. The teacher who understands the real social and emotional needs of children and adolescents will work enthusiastically and patiently with poor and average performers until they are able to secure satisfactions from achievements.

Physical education can contribute in large measure to the important and difficult boy-girl adjustments of adolescence. Wholesome play activities in mixed groups should be permitted and encouraged. Any junior high school teacher can testify to difficulties in bringing boys and girls together as social partners during the early adolescent years. Play activities in mixed groups help boys and girls to adjust to each other in natural and wholesome surroundings. Sports such as volleyball, tennis, badminton, and swimming adapt well to mixed play. Folk dancing is excellent and leads quite naturally to the more individualized social partnerships of social dancing.

Physical education activities provide a most fertile field for social development. Cooperation and competition, both involving real and close relationships with other people, bulk large in physical education programs. Recognition of worth is based upon performance, effort, and sportsmanship; athletics are a splendid medium for social amalgamation. Youngsters learn a good deal about getting along with others as they participate in sports. But desirable social outcomes do not just happen; they are the result of nurture and leadership. Physical education provides a favorable seedbed; growth depends to a large extent upon the quality of leadership exerted by the teacher.

Physical education and emotional needs Social and emotional adjustment are so closely tied up that they cannot be separated. Social maladjustment can be causal to emotional maladjustment. A success pattern is the essence of good adjustment. It should be remembered that success as it relates to adjustment is measured by the feeling of the person involved, not by arbitrary standards or opinions of others except as the standards or opinions affect the individual's own feeling. Growing up and living demand successes; however, failures also are necessary. A success pattern, so essential to satisfactory living, does not mean a long succession of uninterrupted triumphs. It does mean that there must be enough success to provide feelings of adequacy and security that result in personal integration. Ability to meet failures is important to adjustment, but continual failures are pernicious and disintegrating. As the great poet, Rudyard Kipling, once put it, "You'll be a man, my son, when you can meet with triumph and disaster and treat those two impostors just the same."

Emotionally detrimental frustrations occur in physical education activities when students are required, or placed under pressure, to engage repeatedly in activities which bring failure feelings to the individual. Timidity, sensitivity, fear, and dislike for physical activity involving other people are likely results. Satisfying self-expression in sports activities builds up feelings of adequacy and security that contribute significantly to social adjustment because of enhanced social approval and because of added personalized feelings of being able to "take the environment by the tail and twist it."

Adjustment through physical education Repeated references have been made to physical education as a force in helping boys and girls to establish satisfying patterns of personal living which place work, play, exercise, recreation, and rest in proper perspective and give due attention to each. The energetic person who attacks his problems actively, rather than let them accumulate and cause undue concern and worry, is most likely to be well adjusted. Physical education activities, with their demands for active behavior, help in establishing habits and attitudes tending toward direct attack. Exuberant physical health, abundant energy, satisfying accomplishment, good relations with others, optimistic outlook, and habits of active and direct attack assure good mental health. Inclusion of continued physical activity suited to the needs and conditions of the individual, as well as adequate rest, satisfying accomplishment, and stimulating experiences in one's rhythm of living, is a necessity for good adjustment to the complexities of living. Mental health's dependence upon a physical base is well understood; unhygienic living, as well as organic illness, is a large contributor to mental illness or lack of adjustment.

Satisfactions in physical accomplishment can give one a new lease on life. The dub golfer who makes a birdie is likely to be easier to live with for a week! A boy who lacks satisfactions to the extent that his whole pattern of living is out of tune with his world may find a new outlook as a result of accomplishment in physical activity.

GUIDANCE AS A TEACHING METHOD AND AS A SCHOOL SERVICE

There is a general and a specific consideration in discussing physical education and guidance. Generally, guidance can be used to connote the sound educational idea that it is the individual who learns, and therefore the most effective teaching must take cognizance of the unique characteristics of the individual. This in turn implies that the effective teacher must not only understand the basic methodological concepts dealt with in this book, but he also must have skill in understanding the individual learner so he can effectively direct or guide him through the learning process.

Specifically, guidance is a term used to describe a type of service provided by the modern school in which emphasis is placed upon helping the student with problems related to personal, educational, social, and vocational adjustment. Increasing numbers of secondary schools provide personnel whose duties are limited to these areas. One counselor to every 300 students is a presently recommended standard, an ideal which is most often approximated in only the more affluent school districts. Even with the existence of professional guidance personnel the classroom teacher will always have a major responsibility for counseling and guidance work. The teacher of physical education has an especially vital role to play.

Because of the nature of the physical educational program and the general orientation of its teachers, the well-trained physical education teacher often gets much closer to the lives of students than do other persons in the school. If he has developed the necessary competence and understanding, this natural closeness enables him to render effective guidance when students come to him with their problems or when he works with them in close association in the more socially real learning setting of the physical education program. The inherent desire of youth to excel in physical activity and the fact that athletic superiority is the number one peer status symbol among adolescents provide an excellent opportunity for the physical educator to make major contributions to the adjustment problems of youth. Although many technical problems of guidance require the services of a specialist, the teacher of physical education has a major contribution to make in this important school service.

Thus, the role of the physical education teacher in relation to guidance can be summed up in this way: Both the teacher and the guidance specialist are essential to good education. The teacher is the closest contact with the youngster. He is involved in activities with the student which enables him to both understand and assist the student in many helpful ways. Some students have problems that the teacher, even if he could diagnose the cause of trouble, lacks the professional training to help. For example, poor achievement in a subject matter area may be due to lack of motivation or to some physical or emotional problem. If motivational stimulation is the cause, the teacher can be of the greatest help. If the problem is emotional, and not of a transitional nature requiring only support from the teacher to aid the student over a temporary crisis, the help of a specialist will be needed. Ideally, the classroom teacher should have the benefit of consultation services with guidance specialists to assist him in diagnosing student problems and in planning appropriate methods for all concerned.

UNDERSTANDING INDIVIDUALS

Whether one perceives of guidance as enhancing the learning experiences of the classroom or as a specific area of service to the student, it is important that the teacher understand the need for and the techniques of studying the individual student.

Although more similarities than differences exist among human beings and particularly among those of a given age category, the fact remains that no two persons are entirely alike; each is unique in some respects. It is the job and responsibility of the teacher to understand each student as an individual. A teacher equipped with a good fundamental knowledge of the main characteristics of growth and development, with a good understanding of the principal tenets of the psychology of adjustment and of learning, and with sound methods of studying the individual is in a position to understand a great deal about each student, although, of course, he is not equipped to do the work of a guidance specialist.

Some of the means, tools, and methods for studying the individual students are discussed in Chapter 17, Method and Evaluation.

SUMMARY

The summarizing statement for this chapter indicates some major factors about the growth and development of adolescents which give direction to certain of the teaching techniques and procedures recommended in later chapters. Although these implications are not spelled out in this summary, their application becomes apparent when specific methods are discussed.

The typical adolescent gropes toward adult status, simultaneously demanding independence but feeling incompetent to accept the responsibilities of adulthood.

A major consideration of the adolescent age centers around adjustment to rapid changes in the physical body.

Adolescent behavior, unstable and sometimes unattractive in terms of adult standards, is normal to this age group.

The rapidity and intenseness of changes in the adolescent age group increase the need to provide means to assure security and satisfaction with the individual as a self.

Problems, whether of a group or of an individual, are affected by the nature of the school program. The school, therefore, may assist in solving the problems or may increase their seriousness.

Acceptance by peers of both sexes dominates the social orientation of adolescents.

The adolescent age comprises but one aspect of the total growth process and is dependent upon the previous kind and rate of growth.

Individuals vary greatly in their rate and sequence of growth during adolescence.

The adolescent not only lives in an inward world of confusion, but also finds increasing exposure to the outward world, which provides its own elements of confusion and double standards in the present state of civilizations.

Questions and problems for discussion

1. Study several secondary school students of your acquaintance. Note behaviors which relate to their development toward social maturity.
2. Ask several secondary school students to write down their daily schedules. Analyze these schedules from the standpoint of the physical characteristics and needs of the age group.
3. Discuss possible effects upon the adolescent boy or girl of seeming to represent the dub class in all physical activities or of actually having a limiting physical defect. What special problems arise for him, and how may they be resolved?
4. Should every boy in secondary school have the opportunity to participate in an interscholastic sport? Give your opinion in terms of adolescent needs.
5. What common practices in secondary school physical education programs best contribute to meeting adolescent needs? Which contribute the least?
6. List the major physical characteristics of adolescent boys or girls. Derive therefrom at least ten suggestions to guide their participation in physical recreation, both in school and out.
7. What suggestions would you make to a physical education teacher experiencing discipline problems with an adolescent pupil who persistently exhibits negativism?
8. Describe one current fad of teen-agers. Try to track down its origin. What symbolic factors, if any, does this particular fad have? How long do you believe it will last?
9. After reading the material in your text and in the listed references on the extent to which peer groups influence student practices and values, who do you think should write the dress code in a high school? The principal? A parent-teacher group? A student-selected group? Others? Give reasons for your answer.
10. Why might the high school coach have greater influence on the nonathletic conduct of students, including nonteam members, than any other teacher in the high school?

Selected references

Blair, Glenn Myers, and R. Stewart Jones: *Psychology of Adolescence for Teachers,* The Macmillan Company, New York, 1964.

Blos, Peter: *On Adolescence, a Psychoanalytic Interpretation,* The Free Press of Glencoe, New York, 1962.

Coleman, James Samuel: *Adolescents and the Schools,* Basic Books, Inc., Publishers, New York, 1965.

Crow, Lester D.: *Psychology of Human Development,* Alfred A. Knopf, Inc., New York, 1967.

———, and Alice Crow: *Adolescent Development and Adjustment,* 2d ed., McGraw-Hill Book Company, New York, 1965.

Grinder, Robert E.: *Studies in Adolescence,* The Macmillan Company, New York, 1963.

Havighurst, Robert J.: *Development Tasks and Education,* 2d ed., Longmans, Green, & Co., Inc., New York, 1952.

———: *Human Development and Education,* Longmans, Green, & Co., Inc., New York, 1953.

Jewett, Ann E., and Clyde Knapp (eds.): *The Growing Years, Adolescence, 1962 Yearbook of the American Association for Health, Physical Education, and Recreation,* National Education Association, Washington, D.C., 1962.

Krumboltz, John K. (ed.): *Revolution in Counseling,* Houghton Mifflin Company, Boston, 1967.

Patterson, Cecil H. (ed.): *The Counselor in the School: Selected Readings,* McGraw-Hill Book Company, New York, 1967.

Tyler, Ralph W. (ed.): *Social Forces Influencing American Education, Part II, Sixtieth Yearbook of the American Society for the Study of Education,* The University of Chicago Press, Chicago, 1961.

chapter 4

THE OBJECTIVES OF PHYSICAL EDUCATION

THE NATURE OF OBJECTIVES

Objectives are statements of the purposes or goals of education. They give direction to the organization and conduct of educational programs. They indicate the kinds of subject matter, learning experiences, methods of teaching, and administrative and supervisory procedures required, and they serve as the basis for the evaluation of outcomes.

Objectives are guideposts; they point the way. Education proceeding without a framework of objectives is like a trip in a wilderness without a compass. In order to progress toward desirable ends, it is necessary that ends be apparent, that planners lay out signs which direct the journey and which permit the travelers to know their location. Known objectives clarify the selection of procedures and techniques. They indicate when an educational activity has been successful or when procedures or plans should be changed or modified.

THE BASIC PURPOSE OF PHYSICAL EDUCATION

Physical education is a two-headed coin. One side represents development and maintenance of physical characteristics including strength, endurance, good posture, flexibility, balance, and neuromuscular skills.

The other side represents what is happening to the total person as he develops these physical attributes, and that is a growth in regard to self-perception, attitudes, interests, aspirations, social and emotional qualities, and a general feeling of well-being or self-realization.

It may be emphasized that the most important purposes of physical education for a high school student are to help him learn how exercise can contribute to his well-being for the rest of his life and to help him acquire the attitudes and skills which will most likely ensure his determination to incorporate the teachings of physical education into his everyday living in both the present and the future. This *living in physical education* requires that one incorporate physically and mentally healthful exercise into daily and weekly schedules. A physically healthful person with good muscle tone, high energy, good endurance, favorable cardiovascular function, and pleasing posture will feel adequate, generally optimistic, and at home with his environment. Although physical fitness cannot be equated with mental health, no doubt exists that the physically fit person is more likely to be able to adequately cope with the multitudinous tensions and strains of living in our modern industrial society. It is significant that the Educational Policies Commission, in the document entitled *The Central Purpose of American Education,*[1] takes special note of the import of physical and mental health. This document holds that the development of rational powers is central to all other qualities of human spirit, and therefore the basic purpose to which American schools must be oriented is to develop the ability to think. The commission further states that the school must also be concerned with establishing certain conditions that are known to be basic to significant mental development. Among the more important of these is physical and mental health.

The central purpose, then, of physical education in the secondary schools is to assist the individual to acquire the knowledges, attitudes, and skills leading to exercise, including physical recreation, and to assure that these become an integral part of one's life pattern to the end that this will result in optimum physical-psychological development and maintenance.

GENERAL OBJECTIVES OF PHYSICAL EDUCATION

The brief history of the evolvement of modern physical education objectives, presented in the next section of this chapter, reveals three basic trends. First, there has been a shift in emphasis in physical education pro-

[1] Educational Policies Commission, *The Central Purpose of American Education,* National Education Association, Washington, D.C., 1961.

grams in the last fifty years from those characterized as preventive and therapeutic to those centered on the purpose of helping the student develop the essential physical and psychological health to enable him to function effectively in modern society. Second, the basic objectives of the modern program of physical education have changed little in the past half century. Third, there is considerable agreement among present and past leaders in the modern era as to the nature of basic objectives.

FOUR BASIC AREAS IN PHYSICAL EDUCATION OBJECTIVES

An analysis of the statements of purpose and the objectives of physical education that have been made by outstanding leaders of the modern program of physical education, beginning with Thomas Dennison Wood and including Clark W. Hetherington, Jesse Feiring Williams, Jay B. Nash, Clifford Lee Brownell, William Ralph LaPorte, and Seward C. Staley, shows similar basic considerations common to all. Differences appear more in regard to emphasis than in inclusion or exclusion of fundamental viewpoints. Representative statements concerning objectives by each of these authorities deal directly with, or have unmistakable implications for, health, social ends, emotional development, and recreation. In addition each leader singles out biological objectives in organic and systemic development, an area for which physical education has singular and unique contributions. Each of the presentations reveals the maker's concept of needs for living, and each pictures a whole person, not simply a collection of bones, muscles, and organs. Intellectual ends, skills, character, personality, citizenship, and cultural status also receive recognition.

A DEFINITIVE STATEMENT OF THE BASIC PURPOSE AND GENERAL OBJECTIVES OF PHYSICAL EDUCATION

The authors present a statement of purpose that emphasizes both the individual and society, and six general objectives which center about the four basic areas—health, social ends, emotional development, and recreation. Physical growth, development, and maintenance, while thought of as belonging to the health category, receive emphasis as the first objective, because of physical education's unique contribution. The sixth general objective, in the highly important area of balanced living, cannot be said to belong to any one of the four basic areas in objectives of physical education; rather, it affects and pervades all.

The fundamental purpose of physical education is to promote through selected physical activity the establishment and maintenance of competencies, attitudes, ideals, drives, and conditions which enable each individual to establish a pattern of living that provides satisfactory self-expression and adjustment through individual accomplishment and that contributes to group welfare through home, community, state, national, and world citizenship experiences appropriate for each individual.

The general objectives of physical education are:

1. To promote physical growth, development, and maintenance through activities that develop strength, vigor, vitality, skills, and coordinations leading to the ability to do the day's work without undue fatigue and to have additional energy for out-of-work personal and social accomplishment.
2. To contribute to the development of social competencies in the areas of relationships with others, cooperation, competition, tolerance, ethical character, and recognition of the fundamental worth of each individual.
3. To promote emotional development through contributions toward individual adjustment, emotional self-mastery, adjustment to others, relaxation, satisfying self-expression, confidence, poise, and freedom from excessive self-confidence.
4. To provide healthful and integrating recreation for the present as well as to lay bases for wholesome, life-balancing recreation in the future.
5. To promote healthful living through contributions to health habits, attitudes, ideals, and information that lead toward elimination of unnecessary strains, drains, and illnesses, and that enable one to protect oneself and others during times of lowered vitality or illness.
6. To help each student establish appropriate balances between work, play, exercise, rest, recreation, and relaxation in daily living.

EVOLUTION OF PREMODERN PHYSICAL EDUCATION OBJECTIVES

The role of physical education in all cultures and civilizations consistently reflects the special characteristics of the times. Primitive and ancient education emphasized the physical because of the great need of strength and endurance for survival. Sparta overemphasized the physical, while Athens blended the physical and the mental into a fine balance. Athens, during its decline, emphasized the intellectual to the detriment of the physical. Many writers have pointed to the parallel between the decline of attention to physical education and the decline of Athens.

In the Roman Empire the physical took on an aspect of debauchery with excesses in body pleasures. Gladiatorial contests, in which slaves or inferiors and animals performed spectacular feats which caused senseless injury or death, served to entertain and thrill vicarious participants who gave little or no thought to physical education for themselves.

During the period of the early Christians there was considerable tendency to regard only the intellectual as elevating and worthy. Physical aspects of living were not only thought of as inferior but also deemed to be debasing and degrading. Although occasional voices pointed to the importance of the development of the whole person, organized school physical education received little or no attention from the time of the early Christians until the eighteenth century. It should be pointed out, however, that physical activity expressed in games and contests was not entirely lacking in the civilization of that time or any time. Indeed, the natural urges and drives which impel self-expression through physical activity can never be completely suppressed in any healthy peoples.

Chivalry, with its tournaments and jousts, struggled against the influence of ascetism throughout Western Europe from about A.D. 1000 to about 1500.

Even humanists, with their preoccupation with literary and linguistic methods, occasionally gave school attention to physical education. The Italian humanist Vittorino da Feltre (1378–1446) combined physical with mental training in his school at Mantua. Besides instruction in classics, he provided instruction in knightly activities such as dancing, riding, fencing, swimming, wrestling, jumping, archery, and ball games. A few aristocratic continental schools, prior to the general emergence of school physical education during the latter part of the eighteenth century, employed special teachers for exercise and for games, as well as masters of riding, fencing, and dance, to work with the academic group in educating sons of noblemen. Such a school was the Danish school at Sorö where Basedow became impressed with the effort to relate education of the mind and body. And Basedow's school at Dessau, Germany, his Philanthropinum, which operated from 1774 to 1793, represents a starting point and landmark in the emergence of modern physical education.

Eighteenth-century Europe found physical education programs gaining a foothold in schools. The so-called systems spread rapidly in the German countries and in Sweden and Denmark. Later, they were adopted in America and, to some extent, in England. In the nineteenth century, German and Swedish gymnastics found their way into American schools and provided a springboard from which present physical education developed. German and Swedish systems remained popular until World War I, although there was considerable school activity in games and sports starting late in the nineteenth century.

After 1918, American physical education, with emphasis upon natural activities and upon games and sports, rose rapidly. Between the two world wars, play and recreation largely dominated American programs. During World War II development of physical fitness through conditioning activities received renewed emphasis. As the second half of the twentieth century began, there was excellent opportunity to develop an appropriate balance between development of physical fitness, as such, and development of the whole person through physical activity.

Conditions today indicate an increasing need for emphasis on adjustment. World tensions and the highly pitched, very largely unnatural characteristics of American living are so apparent and receive so much attention that they need no review here. However, one of physical education's chief contributions to American society unmistakably lies in helping people to adjust their lives to this complex civilization by establishing workable rhythms of work, play, exercise, relaxation, and rest that permit satisfactory self-expression in all areas of living. It has been estimated that of the babies born during the 1960s as many will require medical and psychological treatment for nervous disorders as will become college students. Clearly, physical education has no more important responsibility than that of helping young people to establish patterns of living which lay a groundwork for adjustment. A consideration of present-day physical education objectives reveals an awareness of the potential contributions of physical education to education for modern society.

EVOLUTION OF MODERN PHYSICAL EDUCATION OBJECTIVES

School physical education in the United States dates from the opening of the first school gymnasium at Round Hill School, Northampton, Mass., in 1825, under the direction of Charles Beck, a follower of Jahn and a political refugee from Germany. Two other refugees and followers of Jahn, Charles Follen and Francis Lieber, also were instrumental in initiating the German gymnastic movement in this country. Follen introduced gymnastics at Harvard and became, in 1826, director of the first college gymnasium in the United States. Lieber succeeded Follen in 1827. Although no one of the three continued professional work in physical education for long (Follen taught German at Harvard, Beck became a professor of Latin at Harvard, and Lieber a professor of law at Columbia), the gymnastics they introduced found its way into a substantial number of schools and clubs.

Prior to the time of these three German political refugees, physical activities in America were a matter of home and private concern. Sports of the day were popular in the Southern colonies. Although New England suppressed sports, believing them to be an idle waste of time and a violation of religious tenets, this did not eliminate sports from the life of the people. New England did, however, very largely reject the rich English sport traditions. The popular activities of the period included hunting, shooting, fishing, horse racing, foot racing, hopscotch, marbles, dancing, skating, some forms of football, and nine pins.

Enthusiastic advocates of various systems of physical education, other than German gymnastics, attempted without much success to secure general adoption during the period between 1830 and 1860. Dioclesian Lewis succeeded in wresting some of the physical education leadership from the turners during the 1860s. His *New Gymnastics for Men, Women, and Children* appeared about 1860, and in 1861 he opened the Normal Institute of Physical Education in Boston. He invented games, used dumbbells and Indian clubs, and advocated light exercise with musical accompaniment. Lewis was a controversial person. Perhaps a strong personality rather than scholarly attainment characterized his work. Energetic and dramatic, Lewis gained public attention. While many people praised him, others considered him to be a charlatan.

Proponents of Swedish gymnastics appeared about 1860. They achieved some success in establishing programs in some schools and localities, but in the United States adoption of the Swedish program never reached the proportions of the German turner movement. The smaller number of Swedish immigrants undoubtedly was a factor. It is likely, too, that the more spectacular apparatus stunts of German gymnastics had more appeal for Americans.

After the Civil War, interest in sports and athletics spread rapidly. Baseball became popular, and interest in football grew. Boys and young men not only played games in informal groups but also organized their own teams and scheduled games. This movement was destined to revolutionize American school physical education. School authorities first attempted to suppress the playing of games by student groups. Later they looked upon organized school athletics with an attitude of sanctioning a necessary evil. Still later, as is well known, educators embraced sports as activities rich in educational concomitants.

The latter part of the nineteenth century and the early part of the twentieth saw a good deal of progress toward American physical education as we know it today. Dudley A. Sargent, at Harvard, directed attention toward the development of health through prescribed exercise and nutrition. He also pioneered a measurement movement that has persisted with varying emphases. Interest in sports continued to grow. Normal schools for the training of teachers were opened and the Young Men's Christian Association school at Springfield. Mass., organized a department of physical education under the leadership of Luther Gulick. In 1885, the American Association for the Advancement of Physical Education, now the American Association for Health, Physical Education, and Recreation, was organized. Ever since its inception, the association has been a focal point for interpretation, clarification, and progress of school purposes and practices in physical education. Basketball and volleyball were added to baseball as popular games of American origin. The organization of the Playground and Recreation Association of America, in 1906, did much to direct attention toward the need for organized play and away from emphasis upon therapeutic and disciplinary values of the gymnastic programs.

Games, sports, gymnastics, rhythms, and conditioning activities make up the five backbones of American physical education today. Aimed at physical development, health, recreation, social development, and emotional adjustment, these five categories of activities are the media through which physical education seeks to help each individual establish a satisfactory pattern of living. Physical education holds that adequate living requires satisfying experiences in work, play, exercise, rest, recreation, and relationships with others. American school physical education is dualistic in that it seeks to provide for satisfactory development, recreation, and adjustment for boys and girls during their school lives as well as to lay a groundwork for a lifetime of successful living.

Young people should have opportunities to engage in a variety of activities for three reasons: (1) to experience joys and concomitant development, (2) to try out a number of activities in order to determine which might provide lasting appeal for the individual concerned, and (3) to develop understanding of and appreciation for a substantial number of physical activities. American programs provide a core of required activities that give all pupils basic experiences in a number of team and individual sports, in games and relays, rhythmic activities, gymnastics, conditioning exercises, and relaxation. In addition they provide elective activities that permit specialization, which give individuals opportunities for self-expression in games or activities of their own choosing.

CLEAVAGE BETWEEN EMPHASIS UPON PHYSICAL OBJECTIVES AND UPON SOCIOPSYCHOLOGIC OBJECTIVES

Physical educators are far from unanimous in their opinions concerning appropriate relative emphasis upon physical objectives, on the one hand, and sociopsychologic objectives, on the other hand. These differences of opinion among physical educators roughly parallel varying opinions among educators in other fields concerning relative emphasis upon subject matter and upon real-life needs. While no competent physical educator ignores either physical objectives or sociopsychologic objectives (and could not do so even if he so wished because of the inextricable involvement of both in physical education activities), marked differences in emphasis demand thorough thinking on the part of young teachers.

The spirit and immediate demands of the time cause a great deal of fluctuation in emphases. During the period between the two world wars, American physical education generally became too much dominated by activities requiring too little physical exertion. During World War II, under the influence of great attention to physical condition, the pendulum swung to the opposite side of the stroke. Although such fluctuations are natural they demonstrate the need for attention to relative emphases. Sound position seems to lie at neither extreme. Rather, it lies between the two, but perhaps closer to the sociopsychologic extreme than to the purely physical extreme.

THE RELATION OF PHYSICAL EDUCATION OBJECTIVES TO GENERAL EDUCATION OBJECTIVES

The objectives of physical education lie within the framework of the objectives of education. There can be no such thing as an objective of physical education that is not also an objective of education. The brief history of physical education preceding illustrates how practices relating to physical education have always reflected the feelings and beliefs of peoples or their rulers toward living and toward the human body. General education objectives define the broad goals of the current society. They are usually expressed as a classification of life's activities indicating the areas in which competence is acquired if one is to become a well-functioning member of that society. Subject matter field objectives delineate the unique contribution of that particular area to the overall goals of education.

THE GENERAL OBJECTIVES OF EDUCATION

The broad goals of education have been variously stated in recent years by a number of national groups, commissions, and individuals. The consensus among educators is to accept as four basic goals of education (1) the development of effective and responsible citizenship, (2) the development of talents and abilities for successful vocational fulfillment, (3) the development of talents and abilities for successful personal fulfillment, and (4) the development of abilities to participate in aesthetic experiences.

Chronological list of significant statements of the general objectives of education It is vital for the physical educator to be conversant with the historically significant and currently meaningful statements or documents dealing with the broad social goals of American education. While it is beyond the scope of this book to deal in depth with this topic the following chronological list is provided for the reader's convenience in reviewing this topic.

1.	1890	Herbert Spencer: *Education,* Appleton-Century-Crofts, Inc., New York, 1897.	First to interpret the objectives of education through a classification of life's activities.

2.	1890	*Report of the Committee of Ten on Secondary School Studies,* National Education Association, American Book Company, New York, 1894.	Made significant proposals on secondary education recognizing that vocational training as well as college preparation was the function of the American secondary school, but that the curriculum for both groups should be basically the same.
3.	1918	*Cardinal Principles of Secondary Education,* Bulletin 35, U.S. Bureau of Education, Washington, D.C.	Proposed seven areas of desired educational outcomes (health, command of fundamental processes, worthy home membership, vocation, citizenship, worthy use of leisure, and ethical character) delineating for the first time outcomes other than specific competence in subject matter.
4.	1924	Franklin Bobbit: *How to Make a Curriculum,* Houghton Mifflin Company, Boston, 1924.	Utilized the method of analysis of life's activities to indicate areas in which education should be directed.
5.	1931	*Implications of Social Economic Goals of America,* National Education Association, Washington, D.C., 1937.	Analyzed the goals of American society and presented educational goals that recognized that there were group goals that could not be obtained by the individual alone, but through united efforts of all concerned.
6.	1938	Educational Policies Commission: *The Purposes of Education in American Democracy,* National Education Association and the American Association of School Administrators, Washington, D.C., 1938.	Described an educated person by presenting 43 objectives grouped under the four headings of self-realization, human relationships, economic efficiency, and civic responsibility.
7.	1944 and 1952	Educational Policies Commission: *Education for All American Youth . . . A Further Look,* National Education Association, Washington, D.C., 1952.	Outlined ten basic needs of youth which all areas of education should make sincere efforts to satisfy. Has particular meaning for physical education.
8.	1958	Rockefeller Brothers Fund: *The Pursuit of Excellence: Education and the Future of America,* Panel Report V of the Special Studies Project, Doubleday & Company, Inc., Garden City, N.Y., 1958.	Emphasized the need for and means of preserving individuality in achieving worthwhile educational goals for America.

9.	1960	J. W. Gardner: "National Goals in Education," in *Report of the President's Commission on National Goals*, Prentice-Hall, Inc., Englewood Cliffs, N.J., 1960.	Defined modern goals of education within the original goals of the United States as set forth in the Declaration of Independence, and recommended programs to achieve them.
10.	1961	Education Policies Commission: *The Central Purpose of American Education*, National Education Association, Washington, D.C., 1961.	Accepted as worthwhile the 1938 statement of objectives; held that the fullest cultivation of rational powers will lead ultimately to the greatest development of each individual (see further comment on p. 76).
11.	1964	National Education Association: *Project on Instruction: Schools for the Sixties*, McGraw-Hill Book Company, New York, 1964.	Identified and clarified twelve decision areas related to instructional issues and made 33 basic recommendations for improving educational practices.

FACTORS AFFECTING EMPHASES ON AND METHODS OF STATING OBJECTIVES

The ever-shifting function of the American secondary school and the increasing use of scientific methods applied to the study of the learner, the school, and society have affected ways in which objectives are stated and have determined the emphasis given to certain of the objectives.

THE CHANGING PURPOSES OF THE SECONDARY SCHOOL

Education in the United States has consistently aimed to assist individuals to live effectively in a democratic society. The secondary schools of this country in their evolution have been especially flexible in reflecting the needs and values of the contemporary society. In fact it is frequently claimed somewhat ironically that the secondary schools' success may be one of its greatest problems. Not only is the American secondary school charged with many diverse tasks; but as changes in our national purpose and in our society occur, it is frequently the secondary schools which are asked to take on additional tasks. It appears that whenever a significant social problem arises, whose solution lies in educable factors, the inclination is to turn first to the schools. For example, as the automobile revolutionized our social and economic lives and brought on its accompanying problems of accidents, driver education was thrust upon the secondary school. Increased mechanization of society, resulting in fewer unskilled jobs with less employment available for the high school drop-out, caused concerted efforts in the directions of revising school curricula and in keeping more of our over-sixteen youth in school. The challenge of the international race for scientific superiority brought forth curricular changes in areas basic to science and in methods of early discovery and nurturing of potential talent. A greater awareness of the many problems of *special education* has brought the handicapped exceptional child into the regular school program, and at present, efforts are being made to include and deal with the emotionally ill through the public school system.

It is quite apparent that the American secondary school is an ever-changing, ever-expanding social institution. The population explosion has served to crowd our schools at the very time when we are seeking to develop creativity and individuality as a bulwark of democratic national strength. Even as the science of psychology has helped us to better understand not only the individual nature of the learning process, but also the nature of an individual's problems, it becomes more difficult to deal with the individual as the school population grows. Test scores, some fragmented and inaccurate, may form the basis of major decisions about a student's future. The student loses his identity in a school system dedicated to the individual's growth. As one student in a large metropolitan high school cynically stated, "The only way to get attention around here is to bend your IBM card." Fortunately the apparent magnification of secondary education problems lies not just in the growth of the population and in the expansion of the school's role, but also in greater awareness of the nature of these problems. Expanded efforts and increasing scientific educational knowledge give promise of aiding the secondary school teacher to meet his great challenge.

ATTENTION TO REAL-LIFE NEEDS

Throughout history thinkers and philosophers have talked and written about education as preparation for life. But organized schools, for the most part, have emphasized the absorption of logically organized bodies of subject matter rather than social, emotional, and physical development. Real-life needs center about (1) needs of the individual and (2) needs of society. Neither, of course, is independent of the other. This country and world of high tensions require complicated individual adjustments for satisfactory individual living, and education must accept a large share of the responsibility for improving fast-changing local, national, and world society.

Objectives express needs as seen by the person or persons who formulate the ideas and statements. Needs may be divided into two categories: individual and societal. Individual needs center about such factors as belonging, recognition, achievement, security, independence, adventure, and adjustment to living. Societal needs center about the welfare and security of the family, community, state, nation, and world. Schools must attend to the desires of individuals and of relatively small groups. But schools also must play a leading role in helping people to be good citizens who contribute to the welfare of society. Complete individualism is as objectionable as complete totalitarianism. Freedom within laws and regulations—laws and regulations made, approved, judged and enforced by citizens, by all the citizens—is the way of democracy. Individual and societal needs blend in the objectives toward which school sights are set. Both are served by democratic procedures which permit all participants the privileges of sharing in the making and carrying out of plans as well as demand of all participants responsibility for success or failure.

ATTENTION TO DEFINING OBJECTIVES OPERATIONALLY OR BEHAVIORALLY

Another current trend in educational practice is the greater emphasis being placed on stating objectives specifically as human behavior. The translation of the desired goals of education into the implied action suitable for classroom use is a persistent problem for all teachers. Many teachers find it difficult to understand the relationship between a single activity in a lesson plan and the remote purposes of education for democratic living. This necessary understanding can be considerably increased if on all levels, even the most general, objectives are stated in terms of the specific kind of behavior we hope to achieve through teaching. Understanding the levels of objectives and the reasons for stating objectives as behaviors will assist the prospective teacher to comprehend the continual interrelationship between the daily activity of the classroom and the total life cycle of the individual in his contemporary culture.

Levels of objectives To avoid confusion in considering objectives, the varying levels of objectives should be understood. Since objectives merely represent statements of the goals or purposes of educational activity, it follows that on whatever level the program operates there can and should be a parallel statement of objectives. Thus a nation providing public education must have a reason for or a purpose in establishing educational programs. A community planning its educational program must state the purposes of the program in terms of its particular needs. The purposes of any specific area of study must be outlined, and these purposes must be translated into units and daily lessons for the precise guidance of learning experiences. If the original societal purposes of education are to be achieved, each succeeding level of objectives must contribute to the overall purposes. One apt way, then, of categorizing objectives is to indicate levels which coincide with the structure of the program itself. This sequence consists of:

1. The overall societal purpose of education.
2. The general objectives of an educational program.

3. The objectives for a given course or program.
4. The objectives for a given unit.
5. The objectives for a daily or specific lesson or activity.

Reasons for stating objectives as behaviors The growing trend to state objectives of education as behaviors is a direct outgrowth of the increasing knowledge of the learning process. Learning is commonly defined as a change of behavior. If the desired objective, then, is stated in terms of a human performance or behavior, the task of selecting the methods and learnings to arrive at that behavior is much more clearly apparent to all concerned, the teacher, the student, and the parent. For example, worthy citizenship is a well-accepted general goal of education. What specifically does a worthy citizen do? How does he act? What does he know? What are his values as manifested by his overt behavior? Since any inference about how effective the teaching-learning process has been must rest on observable behaviors of the learner, it would seem only reasonable that the objectives themselves be stated as human behavior. An excellent example of a comprehensive list of objectives stated as observable student behavior may be found in *Behavioral Goals of General Education.*[2]

Attention to the classification of objectives Through the work of Bloom,[3] Krathwohl,[4] and others, efforts have been made to classify the types of behaviors as a sound basis for the development of inclusive and effectively stated behavioral objectives. Learning, which takes place through experience, results in a change in the learner's thinking, feeling, or acting. *The Taxonomy of Educational Objectives* attempts to classify the particular ways in which the learner will react, think, or feel as the result of participating in a successful learning experience. The original project aimed to classify such objectives under three domains. The first, the *cognitive,* includes recall or recognition of knowledge and development of intellectual abilities. The second, the *affective,* refers to changes in interests, attitudes, values, appreciations, and adjustment. The third, the *psychomotor,* concerns manipulative or motor skill objectives.

The factors isolated are kinds of human responses rather than specific

[2] Will French and Associates, *Behavioral Goals of General Education,* Russell Sage Foundation, New York, 1957.

[3] Benjamin S. Bloom et al., *Taxonomy of Educational Objectives, Handbook I, Cognitive Domain,* David McKay Company, Inc., New York, 1956.

[4] David R. Krathwohl et al., *Taxonomy of Educational Objectives, Handbook II, Affective Domain,* David McKay Company, Inc., New York, 1964.

learnings. For example, in the psychomotor domain the schema developed by Simpson [5] include:

1.0 *Perception*
  1.01 Auditory
  1.02 Visual
  1.03 Tactile
  1.04 Taste
  1.05 Smell
  1.06 Kinesthetic
1.1 *Cue selection*
1.2 *Translation*
2.0 *Set*
  2.01 Mental
  2.02 Physical
  2.03 Emotional
3.0 *Guided response*
  3.01 Imitation
  3.02 Trial and error
4.0 *Mechanism*
5.0 *Complex over response*
  5.01 Resolution of uncertainty
  5.02 Automatic performance

The concept of a taxonomy of educational objectives is relatively new and work is still in the experimental and incomplete stage. Undoubtedly much refining of this idea will take place. Such a classification system has great potential because it calls to the curriculum planners' attention the breadth and scope of kinds of learning in each domain, gives them a framework for deriving behavioral objectives, and serves as a reminder to provide specific and adequate learning experiences for all stated or possible objectives. It further serves as a basis for testing, since the desired learning is more likely to be clearly defined.

FORMULATION OF GENERAL OBJECTIVES FOR LOCAL PROGRAMS

Broad statements of objective supply directives for implementation. But they are directives only; generalized presentations of purposes prove meaningless unless they lead to plans and methods that secure progress toward realization. They function as a frame of reference which provides a guide for the formulation of specific objectives and the execution of procedures that lead to desirable progress. Local schools must work out their own purposes and plans for achieving them. Statements by individuals or groups designed for all schools provide an excellent springboard for local action. However, teacher participation in the selection of local objectives is fundamental to a good curriculum. It follows that teachers of physical education have not only the privilege but also the responsibility of building and continuously revising objectives for their

[5] Elizabeth Jane Simpson, *The Classification of Educational Objectives, Psychomotor Domain,* a report of a project supported by a grant from the U.S. Department of Health, Education, and Welfare, Office of Education, Washington, D.C., 1966.

own programs, objectives through which physical education contributes to the overall objectives of the particular school of which they are a part.

SPECIFIC SUGGESTIONS FOR FORMULATING LOCAL PROGRAM OBJECTIVES

When a physical education teacher or department or a committee representing various segments of the school and community sets out to determine objectives of physical education for their own school, they must first check any statement of purposes that may have been adopted as objectives toward which their school aims. If such a framework of stated school purposes exists, then objectives of physical education should be worked out on the basis of optimum contribution to these larger objectives of education.

Framers of statements of objectives should strive for clarity and preciseness. Objectives can be so broad that they become meaningless or so detailed that they prove too unwieldy for practical use. A director of physical education, irked at what he deemed to be "words, words, words" about objectives, recently replied, "To make men and women out of boys and girls," when a student asked, "What are the objectives of your program?" To him the remark made sense; it connoted many things to him. But what does it mean to others? Probably there would be as many interpretations as interpreters. As a guide to others the statement, by itself, is quite meaningless.

It is equally possible, however, to go to the other extreme in formulating lists of objectives for use as general guides. While it is advantageous to use considerable detail in determining short-range, day-by-day objectives, excessive detail should be avoided in determining a set of objectives which give long-range general direction to a program. Suppose that a committee composed of all members of a school's physical education department, a school doctor, a guidance director, two teachers of other subjects, representatives of the parent-teacher associations, a representative of the community recreation department, and several pupil representatives is considering the adoption, rejection, or revision of a proposed list of objectives for the physical education program of a given school. If the proposed list includes items such as developing ability to combine a perpendicular underarm swing with a shift of body weight in serving a volleyball, developing a cooperative attitude in John Brown's soccer playing, developing a concept of the handshake grip on a tennis racket, and improving Mary O'Brien's foot and toe movements in performing a racing dive, it is hardly likely that the committee would be much interested. And even if some of the committee members evidenced interest, it would constitute a waste of time for such a group to consider the kind of detail stated and implied.

While such a policy-forming committee should not consider a multitude of specific objectives, it can give desirable direction to a program by formulating several objectives such as developing and maintaining organic power, contributing to the development of agility and graceful movement, promoting cooperative attitudes through team play, developing competency in democratic processes through group planning and managing of activities, and developing in each student an abiding interest in at least one team game and one individual activity. Long-range or general objectives give direction to the longitudinal program over a period of years, to the program for a school year, to a unit of work, and to the formulation of specific objectives.

Immediate or specific objectives grow out of long-range objectives and out of the needs of individuals and of individual groups. They represent steps to be taken in the attainment of long-range or general objectives. Without well-formulated, short-range goals, statements of long-range purposes become inert and sterile. The teacher studying his group and the individuals within it, formulates and helps students to formulate week-by-week and day-by-day close-range objectives through which progress toward the general objectives may be achieved.

The value of general statements of objectives is not realized until they are interpreted in light of the individual student or student group. Objectives must fit the individual. Much has been written and said about understanding the individual and about fitting the curriculum to the individual rather than fitting the individual to the curriculum. Schools continue to make progress toward doing a better job of meeting the needs of all students. But relatively little attention has been given to planning for individuals in statements and discussions of objectives. An obvious reason for this is that all-encompassing statements designed to give direction to school programs must be either general enough to permit all situations and all students to function within their framework or else so detailed as to be unwieldy for practical use.

All youth do need development in similar general areas. But they need different kinds and amounts of development brought about through different ways, methods, procedures, and techniques. It remains for those who work directly with boys and girls to take the lead in filling in the bill of particulars by which each may progress toward achievement of the imperative needs. Since this cannot be completely done through formulation of general long-range objectives applicable to all, it must be done by formulation of individualized objectives.

If objectives are guideposts, if they point the way, and if one achieves better when he knows what he is working toward, it obviously follows that planning to meet individual needs requires formulation of individualized objectives. In a tennis unit an appropriate goal for John Doe might be to qualify for city-championship play in a municipal tournament, while a reasonable goal for Richard Roe might be to learn the basic rules of the game and to play at a beginner's level. The goal of developing strength of abdominal muscles and reducing weight might be a desirable major pursuit for a year's physical education work in some cases, but it certainly would not make sense for all.

The important factor here, however, is that a clear statement of the general objectives proves essential to effective planning for individuals and individual groups. This chapter reviews current thinking concerning the social purposes and general objectives of education and physical education, as a base to the derivation of program objectives for a given school and the subsequent selection of learning experiences and teaching methods.

SUMMARY

Objectives represent statements of the goals or purposes of education. They indicate the kinds of subject matter, learning experiences, methods of teaching, and administrative and supervisory procedures required, and serve as the basis for the evaluation of outcomes.

Objectives express needs as seen by the persons who formulate them. They represent value judgments about the most important factors in the culture which should be preserved and taught to the rising generation.

General objectives pertain to the overall societal purposes of education. They give direction to the derivation of program objectives, unit objects, and instructional objectives.

The basic purpose of education in American society centers on the preparation of individuals to live effectively in a democratic society. Current emphasis in statements of educational objectives consists of giving attention to real-life needs, merging social and individual needs, stating objectives behaviorally, and classifying the different kinds of learnings.

Objectives of physical education evolve from the objectives of education. Practices in physical education must necessarily be compatible with expressed purposes of education.

The four basic areas of objectives accepted in the modern physical education program include health, social ends, emotional development, and recreation.

Clear, precise statements of general objectives prove, essential to effective planning for individuals and groups and aid in increasing the compatibility between individual and societal needs.

Questions and problems for discussion

1. Is there conflict between satisfaction of individual needs on the one hand and societal needs on the other? Make a list of such conflicts; or if you see no conflicts, explain how the two kinds of needs interact.
2. Should secondary school, physical education programs differentiate between planned experiences for pupils intending to go to college and those for whom high school will be terminal education? Why or why not?
3. How have changing objectives of education changed direction and goals of physical education? How do goals toward which secondary school physical education now strives differ from those of a half century ago?
4. How has the changing function of the secondary school specifically affected content of physical education programs? Consider problems of urbanization, increased secondary school enrollments, and any other current sociological factors affecting the modern secondary school.
5. List ways in which your high school physical education experiences have helped you adjust to subsequent living. Think of high school acquaintances whose modes of living now differ markedly from yours, and list ways in which you think their high school physical education helped them to adjust to living.
6. Describe ways in which stating objectives in terms of actions or performances will (1) improve instruction and (2) aid in evaluating outcomes.
7. What help would you expect nonspecialists in physical education to give to development of a statement of objectives of physical education for a community-centered high school?
8. With several specific and detailed examples justify the statement "Physical education throughout its history has consistently served the avowed purposes of contemporary society."

Selected references

Brownell, Clifford Lee, and E. Patricia Hagman: *Physical Education—Foundations and Principles,* McGraw-Hill Book Company, New York, 1951.

Bloom, Benjamin S. (ed.): *Taxonomy of Educational Objectives, Handbook I: Cognitive Domain,* David McKay Company, Inc., New York, 1956.

Cardinal Principles of Secondary Education, Bulletin 35, U.S. Bureau of Education, Washington, D.C., 1918.

Educational Policies Commission: *The Purposes of Education in American Democracy,* National Education Association of the United States and the American Association of School Administrators, Washington, D.C., 1938.

Gardner, John W.: "National Goals in Education," in *Goals for Americans,* the report of the President's Commission on National Goals, Prentice-Hall, Inc., Englewood Cliffs, N.J., 1960.

Hackensmith, Charles W.: *History of Physical Education,* Harper & Row, Publishers, Incorporated, New York, 1965.

Krathwohl, David R. (ed.): *Taxonomy of Educational Objectives, Handbook I: Affective Domain,* David McKay Company, Inc., New York, 1964.

Oberteuffer, Delbert, and Celeste Ulrich: *Physical Education,* Harper & Row, Publishers, Incorporated, New York, 1962.

Paterson, Ann, and Edmond C. Hallberg (ed.): *Background Reading for Physical Education,* Section One, "Historical Backgrounds," and Section Two, "Philosophical Backgrounds," Holt, Rinehart and Winston, Inc., New York, 1965.

Report of the Committee of Ten on Secondary School Studies; with the Reports of the Conferences Arranged by the Committee, published for the National Education Association of the United States by the American Book Company, New York, 1894.

Thut, I. N., and Don Adams: *Educational Patterns in Contemporary Societies,* McGraw-Hill Book Company, New York, 1964.

Williams, Jesse Feiring: *The Principles of Physical Education,* 8th ed., W. D. Saunders Company, Philadelphia, 1964.

chapter 5

PROGRAMS FOR SECONDARY SCHOOLS

INTRODUCTION

What programs are needed in secondary schools to help students achieve the objectives discussed in the previous chapter? What essential characteristics do top-notch programs need? Should programs be the same or similar for the various grades, the seventh, eighth, ninth, tenth, etc.? What kinds of programs exist in the United States? What correlation should there be with other school areas? What are appropriate procedures for planners? Are there helpful criteria and guides?

Before these questions are answered, let it be made clear that this chapter deals with the activity content of programs extending over several years of secondary school experience. A basic problem exists when considering and selecting curricular experiences for students. It lies in the tenuousness of direct relationship between stated objectives and the activities or experiences selected to achieve progress toward those objectives. As planners select activities they should forever keep the objectives in mind and refrain from becoming so enthusiastic about some activity that they, perhaps unconsciously, think of it as an end in itself rather than as a means toward the objectives.

For administrative and organization purposes it seems necessary, at least in large high schools, to have a list of activities. Emphasizing this aspect, the present chapter may leave persons who do not read the whole text with the impression that the authors regard activities as such as almost the whole program of experience for students. Those who read further will know that matters of method permeate almost all of this volume and that the authors regard method as a part of program in a quite real sense because program includes all the experiences of students.

CHARACTERISTICS OF A SATISFACTORY PROGRAM

Obviously, secondary school programs, starting with seventh grade, need to be part of an all-grade program or at least built upon an elementary school program. Thus, secondary school physical education programs in community X, which has an extensive elementary school program, should be different from community Y, which has a meager elementary program. If some of the essentials of the general characteristics of a satisfactory program listed below have been satisfied through elementary school experiences it is not necessary for a secondary school program to provide for them. To be of high quality a program needs to assure the following:

1. Underlying emphasis upon providing knowledge and attitudes which seem most likely to induce students to make physical activity a part of their future lives. Knowledge of effects of exercise, attitudes affecting concern for one's well-being, and activities which bring satisfaction to the performer are important bases affecting the probability that a student may decide to make exercise a part of his future living.
2. Continuity of activity strenuous enough to develop strength and endurance and maintain physical fitness.
3. All physically able boys and girls learning and participating in several team games, several individual or dual games, rhythmic activities, group games and relays, water activities, and gymnastics.
4. Adaptive, restricted, or rehabilitative work for those whose physical condition indicates such need.
5. Contact activities such as wrestling, combative contests, or football for boys.
6. Opportunity for coeducational activities.
7. Opportunity to select class activities from among several offered for girls who have satisfied the minimum-breadth requirements described in number three above and for boys who have satisfied numbers three and five above.

8. Opportunity to participate in extraclass recreational, intramural, or interscholastic activities for all who wish to do so.
9. Difficulty adjusted to groups and individuals so that all can have a reasonable measures of success and so that all are challenged.

DIFFERENCES AND SIMILARITIES AMONG PROGRAMS

One can find a variety of secondary school physical education programs in the United States. Some are weak, others strong; some are open to only a few students, others to all; some include weekly classes, others daily; and there are those which have generous intramural, recreational, extramural, and interscholastic offerings. Why is this the case?

First, values vary from community to community. A local school district, after complying with legal requirements, tends to emphasize what its citizens believe to be highly valuable. One community may desire the best possible physical education program for all its boys while another may think of interscholastic athletics as almost all that is needed for a program for boys. One district may insist upon a high-quality program for every girl though another may question the need for vigorous and extensive participation in physical activities for girls.

Second, resources vary. A school district may value physical education highly and want to have the best possible program its professional staff can plan but may not be able to find the necessary money. Such situations exist rather frequently but are only temporary. Districts which value a program highly usually find ways to work it out if given a few years.

Third, opinions concerning appropriate emphases differ among physical educators. The authors, of course, believe that a program in any high school should embody the nine characteristics of a satisfactory program presented above. Not all physical educators will agree. Some may prefer more emphasis upon sports and sport skills and less upon an underlying knowledge and attitude for encouraging physical activity permanently. Some may believe there should be more emphasis upon fitness, strength, endurance, and cardiovascular development; others may prefer the opposite.

Some, especially women, may believe the base should be movement exploration and experiences which feature anatomical, mechanical, and physiological analysis. In secondary schools this usually is called basic movement, or fundamentals of movement, or movement education. More dependence upon rhythmic activities and dance may be desired by some while others may prefer larger dependence upon self-realization, upon expressing oneself through movement.

It is possible that at this point the reader may think that existing programs vary so much that there are few similarities. Such is not the case. There are similarities, perhaps as marked as in various other high school subjects. Among the forces tending to make uniform secondary school programs are:

1. State laws and state departments of public instruction (or of education depending upon titles used in various states). Besides the enforcement of laws, the functions of state departments include the distribution of state-supported money to local schools, advisory and consultant services, and production of written materials. Almost all state departments have one or more publications dealing with physical education as well as one or more concerning health.
2. State associations and the National Federation of State High School Athletic Associations regulate interscholastic activities thus providing considerable uniformity in that important area of the program. With a few exceptions the state associations are voluntary, governed by representatives elected by member high schools. The Michigan and New York associations are affiliated with the state departments of public instruction. More about these associations will be found in Chapter 14, Organizing and Managing Interscholastic Programs. Suffice it here to point out that they regulate eligibility, length of sport seasons, and other conditions of competition.
3. Professional organizations, particularly the American Association for Health, Physical Education, and Recreation and its district and state components, tend to bring about similarity among programs. Notable are the AAHPER Fitness Tests,[1] a platform statement,[2] *Physical Education for High School Students,*[3] the first book on physical education written for high school boys and girls, and the attendant *Teacher's Guide,*[4] both projects of AAHPER. The Division of Girls' and Womens' Sports of AAHPER establishes standards and makes rules thus encouraging nationwide similarity; more about this will

[1] *AAHPER Youth Fitness Test Manual,* rev. ed., The American Association for Health, Physical Education, and Recreation, 1965.

[2] W. K. Streit, and Simon McNelly, "A Platform for Physical Education," *Journal of the American Association for Health, Physical Education, and Recreation,* 21:126, March, 1950.

[3] *Physical Education for High School Students,* fifth printing, The American Association for Health, Physical Education, and Recreation, 1964.

[4] *Teacher's Guide for Physical Education for High School Students,* rev. ed., The American Association for Health, Physical Education, and Recreation, 1963.

be found in the Chapter 13, Organizing and Managing Intramural and Recreational Programs.

4. The President's Council on Physical Fitness (formerly the Council on Youth Fitness), first organized by President Eisenhower and continued and supported by Presidents Kennedy and Johnson, has had a considerable impact upon physical education. Through intensive publicity, utilizing all popular media of communication, the Council has increased public awareness. Their school visitations and regional meetings for selected physical educators have had an effect upon programs. The Council has given powerful force to recommendations which include:

    a. Periodic health appraisals
    b. Identification of the physically underdeveloped through screening tests which measure strength, agility, and flexibility
    c. A daily school program
    d. At least fifteen minutes of the daily program to be devoted to vigorous activity
    e. Formation of state and local fitness committees

    Wide distribution of the Council's publications [5] has affected programs; schools which sponsored little or no physical education program have added required work. Vigorousness, with attention to strength, endurance, cardiovascular development, and maintenance, has been emphasized more in schools which already had extensive programs.

5. Greater participation of Federal and state governments, especially through the availability of funds from the U.S. Office of Education, and larger local districts tend to produce program uniformity. Perhaps not everyone will agree although it seems unmistakably true that as the areas and populations served become larger, and as participation, particularly financial support, of larger units of government increases, the differences among local schools decrease.

[5] Among these, all published in Washington by the U.S. Government Printing Office, are *Youth Fitness, a Community Project,* 1959; *Youth Physical Fitness, Suggested Elements of a School-centered Program,* 1961; *Physical Fitness Elements in Recreation, Suggestions for Community Programs,* 1963; *Adult Physical Fitness, a Program for Men and Women,* 1963; *Fitness for Leadership, Suggestions for Colleges and Universities,* 1964; *Vigor: A Complete Exercise Plan for Boys 12 to 18,* 1964; *Vim: A Complete Exercise Plan for Girls 12 to 18,* 1964; and *Four Years of Fitness, 1961–65, a Report to the President,* 1965.

Example 1 Oak Park and River Forest, Illinois, High School

Girls' physical education program

Oak Park and River Forest High School requires a daily physical education period for each student. The amount, degree, and type of exercise in which each girl participates is determined by her physical examination. Skill tests and skill ratings are also used in making activity assignments. The girls' program, organized to include a number of electives, allows the student who has fulfilled the requirements to elect the class of her choice. After consulting with her physical education teacher, she selects a program which most nearly meets her needs and interests.

A girl's four-year program must include four terms of swimming (one each year), two terms of dance, one term of driver education, one term of fitness, one term of tennis, one term of health education, and, in addition, one team sport and one individual sport. All other physical education classes are elective.

Particular stress is placed upon individual sports and games in which we hope the student's interest and activity will continue after she is out of high school.

The various physical education classes which are offered each semester are listed below:

1st Term	*2d Term*	*3d Term*
First semester		
Hockey	Basketball	
Beginning tennis	Badminton	
Apparatus	Fitness and exercise	
Archery	Folk dance	
Life saving	Beginning swimming	
Driver education lecture	Driver education lecture	
Second semester		
Volleyball	Speedaway	Softball
Posture	Volleyball	Tennis
Stunts and tumbling	Posture	Apparatus
Modern dance	Modern dance	Archery
Intermediate swimming	Synchronized swimming	Golf
Health education	Health education	Catchup swim
Driver trainers	On-the-road driving	On-the-road driving

After-school elective activities for girls

Activities for girls are sponsored after school in apparatus, archery, badminton, basketball, bowling, modern dance (Junior and Senior Orchesis), golf, hockey, softball, speedaway, swimming and diving (including synchronized swimming), tennis, and volleyball in connection with the Girls' Athletic Association. In the intramural tournaments which are held, the four school classes and the physical education classes are the units for competition. Qualified girls represent the school in interscholastic tournaments in two individual sports: archery, badminton, and tennis. In swimming, basketball, and bowling they enter a state telegraphic meet.

Note: Appreciation is expressed to the school, and to Jane Axtell, Head, Girls' Physical Education, LeRoy Z. Compton, Director of Physical Education and Athletics, and Orin Noth, Head, Boy's Physical Education.

ILLUSTRATIONS OF ACTIVITIES

The activity outlines of two high schools are presented with permission. These large high schools are in socioeconomically above average suburban residential districts. Other schools, especially small ones, may have superior programs which include fewer activities than do the two schools presented.

Looking over these activities will help the reader when he considers program planning. They are presented for that reason and are regarded as neither typical nor suitable for all schools.

Example 1 lists the activities offered to girls by the Oak Park and River Forest, Illinois, High School and describes other characteristics of the program for girls. It is shown exactly as it has been distributed to students and parents in mimeograph form. Example 2 lists the activities for boys at the same school.

Note that girls may select from a number of activities; this satisfies point number seven of the nine characteristics of a satisfactory program listed on pages 96 and 97.

Example 2 Oak Park and River Forest, Illinois, High School

Boys' physical education class activities

Freshmen	Sophomores	Juniors	Seniors
Basketball	Soccer	Volleyball	Speedball
Tumbling	Badminton	Tumbling	Volleyball
Swimming	Basketball	Basketball	Basketball
Track and field	Track and field	Swimming	Swimming
Health	Handball	Life saving	Water polo
Apparatus	Apparatus	Golf	First aid
Golf	Volleyball	Wrestling	Handball
Wrestling	Wrestling	Handball	Softball
Tennis	Swimming	Apparatus	Tennis
		Softball	Weight training
		Weight training	Badminton

Example 3 shows boys' and girls' class activities offered by the Hinsdale, Illinois, Central High School, and indicates grade level as well as length of time devoted to each activity. Classes for future leaders, which are given as an alternative to the regular program, are shown for girls. Leadership training for boys is handled as an extraclass activity so is not included in the example which deals only with class activities.

Example 3 Hinsdale, Illinois, Central High School Class Activities

Boys		*Girls*	
Activity	*Weeks*	*Activity*	*Weeks*
Freshmen			
Testing and orientation	½	Speedaway	6½
Basketball	6	Basketball	6
Gymnastics	6	Tumbling	6
Swimming	6	Swimming	6
Wrestling	6	Modern dance	6
Weight training and indoor track	6	Track and field	7
Speedball	3		
Tennis	4		
Total	37½	Total	37½
Sophomores			
Track and field	3½	Body mechanics	3½
Driver education, section A	6	Driver education, sections A and S	6
Touch football, section B	3	Modern dance, section B	
Wrestling, section B	3	Basketball	3
Stunts and tumbling	3	Driver education, section B	6
Driver education, section B	6	Modern dance, sections A and S	
Games and relays, section A	3	Volleyball	6
Weight training and indoor track, section A	6	Apparatus	4
Weight training and physiology of exercise	3	Swimming	4
Basketball	4	Softball	5
Gymnastics	4		
Swimming	5		
Total	37½	Total	37½
		Leadership training	
		Softball	3½
		Driver education	6
		Basketball	3
		Modern dance	2

Example 3 (continued)

Boys		*Girls*	
Activity	*Weeks*	*Activity*	*Weeks*
		Classroom	1
		Tumbling	3
		Body mechanics	3
		Volleyball	3
		Apparatus	4
		Swimming	4
		Speedaway	2
		Field hockey	3
		Total	37½
Juniors			
Swimming	3½	Tennis	6½
Soccer	5	Body mechanics	2
First aid I	3	Swimming	4
Stunts and tumbling	3	Apparatus	6
Basketball	3	Modern dance	6
Volleyball	3	Tumbling	4
First aid II	3	Softball	5
Weight training and indoor track	4	Archery	4
Touch football	4		
Softball	5		
Total	37½	Total	37½
		Leadership training	
		Activity	*Weeks*
		Tennis	3½
		Basketball	3
		Recreational sports	1½
		Team sports	½
		Swimming	4
		Apparatus	3
		Modern dance	1
		Body mechanics	2

Example 3 (continued)

Boys		*Girls*	
Activity	*Weeks*	*Activity*	*Weeks*
		Volleyball	3
		First aid	2
		Tournament planning	1
		Tumbling	3
		Track and field	1
		Badminton	2
		Golf	2
		Speedaway	1
		Field hockey	1
		Archery	1
		Total	37½
Seniors			
Soccer and archery	4½	Field hockey	4½
Touch football	5	Swimming	4
Wrestling	3	Recreational sports	4
Volleyball and Co-rec volleyball	3	Volleyball and Co-rec volleyball	6
Weight training and indoor track	6	First aid	3
Gymnastics	3	Body mechanics	3
Swimming	4	Badminton	4
Softball	4	Softball	2
Basketball	5	Archery	3
		Golf	4
Total	37½	Total	37½

Note: Appreciation is expressed to the Hinsdale, Illinois, Central High School, to Mr. Harvey Dickinson, Director of Health, Physical Education, and Athletics, and to the men and women staff members.

CORRELATION WITH OTHER AREAS

Correlation and cooperation among all areas providing significant experiences for youngsters enhances results and improves education. The tendency on the part of some teachers and departments to adopt the attitude, "You run your class and your department; I'll run mine," lowers the effectiveness of high schools. Schools are for boys and girls, and they do not divide themselves into athletic sections, body sections, mind sections, mathematics sections, social studies sections, science sections, prank-playing sections, teacher's goat-getting sections, human relationships sections, family living sections, and the like. Rather, they bring all the forces that go to make them what they are into every situation and activity in which they find themselves.

Some physical education teachers and directors complain that other teachers, administrators, and citizens do not understand the importance and value of physical education. Almost all these teachers and directors, unknown to themselves, suffer from feelings of inferiority about the status of physical education as they lash out at others in ill-advised attempts to boost their own stock. Knocking others down is the warlike way of attempting to gain; cooperating with others is the educational way to gain.

Physical education correlates so closely with health, safety, recreation, and camping that many people erroneously tend to think of the five areas as one. State organizations and laws contribute to the idea that the several areas belong together. It is true that they have much in common; the relationships and overlappings are so great that grouping together for administrative purposes may be both convenient and effective. A considerable number of school systems successfully combine the several and assign administrative responsibility to an assistant superintendent or to a director of health, physical education, recreation, and safety. When competent specialists, or competent persons who give special attention, are employed in each area, the combined administrative structure works well. But when a staff of persons thought to be competent in all these areas, without special preparation and interests within the groupings, attempt to function in all technical and detailed ways, then "the blind leading the blind" usually results.

CORRELATION WITH HEALTH

Physical education has primary responsibility for instruction in health matters most directly related to physical activities. A line of direct or indirect relationship is impossible to draw with complete accuracy. What, then, are the health matters most directly related to physical activities? They are exercise, rest, recreation, relaxation, and sleep. Physical education has a primary responsibility to teach understandings in these matters and to help students to decide how much, how little, what kind, where, when, and how.

Physical education has secondary or reinforcement responsibilities in areas of health for which other subjects have primary teaching responsibility. To cite an example: A school might assign primary responsibility for instruction in communicable diseases and infections to biology. It is a responsibility of physical education, in this case, to reinforce, to work toward behavior that is consistent with knowledge secured elsewhere by students.

It shares with all other school areas the responsibility for maintaining a healthful environment. Attention to clean and safe gymnasiums, playgrounds, dressing rooms, and shower rooms is necessary. Lighting and heating should be conducive to healthful living. The atmosphere surrounding activities should be pleasant and free from continued tensions; relationships should free students from fears, feelings of inadequacy, and anxieties. Responsibilities as well as prerogatives should be clearly understood by the students.

It is a responsibility of physical education to cooperate with the school health-services program. Under the direction of the school doctor, physical education teachers may help with examinations and make inspections. Medical recommendations for adapted activities, or for rest, must be carried out. Close attention to signs of approaching illness and referrals to doctors or nurses are a necessity. Unfavorable or questionable physiological adaptations to exercise are to be referred for medical attention. Questionable growth patterns, as shown by weight and height records such as the Meredith form or the Wetzel Grid, need early detection and referral for medical attention.

There is the privilege and responsibility of helping to plan and continuously improve the school and community health programs. Suggestions should be made to the proper persons. Membership on health councils and committees should be sought and utilized toward improved practices. Cooperation with doctors and nurses, guidance personnel, and teachers of health courses, science, social studies, home economics, and other courses serves to make the school health program more serviceable to students while lack of cooperation causes disintegration.

COOPERATION WITH SAFETY

All teachers, of course, have the responsibility of preventing avoidable accidents in connection with their activities. Physical education produces more injuries than does any other school activity. Accident prevention should receive high priority. However, risk is inherent in living, and creation of fears of desirable risks should be avoided.

School organization for safety may provide a safety committee or coordinator, and safety instruction may be a responsibility of various classes and school activities. It may assign safety education to the broader area of health education, as favored by the Joint Committee on Health Problems in Education of the National Education Association and the American Medical Association. Or special courses in safety may be provided.

In any case, physical education's responsibility to safety goes further than the primary responsibility for safe conduct of physical education activities. It extends to cooperation with school and community programs through the work of coordinators, committees, councils, and other teachers to the end that schools, homes, and communities may be safer places in which to live.

COOPERATION WITH RECREATION

School and community recreation programs serve best when there has been cooperative planning and when all persons responsible for leadership know what each is doing. Cooperative consideration, under the leadership of school administration, is necessary in order that recreational opportunities and events in sports, music, drama, arts, clubs, and others be broad, balanced, and integrated.

Improvement is needed in correlation between school physical education and community recreation services. School physical education programs and community recreation programs should complement and supplement each other. When integration and cooperation are effective, schools help to equip young people with skills and interests that guide them into wholesome recreation provided by community organizations other than the school. Also, cooperation leads to a sharing of facilities such as gymnasiums, parks, swimming pools, tennis courts, and golf courses. School park combinations seem to aid cooperation.

COOPERATION WITH CAMPING

Physical education has a large stake in camping which provides many desirable physical activities. In schools which sponsor camping, physical education teachers should be an integral part of the camping staff. Their abilities qualify them for useful service in planning and organizing camping programs as well as for leadership of games, sports, aquatics, hikes, and outings of various kinds. Physical educators also should cooperate with nonschool agencies or organizations interested in providing free or low-cost camping for young people.

CORRELATION WITH OTHER SCHOOL SUBJECTS AND ACTIVITIES

Indirectly, through contributions to student well-being, physical education improves the success and happiness of boys and girls in all their schoolwork. There are opportunities, also, for cooperative ventures with other subjects or activities. Some of these provide more opportunity than do others. Music departments are called upon to supply bands for games, music for pageants, accompaniment for rhythms, and the like. Art departments may engage in poster projects, scenery projects, and sculpture, painting, and drawing projects that deal with physical activities. Industrial education departments may assign projects such as building play equipment, boats, skis, sleds, and model planes for use by the builder or builders; some industrial education departments produce equipment for school use, but there is no unanimity of opinion among educators concerning the desirability of school-shop production for school use. It is likely that most shop teachers are more than willing to include projects for the production of school equipment among those from which individual students may choose, provided that no pressure is put on the students to work on something that does not represent a free and unhampered choice. Speech and English frequently find a cooperative ground with physical education in the selection of subjects for speeches and themes. Dramatic and musical productions, with dancing and other physical movements, find common ground with physical education. Journalism finds special interest in athletics. When physical education teachers cooperate actively they not only help youngsters have enriching experiences but also increase the students' respect for physical education.

PROCEDURES FOR PLANNING PROGRAMS

At a glance it may seem simple to plan a physical education program for boys and one for girls in high school X. To make a program outline, is it not necessary only to decide upon activities for each of the grade levels and list them? Yes and no. It is necessary to consider many things in order to make the choices likely to produce optimum student growth and achievement. What are the factors planners need to consider? They include:

1. Objectives, probably those of American secondary education, almost surely those of the school involved, and certainly the general objectives for physical education.
2. The growth and development of adolescents in general, with attention to their physical and psychological characteristics, needs, and abilities.
3. The physical and psychological characteristics of the population of the school involved; the students may differ from a general population and from students of schools in other communities because of environment and past experiences in homes, communities, and schools.
4. The nature of the school and its program; for instance, a school which has for years placed considerable responsibility for their own affairs upon student planners of physical education programs would arrange to involve students in managing and planning more than a school whose students were accustomed to more autocratic controls and to more external direction.

5. The nature of the community with regard to mores; these include dominant nationality, economic conditions, educational level, cultural tendencies, and religious beliefs.
6. The facilities, time, and personnel available; almost all physical educators seem aware of the need for a place and time to conduct classes as well as the need for competent teachers, although some tend to be more resourceful than others in making the most of what is available.
7. The relationships among class physical education and extraclass programs including intramurals, recreation, the girls' athletic association, and interscholastics.
8. The effects of various methods of organizing and teaching, with the recognition that any professional teacher has the freedom to select a method for his own classes as long as he does not interfere with others.
9. Continuous evaluation, which is likely to lead to rather frequent revision.

WHO SHOULD PLAN?

Who should take the primary responsibility for planning a physical education program for all grades in high school X? Should one person do the whole job? Should a committee selected from among members of the physical education staff do it? Should the men's department sitting as a committee of the whole be responsible for planning a program for boys and the women's department for girls? Should school personnel other than physical educators participate? Can curriculum coordinators and supervisors help? Should students be invited to help? What is the role of the general administration office? Should nonschool personnel participate? How do schools now approach planning? Are some procedures quite common? Before these questions are answered, let us note that this discussion applies to planning an entirely new program, although, of course, it also fits considering and planning revisions. Only infrequently is a whole program planned from a clean slate; most planning involves changing existing programs. Let us speak to the last question first and then consider the other nine in the order asked.

How do schools today approach planning? What is done varies a great deal. However, several common procedures give a good picture of the approaches in use. In small schools, with one or two men and one or two women teachers, it is quite common for the men to prepare a program for boys, for the women to make one for girls, then for the men and women to meet to consider the allocation of facilities and supplies needed for each of the programs and make adjustments or revisions which may be necessary to make both of the programs possible. Then, usually, the programs go to the principal for approval or suggestions for revision.

In large schools, with a half dozen or more staff members, it is quite common to have a program committee responsible for a continual study and an annual report to the full department which may accept, reject, or revise proposals made in the committee report. Such a committee is likely to meet at times with curriculum coordinators, representatives of school health services including doctors and nurses, recreation personnel, representative students, and representative parents. In some large schools all department members, as a committee of the whole, undertake the job; in others the director or head of the department alone serves the function.

There is no one answer as to who should take the primary responsibility in planning. In each school it should be clear that some person or group definitely is assigned the task. When a group is made responsible it is necessary that a chairman be named to accept responsibility for leading the group.

One person should not do the whole job, but one person should take the lead. When only one person works on the program, the results are not likely to be wholeheartedly accepted, or at least not embraced by others involved with carrying out the plans. All staff members who will be directly concerned should be involved with planning, at least to the extent of having the opportunity to discuss and to vote.

It is possible that a committee of the physical education staff or the men's or women's department sitting as a committee of the whole could be responsible for planning. Such decisions depend upon local circumstances, one of the most important of which is the preference of those most directly concerned. In the case of a large staff it is advisable that all members have a voice in deciding what planning procedures they prefer.

It is advisable to invite and encourage school personnel other than physical educators to participate. Representatives of the health sciences are in a position to give valuable counsel. Faculty members from any of several departments may be helpful. Since they know the students' behavior and inclinations in circumstances other than gymnasium and playfield activity, they may have information valuable to physical educators, and their participation helps to interpret physical education to the faculty.

Curriculum coordinators and supervisors can help in planning if they are worthy of their positions. They should at least be consulted. They need not be continuous members of a group considering a physical education program nor should they be expected to be. Since they are specialists in helping to improve various school programs, their aid as consultants and specialists should be utilized and their analysis and advice at various stages of planning may be of considerable value.

Should students be members of a program-planning committee or group? Their viewpoints certainly should be considered. How these viewpoints are best expressed differs from school to school. Generally speaking, it is advisable to have students meet with program planners as continuing members of a committee, as a group, or as invited guests. At the least, planners should become informed concerning student opinion.

The general administration office must be informed of and must approve the planning. Representatives of that office seldom have time to regularly meet with planning groups. Since they have the responsibility for all school programs, the more fully they know what is likely to be proposed, the better, and if it is possible to persuade administrators to attend some of the planning sessions, that is all to the welfare of the physical education program, and thus to the boys and girls.

The possible willingness and ability of nonschool personnel to contribute something worthwhile to program planning should be seriously considered. It is highly likely that recreation personnel are more than worth consulting in cases where such persons are well trained and able. Both physical education and recreation programs stand to gain if they support each other, and there may be no better way to encourage support than to ask for help in planning. Doctors and nurses have some knowledge and viewpoints of value. Parents know youngsters somewhat differently from teachers, so discussions with them may bring worthwhile results. As with administrators, curriculum coordinators, and supervisors, it seems advisable to have nonschool personnel meet with program planners at various points of progress but not continuously. Their best contributions are likely to be made as they react to progress reports or proposals by the person or persons primarily responsible for planning a total physical education program or for considering revision of an established program.

CRITERIA AND GUIDES

The characteristics of a satisfactory program listed above serve as partial criteria and give considerable guidance for selection from among many possible activities. Additional criteria which should be considered are posed by the following questions:

1. Does the activity contribute to the achievement of program objectives?
2. Does the activity have greater relative value than other possible choices?
3. Does the activity have meaning in the social life of the learner, or can it be made to have meaning?

4. Does the activity have carry-over value for the out-of-school and adult life?
5. Is the activity of interest to the learner, or can interest be developed?
6. Is the activity within the range of ability of the learner?
7. Will the activity lead to further developmental experiences?
8. Has the activity been adequately presented in a previous grade or within a previous experience of the learner?
9. Can the activity be learned better through an available nonschool agency?
10. Does the activity correlate with other experiences in the curriculum?
11. Is the activity reasonably safe, or does it lend itself to reasonable safety precautions?

As far as possible, programs should be based upon established facts. Anatomy, physiology, biology, psychology, sociology, and history supply information. However, physical education programs express beliefs of planners to a large extent because the route to many objectives escapes exact factual analysis.

The following guides, posed as questions, may be used by program planners to check the validity of their methods and results.

1. Is the program based upon a clear statement of objectives?
2. Are the objectives for the physical education program compatible with the educational objectives of the school system?
3. Has a careful analysis been made of all factors surrounding the program, such as pupil needs, the nature of the school program, and community needs?
4. Have program plans been derived cooperatively with maximum representation of all concerned with the program?
5. Have all activities and learning experiences been selected in light of acceptable criteria such as those listed above?
6. Have provisions been made for the process of program development to be a continuous one, with ample flexibility allowed for both immediate and long-range adjustment in plans?
7. Are working plans feasible in terms of existing conditions?
8. Are projected and long-range plans based upon continuous improvement?
9. Are recommendations included for optimum implementation of program plans on both an immediate and a long-range basis?

10. Are opportunities provided for program planners to progressively improve their techniques in both planning itself and the understandings and skills to participate in derived plans?
11. Have all aspects of the program, class and extraclass,been considered by program planners?
12. Has the extraclass program been planned with the same attention to outcomes as the class program?
13. Has attention been directed to the correlative functions of the physical education program?
14. Have provisions been made to interpret program purposes and procedures to all school personnel, pupils, and patrons?
15. Are basic plans, including statements of objectives, accessible in written form?

SUMMARY

This chapter discusses the long-term planning of programs for the several grade levels in secondary schools. Chapter 11 deals with short-term planning, with units and lessons.

Activities are means through which objectives are pursued. Careful planning is needed to assure direct relationship between activities and objectives.

Nine characteristics of a satisfactory program are listed. Differences exist among programs found in secondary schools in the United States because values vary from community to community, because financial resources vary, and because opinions among physical educators vary. Similarities also exist; forces tending toward uniformity include state laws and state departments of public instruction (or of education), state athletic associations and the national federation of them, professional organizations, the President's Council on Physical Fitness, and movements toward greater participation of Federal and state governments and toward larger local districts.

Lists of activities used in two schools are shown to help the reader think through the planning of a program.

Consideration should be given to correlating physical education with other areas. The areas of health, safety, recreation, and camping almost demand physical education cooperation. Cooperation with other school subjects and activities, such as music, art, industrial education, speech and English, drama, and journalism, may provide mutual benefit.

Planners of programs need to consider objectives, the growth and development of adolescents, the characteristics of students in the particular school involved, the nature of the school and its overall program, the community, the facilities, time, and teaching personnel available, the relationships between class and extraclass activities, the effects of methods, and continuous evaluation. Different schools have different ideas about who should plan programs; some suggestions and illustrations are given. The important thing is to locate responsibility and draw upon various resources for help.

The list of characteristics of a satisfactory program presented early in the chapter serves as partial criteria and gives some guidance for the selection of activities. Later in the chapter, eleven questions pose additional criteria and fifteen questions provide guides.

Questions and problems for discussion

1. Is it possible for a secondary school to sponsor too many physical education activities? Too few? List reasons for your answers.

2. Define the terms physical education, health education, safety education, and camping and outdoor education. What contributions can physical education make to each of the other areas?

3. Support or oppose the statement, "Since softball is a popular community sport, there is little reason to include it in the school physical education program."

4. Explain the advantages and disadvantages of having school personnel other than members of the physical education department serve on a physical education curriculum committee. Do the same for students, community-recreation personnel, and representative parents.

5. Review legislation concerning physical education in your state. Indicate ways in which this legislation affects secondary school programs.

6. After consulting several of the references at the end of this chapter, make a list of implications of the concept that students' needs and interests should be considered in curriculum planning. Do the same for the nature of the school program, the facilities and time available, and any other important factors.

7. Describe various ways in which students may practice living in a democracy while engaging in physical education activities.

8. Assume that you have been invited to evaluate the physical education program of high school X. List criteria which you would use as a basis for such evaluation. If you propose to use those listed in this chapter, defend each criterion.

Selected references

Brown, Camille, and Rosalind Cassidy: *Theory in Physical Education; A Guide to Program Change,* Lea & Febinger, Philadelphia, 1963.

Cowell, Charles C., and Helen W. Hazelton: *Curriculum Designs in Physical Education,* Prentice-Hall, Inc., Englewood Cliffs, N.J., 1955.

Douglass, Harl Roy: *The High School Curriculum,* 3d ed., The Ronald Press Company, New York, 1964.

LaPorte, William Ralph: *The Physical Education Curriculum,* 6th ed., College Book Store, Los Angeles, 1955.

Moss, Bernice R., Warren H. Southworth, and John Lester Reichert (eds.): *Health Education,* Joint Committee on Health Problems of the NEA and the AMA, National Education Association, Washington, D.C., 1967, paperback edition.

Nixon, John E., and Ann E. Jewett: *Physical Education Curriculum,* The Ronald Press Company, New York, 1964.

Oliver, Albert I.: *Curriculum Improvement: A Guide to Problems, Principles, and Procedures,* Dodd, Mead, & Company, Inc., New York, 1965.

Saylor, John Galen, and William M. Alexander: *Curriculum Planning for Modern Schools,* Holt, Rinehart and Winston, Inc., New York, 1966.

Taba, Hilda: *Curriculum Development,* Harcourt, Brace & World, Inc., New York, 1962.

Woodring, Paul: *Introduction to American Education,* Harcourt, Brace & World, Inc., New York, 1965.

part 3
INSTRUCTIONAL PATTERNS AND MEDIA

INTRODUCTION

Apt selection of teaching methods depends upon skill in analyzing the unique conditions of specific teaching situations. A method which may prove effective under one set of circumstances may be equally ineffective in another even though surface factors appear similar. Nevertheless, proper adjustment of method to specific problems depends upon a sound understanding of underlying factors and principles.

Part III presents basic concepts, types, styles, procedures, and techniques of method which apply generally to all parts of the physical education program and to varying kinds of activities. Chapter 6 deals with general instructional styles and patterns. Chapter 7 describes basic teaching procedures which relate to each of the three main areas of learning in physical education, i.e., cognitive (knowledges and understandings); affective (attitudes and appreciations); and psychomotor (motor skills). It also includes basic teaching procedures for a variety of instructional problems, including such topics as grouping, safety, discipline, cophysical education and the like. Chapters 8 and 9 discuss procedures for each of the special types of activities commonly used in physical education. These include team and individual sports, apparatus and tumbling, basic movement, combative contests, conditioning activities, group games and relays, posture, rhythm and dance, rope jumping, swimming, and track and field. A general characterization of the value of each is followed by suggestions for teaching.

Chapter 10 explains the use of audio-visual materials in teaching physical education. It gives consideration to their scope and value and discusses their use as a means of teaching motor skills. The chapter also includes criteria for selecting audio-visual materials, a description of basic steps in their use, and a description of and suggested uses for selected audio-visual devices and materials in teaching physical education.

chapter 6

BASIC TYPES OF METHOD

INTRODUCTION

To have his students learn, a teacher must do certain things in certain ways. He must know his subject, have clearly in mind what he wishes students to learn, and be able to lead them in activities which will result in learning. He must understand how the teaching methods he uses affect student learning.

Selection of methods is the heart of the instructional plan or the *teaching strategy*. The teaching strategy (defined as a plan for producing learning giving attention to both reasons for the plan and means of executing it) has three phases: (1) the orientation of the learner to the experience—he determines what response is expected of him; (2) the learner's interaction—he tries to produce the desired response; and (3) feedback to the learner—he learns through various clues if he is making the right response.

The true complexity of this process often defies the imagination. The variables within and among such factors as objectives, the learner's needs and abilities, the learning process itself, the teacher's skills and personality, and the physical and social climate of the learning situation preclude there being any simple formula for selecting teaching methods. Only as the complexity of teaching is clearly understood can the need for maximum skill and ingenuity in selecting teaching methods be fully realized.

The terms method, procedure, and technique are applied rather indiscriminately in referring to what the teacher does when he is interacting with students whom he is teaching. The reader is referred to Chapter 1, The Role of Instructional Methods in Education, for a discussion of the complexity in defining common usages of the term methods. This chapter explains some of the underlying concepts and basic types of method which apply to teaching physical education in general. Later chapters present additional procedures and techniques which apply particularly to special kinds of learning or types of activity.

TEACHER PERSONALITY AND METHOD

The personality of the teacher will be a major determinant of the way he uses a specific method and the success he will have with it. A careful analysis of current research on teaching methods reveals this statement to be well supported. "Very few studies provide data indicating the way in which one method of teaching differs from another. Research workers usually report how the methods *are alleged* to differ, but few studies provide data indicating how the methods actually differ in terms of the recorded behavior of the teachers in the classroom." [1]

Teacher personality does affect how well an individual executes a particular procedure. For example, one teacher may be quite poor at presenting a demonstration of a close-order-precision gymnastic drill, but excellent in producing a completely student-designed demonstration. Some teachers could do both of these extremes; some could do neither but something equally good in between.

Not only does a teacher's personality affect how well he can use one method or another; it also affects his success in working with different types of students. Matching the personalities of teachers and students has obvious effects. Some students feel restricted and frustrated in closely structured or authoritative situations, whereas others find comfort in a restrictive situation and become confused when overpermissiveness is the class pattern. The alert teacher understands his own personality, the demands of the particular teaching situation, and the individual personality of his students and tries to make a mutual adjustment which will result in maximum learning for all concerned. This implies that teacher education recruitment efforts should be directed toward finding young people who are intelligent and well adjusted, who have been exposed to a superior teacher education program in college, and who are devoted

[1] R. M. W. Reavers, *Essentials of Learning,* The Macmillan Company, New York, 1963, p. 4.

to the idea that the strength of the democratic system lies in its educational program. It further implies that a school system, recognizing that different personality types will utilize different teaching modes and methods with equal success, should give primary consideration to finding individuals of superior quality.

CATEGORIZING TYPES OF METHODS

Despite the difficulty in accurately defining broad patterns of teaching methods, there is value in recognizing various ways in which classroom procedures have been described. The various types of methods listed in the remainder of this chapter reflect both traditional and new modes of teaching methods or classroom activity. Use of traditionally stated modes does not imply that the latest knowledge about how the individual learns is overlooked. For example, traditional recitation and response-to-command methods have a negative connotation in some respects to be sure, but the latest research on the importance of drill to promote some kinds of learning supports judicious use of these methods. Perhaps a new word for an old form would actually serve only to obliterate negative stereotypes and would not actually any better describe a useful basic pattern.

As a corollary to the above statement it is further noted that it is somewhat dangerous to equate a priori a certain teaching style or method with degree of desirableness of outcome. For example, use of the problem-solving method will not necessarily guarantee improved or more complex learning outcomes. Use of response-to-command styles will not necessarily limit learnings to mechanistic detail. The effectiveness of style or method can only be equated with the true reality of the situation in terms of objectives, learners' needs, administrative feasibility, and all other factors of the teaching-learning process described in Chapter 1.

In addition, many of the precise descriptions or models of teaching styles and methods are made either to delimit a topic for research purposes or to isolate and describe basic areas for more clarity of presentation. Actually in a typical school classroom teaching situation the dynamics of operation demand an ever-shifting, ever-flexible series of teacher-student interactions. In a typical physical education class period the teacher may employ a number of different teaching styles and patterns. Thus he (or a student leader) might lead the class in warmup exercises using a response-to-command technique. He may next divide the class into groups for diverse activities. One group might work on defense strategies in basketball using problem-solving techniques. Another group may work on layup shots using a film loop for a model. Another may practice free throws. Before working with each of these groups individually, the teacher (or student leader) may first aid a group of less well-coordinated students with elements of passing and catching. In his interpersonal relations with students he might give one a direct order, challenge another with a provocative question, and reinforce one with praise but another with direct admonitions to try again and keep his attention on the task at hand.

When one has a simple objective and a quite homogeneous group of learners, it is relatively easy to design a workable, accurate, and efficient model of the teaching strategy. The reality of the issue is that in the typical classroom or gymnasium period the teacher is faced with a large number of students with quite varying abilities and needs, and a complex set of learning objectives. For this reason it is important that the teacher be aware that flexibility of style and pattern of method is more important than mastering the technique of one particular approach.

It should be noted that some of the patterns described below are not parallel in scope. Headings cover the terms likely to be encountered. There is some overlapping. Many of the so-called methods are really generalized approaches, making use of a wide variety of subtechniques. Thus the socialized class method would be likely to utilize at some stages all the methods suggested in this section. On the other hand, the lecture method may be complete within itself, although it too can be combined with other techniques. The absence of a similarity in scope is due to a lack of consistency of terminology. The terms are used in this chapter according to common usage.

RECITATION AND RESPONSE-TO-COMMAND METHODS

The recitation method as a classroom technique and the response-to-command method as an activity or gymnasium method have much in common. Both represent a traditional approach with emphasis placed on external discipline and a narrow scope of outcomes. In the classroom, formal recitations consisted of teacher-dominated procedures in which students studied, read, or carried out other learning assignments and in turn recited or answered questions posed by the teacher. In the gymnasium the response-to-command method found the teacher giving precise directions, often preceding, following, or concurrently with demonstrations, with all students responding to the directions in like form.

Both these methods traditionally gave little attention to individualization. They emphasized subject matter rather than its significance to students and provided little or no opportunity for socialization during the process.

When freed from their narrow and traditional concept, both methods have use in modern teaching. The recitation method may serve as a good means for review of many learnings. For example, a group may have been assigned to study a section of the rules for a game. An excellent way to check on progress and to reinforce individual learning is a brief recitation period skillfully led by a teacher adept at posing pointed and apt questions.

The effectiveness of the recitation method often depends upon the teacher's skill as a questioner. The questions should be prepared in advance with emphasis placed on asking questions which will stimulate answers that reveal an understanding of the information learned. Rote answers should be discouraged, except for material where exact wording is pertinent. Questions should be posed so that the purpose will be clear; tricky questions should be avoided, and opportunities to respond should be well distributed among the class members.

The response-to-command method finds use in situations where drill or unison practice has value. Some forms of gymnastics are based entirely on this method. An informal approach using this method is helpful in teaching all types of dance. A beginning square dance group, for example, may walk through the steps of a new dance, proceeding to each new step in response to directions. Minimizing the rigid unison aspect and formal spacing and lines will help to focus attention on the purpose of the drill or activity rather than on the externals of the class procedure.

PROGRAMMED-INSTRUCTION METHOD

The programmed-instruction method which includes the use of many kinds of autoinstructional devices is a product of our scientific age. Research on reinforcement and conditioning learning theories (see page 29) and on educational teaching-learning processes, combined with technological advances, have produced a highly sophisticated and valuable teaching method.

Programmed-learning techniques follow a number of basic principles. After careful analysis behavioral objectives are established and content is selected. Material to be learned is presented in small, discrete steps, each one depending upon the preceding for its full comprehension and mastery. The learner must make his own response to the material to be learned. Depending upon the type of device, his overt means of making the proper responses may be pushing a button, pulling a lever, using a stylus to punch a hole or make electrical contact, or writing an answer in an appropriate space.

Immediate feedback is a characteristic of this method. Success is reinforced by a knowledge of results and the reward of being able to proceed to the next step. When a student makes a mistake he is required to repeat the step in one of several ways, depending upon the machine used. In some instances feedback is delayed to the end of a larger sequence; in others it is simultaneous with his mistake. He either repeats the previous pattern or is directed to a branch. The branching technique is used to send the student down a separate track to help him gain sufficient supplemental knowledge to proceed and also to enable an advanced student to progress at his own speed, skipping intermediate material.

Programmed instruction makes use of many different types of autoinstructional devices which can be described in two categories: teaching machines and programmed textbooks. Machines can range from highly complex computer-type devices containing thousands of response-producing frames and entailing complicated systems of reacting to the learners' responses, to simple sets of cards in envelopes or single mimeographed sheets. Other machines use tapes, films, or slides, or a combination of these. Programmed textbooks are constructed on the same principles as machines. Both isolate discrete learnings. Some texts present material in a logical order and put the desired response on the next page for easy reference; others, such as the intrinsic textbook, require the student to follow a different page sequence depending upon the nature of his response.

Programmed learning gives promise of being valuable in several different ways. It can free the teacher from tedious tutorial tasks, giving him more time to spend with learning problems which cannot be reduced to programmed learning. It can allow for individual differences by permitting the student to proceed with a learning sequence at his own rate. Use of more sophisticated machines which include sufficient branching variables can enable students to pursue learnings of varying difficulty. Programmed learning requires careful attention to delineating and stating objectives as behaviors. This requisite has had a salutary effect in promoting this desirable practice generally in education. The clarity of objectives in programmed instruction and the sequential nature of the learning plan enables both the student and the teacher to better understand the learner's progress. This knowledge can give valuable direction to the student in his own self-improvement efforts and to the teacher in guiding or motivating him.

Criticism of programmed learning does exist. Its effectiveness as a learning technique has been challenged, and its misuse in the sense that learnings adaptable to programming may be given priority over more valuable but more difficult to teach objectives has caused professional concern. Fortunately programmed instruction is now sufficiently established and understood so that its proponents tend not to overzealously proclaim it as a panacea for all our educational ills, nor do its opponents fear it as a threat to reduce education to a system capable of producing only well-trained robots. Programmed instruction has emerged as another important methods and materials dimension for the modern educator. It does give great promise provided it, like any other method or tool, is used in the proper way to achieve desirable goals.

Programmed instructional materials for physical education are still meager. Actually many kinds of verbal or cognitive learnings in physical education would readily lend themselves to programming. Of particular value, to illustrate many possibilities, would be programmed textbooks or materials for learning the official rules of sports and the field positions of set plays in team sports.

As a whole, materials and experimentation in programmed instruction have been confined to cognitive learnings. A major exception to this is in the realm of teaching languages (to the extent that vocal response is psychomotor). Reasons for the lack of major attention to programming the types of psychomotor learnings with which physical education is concerned lie perhaps in the realm of practicality rather than in the inability to apply principles of programming to teaching motor skills or in a priori objections to exploring this means of instruction.

Chapter 10, Use of Audio-Visual Materials, describes some teaching devices which produce sequential frame pictures such as the film loop, movies, instant replay video tape, and the Polaroid sequential frame camera and which could provide the technical basis for programming motor skill learnings. For example, the student could study a pictorial model presented on one of these forms, practice, then have a duplicate format picture taken of his performance to compare his results with that of the standard model. Typical uses of these devices do not meet the conditions of true programming. If the student is evaluated by another student or a teacher after study of a pictured model and practice, the autoinstructional criterion of what constitutes a programmed instructional device would not be met. Use of a pictorial model followed by teacher evaluation is a sound teaching technique, but it is not programmed instruction. Programmed-instruction techniques are designed for self-teaching, aimed toward the student learning with little or no outside help. The system also requires the inclusion of accurate ways of self-evaluation. Obviously, programmed instruction would have some value for teaching psychomotor skills. How much value rests upon the development of practical instruments (time and cost) and upon research to determine what kinds of psychomotor learnings could be effectively taught by this method.

LECTURE METHOD

The lecture method is perhaps the oldest formal teaching method. Its original value lay in the fact that textbooks and other study materials were unavailable, so knowledge was passed on from the master teacher, or expert, by word of mouth. Obviously the existence of written materials and other communication media does not preclude the value of the lecture. It serves a basic purpose in organizing large fields of material, segregating a particular body of information of immediate pertinence to the present group, presenting little-available or new information, and synthesizing information from a wide variety of sources. The lecture method has been found to be most valuable with mature and abler students and those individuals with a high degree of auditory perception.

The lecture method as discussed here presupposes a planned presentation covering a specific topic. It implies a more comprehensive talk than one involved in merely giving directions and short explanations. The discussion in Chaper 7 on explanation procedures for teaching motor skills (pages 152–153) contains suggestions pertinent to shorter talks. A review of that section will point up problems relative to factors of attention, voice level, clarity, use of rest periods, and vocabulary level, also applicable to the lecture method.

When time is not too restricted for physical education, regular classroom periods are desirable. Students will accept this phase of physical education as an important part of the program. It would be impractical to suggest that in schools where but two periods a week are allowed for physical education, many periods should be used in this manner. However, most programs have days at the beginning and end of the school semester and shortened periods throughout the semester that could be used to advantage for carefully planned classroom activities.

The lecture may be used in presenting any type of physical education information. When it is used, attention should be given to the fact that a group of students dressed for activity are not likely to be interested in a protracted lecture. If learning goals indicate an extended lecture, students should be seated in comfort, where they can hear clearly. When possible, a classroom should be procured for the period; if this is not feasible, chairs or other seating arrangements should be provided before the beginning of the period. A class straggling into the gymnasium, with individuals playing with available equipment or scattered about the floor, will take several minutes to call together and assemble for proper attention.

Needless to say, all lectures should be carefully prepared. The purpose should be clear to students and the material to be covered outlined for them. All possible devices to hold interest, such as charts, diagrams, and materials, should be used. Too often physical education teachers assume the attitude, "The students would rather be playing; the lecture period is a necessary evil, so let's get it over with!" A lecture on any topic can be stimulating, interesting, and motivating to students if it is properly prepared.

The lecture method often proves more beneficial when used in conjunction with other methods. Use of films, in addition to other visual materials, is of considerable advantage. Other effective combinations include question and answer periods and panel or group discussions.

A teacher using the lecture method must recognize its limitations: (1) The method constitutes a teacher-centered activity and may encourage lack of participation on the part of students; (2) many students lack the ability to learn effectively by the lecture method; (3) the seeming efficiency of the method may lead teachers to neglect trial of more effective methods; and (4) the attention span of the more immature secondary school students may limit its value when used for a full period. Most of these objections can be circumvented by using the method judiciously.

PROJECT METHOD

The project method is generally thought of in connection with classroom activities particularly in those subject matter areas where learning centers around problem areas. There is no clear-cut definition of the project method. Its original aim was to enable students to put into practice what they learned in class. It generally was considered outside work, although numerous modifications have appeared in educational practice. Its chief feature is that subject matter learnings are held secondary to a real-life purpose.

Physical education has made less use of such methods chiefly because the activities themselves, particularly the natural activities including games and sports, are inherently interesting to students as ends. Certain advantages may be found in placing physical education activities in a broader setting. Preparing for a county field day or play day, preparing to assist with the noon-hour or community recreation program, preparing for leadership in any phase of the school program, composing dances for use in a school play or festival, preparing for a swimming or gymnastics demonstration—all serve as motivation and widen the social significance of the activity. Physical education does make use of these devices. Extended use, which would tend to encourage the learning of physical activities for broader social purposes, would be desirable.

The project method may also be of special use in assisting students to learn related information. When time is brief in the regularly scheduled program, outside projects, such as compiling scrapbooks or notebooks on rules, form, and sportsmanship, studying recreational opportunities in the community, and observing sports events, represent invaluable aids to teaching.

As originally conceived, the project method was an individualized technique, with each student pursuing his project on his own. It does serve as one of the better techniques for individualizing instruction. It is equally effective when used for group projects, but the size of the group depends upon the nature of the project.

DIRECTED-STUDY METHOD

Closely akin to the problem just discussed is the assigning of outside work to students. Traditionally, physical education has made minimum use of this device primarily because emphasis has been placed upon the motor-skill aspects of physical education. Other deterrents included the lack of instructional materials for students and the lack of time to give and score tests.

Outside study in connection with physical education helps students learn activities and develop interest in them. If students are to reach acceptable standards in knowledge and understanding, it is necessary that a certain amount of study accompany actual participation; through outside assignments, valuable class time can be saved for activity. Fortunately, a current development in education recognizes the need for textbooks in physical education, and these are becoming more numerous. School libraries are showing an increasing interest in books on activity and on other physical education subjects. Many of the books in these categories written for the general public are suitable for use by high school students. The number of paperback books now available on sports, sports figures, and physical fitness topics provide an excellent means of encouraging students to do outside reading in connection with the physical education program.

The effectiveness of outside assignments depends upon several factors. When an assignment is given, it should be clear to all. Exact directions should be given, and there should be an opportunity for the students to ask clarifying questions. Assignments should be of reasonable length. Allowances should be made for different types of learnings: studying a series of rules may take careful memory work; reading material on an activity may increase one's interest in that activity. Further, assignments should be pertinent to the course and closely related to the total activity.

When possible, assignments should be prepared in mimeographed form. Very often students do not come to the gymnasium with a pencil and paper in hand. In fact, it is hazardous to have loose papers and pencils lying around during activity periods. When it is necessary to have students write down an assignment, provisions should be made to have pencils and paper distributed at the proper point. Another plan suggests placing assignments on a blackboard or bulletin board. Students can copy them down before or after class.

Provisions should be made to check on assignments by such means as brief question periods, take-home or class quizzes, or written reports.

The institution of assignments as a regular part of physical education classwork will do much to increase the status of physical education as a credited school subject.

DIRECTED-PRACTICE METHOD

Outside assignments for practice of motor skills and for development of condition are desirable. Concepts of the skill to be learned and of needed practice procedures may be presented in class, and skills may be developed through out-of-class practice. It is apparent that outside practice is essential to achieving desirable goals in almost any activity from the standpoints of conditioning and skill improvement. Few physical education programs offer sufficient in-class participation for a student to fully develop his potential.

For some activities outside practice is necessary if the activity is to be taught at all. For example, some schools teach golf in indoor cages if proper facilities are lacking; similarly, tennis sometimes is taught indoors when there is no sufficient opportunity to play on regular courts. On weekends or afternoons, students play on available courses or courts without school supervision and turn in their score cards or report results to the high school instructor. Girls in conditioning and grooming classes are sometimes requested to walk a minimum of four miles a day or are given a set of prescribed exercises to perform at home. Football players and candidates for all varsity teams frequently are requested or advised to get into condition prior to the opening of the regular practice season. An exercise program for out-of-class, out-of-regular-practice-session use, designed to produce desirable condition, may be suggested or prescribed.

Obviously, the question arises as to the faithfulness of students in actually carrying out these directed-practice procedures. The problem here, however, proves little different from that for any school subject. Success depends upon motivation and general rapport.

PROBLEM-SOLVING METHOD

Psychological research on problem solving and discovery as learning theories has given rise to attempts to translate the principles of these theories directly to teaching theories. These theories consider the learner in terms of goal-seeking behavior. He formulates hypotheses about the goal he is seeking and how he can best achieve the goal. Through feedback during the learning experience, he evaluates his progress toward his goal and may reformulate either his working plans or the goal itself. From a teaching-learning standpoint, for a true problem situation to exist one of these conditions is necessary: (1) the goal is clear to the learner, but the means of attaining it are not; or (2) the goal is vaguely defined and therefore both the goal and the relevant means of achieving the goal are not immediately clear to the learner.

Thus, the problem-solving method requires that, in the process of a learning experience, the student become aware of and accept a goal which is meaningful to him and explore means of achieving that goal. It also implies that the problem can be *presented* to the learner or *discovered* by him. Presenting a problem simply means that the teacher outlines a problem, which may or may not be known, to the student who must understand and accept the value of the problem. On the other hand, the teacher may introduce a broad issue and let the learner discover for himself what the problem really is. Sometimes neither the teacher nor the student knows what the real problem is and they seek to discover its nature together; at other times the student alone tries to define the nature of the problem. The solution, too, follows these dimensions. The teacher may know the solution to a problem but let the learner discover it for himself; or the solution to a problem may yet be unknown.

Klausmeier and Goodwin [2] propose the following model for developing problem-solving abilities:

Generalization	*Principle*
1. Productive thinking originates with dissatisfaction about a problem.	1. Activate solvable problems.
2. Preparation for problem solving requires the recognition and focusing upon the problem.	2. Assist students in stating and delimiting problems.
3. Background information and methods are necessary in order to avoid random trial, error, and subsequent failure.	3. Assist students in finding information.
4. Problem solving requires the application, analysis, and synthesis of information.	4. Help students process information.
5. The formulation of hypotheses and their subsequent conditional rejection or acceptance is essential.	5. Encourage the stating and testing of hypotheses.
6. Continuous improvement in problem solving is engendered through independently discovered methods and solutions.	6. Encourage independent discovery and evaluation.

The problem-solving method of teaching has gained increasing attention because it is compatible with the true goals of education. As a nation

[2] Herbert J. Klausmeier and William Goodwin, *Learning and Human Abilities*, 2d ed., Harper & Row, Publishers, Incorporated, New York, 1966, p. 278.

we need creative and rational individuals who are able to identify and solve the complex problems of our social order. Rote learning alone of existing knowledge will not push through to new frontiers in science, philosophy, aesthetics, and social organization.

Three basic claims are made for the value of the problem-solving method of teaching. (1) Although research evidence is not definitive, there is some justification to believe that the way in which a student learns a generalization may affect the way in which he uses it. More transfer, therefore, is likely to occur when the student learns by the discovery method rather than being told the rules, principles, or facts by the teacher. (2) There appears to be enthusiasm by the student for the kind of work included in this method, resulting in greater effort and thus more learning on his part. (3) It is also held that by discovering something for himself or solving a problem, the student learns a "set" to discover or solve problems which is more likely to apply to other life situations.

Arguments commonly found against the problem-solving method are likely to deal not with what it claims to do, but rather in limitations of its use in certain school settings. The usual criticisms which accompany the use of any type of complex, multiple-goal, student-centered method in an educational program have their elements of truth. Situations can be described in which the problem-solving method is cumbersome, wasteful of student and teacher time, expensive, helpful for some students but not for others, lacking in administrative feasibility, and effective for some kinds of learnings and not for others. In judging the value of a method, one should recognize both its practical and theoretical strengths and limitations. As long as the teacher recognizes that *there is no one best method* it is necessary in a text of this kind only to describe a method, not to condemn it just because it could be misused.

The use of the problem-solving method in physical education teaching no doubt has many valuable applications. Applying problem-solving techniques to cognitive and affective learnings in physical education involves the same issues as the method does in other areas of education. Applying it to psychomotor learnings, the teaching of motor skills, gives rise to the consideration of some additional problems. The eternal aim of education, that of understanding rather than merely imitating or parroting, is equally important in physical education. From finding a simple way to jump a stream or lift a box with the correct elemental basic movement to solving a complex team maneuver in football or creating an artistically choreographed dance, the problem-solving method has important learning-producing potential. Courses in modern dance and in basic movement which endeavor to help the student discover the true kinesthetic resources of his body are two areas of physical education that have made particularly effective use of the problem-solving method. This method, further, has a great potential for teaching psychomotor skills since it is obvious that because of variation in body builds each individual will perform aesthetically or efficiently in slightly different ways.

Use of the problem-solving method has certain limitations in teaching specific motor skills. Because of the way in which motor skills are learned, immediate feedback is especially important. Continued practice of a skill without redirection at the crucial point may simply result in the wrong patterns being learned. The problem-solving method suggests that the teacher should not demonstrate. If he does, the student has learned by imitation rather than by discovery or problem solving. This means that the teacher must use only verbal clues in setting the goal or helping the student "process information," and many motor skills cannot really be explained verbally. Controversy exists in some quarters over any use of this method in teaching motor skills, but like any other method its application is specific to time, place, the individual learner, and the skill to be learned. It is possible that its most effective use will be found in teaching those physical education psychomotor activities that involve a maximum of perceptual components, and in an educational climate where administrative feasibility for this method is optimum. (See pages 213–214 for a discussion of the application of the problem-solving method to teaching basic movement.)

GROUP METHODS

In recent years a new social science has emerged. This science deals with the dynamics of group action. It has long been recognized that to realize the potential of a democratic social form of government, skill must be developed in the process of group action. Problems and issues must be solved over the conference table, in groups of various sizes and kinds, and by peaceful cooperative means. *Group dynamics,* as now used, refers to the forces or factors within a group which cause members of the group to behave the way they do. It does not refer to some special set of methods or procedures. A goal, of course, of those concerned with the study of group dynamics is to develop ways and means of implementing the effectiveness of group behavior. They are concerned with such problems as these: what motivates individual members of a group, how do they interact with each other, what are the most effective means of communication, what factors give status within a group, how do leaders emerge? On the basis of their findings, new modes of group action inevitably emerge.

Group dynamics, then, is simply the study of what happens within a group. It should not be confused with a series of techniques which may be used for more effective group action. Group dynamics is in operation whenever two or more people come together for any reason whatsoever. Educators and social scientists have now begun to apply scientific study procedures to understand better the forces at work in any group situation.

Since modern education is fundamentally a group activity, many of the findings of this new science are directly applicable to the school program. Chapter 15, Method and Supervision, includes further discussion of some of the techniques useful in working with groups.

Good teaching requires an understanding of the group behavior of students. While the area of group dynamics offers no panacea to solve all teaching problems, it can assist one to work with groups more effectively through better insight into group processes. A review of the area actually reveals that teachers have long been doing many things consistent with recent, more scientifically verified recommendations. A good example of this is that group discussion has long been a popular method in more progressive educational programs. The science of group dynamics has simply aided in the development of new and sounder techniques for carrying on this fundamental democratic skill.

The following types generally represent group methods.

SOCIALIZED CLASS METHOD

The chief characteristic of the socialized class method is that the work of the class is undertaken as a group project. All participate in planning instruction and deciding upon what methods and activities to use and what project to pursue. All contribute to carrying out the learning tasks and evaluating outcomes. The teacher avoids domination of the class and serves as leader and guide. This development in instructional methods came as the outgrowth of changing concepts of the function of schools—when it was recognized that schools must be concerned with all aspects of preparation for citizenship and that limitation to a few narrow intellectual learnings was inadequate. It became apparent that to develop social competencies of many kinds greater attention to providing truly social opportunities for learning was requisite, that the emphasis must be placed on organizing learning in social settings comparable to life itself.

In truth, it is difficult, because of the modern crowding of the schools, teacher load, and other administrative barriers, to carry the principle of the socialized class method to its ultimate goal. In the teaching of physical education, the chief weakness is in finding time for pupil participation in planning. Despite the limitations, however, the very nature of physical education, with its potential appeal to students, its basic group structure, and its reality to the life of students makes it possible to have the spirit of the socialized class method dominate physical education teaching.

Success of the socialized class method depends upon the development of the students' willingness to cooperate and work together, the development of their skills of both leadership and followership, and the ability of teachers to assume the role of democratic leader and guide. Merely introducing this method will not result in these qualities; but rather the success of the method depends upon their development. This suggests that the initiation of socialized procedures must of necessity be a gradual one. In a highly formalized school program where students are likely to lack such skills, the intramural program proves an excellent place to begin. Committees to plan the program, arrange tournaments, set policies of participation, and officiate provide ideal laboratory experience to develop essential skills. This method can be gradually applied to the class program, particularly in those areas to which it lends itself, such as team sports and other activities in which group participation is basic. Obviously the socialized method represents an approach rather than a series of procedures and techniques and would make use of many types of method such as student-teacher planning, use of student leaders, and other procedures discussed elsewhere in this volume.

THE TEACHER-STUDENT PLANNING METHOD AND THE EXPERIENCE-UNIT METHOD

The teacher-student planning method is inherent in the previously discussed socialized class method, but it is noted here since it often appears as a separate listing as one of the basic methods of instruction in the category of democratic group methods. This form may be used in conjunction with any of the other instructional methods, its chief characteristic being student participation in instructional planning. Chapter 11, Planning Instruction, discusses this topic. The basis for mentioning it as an instructional method rests on the recognition that participation of the student in planning represents one of the best ways to orient him to learning goals, to develop an interest in him requisite to learning, and to motivate him to participate actively in the selected activities. In addition, by participating in the process of planning, he is learning the fundamental techniques of the group process as well as the many incidental learnings associated with making choices of specific learning activities.

The experience-unit method uses teacher-student planning as its central technique. The experience unit describes a classroom pattern in which the desired learnings are organized around a meaningful activity for students. The experience unit consists of what the students actually do in the course of arriving at a given goal. Since it must evolve through teacher-student planning and requires active participation of the students in both the planning and the execution of plans, any plans made by the teacher are purely preliminary. The anecdotal record of the completed plan constitutes the experience unit. Thus, from the teacher's point of view, an experience unit is an operational plan centered on process objectives rather than on subject matter objectives. The teacher is as interested in the ways in which the students select and pursue learning activities as he is in the subject matter they learn. Teacher-student planning as a method is illustrated in pure form in the experience-unit plan of organizing instruction.

GROUP-DISCUSSION METHOD

To acquire all the skills, knowledges, understandings, attitudes, and appreciations physical education aims for, extended use may be made of the group-discussion technique. In any democratically organized physical education program many problem-solving situations will occur. When a group has a mutual problem to solve, they should understand the techniques which will lead them to a satisfactory solution.

Group discussion is an educational technique primarily designed for use in situations where a problem needs solution. The problem may be either of a practical nature or one that involves the definition of values. The discussion method should not be confused with a question-and-answer-type classroom procedure where review or seeking of information is the basic goal.

There are many kinds of situations which arise in a typical physical education program where the group-discussion method may be employed to good advantage. Typical examples include planning for any part of the program, such as selecting activities for the class or extra program, setting program goals, setting policies for class management, selecting themes for demonstrations of swimming and dance or for other programs, planning award systems, defining the role of good sportsmanship in modern life, developing ways to improve student behavior at athletic contests, improving mutual understanding of the boys' and girls' physical education programs, devising means of correlating physical education with other program aspects, and conducting the business and work of all clubs, programs, and the like.

Group discussions are carried on in the regular class period, in extraclass activities, and in the cocurricular activities such as school assemblies, community programs, and parent-teacher association meetings.

The group-discussion method has both individual and group value. It aids the individual to learn to express himself in front of others, be tolerant to the opinions of others, and improve his ability to think critically about the issues of a problem. From the group standpoint, it develops commonness of purpose and assists in crystallizing group goals and means to achieve them.

The effectiveness of the group-discussion method depends upon the leader's facility with a variety of techniques. In introducing this method in physical education programs where students have had little practice with the method, the teacher should serve as leader. As they develop skills both in leadership and in participation, they may gradually take over the leadership roles.

Examples of the kinds of techniques a leader may use in promoting better group discussion follow: The basic principle to govern his approach is that the discussion belongs to the group, and his role is to glean ideas and comments from the group which will contribute to solution of the common problem. The leader must avoid domination of the discussion. His leadership role does not give him license to impose his solution to the problem on the group. His chief jobs are to stimulate contributions from the group and to keep the discussion on the point. Several ways are suggested for his doing this. He may write the topic on the board and spend a brief time clarifying the issues and seeking group consensus on the delineation of the problem. If the discussion wanders, he may refer back to the initial topic and limitations before them on the board. All questions he poses to stimulate discussion should be phrased so they cannot be answered by yes or no. When a question is asked by a member of the group, he should refer the question back to the group rather than answer it himself. He should summarize frequently, giving credit to the group for any progress and to individuals who contributed major ideas. No contribution should be belittled; its merits rather than its weaknesses should be commented upon.

When students are skillful enough to assume leadership of discussion sessions, the teacher's responsibilities change but do not lessen. He continually evaluates group progress to ascertain that straight thinking dominates the process. He sees that necessary information is at hand or available and serves as a resource person when necessary. He continues to work with the group or individuals within the group to develop their skills in the discussion method. Sometimes this consists of a brief evaluation period when he discusses the processes with the group and points out strengths and weaknesses. Occasionally he may wish private discussion with individuals or small groups who through poor attitude or lack of skill impede group progress. He keeps primarily in mind that the discussion period is a learning period and that the time should be used wisely in terms of the total educational job.

DRAMATIC METHOD

With the dramatic method, subject matter is dramatized in various ways. Formal and informal plays, skits, tableaux, role playing, sociodramas, and other dramatic forms are utilized to emotionalize and visualize materials.

The dramatic method finds use in physical education teaching, particularly in interpreting the purpose and values of the program to the public, developing desirable attitudes toward certain phases of the program, indicating the social and health values of physical education, and motivating interest. Dramatic presentations may take place on radio or television programs, at PTA meetings, at school assemblies, as a part of classwork, at special programs, and the like.

Probably the best use of the dramatic method for physical education is in correlation with other subjects, or as special student projects, or as an extraclass club activity. For example, students in a health or English course may prepare a skit or play on safety in recreational sports; a group from a physical education class may take as an outside assignment the preparation of a skit on how to watch a football game for presentation at a school assembly; the aquatics club may develop a noon-hour tableau to recruit participants for a lifesaving course.

The dramatic method proves especially adaptable to group procedures, since most such projects involve several performers.

DEMONSTRATION METHOD

The demonstration method directs the organization of classes toward preparation for a public performance of some kind. The demonstration of physical education activities presents one of the oldest practices in physical education. The goal of many who engage in physical activities is a public performance, either in competition, i.e., gymnastic, swimming, or track and field meets, or athletic contests, or in a demonstration such as a dance program or gymnastics. Demonstration refers more precisely to noncompetitive-type public performances with emphasis placed on skill and form. The demonstration method, as used here, describes the organization of the teaching of physical education classes or club programs solely around learnings which will become a public demonstration when concluded.

Demonstrations are of value, if properly directed, to both performer and viewer. Several disadvantages, however, mark the demonstration method as a technique for class use. (1) It tends to restrict the scope of learnings. All subject matter selected must be circumscribed by the conditions of the demonstration. For example, a given dance may be selected only on the merit that its floor pattern is restricted enough to be performed in the stage space available for the demonstration. (2) It tends to utilize existing talent rather than develop new skills. Time is usually a factor, and in order to master the mechanics and organizational detail of putting on a show, students who are already star performers generally are picked for leading roles, and others just fill in by taking less skilled roles. They often merely do what they had previously learned, and time is spent on putting the show together. (3) A not uncommon disadvantage is that the teacher spends a disproportionate amount of his time with the skillful students, polishing their performances and neglecting those who may be so lacking in skill they cannot perform at all or who have minor unskilled jobs, such as flag-bearer or prop boy.

Demonstrations do have value in the physical education program. They stimulate the learner and are a natural fulfillment of skill achievement in the noncompetitive sports activities. Also, they serve as an excellent means of publicizing the physical education program. When used as a basis for class method, however, care should be exercised to circumvent the stated disadvantages. Demonstrations of classwork should be final presentations of the outcomes of properly selected curricular experiences. All students in the class should have a part to play. For polished demonstrations, the necessary practice should be put on a club or extraclass basis. When an expert group of students is drawn from a regular class to perform a dance for an assembly program or PTA meeting, additional practice should be provided in extraclass time. The teacher should avoid devoting a major portion of his time and facility use to the special group, to the neglect of the remainder of the class or the progress of the group as a whole.

When the physical education teacher receives a request to put on an all-school demonstration, such as a Flag Day parade and mass flag drill, he should strive for effectiveness through simplicity. The least possible number of physical education periods should be devoted to learning formations which will have limited enduring values to students. Cues and devices should be used so even the inept student may perform accurately with a minimum of practice. No one should be excluded. The teacher should provide such cues and devices as marked lines on the field rather than spend an excessive amount of time practicing to keep straight lines. Another practical device suggests use of volunteer leaders who will assemble for extraclass practice and serve as guides for the remainder of the group. The basic principle in regard to practice for demonstrations is to give primary consideration to the learning value and the continued growth of students. This must be held primary to spectator pleasure.

The demonstration method finds its best use in the club program. An aquatic club, for example, may well build its entire program around preparation for a water carnival. The same precautions should be followed, however, so as not to neglect valuable learnings outside the skills involved in the water carnival and to ascertain that individual needs are served.

The demonstration method serves as an excellent group method. Traditionally, it represented a teacher-dominated activity, particularly those demonstrations involving mass gymnastics. The current use of demonstrations based upon group work and utilizing student responsibility in planning and organizing demonstrations makes this type of method a potentially valuable one.

TEAM TEACHING

Team teaching is a method of organizing and planning a learning experience which involves several teachers working together to plan and carry out a course of study for a group of students. Team planning might be a more accurate term because usually one teacher at a time does the teaching to the group although on occasion several may be working simultaneously, each with a smaller section of the total group. The actual methods each teacher uses will vary greatly, but the system does promote the development of competency in large group instructional techniques. The practice of team teaching arose in the elementary school as a means of overcoming some of the weaknesses of the self-contained classroom. The plan is based on the assumption that it is unrealistic to expect that even an excellent teacher will be totally effective in working with all types of students and with many different subject matter learnings. The plan recognizes that a teacher has both strengths and weaknesses; by combining staff efforts the teacher is able to do what he can do best. It also aims to cut out duplication among subject matter areas within a discipline and to make the interrelationships between disciplines more meaningful to students.

Although the team-teaching concept originated in the elementary school it has spread to the secondary school, but to a much lesser degree. Team teaching in secondary schools can either maintain subject matter lines or integrate separate courses. An example of integration is the combining of formerly separate courses in music, art, literature, history, and dance into a course entitled Humanities, Integrated Arts, or some other title emphasizing aesthetic objectives or any common goals. Most such courses are on the experimental level since it is difficult to break through traditional credit requirements patterns.

The more common way to use team teaching in the secondary school is to combine students of like abilities into a large group and assign them to a team of teachers from three or more different subject matter areas, e.g., English, science, and social studies. The time is blocked so that sometimes the students meet in their large group and at other times in smaller groups. For example, the whole group can take a test in one period thus saving the teacher spending the usual three periods giving the same test three times. Many other activities such as showing films, giving special lectures, or assigning study periods are as effective in a large group as they are in a small group. This leaves the teacher free to work with individuals and small groups and to spend more time in planning.

It is difficult to make a direct comparison of the essence of team teaching to physical education primarily because physical education has long made use of the basic concepts of this technique. A football coaching staff, with its line coach, backfield coach, and as many other specialists as school size will allow, who work together in planning practice procedures and game strategies and each of whom takes the teaching responsibility for a special area is an accurate picture of the way in which a team-teaching unit works in subject matter fields. Another example, frequently found in large schools, is having all classes which meet in a period gather in the gymnasium for warmup exercises for the first part of the period and then split into separate groups for a variety of activities under specialists.

On the other hand, one cannot find too many examples in secondary school core programs which include physical education with other subject matter areas using a team-teaching approach. Dance personnel have been included in experimental humanities courses, but most examples of team teaching in physical education are confined to efforts within its own field.

SUMMARY

To have his students learn, a teacher must do certain things in certain ways. He must know his subject, have clearly in mind what he wishes his students to learn, and be able to lead them in activity which will result in learning. He must understand how the teaching methods he uses affect student learning.

Teaching methods may be defined as that phase of the work of the teacher concerned with organizing and conducting learning activities. Selection of methods is the heart of the instructional plan or the teaching strategy.

An analysis of research reveals that there is no best method. Validity of a method is specific to time, place, the nature of the learning, the teacher, and the learner. The personality of the teacher is a major determinant in the kinds of methods he can use most effectively. Similarly students react differently to both the type of methods used and the teacher's personality.

While it is not possible to neatly categorize types of methods, an understanding of how some of the general patterns of instruction have been described should be helpful to the teacher. Many of the traditional modes are still useful provided they keep within the modern aims of education.

The recitation method as a classroom technique and the response-to-command method as an activity or gymnasium method both characterize a traditional approach with emphasis placed on external discipline and a narrow scope of outcome. The preferred way to use these methods requires minimizing the rigid unison aspects and maintaining formal spacings and lines. It also suggests their use only after due attention has been given to problems of individualization.

The programmed-instruction method is designed for autoinstruction with little or no outside help. It makes use of either teaching machines or programmed textbooks. While principles of programming could be applied to teaching psychomotor learnings, most of the presently available materials and research efforts have been directed toward cognitive learnings.

The lecture method serves a basic purpose in organizing large fields of knowledge, segregating a particular body of information of immediate pertinence to the present group, presenting little-available or new information, and synthesizing information from a wide variety of sources.

The original aim of the project method was to enable students to put into practice what they learned in class. Its chief feature is that subject matter learnings are held secondary to real-life purpose.

The directed-study method relates to the assignment of outside work to students. Outside study in connection with physical education helps pupils learn activities and develop an interest in them.

The directed-practice method proposes outside assignments for practice of motor skills and for development of physical condition. Students generally need more practice to master motor skills than can be provided during scheduled class periods.

The problem-solving method evolved out of attempts to apply problem-solving and discovery learning theories directly to classroom teaching. A problem is either presented by the teacher or discovered by the student himself; the student then attempts to solve the problem on his own initiative. The teacher gives support and assistance but no direct help in finding the solution. The concept of this method is consonant with the goals of education. Its use in teaching psychomotor skills has potential, but much remains to be learned about the most effective and administratively feasible way to use this technique in the physical education program.

Modern educational practice is based primarily on group activity. Good teaching requires an understanding of the group behavior of students. Many of the findings of the science of group dynamics are directly applicable to school programs.

Undertaking classwork as a group project is the chief characteristic of the socialized class method. Success of the socialized class method depends upon the development of students' willingness to work together, the development of their skills of both leadership and followership, and the ability of teachers to assume the role of democratic leader and guide.

Teacher-student planning is essential to all socialized and other types of group methods. Since students also learn through the process of planning, teacher-student planning can be considered a type of method. The experience-unit method is an example of a plan in which the central purpose of the learning experience is the way in which students plan and carry out the activities rather than the subject matter learned itself.

The group-discussion method proves useful for dealing with all problem-solving situations which arise in connection with physical education programs. A student-centered program requires extensive use of this method.

With the dramatic method subject matter is dramatized through informal plays, skits, tableaux, sociodramas, role playing, and other dramatic forms which emotionalize and visualize materials.

The demonstration method directs the organization of class or group work toward the preparation for a public performance of some kind.

The team-teaching method is actually more concerned with a plan for organizing learning than with methods per se. The chief purpose of this plan is to pool the abilities and time of a group of teachers so better teaching will result. The concept, while considered somewhat new in academic fields, has long been a practice in physical education.

Questions and problems for discussion

1. Describe a likely purpose, and prepare an outline for a lecture which would be suitable to the occasion. Include a description of all devices you would use to create and maintain listener interest.

2. What type or types of method described in this chapter are most commonly used in coaching a varsity team? Do you consider these the best methods?

3. Discuss the possible effects of teacher personality on choice of and success with methods.

4. Describe a number of circumstances for which the dramatic method would be appropriate in any aspect of physical education. Include also a description of the dramatic form which would be most suitable for each circumstance.

5. What factors have caused more extensive current use of socialized methods and problem-solving methods in physical education teaching? What factors cause some continued use of response-to-command and other teacher-centered methods?

6. Prepare a guide for students entitled *Responsibilities and Duties of Squad Leaders.* Assume that they will operate in a student-centered program.

7. Distinguish between understanding the individual and the group behavior of students. Why are both important in selecting instructional methods?

8. Describe several appropriate projects for use in class physical education which are either individual projects for in-class or out-of-class work, or group projects for in-class or out-of-class work.

9. Indicate ways for physical education teachers to check on the effectiveness

of out-of-class assignments, including both informational study and practice of motor skills.

10. Take any one section from the official rulebook of any sport and prepare the material in programmed form. Do you think it would be easier for a high school student to learn the rules in this form?

Selected references

Amidone, Edmund J., and Ned A. Flanders: *The Role of the Teacher in the Classroom: A Manual for Understanding and Improving Teacher's Classroom Behavior,* Paul S. Amidon, Minneapolis, 1963.

Benne, Kenneth D., and Bozidar Muntyan: *Human Relations in Curriculum Change: Selected Readings with Especial Emphasis on Group Development,* The Dryden Press, Inc., New York, 1952.

Charters, Werrett W., Jr., and N. L. Gage (eds.): *Readings in the Social Psychology of Education,* Allyn and Bacon, Inc., Englewood Cliffs, N.J., 1963.

Fry, Edward Bemand: *Teaching Machines and Programmed Instruction,* McGraw-Hill Book Company, New York, 1963.

Kozman, Hilda Clute (ed.): *Group Process in Physical Education,* Harper & Row, Publishers, Incorporated, New York, 1951.

Jacobs, Paul I., Milton A. Maier, and Lawrence H. Stolurow: *A Guide to Evaluating Self-instructional Programs,* Holt, Rinehart and Winston, Inc., New York, 1966.

Luft, Joseph: *Group Processes, An Introduction to Group Dynamics,* National Press, Palo Alto, Calif., 1963.

McDonald, James B., and Robert R. Tuper (eds.): *Theories of Instruction,* Association for Supervision and Curriculum Development, Washington, D.C., 1965.

Torrance, E. P.: *Creativity: What Research Says to the Teacher,* Bulletin No. 28, National Education Association, Washington, D.C., 1963.

chapter 7

BASIC TEACHING PROCEDURES

INTRODUCTION

This chapter describes basic teaching procedures which are used within the broader framework of the basic types of method discussed in Chapter 6. Later chapters in Part II apply these procedures to various activities of a physical education program.

The frequent reference to objectives throughout this text calls attention to the considerable scope of objectives related to physical education. Acquiring knowledge and understanding should accompany development of motor skills. Attitudes and appreciations need primary consideration because they serve doubly: they motivate toward achievement or lack of it in school physical education and toward inclusion or exclusion of planned physical activity in one's out-of-school and adult living. All types of activities and all parts of a physical education program are considered in this chapter which first describes methods for teaching motor skills by dealing with (1) general procedures, (2) wholes and parts, (3) steps, (4) demonstration, (5) explanation, (6) drill, and (7) questions for self-evaluation of brief teaching periods. Attention then turns to teaching (1) knowledge and understanding, (2) attitudes and appreciations, (3) motivating, (4) transfer, (5) discipline, and (6) several other basic procedures.

GENERAL PROCEDURES FOR TEACHING MOTOR SKILLS

To learn motor skills the learner must have a concept of the movement or movements. In almost all cases there must be analysis of the performance unless the learner happens to hit upon an entirely satisfactory performance immediately. In teaching any motor skill, then, the tasks center on helping the learner to create concepts, on arranging for practice, and on analyzing the learner's movements and (or) encouraging him to do so. Teaching motor skills can be largely a process of demonstration, explanation, and providing for practice. It also can be guiding students toward discovering concepts by asking questions which lead the student toward this discovery. Teachers can present problems for students to solve. They also can encourage creativity by permitting students to experiment. An analysis of the movements made during practice provides information showing the need for more demonstration, more explanation, or more practice, or the need for more guidance to lead students to discovery, more delineation of problems for the student to solve, or more experimentation.

In helping the learner to create a concept, the teacher may provide a model by demonstrating, by arranging for others to demonstrate, by explaining, by using pictures or diagrams or films or kinescopes, by assigning or encouraging reading by asking leading questions, and by allowing students to experiment. Practice should be introduced very early. The teacher should not attempt to have a learner conceive a perfect pattern before engaging in practice. Rather, practice should follow perception of the big idea. Demonstration games, movies, talks by experienced performers, reading assignments, television-viewing assignments, guiding students toward discovery or problem solving, and the like frequently are worthwhile for introducing new or complicated activities.

Analysis of performance is the making of judgments concerning movements made by the learner himself as he practices. What is he doing that is correct and therefore needs reinforcement? What is wrong and hence needs correction and perhaps extinction? Analysis tells the teacher and student what further teaching and practice are necessary. It is clear that teaching has not been completed when there has been only one attempt to teach concept and a practice period. Rather, the teaching process emphasizes analysis so that correct movements may be encouraged and faulty ones corrected. A teacher demonstrates, explains, asks leading questions, presents problems, encourages experimentaion, and guides and directs practice. As practice proceeds, a teacher gathers information about student progress. The results of his diagnosis tell him what additional teaching is needed.

TEACHING MOTOR SKILLS BY WHOLE AND PART METHODS

In a whole method one starts by presenting and having learners practice a unitary act or a natural subdivision of a large unit in its entirety. Whether or not the teacher decides to have learners continue practice of the large unit or whether he later segregates one or more parts for special practice by one or more students depends upon his analysis, his diagnosis of needs. In a part method a teacher analyzes component parts of a movement or activity to identify a logical sequence of parts from the simple toward the more complex. After determining the order, he starts with one part, has learners practice until there seems to be satisfactory mastery, then proceeds to the next part, and the next, with the plan of adding the parts to make a whole.

Chapter 2 presents the theory of and reviews literature concerning whole and part methods. Three points are made. First, it is held that a whole-method approach is always superior to a part approach when a whole is defined as the largest whole or unified whole part which the learner can grasp without undue confusion. This concept places emphasis upon diagnostic teaching, upon teacher analysis of learner performance, because successful use of a whole-method approach demands that a teacher judge well what part practice, if any, to prescribe while employing a whole method.

Second, individual differences in abilities to learn cause some to learn best by using large wholes as a basis whereas some individuals may progress more rapidly by practicing smaller units. It seems probable, as a number of writers have suggested, that more intelligent persons or fast learners profit more than slow learners from whole methods. It also seems likely that well-adjusted and self-confident learners do better with a whole and that some may need the security of a step-by-step part approach. Third, the authors recommend that if a teacher is in doubt concerning the size of unit to start with he should select the largest from among all he considers.

It is important to provide experience in a whole activity as early as possible because (1) learning takes place through purposeful self-activity, (2) the learner must relate his activities to his goals, and (3) accomplishing steps 1 and 2 is difficult if not impossible without early contact with the whole activity. For example, in teaching a team game it is possible to create some concept of the whole game in the learner's mind through use of various procedures as discussed above; however, in order to expand the original concept, to give it more breadth and depth and insight, early trial experience with the full game is recommended. Such early attempts to play a full-team game lead to more purposeful self-activity during future practice of smaller parts and to a clearer understanding of relationships of such practice to goals.

ADDITIONAL REASONS FOR EARLY PARTICIPATION IN THE WHOLE

It is, of course, well known that repetition of correct movements of the kind best organized through drills is necessary to achieve rapid progress in skills fundamental to team games. Why, then, should there be early practice in the playing of the whole game?

In early performance of the whole, the learner rapidly expands his insight into the skills necessary to play a game. By trying out, he sees and feels the need for his own development of various skills. Before such a tryout a boy may feel that he has sufficient fundamental skill to play a game of soccer satisfactorily. During an early tryout in soccer, he may have an opportunity to kick a goal. If he muffs the kick, an inwardly felt need to develop his kicking skill may become very real to him. He may approach to play a ball just as an opponent does the same thing. He may kick away at the ball only to find that he kicks nothing because his opponent has deftly tapped the ball a yard to the side preparatory to making a long kick. When these and other similar things happen to a student early during the learning period, readiness for drill in skills increases. It becomes quite certain that he will relate practice of skills to their use in a game and that appropriate repetition of skill movements will become purposeful self-activity, whereas prior to these experiences in playing, such drill might have been boring and seemingly useless to the boy or girl. During early tryout experiences, the learner assesses his own abilities.

Another function of early performance in the whole activity is to permit the teacher to learn more about the abilities of each of his students. The teacher knows what skills a player must have in order to play well. What he does not know at the outset is the abilities of his students. Observation during the playing of a team game by class members permits the teacher to plan practices with intelligence. He can then plan on the basis of more information about the learners because he will know their needs better. Also he can plan with the students more effectively because they will feel and see their own needs realistically.

STEPS IN TEACHING MOTOR SKILLS

Traced below are the major steps through which complex motor skills are taught. The whole-part-whole method is assumed to be superior and is advocated. Note that the steps relate to complex skills. They do not hold for closely knit units, such as throwing a ball, which are learned more efficiently by whole rather than whole-part-whole approaches. They do hold for games such as basketball, baseball, volleyball, tennis, and handball which are made up of many parts which, in themselves, present unitary wholes or gestalts.

1. *Establish concept.* The learner must get the picture, understand what the movements and ideas represent. Demonstration, explanation, observation of whole performances by experienced persons, reading, pictures, movies, questions, and limited discussion are resources which teachers use in helping learners to create a concept.
2. *Provide experiences with the whole.* Immediately following a reasonably good mental concept there should be a tryout experience with a whole. Reasons for this were discussed above.
3. *Analyze the performance.* The emphasis in this stage should be upon diagnostic procedures. Once practice begins, teaching should concentrate upon detecting and eliminating any particular difficulty of an individual which is blocking his progress. A teacher who uses mass-drill methods which require all members of a group to do the same thing for the same amount of time, without regard for individual differences in abilities and difficulties, not only wastes time but also kills interests. Students also analyze their own performances; however, their conclusions are seldom complete, and frequently they are wrong. The teacher and student, together, arrive at diagnoses that guide learning into rewarding channels.
4. *Provide for practice in parts as needed.* Repetition is necessary for the learning and perfection of motor skills. Considerable repetition is necessary to "fix" complex movements. Parts causing difficulty should be singled out for special attention. The principal reason for considerable drill in the teaching of games is that practice of the whole does not provide sufficient opportunity for repetition. A game such as singles in handball provides many opportunities for repetition of the various strokes and may be learned effectively through major use of the whole method. In a nine-inning baseball game an outfielder may have very few chances to catch fly balls. Obviously, sufficient repetition to develop skill in fielding requires part practice if catching fly balls is defined as a part. A golf player makes only eighteen drives in several hours of actual play. Development of skill in driving will be much more rapid if specific practice in that phase of golf is provided in situations permitting many more repetitions.

The importance of keeping part practice meaningful and purposeful to the learner cannot be overemphasized. Mere repetition of parts for which the student sees little reason is wasteful. Relationships to a larger context should be understood and stressed. Part practice brings results when the learner is anxious to develop skill which will permit him to develop desired improvement in a larger pattern of movements and when he believes that part practice is the best means for reaching his goal. Drill is worse than ineffective when learners dislike it because they see no reason for it but submit because of pressures or compulsion.

5. *Again and continuously, reanalyze performance.* As part practice progresses, both teacher and learner analyze performances so that correct and effective movements may be made and so that difficulties may be eliminated. "Practice makes perfect" is only a partial truth; practice makes permanent is much closer to the full truth. Practice of incorrect movements tends to fix wrong responses, to develop bad habits.

6. *Reestablish the whole performance.* Frequently the parts singled out for specific practice or drill should be put back together again through performances of the whole. Note that the above sentence says "frequently." It does not mean that the whole-part-whole method requires only that learners should practice the whole, then parts as needed, then the whole, amen. It means a continual and repeated process of putting the game or skill together, breaking it into parts as needed, putting it together again, dividing it up again, and so on, with continual analysis at all points throughout the learning period. Thus further steps in teaching motor skills might be expressed as:

7. Again analyze.
8. Again provide for practice in parts as needed.
9. Continue analysis.
10. Again provide for the whole performance and repetition of the cycle with emphasis upon part practice only as needed and as pupils feel the need.

DEMONSTRATION PROCEDURES FOR TEACHING MOTOR SKILLS

Demonstration of new skills plays an important part in the teaching of physical education activities. Motor skills involve complex coordinations, and seldom, if ever, can students receive a clear view of a motor skill by verbal explanation alone. Demonstration of motor skills can be accomplished through several media. Chapter 10 discusses the use of audiovisual materials. Suggestions here refer to demonstrations of motor skills performed by the teacher, a selected student, or some other expert performer.

In conducting demonstrations, the first step involves preparation. The teacher should review the objectives of the lesson, ascertain the precise need for the demonstration, and define the purpose for which the demonstrated skill will be used. All necessary equipment should be at hand, the appropriate space selected, and the students carefully arranged so that all can see with ease. Student comfort looms as a problem in physical education demonstrations. Such factors as excessive chilling outdoors or poor seating or viewing arrangements indoors may detract from the demonstration. A playground demonstration, where a teacher must compete with passing traffic noise, for example, should be moved to a remote area where privacy permits primary attention.

Preparation also includes mastery of the skill by the demonstrator. It proves of little worth for a demonstrator to muddle through explaining where he made his mistakes. Students are likely to duplicate what they see. Very often teachers use students to demonstrate not only in cases where one is a superior performer but also to set a performance pattern that the others may expect to approximate immediately. In either case, the demonstrator should be well coached and adept at the skill he is to present.

The second step is to orient the learner to the purpose of the demonstration. The pertinent factor rests on the point that for effective demonstrations students must be aware of the purpose, its application to their own needs, and the use they can make of it in a larger setting. Explanation used with demonstration should call attention to what the performer is showing; it should avoid distracting attention, which overexplanation frequently does.

The third step relates to the actual performance or demonstration, to showing how. The demonstrator should start from the same position the learners will use for starting. For instance, if a teacher shows how to do a dance step or a calisthenic exercise while facing class members and starts to the left, that will appear to be the right to the audience. The demonstrator should either turn his back to the class or perform in a reverse direction which will be moving with the class.

The skill may be performed slowly while students observe the focal points. In demonstrating a motor skill, such as the one-handed push shot, the teacher may wish to perform it at regular speed several times to set the total picture, then proceed to slower trials. Trials should be interspersed with concise explanations, and opportunities should be given for questions and answers.

All demonstrations should be conducted as quickly as possible. Students usually are eager to try the skill themselves and often become bored or lose interest in an unduly prolonged demonstration. It may prove advantageous to summarize the crucial points very briefly after demonstrating. However, it is better to do this between two demonstrations of the same movement.

After students have an opportunity to practice, the demonstration may be repeated with attention directed to common problems which have arisen. Demonstrations can also be conducted with students performing simultaneously with the demonstrator when space, equipment, and the nature of the skill permit.

Other kinds of demonstrations in addition to the type described in the foregoing paragraphs are commonly used in physical education teaching. Closely akin is the type which involves the interrupting of an activity or game to indicate points of error or fine performance. For example, a team may have mastered a complicated screen play; the teacher halts the class and has the players demonstrate the play. Whether prearranged or spontaneous, the steps of preparation, explanation, performance, and reinforcement should be carried out as described for the more planned type of demonstration. Factors of attention, clarity of purpose and explanation, and the like apply equally.

EXPLANATION PROCEDURES FOR TEACHING MOTOR SKILLS

Any explanations, including those accompanying demonstrations, should be brief. Verbal explanations simply provide a means to assist students to understand, to clarify what is expected. The eagerness of students to participate actively increases the usual impatience of youth. Motor skills are learned through practicing them. Precious time should not be consumed by overlong explanations.

The language used should be simple. Fortunately, the vocabulary of physical education is usually familiar to the average sportsminded person. The development and use of cue terms and phrases promote efficiency in teaching. When unfamiliar terms are introduced in connection with new activities, care should be taken that these are carefully explained. Supplementary teaching means, such as blackboard and bulletin-board lists or mimeographed instruction, can be used, or the terms can be explained in orientation lessons.

Allowances should be made for the acoustics and the fact that both in and out of doors students very often are scattered. While it is generally desirable to call students together into a group for major explanations, brief explanations during play may be made while students remain in playing position.

The voice should be kept at a conversational level. The teacher who consistently shouts to be heard above the din merely promotes inattention. If students are beyond normal voice range when explanations are in order, the group should be brought more closely together rather than the voice being raised unduly.

Some of the learnings of physical education require extended explanations. An entire period or major portion of a period might be spent on rules or officiating, on the history of the sports or activity, on orientation to the physical education program, and the like. Factors involved in these situations are discussed under Lecture Method on page 125–127.

When learnings which center on verbalization are the desired outcomes, a classroom atmosphere, with participants not dressed for active play, is more conducive to good results. It is an uneconomical use of time to allow fifteen or more minutes for dressing and then devote a major portion of the period to nonactivity learning.

A common practice in physical education is to save explanations until a rest period. Some explanations lend themselves to this procedure, but care should be exercised. If students are truly fatigued enough to need a rest period, they may not be of a mind-set to give proper attention. Also, the timeliness of the point may have passed, and interest is elsewhere. Then, too, very often the explanations given during rest period tend to become too lengthy, and interests wane as the students chafe to return to activity. The average person recovers from fatigue in a matter of approximately two minutes or less when the activity has not been highly strenuous. This fact should be taken into account both in beginning explanations and in terminating them.

DRILL PROCEDURES FOR TEACHING MOTOR SKILLS

Drill, or practice in the performance of specific skills, is a prime essential in the learning of physical skills because students learn by doing. It is not possible to achieve a high degree of skill in a complicated movement without repetition in performance. Most physical education activities require a myriad of specific skills, many of them complicated. It follows that a teacher of motor skills must provide for repetitive practice.

A mental analysis of a movement aids in the learning. Without this concept, learning activities will be relatively purposeless. But a clear picture, which can be formed by watching performers, by listening to explanations, and by early and limited performances in a game, is only a start in learning the motor skills. It is only through repetition that a skill becomes part and parcel of the reactions of a person.

If the playing of a game provided opportunity for sufficient repetition in the performance of all the component parts, it would not be necessary to provide for drill in smaller parts. Indeed, if repetition to make permanent occurred with frequency during the playing of a game, economy of time and efficiency of learning would be achieved without drilling the parts. The reader may remember illustrations concerning this presented in (4) under Steps in Teaching Motor Skills above.

DRILL PROVIDES REPETITION AND PERMITS TEACHER ANALYSIS

When a kicking drill is organized properly, with not less than one ball for each team of 11 players, each player will kick the ball once in approximately forty seconds or less depending upon the length of the kick and the ability of the players. So in eight minutes each player will have 12 kicks, or 12 repetitions, in contrast to perhaps three opportunities in thirty minutes, as in the case of playing a game. In addition to providing for frequent repetition, a drill on a part, such as a kicking drill, provides superior opportunities for the teacher to make sure that each player is developing the proper movements. Movements can be observed, analyzed, corrected, and fixed during such drills.

MAKING DRILLS ATTRACTIVE AND EFFECTIVE

Drills should be interesting and satisfying. Learning is accelerated if the experience is satisfying; it is retarded if the experience is repugnant. A good concept, student participation in planning, and early performance in the whole activity to acquaint the learner with the game and with his own playing assets and liabilities all contribute toward the probability of student satisfaction in drill. The type of drill selected also affects the degree of satisfaction.

Although it is advisable to isolate a single skill for concentrated attention at times, combinations of several skills in one drill should be favored. Players need, of course, to learn correct patterns. When attention needs to be concentrated on one movement in order to get the correct response started, drill on one movement only is appropriate. But, since learning by wholes or comparatively large whole-parts brings superior results, it is important to use isolation of small parts sparingly. It should be remembered that team-sport skill drills sometimes become terribly formal and uninteresting. This should be avoided.

Drills should increase in complexity as playing skills increase. Drills should approach performance conditions; dance drills should aim for form, style, and quality; combinations that resemble a game situation as nearly as possible are to be favored. Simply kicking a soccer ball in a practice drill is worthwhile for a limited time with beginning players, but the addition of skills such as found when two players pass to each other and attempt to take the ball past an opponent adds to the satisfaction. Such additions, or combinations, should be made early in the learning process.

COMPETITIVE ELEMENTS IN DRILLS

Competition between teams or squads adds zest. There may be competition for speed or for accuracy or both. Soccer dribbling drills provide good opportunities for speed competitions. Goal-kicking drills lend themselves to accuracy competition among squads. A two-against-one or a two-against-two or a three-against-two drill provides competition because it measures the success of the offensive players in taking the ball past the defense, as well as the success of the defensive players in blocking and tackling.

VARIETY IN DRILLS

Repetition of the same drill may lead to monotony. There should be variety. However, drills which contain important elements of game situations and those that provide practice in several skills or combinations of skills may be repeated frequently without loss of interest. A soccer drill which consists of dribbling, passing, and shooting as well as defenses against these offensive maneuvers is likely to capture and hold the interest of the most advanced and expert players. When signs of monotony appear, it is time to change, to add variety.

DRILLS SERVE BEGINNING AND ADVANCED PLAYERS

Drills, properly introduced and used, not only are useful in the presentation of elementary skills to beginners but also serve to improve the abilities of players at any skill level. Besides the function of improvement of skills, drills provide for desirable warmup activities which are needed to prepare players for the more violent play that is to follow. It has been said with a great deal of truth that the best basketball coaches are the ones who have the best fundamental drills in their practice repertoire. The same can be said for all physical activities. Drills which give players satisfaction and put the performers in performancelike situations bring superior results.

QUESTIONS FOR SELF-EVALUATION OF BRIEF PERIODS OF TEACHING

The following questions concerning self-evaluation of one's teaching of motor skills represent a level of subject matter different from the material preceding and following in this chapter. Nevertheless, including them at this point following the discussion of teaching motor skills and prior to turning attention to the teaching of knowledge and understanding seems appropriate because they can help a teacher analyze and evaluate some of his own brief periods of teaching. Let it be clear that these questions are intended for analysis and evaluation of the teaching of one lesson or a part of one lesson. They are not appropriate for self-evaluation of teaching over a long period of time and are not meant for evaluation of accumulative results of teaching. They serve as a basis for evaluating one's own teaching shortly after the teaching. They may serve as a foundation for mutual cooperative evaluation of teaching by two or more persons at the discretion of those directly involved.

Did you (or the teacher)

1. Help students get their minds and attention on the subject or activity?

2. Help students develop a curiosity likely to lead them toward exploring and questioning?
3. Help students develop readiness to undertake the task?
4. Help students get the concept, the big idea?
   a. Show how effectively?
   b. Ask leading questions?
   c. Encourage student exploration?
   d. Encourage students to help one another?
   e. Tell how effectively?
      (1) Use too many words? Too few?
      (2) Direct the minds of students to easily grasped "big pictures"?
      (3) Befuddle students with a description of too many details at one time?
5. Give students a chance to try, to perform the act, as soon as possible?
6. Use diagnostic teaching, analyze performance and encourage students to do so, teach on the basis of need shown by diagnosis?
7. Emphasize main points?
8. Help students develop additional and accumulative motivation during practice?
   a. Manipulate feedback?
   b. See that favorable responses were reinforced?
   c. Help students develop goals?
   d. Help students feel success?
   e. Help students see their own progress?
9. Provide for continuity, and relate the current activity to previous and future activity?
10. Assign or suggest out-of-class practice?
11. Assign or suggest out-of-class study?
12. Psychologically support students and refrain from sarcasm or destructive criticism?

BASIC PROCEDURES FOR TEACHING KNOWLEDGE AND UNDERSTANDING

The terms knowledge and understanding often are used loosely as synonymous terms. Specifically, however, *knowledge* refers to information which the individual acquires, and *understanding* implies that he has a functional comprehension of the information. A student, for example, may recite in class a rote-learned rule yet fail to understand its application to the game. Effective teaching always strives for acquisition of understanding as well as knowledge. For this reason, teaching methods have aimed for maximum application and practice in lifelike situations.

The sequence of learning does not vary for different kinds of learning in a fundamental way. The steps outlined in relation to motor learning apply in mental learning—there must be concept, experience, initial discovery of the correct response, and practice and fixation of the correct response. The physical education teacher can make use of all knowledge common to classroom teaching to assist him in teaching information. No attempts will be made to review this entire field, but certain suggestions growing out of the nature of the physical education program are included.

The first requisite for adequate teaching of knowledge and understanding implies ample provision for such learning in preliminary plans. Too often teachers assume that participation in physical education activities will produce all desired mental learning almost automatically. Obviously, some will accrue, but unless there is selection of material to be taught and planning for methods of teaching, the results will be fragmented and skimpy.

Although one may learn the rules of a game as he learns the physical skills necessary to play, there are many kinds of important information which are not necessarily an outgrowth of this learning. A boy might play basketball for years without knowing its history; one might become an all-star soccer player without knowing the worldwide popularity of this game; a person might square dance for years without learning much about the cultural aspects of this form of dance; a class might complete a course in badminton and fail to learn how to care for equipment.

Again, a class might exercise over a long period of time and become physically fit without learning much at all about how exercise may serve them for the rest of their lives, about the effects of exercise, about its role in physical and mental health, about anatomy and physiology, about body mechanics or posture with the attendant relationships to back pain, sore feet, or psychological and aesthetic aspects. One might take school physical education for years without learning about relaxation, without knowing that there can be no nervous tension if all muscles are relaxed. It becomes obvious, does it not, that adequate teaching of knowledge and understanding appropriately associated with physical activity requires thought, organizing, and planning on the part of the teacher?

Steps should be taken to encourage acceptance by students of the need for acquiring knowledge and understanding as a part of physical education. Outside assignments should be an accepted part of physical education classwork (see Directed-study Method on page 128).

Effective teaching of knowledge and understanding requires drill or practice. The problem of drill was discussed at length in relation to the teaching of motor skills. Similar principles apply to the teaching of information, except that in many instances the learning is swifter and some information and understanding are acquired by pure insight. Immediate grasp of the factors is sometimes achieved at first exposure to the learning experience. The selection of adequate response and the fixation of the response as a part of the behavior of the individual vary both with the learner and with the kinds of learnings. Practice or drill supplies opportunities for exploratory experiences which contribute to both selection and fixation of the desired response. When memorization is desired, drill becomes highly important; when general understanding is desired, reading, thinking about ideas, and summarizing, rather than practice or drill, is appropriate.

The teaching of knowledge and understanding should be closely related to the activity phase of the program. Study of the rules of basketball can be most effective when presented in connection with practice of the related motor learnings. An outside assignment to study rules, for example, is likely to be most effective when preceded by a preliminary practice of a game situation calling for use of those rules and when followed by the same to reinforce outside study. Study of the history of the dance should accompany the unit or semester's work on the dance, rather than be taken up at a time unrelated to actual participation, in order to benefit by motivation which may occur from both directions.

Students should be encouraged to draw facts and implications from playing procedures presented during the activity phase of the lesson. For example, each time a situation calling for a new rule arises in the course of play, a student might write the new rule on a blackboard. A few minutes taken at the end of the period to summarize new knowledge may add clarity and aid retention.

It should be remembered that students acquire information from the very organization and conduct of the program, just as they acquire attitudes through exposure to various aspects of their environment. Information about showering after exercise grows indirectly out of school showering policies. All conditions of the environment should be analyzed to determine their possible effects in this regard. Learnings of this type may need reinforcing by more formal teaching procedures.

The presentation of information to classes should be done at opportune times when attention and readiness to learn are optimum. Talking to a class panting from an activity or widely spread over a gymnasium or playing field is not conducive to good learning. Presentations should be appropriate to existing conditions, and generous use should be made of such things as bulletin boards, pictures, anatomical charts, posture diagrams, pictorial and short word descriptions showing and telling how to perform some skill or stunt, and safety bulletins.

BASIC PROCEDURES FOR TEACHING ATTITUDES AND APPRECIATIONS

Attitudes are generalized emotionalized feelings about anything. They are characterized by the quality of intensity, which means they can be either positive or negative, with intensity ranging in all degrees from strongly for to strongly against. Appreciations, also an attitudinal reaction, refer to emotionalized feelings about the aesthetic qualities of anything.

Although authors agree on the basic characteristics of attitudes, they do not agree on a definition. Early psychologists regarded an attitude as simply a tendency to seek or avoid something. Some define them broadly as emotionalized feelings about things, people, and ideas. Lee J. Cronbach [1] uses a one-sentence definition: "Attitudes are meanings one associates with a certain object, which influence his acceptance of that object." In conjunction with his definition, Cronbach makes it clear that he includes ideas within his meaning of "object" and that unlike knowledge, which can be described as true or false, attitudes are largely personal; one's attitudes cannot be regarded as right or wrong on the basis of a standard completely acceptable to all, although every teacher has good reasons for wanting to teach certain attitudes because they influence learning.

Attitudes, including appreciations, play an important role in learning and teaching. They form a basic part of an individual's readiness to learn. His attitude about anything conditions his reaction to associated events. An overwhelming attitude of fear toward the water may block one in his efforts to learn to swim. On the other hand, a dominant feeling, such as his desire for peer approval, may lead him to conquer his initial fear and attempt the learning sequence.

The acquisition of attitudes constitutes a learning similar to the learning of motor skills and knowledge and understanding, a change in attitude likewise representing a change in behavior. The process of acquiring attitudes is generally less observable and less consistent in pattern, relatively speaking, than in other learnings.

Attitudes usually are acquired through five means. These include, first, long exposure to cumulative experiences which influence the individual. For example, a boy who has participated continuously in a dance program from elementary school into high school under circumstances of accepted approval by pupils, teachers, and parents may accept dance as a desirable high school activity for the boys' program. Conversely, if every experience in dance has been met with ridicule by peers or other signs of social disapproval, his attitude may be negative.

A second way, closely related to the first, suggests that attitudes may

[1] Lee J. Cronbach, *Educational Psychology*, 2d ed., Harcourt, Brace & World, Inc., New York, 1963, p. 461.

be acquired through the process of analyzing a variety of experiences and differentiating among them. For example, a student may elect to participate in a given activity to explore its possibilities of satisfaction to him. After due experience he may crystallize an attitude of some degree of intensity about it. Or he may set about to explore a variety of activities and may develop feelings about their relative worth.

A third way to acquire attitudes is through traumatic or strong experiences involving great pain or pleasure. For example, the boy with fear of the water may have seen a playmate drown. Or another lad may have won a small prize at a picnic foot race, the pleasure of which launched him on a lifelong interest in track.

The fourth way attitudes are acquired is through identification with and emulation of either a person or an institution. A boy's pride in his athlete father may determine his love of sports, or an athlete's son may reject sports if he feels his father expects more than the son feels possible. Honesty or dishonesty observed in an admired person may cause attitude development. A group such as the Boy Scouts leads youths to accept scout values as their own.

The final way attitudes are learned is through associating related things with something about which a person already has developed an attitude. For example, one who likes a sport may like all sports, or one who fears swimming may also dislike boating. Stereotypes of social types and prejudices such as those involving religious, racial, or political groups are learned partially through association and partially through long exposure.

It can be noted that all the examples cited make use of the modifier "may." The acquisition of attitudes is a highly individualized matter. An experience which may result in an attitude for one person may have quite a different effect on another. Despite the complexity of the process of acquiring attitudes, the teacher should keep in mind that since attitudes are a learned response, they can be taught. Following are some suggested procedures for developing desirable attitudes through the physical education program.

1. Teachers should set good examples, be good models; they should epitomize various qualities which they wish to establish in their students, including those of sportsmanship, democratic outlook, and adherence to rules of clean living. The teacher of physical education in his close personal contact with students has considerable opportunity to be a respected leader. In any case, his actions will inevitably influence student attitudes either favorably or unfavorably. A coach who condones rough play or places more value on winning than the means by which victory is achieved may be expected to have players whose attitudes are similar. Boys sufficiently mature socially to be

repelled by the coach's attitude may be driven from the program or face conflicts which deprive the activity of much of its pleasure for them.

2. The entire social and physical environment should be pleasing to students. Many adults today who speak in slighting terms of physical education often describe their own unfavorable experiences in school gym classes, which they recall with boredom and distaste. These same adults may have favorable attitudes toward professional sports and follow a major team with extreme eagerness because of pleasurable associations.
3. All reasonable safety precautions should be carefully followed, both in organizational matters and in care of equipment and facilities. A student who falls unguarded from a piece of apparatus in the early stages of practice may lose his flavor for the activity. Safety, of course, implies elimination of needless hazards and should never dilute the challenge or thrill of physical activities.
4. Teachers should strive for continuity and consistency of favorable student experience because attitudes often result from long accumulative experiences. If youngsters are consistently impressed with the high value and worthwhileness of physical education, attitudes of acceptance, appreciation, respect, and interest will develop. Such attitudes may lead one toward participating in physical activities for many years.
5. Efforts should be made to do the best possible job of teaching skills, knowledge, and understanding. Research reveals that information does change attitudes and that success in motor skills increases interest in an activity. Barring the presence of dominating outside incentives which compel the student to learn despite a lack of inherent interest in the activity, favorable attitudes will accompany increased insight and skill into the learnings involved.
6. Motion pictures and other highly pictorial influences should be used whenever feasible. Numerous studies have revealed that motion pictures have a significant influence on children's attitudes. This effect, however, tends to diminish with age. Nevertheless, movies of selected sports and physical activities may be effectively used to create interest and favorable attitudes toward activities and ways of conducting them. Similarly, inviting outstanding speakers whom the students accept may influence their attitudes favorably.
7. Provisions should be made for the individualized nature of attitudes. Differences in attitudes are likely to be far greater than physical or even skill differences among a typical high school class. In a single swimming class, attitudes may range all the way from rigid fear of the water to extreme foolhardiness, causing the fear-stricken student

to refuse to enter the pool and the one lacking in cautiousness to jump into the deep end. Only by considering individual difference and striving to know and understand each student can effective work in attitude development be forthcoming.

8. Any student found to possess extremely negative, hostile, or disruptive attitudes about anything should be referred to the guidance program for more complete diagnosis. Individuals with highly emotionalized attitudes often prove to have problems of inner emotional security and may be in need of expert guidance.
9. Care should be exercised about which factors in the physical education program embody the most prestige. Attitudes toward the intramural program and resulting participation may be unfavorable if the program has little standing in the school and if all attention is directed to the interscholastic program. Also, it is possible that negative behavior, such as cutting physical education classes, may be the source of prestige in some student groups. This may result in a general lessening of respect for the program as a whole.
10. Provisions should be made for practicing the outward acts of a desired attitude. If the program of physical education aims to promote attitudes of good sportsmanship, then students should be encouraged to practice outward signs of good sportsmanship, such as applauding a good play by an opponent, congratulating the winner, cheering for the opposing team at the end of a contest, refraining from jeering officials, and replaying close or questionable decisions. Such procedures are likely to lead to acceptance of the worth of this conduct.
11. Finally, the teacher should recognize that attitudes can be taught. The teacher should be very conscious of what attitudes he wants to teach. He must define them and plan thoroughly for teaching them, recognizing that attitudes usually are learned slowly since, of the five means through which attitudes are acquired, only one, traumatic experience, makes rapid learning possible. Both in planning and during the progress of teaching and learning, one should think carefully about how teaching, how student experiences, how the whole environment affects attitudes.

PROCEDURES FOR MOTIVATING LEARNING

Discussion in Chapter 2, Teaching and Learning, indicated that motivation is essential to learning. Learning requires activity on the part of the learner. Unless he is motivated to participate in the learning activity, learning cannot take place. It was further pointed out that there are two basic types of motivation: intrinsic, which stems from the nature of the activity itself, and extrinsic, which places value on factors secondary to the focal learning itself. Obviously, motivation is an essential to learning in physical education as it for any type of learning. What are the most desirable ways to motivate students to learn in physical education?

One thing is certain, the most desirable ways to help some students motivate themselves will not be the best ways to motivate all. Individual differences concerning motivation are as great or greater than those in motor and mental ability. Both level of aspiration and self-concept—ego—strongly affect one's reaction to various motivational factors. If a teacher helps a youngster who is lacking in confidence to increase either his level of aspiration or his self-concept or both, the teacher can be sure the level of motivation has increased.

Praise or level of success which spurs one person may actually deter another. It is natural to want to do well, to fell that we have done something worthwhile, so we like to do what we feel we can do well. Because of this, the motivational power of teacher support can hardly be overrated. Also, people tend to accept constituted authority; they want to do what is expected of them and find a pleasant feeling of security when they please others, including teachers. For this reason promise of reward for doing something and threat of punishment for not doing it serve as moving forces for many. If a student's determination to succeed has been increased by the prospect of reward for success or punishment for failure, then motivation has been increased. So either extreme, praise and blame, reward and threat, may be effective in a given situation.

STUDENT UNDERSTANDING AND ACCEPTANCE OF GOALS

Perhaps the most desirable way to motivate youngsters to learn is to increase their understanding and acceptance of the goals and the means used to achieve those goals. That is to say, if a student desires to achieve the goals of any educational activity and sees that the activities involved have purpose or meaning in achieving those goals, better learning is likely to result. Generally speaking, physical education activities are inherently interesting to secondary school students. Objections and poor attitudes usually stem from administrative or teaching-procedure factors in the program. One of the best ways to increase student responsiveness to the physical education program is through use of democratic procedures including student participation in planning and managing—by developing student involvement (see page 192 for a fuller treatment of this topic).

SUCCESS

Success, too, represents one of the primary forces in the motivation of learning. Failure tends to result in lack of responsiveness, withdrawal, and diverting activities which may take on an asocial or disrupting form. One who experiences success in his performance finds encouragement to continue. Teachers can capitalize on the moving power of success by using various procedures such as carefully selecting subject matter or learning experiences which are well within the potential range of participants, providing for individual differences so that poorer performers may succeed and better ones still be challenged, and setting standards appropriate for those involved. Care must be exercised, of course, to avoid use of false standards of a low level just for the sake of success.

The provision of variety in physical education programs adds to the possibility that all students will find some success. It is unreasonable to expect that all students should find success in the same sports. One of the great attributes of physical education rests on the breadth of suitable activities. The tall, fragile boy who may lack the power and ruggedness to play football or basketball may achieve equally worthwhile goals through participation in badminton, high jumping, or some activity more suitable to his body build. A girl who feels failure in sports may find satisfaction of accomplishment in dance.

In the last analysis, the effect of success or failure on learning is closely related to the individual's level of aspiration. An achievement which encourages one individual to proceed with an activity may actually deter another. A not isolated case is the young man who gave up golf in disgust when he finally came to the conclusion that he would never break 75! His aspirations toward a professional golf career set these high standards. Now, as a businessman, he does not even enjoy golf as a recreational pursuit; his partner golfs each weekend, and a score below 80 gives him cause for celebration.

REWARD AND PUNISHMENT

One of the difficulties in conducting and interpreting research on the relative merits of rewards and punishments as motivating factors in learning is the difficulty in defining or isolating reward and punishment. Too often they are merely manifestations of a given situation. A B grade may represent a reward to one student who is pleased to have gained that much recognition, but it may be a punishment to another who sought an A. Research on this subject also indicates that results are situational and individualized. A considerable amount of recent research emphasizes that personal satisfactions strongly affect motivation; these may be created by rewards, including those of a monetary nature, or by status-giving recognition of achievement or worth. Many who write about student motivation urge that reward and punishment as well as praise and reprimand be used judiciously and that efforts to encourage intrinsic motivation be emphasized. Some studies have found that reward may have a pervasive effect for good, but that punishment may disorganize and divert the learner. Operationally, teachers will do well to study their students and then use reward and punishment as they think it will favorably affect the students involved.

Since motivation is central to learning, various parts of any book on teaching relate to this topic. Helpful foundational material may be found in Chapter 2, Teaching and Learning, and in Chapter 3, Understanding and Guiding Today's Adolescents. The section on discipline later in this chapter has relevant ideas as does the discussion of awards in Chapter 13, Organizing and Managing Intramural and Recreational Programs, and of marking in Chapter 17, Method and Evaluation.

OTHER MOTIVATIONAL FACTORS

All factors which affect learning favorably may be said to motivate learning. The reader is referred to certain other topics discussed elsewhere in this text as follows: (1) Importance of Feedback (page 414). Giving students a knowledge of the results of their learning efforts motivates learning. Although results can be given in such a way as to completely discourage an individual, understanding his progress and success contributes to effective learning. (2) Teacher-student Rapport and aspects of Teacher-student planning (pages 170, 273). It has been found that teachers who are well liked by students and who have won their respect contribute to learning through student identification and the desire to win the teacher's approval. (3) Interests (page 56). The utilization of interests which already exist serves as a foundation for initial progress in new activities or continued improvement in old ones. (4) Objectives (page 34). Understanding the direction of desired learning and expected achievement levels contributes to learning.

PROCEDURES FOR PROMOTING TRANSFER

Transfer logically appears essential to effective education. An experience can never repeat itself in exact form because conditions of neither the environment nor the individual ever remain constant. Learning, to be effective, therefore, must transfer. The discussion of transfer in Chapter 2, Teaching and Learning, presents several theories of the way and the extent to which transfer takes place. Even though understanding of this subject still eludes exact definition, certain suggestions appear to be plausible in assisting teachers of physical education to increase the likelihood of transfer.

The teacher should try to define the common elements of his field and indicate to students where these similarities exist. For example, for the many games which use a ball, or some other implement in motion, keeping one's eye on the ball is basic.

Another way to encourage transfer suggests that provisions should be made for opportunities to practice the learning in the setting similar to those that will be encountered in real life. A football coach does not confine his tackling drill to work on dummies, knowing that this form represents but one basic pattern in tackling. He supplements this technique with actual tackling in a gamelike scrimmage.

Transfer may also be promoted by helping students to make generalizations about specific facts or individual skills. What is similar about throwing a baseball and a football? What has head position to do with body balance in tumbling and diving? Why is volleyball a good game for cophysical education programs?

Calling attention to opportunities for transfer increases the probability of considerable use of skill and knowledge in differing situations. Questions such as those asked in the preceding paragraph should be posed to students, or, at least, answers to them should be communicated if the teacher seeks maximum transfer.

Finally, the likelihood of transfer can be enhanced by seeing that understanding accompanies information in mental learning. A student may correctly repeat a rote-learned phrase from the rulebook, enter the game, and promptly violate it. In motor learning similar assurance should be made that the student is not merely imitating a model but can actually perform the skill in a game situation, and will not revert to habits developed in a part practice situation without adapting to the new context.

PROCEDURES FOR ESTABLISHING DISCIPLINE

Good discipline is necessary to satisfactory progress in physical education as well as in any school pursuit. Without good discipline objectives cannot be realized, nor can either educational ideals or favorable growth patterns.

What is good discipline? It exists when satisfactory progress toward objectives occurs. In physical education, satisfactory behavior requires quiet and attention if the teacher wants to speak to a whole class; however, noise usually accompanies physical activity and in many cases the more noise, the better the discipline. Whenever any student interferes with another, discipline is bad. A youngster wasting his own time without interfering with others may be poorly disciplined and correction is in order, but this can be regarded as a teaching problem rather than a disciplinary one in the sense of maintaining satisfactory class discipline.

INDIVIDUAL RESPONSIBILITY FOR BEHAVIOR

A student's acceptance of responsibility for his own behavior is the ideal. Teacher authority should withdraw and change to leadership and guidance as evidence of a student's ability to manage his own affairs appears and develops. When child growth is recognized as a total process, discipline is conceived as expanding freedom which should not be greater than the youngster can handle. There must be limits to freedom, and teacher guidance should be available. Some external controls are necessary in all school situations. Sometimes teachers must insist upon conformity whether or not the student sees the reason at the time.

The concept of freedom for students is not always interpreted with soundness by beginning teachers or, for that matter, by experienced personnel. Freedom with responsibility always is in order; freedom with license should never be tolerated. How can one be reasonably sure that his judgment of appropriate student freedom is sound? Getting one's attention centered on two things, the students and the objectives, and avoiding attention to himself helps the teacher immeasurably.

When thinking about students and objectives, one should consider the fact that teachers tend to want students to be obedient and industrious, that they favor high IQ students over highly creative ones. Teachers, then, may tend to be unable to accept "different" behavior which is necessary for nurturing creativity; hence schools may suppress creative thinking and acting rather than encourage it.[2] Freedom to learn should include freedom to be creative. Teachers should distinguish between unruly rebelliousness on the one hand and independent, responsible individuality on the other, and should not confuse honest appreciation for individuality with sentimentality for "cute" behavior. We need discipline. When discipline is poor, something is wrong, and students as well as teacher are unhappy. We also need some rebellion.

One of the authors has noted that in quite a number of methods classes he has taught to senior majors in physical education, a general opinion among students has been, "We should have freedom but high school students should not." Why? "We are college students; that makes the difference." Well, they have a point. What they miss is that there can be no point in one's life when he changes abruptly from an outer-directed to an inner-directed person, from living without freedom to living with a large amount of it.

Groups of experienced teachers have been known to hoot when a

[2] See Jacob W. Getzels and Philip W. Jackson, *Creativity and Intelligence*, John Wiley & Sons, Inc., New York, 1962; and Ellis Paul Torrance, *Guiding Creative Talent*, Prentice-Hall, Inc., Englewood Cliffs, N.J., 1962, and *Gifted Children in the Classroom*, The Macmillan Company, New York, 1965.

theorist answered in response to a question about discipline: "Motivation is the base; if you are successful in developing motivation there will be no disciplinary problems." Well, there may be reason for such hooting. The best teacher in the world cannot handle motivational procedures so well that everyone in a high school class will be highly motivated every minute of each of 180 days of a school year. If the theorist were a teacher in an inner-city school or in any school fraught with disciplinary problems, he, too, might have need for disciplinary controls of a different nature. Still, at the base his answer had soundness. A student who is motivated to master whatever subject matter or skill a teacher requires will not be a discipline problem. Youngsters will work hard if they can see a payoff in the not too distant future.

From the standpoint of immediate teacher comfort and work, it is likely to be much easier to operate on the old basis of discipline through punishment. At least this is true when one works with youngsters who have a background of control through fear of punishment. Acceptance of responsibility for all or most of one's actions does not appear suddenly. It develops gradually. One needs only to view development from infancy to realize this. The baby is unable to be responsible for itself other than to give signals of hunger and discomfort, to wriggle in response to a need for activity, and to sleep when tired. By the time the youngster is ready for school, he usually can be depended upon to be responsible for such things as going to and from school, crossing streets safely, caring for his own physical needs for water and elimination, self-feeding, and self-dressing, for the most part. As the child progresses through school, self-responsibility normally grows gradually. But the extent and speed of such growth depends to a large extent upon the degree to which home, community, and school permit and encourage freedom with responsibility. Youngsters accustomed and habituated to control through direct orders from adults become confused when suddenly confronted by freedom. All youngsters, regardless of their favorable growth in self-responsibilities, become overwhelmed by too much freedom. They must look to adults for guidance, for cues, and for directions. Although a teacher may find it easier to give all the answers and directions, it must be recognized that in a democracy development of self-responsibility is basic to individual and societal success. It may be easier for a teacher to do things for a student than to help him do things for himself, and this procedure may give students a pleasant feeling of security because they are relieved of the necessity to make some hard decisions. But a teacher's function is to help boys and girls achieve ascending degrees of maturity, and a fundamental difference between maturity and immaturity lies in ability to take responsibility for self.

NECESSARY CONTROLS

Schools must exert controls. Education is compulsory, and attendance in a given school is required unless the parent assumes private responsibility for education. Days and hours of attendance are fixed, certain subjects are required, and regulations designed to protect pupils and to permit orderly procedure must be made.

What controls, other than required attendance, are needed for physical education classes? Some of them are (1) time controls which indicate time of appearance and dismissal, (2) program controls which specify types of activities, (3) safety controls which protect against injuries, (4) clothing controls which insure freedom of action, protection of clothing, protection of the student and of equipment such as gymnasium floors and mats, and (5) procedural controls which permit the teaching-learning process to proceed in orderly and efficient ways. The first four of these controls hardly need further elucidation here. The fifth, procedural controls, involves behavior such as attention to the business at hand, avoidance of interfering noises and disturbances, extraneous "horseplay," and violations of the rights of other members of the group. Stimulation of interest in worthwhile activities, rather than insistence upon acceptance of a multitude of specified regulations, should be emphasized in the establishment of procedural controls. Needed regulations should be established as routines by consistent use and by a never failing disapproval of violations.

CAUSES FOR BREACHES OF DESIRABLE DISCIPLINE

Lack of satisfaction through approved activities is the basic cause of disciplinary difficulties. The teacher who stimulates interest through the use of activities appropriate for the individual or group concerned, through interesting and attention-capturing teaching methods and through enthusiastic teaching and leading, finds few breaches of desirable discipline in physical education classes. Most breaches of discipline spring from boredom, on the one hand, and confusion, on the other. Students bored with teacher-approved activity look elsewhere for satisfaction, whereas students confused by class procedures also find outlets elsewhere. Both the bored and the confused are likely to strive for attention by misbehavior such as teasing, pushing, tripping, "teacher egging," shouting, and refusing to follow approved patterns.

The physical education teacher who attempts to force students to attend to activities which lack challenge for them is courting difficulties that are certain to arise from boredom. Worse, he is arranging a sterile learning situation in which little progress will be made. Similarly, the teacher who attempts to insist upon attention to an activity that is too difficult for the youngster concerned contributes to confusion that not only causes rebellion but also makes satisfactory learning progress impossible. It is necessary, then, to gear activities to the abilities of various members of whatever group is involved.

RELATIONSHIPS BETWEEN TEACHERS AND STUDENTS

The teacher must regard each student as a person of worth and importance. Good teachers respect young people and tend to like students; they also find satisfaction in good progress by youngsters. The opinions and beliefs of every person are to be respected and recognized. Teachers of young children serve as parent substitutes; pupils need to be able to depend upon them. Teachers of preadolescents and adolescents must recognize that while their students will place great importance upon approval from their peers, they also long for adult friendship, understanding, and guidance. The very essence of excellent teacher-student relationships is found in a friendly atmosphere of mutual trust and regard in which the student can depend upon the teacher for help in solving problems. Ridicule and nagging are out of place; analysis, suggestion, and good example make for good relationships.

Students recognize, like, and respect teacher qualities of pleasantness, decisiveness, fairness, poise, ability to empathize, desire to be helpful, and competence in subject matter or activity. Although individual person-to-person relationships are emphasized here, the quality of whole-class reaction to the teacher is based upon individual relationships; there is a tendency for group reaction to snowball. When youngsters talk about good or poor qualities of a teacher as they see them, there is a tendency for the group as a whole to think in terms of good or bad, white or black, without full analysis. When youngsters like a teacher and believe in him or her, they are anxious to cooperate. Students who, on the whole, like and respect a teacher will accept regulations and demands which they would reject if they came from a teacher they neither liked nor respected.

RELATIONSHIPS AMONG STUDENTS

Friendly relationships of mutual respect and understanding are as important among students as between a teacher and his class members. An overtense situation produces irritability and strained relationships. Poor discipline as well as confusing instruction make for poor relationships within a group. Overstress on competition produces a selfishness that causes relationships to deteriorate.

Establishment and maintenance of an atmosphere of friendly relationships demand recognition of and respect for the rights of others as well as a feeling of group solidarity which comes from group cooperation. Since students want and need the approval of their fellows, it becomes an important task of the teacher to lead toward rich relationships among students. Talk of the preaching kind is ineffective. Provision of opportunities for each student to achieve something worthwhile in the eyes of his peers brings results. Repeated teacher approval of good student-student relationships and disapproval of questionable behavior is effective.

Students should be permitted and encouraged to discuss points concerning an activity or a problem rather than be required to remain silent when talk does not interfere with the ongoing activity. A bit of kidding and happy byplay not only makes for good relationships but also facilitates learning by increasing interest. Recreation is an important part of physical education; a happy atmosphere is just what is needed. Physical education classes should bring forth chuckles and good laughs. When a pleasant atmosphere exists, students almost always will provide a bit of desirable merriment.

PREROGATIVES OF STUDENT AND TEACHER

Each student has a right to consideration by all other group members including the teacher. Each has a right to make suggestions and express opinions at appropriate times. Also, each has a responsibility to consider the others and to abide by constituted authority, whether such directives come from the teacher or from a majority of the class or group involved. The teacher is responsible for the conduct of his class. He represents not only mature judgment but also specialized professional training and experience, and he is responsible for leading the class. Students should recognize the necessity for controls and regulations which serve the common good. They should recognize that in cases where group agreement is not feasible or not possible the teacher must make decisions which affect all. They should recognize that no class member has a right to freedom without the attendant responsibility.

OTHER BASIC PROCEDURES

Procedures which concern formal and informal teaching, mass, small-group, and individual approaches, grouping, student leaders, and co-physical education are applicable to all teaching of physical education. Each is discussed for the purpose of identifying basic concepts relative to their use.

FORMAL AND INFORMAL PROCEDURES

What constitutes a formal procedure and what an informal one? Formal procedure in physical education is not easy to define, for the term does not mean the same thing to all people. To many persons, formal physical education implies activities rather than methods of presentation, activities such as those of the so-called German or Swedish systems, or calisthenic drills, or grass drills. But in reality, activities cannot be classified as formal or informal. A more accurate description of the types of activities is "natural and artificial."

Methods of presentation may stress formality or informality. Associated with formal methods are military-type procedures, exact formations, teacher commands, and student response to commands. Informal methods involve freedom of student action, instruction by example and suggestion, and pleasant, helpful relationships between teacher and class. Activities frequently referred to as formal may be taught informally. Calisthenics, for instance, are taught by an informal method when students perform them at their own time and pace as the teacher makes helpful suggestions when the need is indicated and upon request for help. Tennis, usually thought of as an informal game, is taught formally when the teacher breaks a stroke movement into segments and commands or counts as all students respond in unison.

Some people have condemned formal approaches to teaching physical education as inappropriate in a democratic education that stresses the development of self-responsibility. The condemnation is justified if it objects to teaching procedures which call for continuous and dominant reliance upon formal method. But when all use of formal procedure is condemned, the objection is not valid.

MASS, SMALL-GROUP, AND INDIVIDUAL PROCEDURES

In teaching physical education there is a place for mass, small-group, and individual procedures. The extent of desirable emphasis depends upon the type of activity and upon the situation in which the teaching-learning process occurs. Mass procedures are appropriate whenever there is need for a large number to perform the same pattern of movements at the same time. An example of mass procedure made appropriate by the activity is the practicing of defensive footwork in basketball in which a large group of boys or girls move in unison at a signal, command, or movement by the leader.

An example of mass activity made appropriate by the situation is found in golf. It may be decided that instruction in golf is desirable even though facilities for practice and play are limited. Teaching this sport in such a situation might well include mass drill in which all members of the group practice swings at cotton balls in unison as the leader commands or gives signals. If such practice takes place in a gymnasium or on a small outdoor area, mass unison is necessary in order to permit students to retrieve their balls without considerable risk of being hit by a club.

Although it is unmistakably true that emphasis should be upon instruction that fits the individual, it also is true that judiciously selected and infiltrated mass procedures produce efficient learning. Practice or drill on the same thing by many is particularly appropriate during the early phases of instruction in an activity new to the students. There may be and frequently is a considerable amount of individual instruction during the progress of a mass activity. As the teacher observes and analyzes some of the individual performances, he may, during the progress of a mass drill, give verbal or demonstrative cues which help to improve performance and understanding in individual cases.

Small-group procedures are effective in the teaching of many physical education activities. One group may be working with volleyball, another with badminton, another with apparatus, and still another with table tennis. Several groups may be learning speedball, with each group engaged in practicing different component parts of that game according to the needs of each group as indicated by their skill level. Again, various groups may be practicing the same basketball skill or skills, with the groups formed either to make fuller use of the facilities or to provide greater homogeneity, or both.

Individual instructional procedure takes place in conjunction with both mass and small-group procedures. It also is utilized as a method apart from its use in conjunction with mass and small-group methods. Thus, one student may be engaging in corrective exercises designed entirely for him. Another may be practicing certain skills quite independent and differentiated from the activity of others; another may be working out a dance pattern of her own creation, while still another may be performing conditioning exercises. Complete individualization in the sense that each student works independently of all other class members is hardly possible, and it would be undesirable if it were possible. Physical education almost always is and should be carried on in a social setting in which people work and play together.

GROUPING PROCEDURES

Public education customarily relies principally on group teaching methods. Individual instruction, of course, occurs and is encouraged within a group setting, as well as in special situations such as counseling and remedial work. Some hold that private instruction, a one-teacher and one-student procedure, would be superior. In some cases this might be true, but it would be literally impossible to provide complete individual instruction in American public education. Even if it were possible, desirability would be questionable since experiences in a group teach the skills needed for participation in society, business, or government. Further, learning with a group provides the stimulation of coparticipation. Physical education uniquely lends itself to group instruction not only because team sports and other group activities require many participants, but also because the social nature of activities which require only one or two participants attracts participation by groups.

As pointed out later in Chapter 16, Method and Administration, group composition should represent reasonable synonymity of purpose among its members to make teaching effective. The greater the extent to which a group is homogeneous in the focal point of the learning experience, the better the results that are likely to accrue. Groups have been formed on the basis of scores on intelligence tests or results of achievement tests in reading and arithmetic, and many people think of homogeneous grouping in these terms. Such classification may work well as a whole for teaching subject matter which requires a high level of abstract verbal ability or excellence in mathematics. Nevertheless this type of grouping is pertinent to only some of the learning goals of education and then not necessarily for all individuals. The crucial point in grouping is to have a school structure which makes it reasonably simple for groups to form and re-form on the basis of the particular job to be done.

Grouping for physical education presents several problems. Obviously, school groupings based upon intelligence have little pertinence to physical education teaching since, consistently, research has shown only a small positive relationship between athletic ability and intelligence. In addition, it is doubtful if complete homogeneous grouping is either possible or desirable. Since the outcomes from most learning experiences in physical education center on social and emotional learnings as well as on physical outcomes, difficulty arises in identifying homogeneity in all these aspects. Also, individuals may vary considerably in their development in regard to each of these factors, and it is difficult to provide sufficient administrative flexibility to allow for the number of different groupings which would be required during the course of a semester's work in physical education. The chief factor to govern procedures in this regard includes consideration of the focal purpose of the principal activity.

PROCEDURES FOR USE OF STUDENT LEADERS

Physical education offers many opportunities for the development of desirable leadership traits and skills. Student leaders may be used as squad leaders, referees, managers, assistant teachers or coaches, and as members of committees or policy and planning groups on all levels and in all parts of the program. A basic concept concerning student leaders is that their experience should provide learning opportunities for them. A student-leader program cannot serve as a means for hiring fewer teachers or maintenance personnel. When a leader has exhausted the educational value of some function, such as serving as a towel attendant or a roll checker in class, he should not continue in that assignment because it has become educationally sterile.

One necessary procedure in the use of an organized student-leader plan is to prepare the leaders for their tasks. Youngsters cannot be expected either to have educationally valuable experiences or to be helpful to other students and to the teacher if they have little or no preparation for their assignments. This requires organization and operation of a training program. Successful procedures which are used for preparation of leaders include (1) individual and (or) group conferences between teacher and prospective leader, (2) extra group meetings before or after school for the purpose of instruction concerning the work of leaders, (3) formation of a class for leaders or for gifted boys or girls (for example, forming a class of juniors from among sophomores who apply), and then, in effect, teaching on a speedup basis, covering both junior and senior physical education in one year as well as preparing the students for leadership roles during their last year in high school, and (4) use of written materials describing the function and work of leaders, a procedure which is likely to be used in conjunction with any or all of the first three procedures.

Although there are many advantages inherent in an organized plan for developing and using student leaders, two pitfalls bear attention. One is that it is possible to develop an elite corps which receives favoritism and privileges while the rest of the students get no opportunity to lead. This, of course, should be avoided, and can be, by the use of flexible qualifications for membership in a leaders' corps and by having helpful and unobtrusive leaders. The other pitfall is that it is possible to discourage emerging leadership, that is, to lessen leadership by various class members who feel that they can show or tell others something worthwhile. This pitfall can and should be avoided by encouraging and approving such unofficial and unplanned leadership. Further, providing ample opportunity for emerging leadership also serves as a deterrent to the first pitfall mentioned above, that of developing an elite corps.

PROCEDURES FOR CONDUCTING COPHYSICAL EDUCATION ACTIVITIES

Joint participation by boys and girls provides opportunities for promotion of social adjustment and recreational satisfaction and hence helps youngsters to make progress toward social and recreational objectives of the school and of physical education. Heterosexual adjustment comprises one of the major developmental tasks of youth, and coparticipation in wholesome recreational activities serves as one of the avenues through which this development occurs. A discussion of the teaching procedures likely to enhance the value of coparticipation and to circumvent problems which sometimes occur follows.

Coparticipation may be included in either the class or extraclass programs. The latter is preferred for schools which are initiating such a program. Recreational activities such as school dances, field days, noon-hour recreation, and class days provide natural opportunities for organizing and furthering coparticipation. Using extraclass activities as a springboard toward more extensive class activities involving both boys and girls lessens the probability that students, not yet used to the idea, will become self-conscious and create opposition.

In well-planned systemwide programs of physical education which provide for continuity from elementary through secondary school, best practice suggests that early elementary school patterns of coparticipation never be entirely broken. There is good reason for separating boys and girls sometime during the intermediate grades for most of their physical activity. This does not imply, however, that they be separated in all activities. There is good reason to conduct part of their physical education jointly, and if this is done no problem of reestablishing a pattern of mixed classes in the secondary school will arise.

A second basic consideration in conducting cophysical education relates to the types of activities used. There are many activities, such as tennis and badminton, in which mixed-doubles play is widely popular, or various forms of dancing, roller skating, ice skating, and the like, which are normally done in mixed groups. Another category of activities, including bowling, archery, hiking, golf, swimming, and many other individual and dual sports, is equally adaptable to mixed play. Only activities which are completely suitable to mixed participation should be emphasized. Occasionally for recreational purposes a mixed group will wish to play softball, volleyball, or even basketball. When activities of this type, in which boys are generally quite superior to girls, are used, rules should be adapted to equalize competition. In volleyball, for example, girls cannot usually compete against boys who play the game on an expert level with highly skilled blocking and spiking. No problem exists if play is on a lower skill level in which serving and volleying are the major skills used. When players are more expert, however, a simple rotation plan can be worked out in which the front lines of the two teams are either all girls or all boys opposing each other. This requires a line-rotation plan rather than a circular player-rotation plan. Needless to say, teams should always be mixed, rather than pitting a boys' team against a girls' team.

It has already been suggested that initial introduction of cophysical education be promoted in the extraclass program. It further follows that first attempts at mixed classes during the regular instructional program be offered on an elective basis. Success for such elective classes will inevitably lead to mixed classes in certain activities being taken as a matter of course by students, parents, and other school personnel. For example, a logical sequence would begin with afterschool square dance sessions in the recreation program. Interest created in this medium would suggest opportunities to increase skill through a class offering. The class, set up on an elective basis, would be open to both boys and girls. If the square dance program became highly popular in the school and community, a final step would indicate that all ninth-grade students participate in a square dance unit during the class program. Having mixed classes would be the logical result of the preliminary buildup.

Another way to introduce coparticipation into the class program is to combine boys' and girls' classes for special learnings. For example, a boys' badminton class and a girls' badminton class may meet separately for most of the unit. Sometime during the unit the two groups could be combined for several periods to learn the rules and techniques of mixed-doubles play. Similarly a special speaker or performer, in golf for example, may be invited to the school. Boys and girls may well be combined into a single class to benefit from help from the specialist who has but one day to spend at the school. Also, it should be remembered that some learnings in physical education do not involve motor skills. Mixed groups to hear lectures or other programs on sports appreciation, spectator conduct, information on the recreational opportunities in the school and community, and the like all serve to bring boys and girls together for instructional purposes.

A careful definition of objectives often solves any problems on the desirability of conducting a class on a mixed basis. One merely has to ask what learnings dictate the advisability of conducting a class on a mixed basis. A central purpose directed toward developing motor skill, motor fitness, or skill in typically masculine or feminine activities usually indicates separate classes. When social and recreational skills are paramount or objectives relate to acquiring specific skills in actual techniques of mixed participation, such as techniques of mixed-doubles play in tennis or ability to social dance, coparticipation often provides the best learning environment.

SUMMARY

The tasks of teaching motor skills center on helping the learner to create concepts, on directing or leading practice, and on analyzing the learner's movements.

The whole method advocates that the complete act or a natural subdivision of a large unit be presented in its entirety. The part method is based upon analysis of the component parts of an activity for the purpose of identifying a logical sequence of parts for presentation from the simple to the complex. The whole approach proves generally superior to the part method when a whole is defined as the largest whole, or unified whole-part, which the learner can grasp without undue confusion.

The precise steps in teaching a motor skill by the whole method include (1) establishing concepts, (2) providing experiences with the whole, (3) analyzing the performance, (4) providing for practice in parts as needed, (5) again and continuously reanalyzing the performance, (6) reestablishing the whole performance, (7) again analyzing, (8) again providing for practice in parts as needed, (9) continuing analysis, and (10) again providing for the whole performance.

Appropriate demonstration procedures for teaching motor skills emphasize careful preparation, mastery of the skill by the demonstrator, orientation of the learner to the purpose of the demonstration, accurate performance of the act during the demonstration, promptness of presenting and terminating the demonstration, and provision of immediate opportunity for students to practice.

Appropriate explanation procedures for teaching motor skills emphasize brevity, pointedness, clarity, use of meaningful vocabulary, and holding attention with the voice at a conversational level.

Drill plays an important part in learning motor skills. It provides for the repetition necessary to perfect a performance. With careful organization drills can be meaningful, interesting, and motivating to students.

The sequence in learning information and understanding does not vary from learning motor skills. Information may be acquired by rote without the student's having a functional understanding of it. Teaching methods should allow for maximum opportunity to apply and practice information in lifelike experiences.

Attitudes consist of generalized emotionalized feelings about anything. They have the quality of intensity and can be either negative or positive. Appreciations, also attitudinal reactions, refer to emotionalized feelings about the aesthetic qualities of anything. Attitudes serve as motivating agents which condition a student's orientation to learning and direct his use of the learned skills, knowledge, and understanding.

Motivation is essential to learning. Learning requires activity on the part of the learner, and unless he is motivated to act, no learning can take place. Motivation, though a highly individualized problem, can best be accomplished by such means as helping students to understand and accept learning goals, providing opportunity to experience success, and emphasizing rewards rather than punishments. In general, intrinsic motivation proves superior to extrinsic.

Transfer of learning is essential to effective education since an experience can never repeat itself in exactly the same form because of changes in either the physical or emotional environment. A teacher can increase the likelihood of transfer by understanding the factors inherent in the problem.

Good discipline is necessary for satisfactory progress. The best discipline is conceived as a gradually expanding freedom for self-discipline, Which should not permit greater freedom than the student can handle responsibly. Students must accept authoritative regulations necessarily imposed for the common good.

Methods of presentation may stress formality or informality. Intended outcomes determine the desirable degree of formality or informality for various learning activities.

In teaching physical education there is a place for mass, small-group, and individual procedures. The extent of desirable emphasis depends upon the type of activity and upon the situation.

To make group teaching effective, group composition should represent reasonable synonymity of purpose among its members.

Extensive use of student leadership proves essential to a sound student-centered physical education program. The basic concept in relation to use of leaders recommends that all such assignments for students provide a real learning opportunity.

The values of cophysical education activities can be considerably enhanced by attention to appropriate teaching procedures. Careful selection of activities, adaptations of rules, and organization and conduct of class or recreational periods serve to increase likelihood that full advantages of coparticipation will be realized.

Questions and problems for discussion

1. Apply the steps in teaching motor skills to a simple motor skill, such as the underhand ball throw, and to a more complex motor skill, such as the basic bowling roll including the running approach.

2. Make a list of various attitudes and appreciations which might be among the desired outcomes of a teaching unit in basketball (or any activity) for a class of ninth-grade boys or girls. Show how various teaching methods or procedures would contribute to or hinder achievement of these learning goals.

3. Observe a high school physical education class over several periods. Make a list of all influences in the environment for learning which might have an effect on the attitudinal learnings of students.

4. As a physical education teacher, which school policy would you prefer: one that required immediate referral of any classroom discipline problem to the principal or one in which the principal completely washed his hands of any but major infractions of school regulations? Give your reasons.

5. What motivational factors are found in interscholastic participation? Which of these factors promote the best all-around learning? Which are least desirable?

6. Draw up an operating code for a student leaders' club. List ten general policies to guide teacher use of student leaders.

7. List five activities which lend themselves to large-group teaching. Suggest ways of organizing groups to facilitate learning. List several activities that are less effective for large groups and give reasons.

8. Assume that school A emphasizes formal teaching procedures while school B emphasizes informal, although the facilities and number of students are equal. What factors or influences seem likely to account for such difference in emphasis?

Selected references

Alcorn, Marvin D., James S. Kinder, and Jim R. Shunent: *Better Teaching in Secondary Schools,* Holt, Rinehart and Winston, Inc., New York, 1964.

Burton, William Henry: *The Guidance of Learning Activities,* 3d ed., Appleton-Century-Crofts, Inc., New York, 1962.

Collins, William Milton: *Methods of Teaching in the Elementary and Secondary Schools,* Pageant Press, Inc., New York, 1965.

Johnson, Perry B., Wynn F. Updyke, Donald C. Stolberg, and Maryellen Schaefer: *Physical Education: A Problem-solving Approach to Health and Fitness,* Holt, Rinehart and Winston, Inc., New York, 1966.

Mosston, Muska: *The Teaching of Physical Education,* Charles E. Merrill Books, Inc., Columbus, Ohio, 1966.

Oliva, Peter F., and Ralph A. Scrafford: *Teaching in a Modern Secondary School,* Charles E. Merrill Books, Inc., Columbus, Ohio, 1965.

Shipley, C. Morton, et al.: *A Synthesis of Teaching Methods,* McGraw-Hill Book Company, New York, 1964.

Smith, Herbert Frederick A.: *Secondary School Teaching: Modes for Reflective Thinking,* Wm. C. Brown Company, Publishers, Dubuque, Iowa, 1964.

chapter **8**

TECHNIQUES FOR TEAM AND INDIVIDUAL SPORTS

INTRODUCTION

While teaching any physical education subject or activity, one should use techniques consistent with the principles discussed in Part II, Bases to Method, and in Chapter 7, Basic Teaching Procedures. To do this it is necessary to adapt to the practical problems presented by various activities. Of course, the teacher must know the subject matter, the activities. Further, he needs to know the principles of learning, understand adolescents, know what results he seeks (objectives), and have the ability to decide how to teach a given activity.

This chapter discusses methods for teaching team and individual sports, two important areas in high school physical education curricula. Dealing with teaching procedures, with method, it makes no attempt to treat the sports or the techniques of performing various movements. The teacher-education program provides various courses for learning the sports themselves, and books treat sports in detail.

TEAM GAMES

Little need be said here concerning the reasons for having team sports in secondary school programs. Their contributions to physical, emotional, and social development of adolescents are well accepted. Are physical educators in unanimous agreement concerning the place of these sports in the program? Yes and no. Yes, they agree that team sports should be included. No, they do not agree about appropriate relative emphases. All recognize that team sports provide splendid opportunities for social and emotional development. Being a member of a team, cooperating, surely affects social development and probably produces emotional changes. Competing, with its inevitable emotion-producing situations, surely affects emotional development and probably produces social changes. Note that the above two sentences use the words "affects" and "produces" in discussing social and emotional changes or development. Does playing team games assure that the changes always will be favorable? No, it is quite possible for deterioration or negative development to occur because of unwholesome surroundings. To assure favorable development, the teacher must plan and teach for wholesome social and emotional surroundings and for reinforcement of appropriate behavior.

All will agree that the big-muscle activity of team games can provide desirable satisfactions and to help to develop agility and skills. Some have higher regard than others for the value of team games as developers of strength and endurance. Teachers who believe it highly important to develop cardiovascular strength and endurance to a maximum will intersperse large amounts of runnning and other conditioning activities as they teach team games (this applies as well to individual games, discussed later). Those who believe that a moderate amount of strength and endurance is sufficient may intersperse less exercise specifically for conditioning or developing of physical fitness. Some team games inherently provide considerable continuous exercise, whereas others provide intermittent rather than continuous muscular work. Youngsters playing speedball or soccer (if they play it rather well) may run for quite long periods of time. Those playing touch football or softball will be physically inactive a good deal of the time. It follows, of course, that more exercise for the specific purpose of developing, and (or) maintaining, fitness should be interspersed with touch football and softball than with games which in themselves demand continued muscular work over longer periods of time.

Young people usually are keen to get into condition to play team games. They may become highly motivated to develop strength and endurance in order to become better players. This may be a springboard toward genuine interest in exercise as a producer of strength, endurance, and feelings of well-being.

LEVEL OF SKILL NEEDED

The development of highly specialized skills is not necessary to the successful reaching of the goals of physical and social development. It is necessary, however, for the individual to attain sufficient skill so that he may play the game with satisfaction. Satisfaction, of course, is individualized. A level of skill which satisfies one person may not satisfy another.

A principal measure of satisfaction comes from progress, from improving ability. The pleasure of the journey itself is great. While highly developed specialization, such as is called for in interscholastic competition, is neither necessary nor appropriate for class or recreational or intramural team games, continuous upgrading in ability to play is basic. Without the improvement of skills, neither development nor enjoyment on the part of students can be adequate. The educative process associated with team sports in physical education programs falls flat if boys and girls do not experience the joys and satisfaction of increasingly able performances.

How much skill is required for satisfactory participation in games? Frequently the answer, "A reasonable amount," is given. While this is true, it is not a complete answer. A better answer is that there must be sufficient skill to provide satisfaction and growth for the individual involved. A person with little or no ability, with few or no skills, cannot participate with satisfaction because he will feel ill at ease, out of place, insecure, self-conscious, and even ashamed. The teacher's responsibility with such a student, and it is a responsibility which requires patience and understanding of the person's feelings, is to guide the student through rudimentary development of skills to a point at which the individual may participate in a game with satisfaction to himself. After that is accomplished, further development of playing ability both through playing the game and specific practice of component skills is needed.

ILLUSTRATIONS OF COMBINATIONS OF FUNDAMENTAL SKILLS

Teaching principles which apply to all team games will be presented after two illustrations showing combinations of fundamental skills, one for teaching basketball, the other for volleyball. Why these illustrations, dealing only with combinations for teaching basic skills of basketball and volleyball? (1) They show a rationale for the kinds of skills the teacher should have the student practice, and (2) they clarify seeming differences between two points of view, one which says, "We must teach the fundamental skills before letting the learners play," and one which says, "Let them play and they will learn the game."

Note that the second reason above mentioned "seeming differences." Experiences of the authors with upper-level students, teachers, and literature have shown not only contrasting points of view but also contentiousness between some who say, "We must *teach skills* and not just let the students play," and some who say, "*Let them play;* that is the best way to progress toward worthwhile objectives." However, when you get the shells cracked, frequently the only difference of viewpoint concerns how skills are learned best. In other words the differences lie among those who adhere closely to a part-by-part conditioned-response theory of learning, and those who incline toward a gestalt theory and believe that practice of unified wholes produces more efficient learning (see Chapter 2). Both seeming extremes want the same end result—ability to play the game. Both know that to play the game it is necessary to perform fundamental skills.

One probable reason many lean toward the idea that you must teach each skill independently is that the various games have been learned that way in courses and from books. Naturally, and appropriately, when teaching or writing about a game and its basics, you necessarily must isolate parts to analyze them. Similarly, a psychologist isolates each of various human traits to discuss it but does not suggest that any single trait operates independently. Another probable reason stems from exhortations to "Teach; don't just throw out the ball." The erroneous assumption sometimes made is that the teacher continually must be telling and showing. Indeed, "Teach, teach, teach." The question is how does one teach, or, better, how does one see that students learn?

If the illustrations serve their purpose they will clarify such differences and will show combinations which are effective for learning fundamental skills. Let it be crystal clear that the illustrations apply to teaching games to classes, not to interscholastic teams, not to groups devoting large amounts of time to developing high levels appropriate for specialists. It should be remembered that polish comes last, that one first learns to perform in reasonable fashion and polishes toward perfection later.

The illustrations deal only with appropriate combinations of skills for teaching basketball and volleyball to high school classes. They deal neither with other aspects of teaching nor with day-by-day development. Rather, they indicate combinations to start with and general trends in selection of combinations later on.

Basketball There is a reason for selecting this game for illustration. The authors feel that, especially in this game, far too many teachers feed in the parts too slowly, that they use time inefficiently by practicing segments of the game which are too small for optimal learning of all that needs to be covered, that they use techniques in classes which would be appropriate for coaching a team but not for the purpose of providing the best experiences for a class.

Situation: (1) a freshman class; (2) not less than 12 and not more than 24 class days available; (3) enough balls and baskets so that at least one ball and one basket is available for ten students; i.e., if there are 40 students, not less than four balls and four baskets, and (4) that none, or only a few of the students, has had much basketball playing experience, that most have played some, and that all, or almost all, have at least seen someone play.

Several days before basketball instruction is to start, give information about the approaching unit, stir up interest with announcements, bulletin board notices, or displays, suggest titles and sources of appropriate articles or books including, of course, *Physical Education for High-School Students.*[1]

First day:

1. Have balls available for early students, encourage shooting, passing, rebounding, dribbling, one versus one, two versus two.
2. Have all, not more than ten to a basket, engage in a short-shot setup with one student shooting at a basket, another rebounding or getting the ball and passing it to a third who in turn dribbles once or twice, shoots at the basket; then a fourth student rebounds and passes, etc., until each has practiced rebounding, passing, dribbling, and shooting about a dozen times. The teacher teaches as students practice or as they wait their turns. He deals with details according to student needs.
3. One versus one. One on defense who attempts to prevent his opponent from scoring, one on offense who attempts to score, one passer who may receive a pass from the player on offense and pass to him, but not help otherwise. Give each student a specified minimum number of trials on defense and on offense; encourage rebounding. Teach as this practice continues.
4. If time will allow, two versus two. Two on defense, two on offense with each student having as many turns as time will allow.
5. Tell about the next lesson, suggesting outside reading and (or) practice if deemed useful. Although this is step 5, it is excellent teaching procedure to intersperse this here and there during the lesson instead of saving it for the last item during the period.

Second day: Depends upon progress the first day. Possibly only the first day's practice will be repeated. More likely this lesson will repeat steps 1, 2, and 3 of the first day and then practice three versus three, five versus five, which would be an informal full game, either a full-court or a one-

[1] American Association for Health, Physical Education, and Recreation, *Physical Education for High-School Students,* 1960. Available from National Education Association, 1201 Sixteenth Street, N.W., Washington, D.C.

basket game. Divide the class into several ability groups to facilitate teaching, and practice appropriate to level of skill.

Third day:

1. Substitute shooting from a distance and following with a short shot for the short-shot set-up of the previous days. Have students in a semicircle shoot from a distance of about 15 feet, follow up their own shots, and take another from wherever they recover the ball. Competition among players of near-even ability might be used; the youngsters might play 21 or 50 by teams, counting two points for a long shot, one point for a short shot.
2. Practice offense and defense against opposition. Select one or more from among one versus one, two versus two, three versus three.
3. Five versus five, which may be presented as informal competitive play of the whole game.

Fourth through tenth days: Select combinations previously used according to (a) teacher observation of student progress and (b) student expression of preference if teacher sees fit. Regroup if demonstrated ability warrants.

1. Add two versus one and three versus two.
2. Use competition in some of the practice drills.
3. Introduce team play on offense and defense if it would be helpful.
4. Form teams for later competition.
5. Devote progressively more time to informal games (or five versus five).
6. Prescribe part practice as various students show need.
7. Stir interest in and prepare for games.

Eleventh and later days: Competitive play, providing practice with warmup, if 15 or fewer days are allotted. If more than 15, lessons similar to those given on the fourth through tenth days may be continued for several more days before competitive play starts.

Volleyball As for basketball, several days before the unit is to start, give infomation, stir interest, suggest reading sources, etc.

Situation (similar to basketball): (1) a freshman class; (2) not less than 12 and not more than 20 class days available; (3) enough balls and courts so that at least one ball is available for six students and one court for 12 (if fewer courts are available play may be rotated, with some practicing while others play); (4) about half have played some volleyball, about half of those who have not played know something about the game, and the rest know nothing of volleyball.

First day:

1. Divide into teams and play volleyball for half of the period. Do not instruct, other than to say something like, "Serve like this (showing), or if you wish, throw the ball over the net to get started"; or, "Get the ball back to the other side of the net by playing it like this (showing); no catching the ball", or "Play it as often as you want to for now, just so you do not catch it. Now go to it." If questions are asked, say something to the effect of, "Sorry, play as best you can; questions in order later."
2. After students have played for half a period answer a few questions if asked.
3. Practice passing from circle formations, about six to a group with one in the center. Path of the ball (1) from one student in circle to the one in the center, (2) to the next student in the circle, (3) to the center, (4) to next in circle. Continue until each player in circle has passed a specified number of times; then the youngster in the center changes positions with the one in the circle and the sequence is repeated until everyone has had a turn in the circle. Teacher teaches, of course, during practice.
4. If time permits, practice serving, using double-line or rectangular formation with students serving to each other from a short distance, perhaps 15 feet.

Second day:

1. On this day, and all subsequent days, have balls available for early students. Encourage them to volley, practice passing or serving, bounce a ball against the wall. (On subsequent days after feeding, boosting, spiking, and perhaps blocking and recovery from the net have been taught, encourage early practice of any of those skills as well as those mentioned specifically for this second day.)
2. Repeat circle-passing practice of first day.
3. Practice setting-up, same circle and idea as above.
4. Repeat serving practice as described for first day, or introduce it if there was no time for it the first day.
5. Play informal games, continue allowing unlimited number of plays (not just three according to the rule), permit serving from close up, or permit throwing instead of serving. Teach as play continues. At some time interrupt play briefly to demonstrate a spike.
6. Divide class into ability groups for future teaching, practice, and play if teacher sees fit.

Third day:

1. Again, as indicated, encourage early arrivals to play or practice today and all days.
2. Circle-passing practice.
3. Circle–setting-up practice.
4. Circle or double-line or rectangular serving practice.
5. Informal play, teaching as play progresses, encourage students to help one another.

Fourth day:

1. Early arrivals practice and play.
2. Have students practice setting-up and spiking. A good arrangement is (1) have three students on one side of net, three on other side, with two of each set of three near the net about 6 feet from each other, one about 12 feet from net; (2) player about 12 feet from net passes ball to a teammate who sets it up for the third teammate, who spikes; (3) players on opposite side of net perform as did the others in step 2 just above, (4) repeat this sequence until each player has had a specified minimum number of turns; (5) players exchange positions so that those in passing positions go to set-up positions, those in set-up positions go to spike positions, and those who have been spiking become passers from about 12 feet back; and (6) repeat procedure until everyone has had the specified minimum number of turns to practice each of the three skills.
3. Play informal games.

Fifth day:

1. Early arrivals practice and play.
2. Circle-formation practice of passing and setting-up.
3. Selection of another one or two skill-practice drills from among those used on previous days.
4. Play informal games.

Sixth day:

1. Early arrivals practice and play.
2. Circle-formation passing and (or) set-up practice.
3. Practice setting-up and spiking as in step 2 of fourth day with addition of practice of blocking and recovery-from-net added to this three-on-one-side-of-the-net, three-on-the-other-side arrangement.
4. Play informal games.

Seventh day:

1. Early arrivals practice and play.
2. Form teams.
3. Select practice procedures used on previous days as teacher sees fit. He may well make his decision after listening to student suggestions.
4. Play informal games.

Eighth through twelfth days:

1. Early arrivals practice and play.
2. If only 12 days are available, start with competitive games. Before games start, warm up with either volleying or circle-passing drill.
3. If up to the maximum of 20 days are available, select practice according to judgment of teacher and felt needs or expressed interests of students. Also play informal games, and extend time devoted to them.

Thirteenth through twentieth days: Competitive games preceded by practice as deemed advisable.

TEACHING-LEARNING PRINCIPLES COMMON TO ALL TEAM GAMES

Although each team game may require a somewhat different application of basic principles and selection of combinations of skills differing from the above illustrations, the following represent principles common to the teaching and learning of all team games.

Create a concept of the whole The first step in teaching a game is to help the learner build a picture of the total activity. Suppose one sets out to teach volleyball to a group of boys who know nothing about the game, who have neither played nor seen the game. Suppose, further, that one decides that it is only logical that these boys must first learn to serve the ball, then learn to pass from the back line to the front line, then learn to set the ball up for a spike, then learn to spike, then learn about rotating, then learn about team attack and team defense, then learn about scoring, and then be permitted to play. Such reasoning may seem sound from a logical viewpoint, but it is unsound psychologically. The various parts must be seen not as independent parts but as parts fitting into a whole pattern.

Verbal description by the teacher helps students create a concept, see the picture. It should center on key or principal points. The details can be grasped by students better after they get the big idea, after they have formed a concept of the whole. Since word pictures are less clear than more concrete pictures, it is wise to show neophytes pictures of a game. Arrange a demonstration game, show pictures, show a film, let students who know the game show beginners how the game is played.

Provide for early performance in the whole game or in unified whole parts Some teachers believe that it is senseless to permit inexperienced students to attempt to play a whole game because very often first results seem chaotic. Broken rules cause interruption, poor skills cause balls to go awry, and the like. When using a unified-whole method to give early experience in playing an entire game, teachers should reconcile themselves to some confusion. They should present just a few basic rules and suggestions for play so activity can proceed with some enjoyment and some progress. For example, in giving a group of high school girls a chance to play basketball for the first time, a few familiar lead-up games such as captain ball and take-a-way may be briefly introduced. Then in playing the game of two-courts basketball, playing positions should be briefly described and play allowed to proceed with one or two simple rules. These rules could include: *Do not run with the ball,* and *Do not touch an opponent or hit the ball when it is in her hands.* If either of these faults occurs, the other team takes possession of the ball. Refinements such as the differences between fouls and violations, technical and personal fouls, and the like can be introduced at a later date. The need to learn guarding tactics, bouncing and juggling, and, most of all, shooting becomes immediately apparent, and practice drills introduced at subsequent sessions become meaningful and stimulating.

Another consideration in the early introduction of a whole game rests upon safety factors. An element of danger may enter if students do not have sufficient skill to handle a game situation. Obviously, in teaching water polo, players must know how to swim, and it would be dangerous to have a player who cannot catch a ball play behind a batter who is also likely to throw his bat. In such cases the use of lead-up games provides basic experience in meaningful whole activities to prepare for more skilled games. Students who have had adequate programs of physical education in elementary schools probably have acquired sufficient skill in fundamental movements to undertake with perfect safety and some skill any of the more complex team games. However, many high school teachers find students entering secondary school with little previous physical education experience, necessitating teaching of simple skills such as catching and throwing. This is a particular problem with girls; most boys find such experiences in informal play life. A problem to men teachers is the poor skill habits of untutored boys, such as batting cross-handed and the like. Sometimes such poor habits prove difficult to change.

Provide for specific practice of small or isolated parts as it is needed by individuals Students may need specific practice in basic skills of team games for either or both of two reasons. First, although some may perform the component parts very well when practicing rather large wholes, others may need breakdown practice of some parts to learn well. Second, team games may not provide opportunity for sufficient repetitions. For example, a soccer goalie might need considerably more practice in blocking shots than playing the whole game would provide. Playing volleyball, however, with its rotation of player position might provide sufficient opportunity to practice the various fundamental skills of the game.

Participating in a whole game is necessary for perfecting a skill but seldom provides enough practice. This is true of team skills as well as fundamental game skills. In regard to team skills, a screen play may be used only two or three times in a game. The play may be taught in a practice drill, then further practiced in a game situation. That is to say, each time the ball is brought down the floor, the offensive team attempts a screen play, while the defensive team practices appropriate maneuvers against the play. Drill on the screen play under these gamelike conditions is as important as the initial nongame drills.

In football often one or two plays may be run repeatedly against full defense. Time need not be taken to observe downs and give up the ball to the other team, but most elements of full-team participation are kept while combined with a drill approach, thus providing practice in a gamelike situation.

Drills can be attractive and interesting. They provide for repeated practice necessary for the learning of a motor skill. Team sports, with their complex fundamental and team-tactic skills, require extensive opportunities for repeated practice on the many different elements of play, both for individuals to improve individual skills and for two or more members of a team to improve team performance.

Is it possible to indicate proper balance between drill and play? Above it was pointed out that both are needed. To what extent each is needed and the way in which a teacher determines how time should be divided between drill and play depend upon the groups involved and upon the individuals within a group. Some persons in almost every group are more ready for competitive play than others in the same group. This means, of course, that selective practice in skills is indicated. A basketball player whose hand skills are highly developed but whose foot skills are faulty needs to stress the improvement of his foot movements through specific practice.

A group of high school seniors who have had considerable experience in volleyball will need less practice than will a group of ninth graders who have had little or no previous volleyball experience. The ninth graders will need more concentrated ball-handling practice. This may be provided by drills and by modification of rules such as requiring six plays on the ball before it may go over the net or requiring a player who plays the ball to play it twice.

As a guide to deciding the relative distribution of time between playing and practicing in physical education classes, it might be estimated that, generally speaking, about 30 to 35 percent of the time should be spent in competitive play. Approximately 15 to 20 percent of the time may well be devoted to short informal games near the end of a period which has been spent largely on practice and 45 to 55 percent to practice of component skills.

In determining time distribution, the following three criteria should be considered:

1. Ability level of the group and of individuals. More highly developed abilities make more competitive play desirable.
2. Ability of the individuals to play with satisfaction. This differs from ability level in that a group of relatively low ability may be able to compete with teams of equal ability and find satisfaction as well as improvement in their play in so doing.
3. Development of playing ability. The test of satisfactory progress in learning is found in progressive bettering of skills. If competitive play provides for repetition of the movements that most need development, then playing ability develops during the playing of the game. If, on the other hand, adequate repetition is not provided during a game, it is necessary to provide for practice of certain component parts in situations where repetition is facilitated.

Provide for student participation in planning, organizing, and managing For effective learning to take place learners must accept the project. They must feel that it is their own; they must be with, not against, the leader. Teaching a game is not a process of pouring in by the teacher; rather, it is a process of providing an environment in which the learners may grow. Does a person do best work when he works for someone else, or does he perform with more zest, more sparkle, more animation, enthusiasm, and energy when he works for himself? When a project is his own, he really wants to make it go and see it through.

Team games present rich opportunities for student participation in planning, organizing, and managing. Students, all of them or some of them, can share in the selection of a game, in planning the overall methods of attack, and in doing the things that carry the learning process along at a high pitch. The process of planning and the experiences while planning represent a practical laboratory in democratic living. The boys and girls live the process of cooperative planning and self-government, important cornerstones of democracy. Frequently, it is easier for the teacher to do all the planning than it is for him to lay the foundation for student planning and see it through. When temptation to forgo student planning presents itself, one should consider well not only the effect upon the immediate success of the game at hand but also the fact that democratic living in the present is the best preparation for future citizenship in a democracy.

Provide for recreational play in competitive games Team games are to be played for fun and satisfaction. Part practice of various skills helps to develop abilities which permit learners to play the full game with satisfaction. Playing opportunities must be provided if the learner is to have a complete experience. Looking forward to playing a game gives meaning to practice procedures and experiences; it enables the learner to relate his activities to his goals; it makes the various experiences purposeful. Opportunities for realizing innate possibilities for rich social and emotional development through team games are found in playing games more than in practicing for them. Competing, being a member of a team, may change one's attitudes and habits of sportsmanship, character, personality, cooperativeness, leadership, and contributory group membership.

Competitive play should be allowed in classes Some have presented the false idea that class instruction in team games should be devoted only to skills, that playing of games should not be permitted in classes, that experiences during class should bring the student to a skill development point which encourages him to play games in out-of-school, or at least in out-of-class, situations. However well intentioned proponents of this idea may be, following their specious proposal would be detrimental to learning for two reasons.

First, learning of skills will be inefficient because of fragmentation, isolation, overuse of practice on parts, and deprivation of opportunity to fit all the parts into a whole game. Second, if students are not given the opportunity to play games in classes those with below-average ability very likely never will play.

It is a truism to say that one likes to do what one can do well. All like to succeed, all like to show well, and most tend to avoid entering activities in which they think they are likely to perform poorly. A school cannot expect that any great proportion of the less able and inexperienced boys and girls are going to play team games outside of classes, without first having full playing experiences in their classes. Where are the boys and girls going to be initiated to the extent of developing impelling desires to play if not in the classes? The answer is that many of them will not. On the other hand, substantial playing experiences in the required classes will assure all an opportunity to compete against others of similar ability. Further, after developing abilities, interests, and self-assurances while playing in classes, students are much more likely to enter team-game competitions in extraclass school activities and in out-of-school community situations. It is clear that if we believe that the many should have realistic opportunities to participate in team games, we should not only permit but also encourage and stimulate playing of games during class periods.

Competition and cooperative planning add zest Competitive games add zest to the program. Recently the authors observed two different classes of high school boys, each engaged in a unit of touch football. One teacher conducted the unit by using various skill drills from day to day and occasionally organizing games by having the boys count off. The boys did not know from day to day what they were to be asked to do. The response was dull. There was little zest and little learning. The skill drills were accepted passively; the games were played with little enthusiasm and with little or no development of team offense or defense. Another teacher introduced the unit by saying that four weeks were to be devoted to touch football, that there would be practice, and that there would be games. He asked the boys how they would like to organize for the games and for practice. The boys and the teacher decided that they would organize four teams, that the teams would play a double-round-robin schedule as a climax to the unit, and that the teams would practice skills as groups. This class took hold of their touch-football unit. It had meaning for them. The enthusiasm and zest for the skill drills was at a high level, and the games were a pleasure to behold, with the boys putting themselves into the activity with their whole hearts. These two classes seemed quite similar in makeup; the difference seemed to be due almost entirely to the method used.

It seems apparent that planning competition as a climax to a unit provides a splendid basis for letting pupils have a part in the planning. It is one of the best approaches to bringing the boys and girls into the planning, and it is one of the most effective means of making a unit-cooperative venture in which the teacher works with the students to accomplish determined goals. Such approaches cause a class to be with, not against, the teacher. The teacher helps the boys or girls to accomplish something which they have accepted as their own project.

BASES FOR SELECTING TEAMS

Best results accrue when competition is between teams of approximately equal ability. How then should teams for intraclass competition be selected? Two approaches are (1) distribute good, average, and poor players evenly among the various teams in a class, and (2) organize teams so that teams are composed of players about equal in ability, and schedule games only against teams similarly selected.

If a scheme of distributing good, average, and poor players evenly is to be successful, it is necessary for the more experienced and better players to help the less able during play and during practice. If the better players monopolize play rather than encourage development among the less experienced, this distribution of players will not work. On the other hand, if the better players share responsibility with the teacher for guiding the less able, then the learning situation becomes meaningful for all. Superior players feel satisfaction in playing leading roles, and they thrill at helping others. The less able performers appreciate help given by others. The whole group shares in cooperative learning experiences at their best. This represents education at a high level.

When a class or group is divided into teams or subgroups of players of like ability, it becomes easier to select logically arranged skill drills because the players involved are likely to need practice in the same skills at about the same level. There are advantages in this. Theoretically, at least, it enables students to progress at their own rate without being held back by a slower group or without being frustrated by a superior group.

Is it better to distribute good players evenly among several teams, or is it better to group according to ability? The answer is not entirely clear. Either or both may be appropriate. It depends upon the group, the school organization, and the encouragement or acceptance of teacher-student sharing.

INDIVIDUAL GAMES AND SPORTS

Let us clarify, immediately, the sense in which this heading is used. The specific activities discussed are archery, badminton, bowling, casting, golf, handball, tennis, table tennis, and wrestling. The word "sports" is included to cover archery, casting, and wrestling to which the word is more applicable than the word "games." They are grouped with the others, commonly called games, because they seem to fit together from the standpoints of program and teaching. Readers also should know that the authors intend to include dual and team aspects of these games and sports within the word "individual." Of course, when any game or sport is one player against one it is individual. Doubles in tennis, for instance, makes a dual game. Five participants against five, as in bowling, may be called a team game. Such imprecision of the word "individual" may be disapproved by some who are interested in exact taxonomy; it will be approved by those interested in groupings of activities according to similarities concerning program and teaching. The word is used broadly —not according to Webster—here.

Almost all educators agree that individual sports have value as school-program activities. Along with team games and other large-group activities, they help to meet the immediate needs of youngsters. They are healthful, wholesome, and enjoyable sports which contribute to favorable growth and to development of vigor and coordination. They help satisfy needs for recreation, provide socializing experiences, and may improve emotional adjustment and enhance feelings of well-being and self-mastery.

Besides helping to meet immediate needs of youngsters, individual sports are activities adults are likely to engage in over a long period of years. Of course, all physical education teachers would like to feel that each of their present students will embrace physical recreation or exercise during his adult life. Individual sports are quite likely to be so embraced by at least some who learn them as high school students. There does seem to be a tendency on the part of adults to participate in the sports they learned as youngsters. It also seems true that mature persons generally are reluctant to take the first steps necessary to learn a new game, although, of course, some do.

Individual games can be played on one's own terms: They are adaptable to individual vitality, energy, and vigor; they can be played strenuously or mildly according to needs. They adjust to individual differences in ability: Mediocre players can enjoy playing with others of similar ability; excellent players can find others who can challenge their abilities. A high school program which seeks to prepare its students for life will give opportunities to learn individual sports, to develop skills and interests in them.

The physical education teacher who desires to emphasize individual sports frequently encounters real difficulties because of the lack of adequate facilities. Tennis courts, handball courts, archery ranges, badminton courts, and golf courses are at a premium. Only a few schools have facilities sufficient to permit all members of a class to engage in full play in an individual sport at one time. It is difficult to arrange for sufficient whole experiences with these sports.

There are several approaches to solution of the difficulties presented by limited facilities. One is to combine several activities for simultaneous class participation in order that maximum use of available facilities may be made. Several individual activities progressing at one time may relieve the pressure, or the combining of an individual sport with activities in which larger numbers can satisfactorily be accommodated may solve the problem. This approach, of course, requires teaching procedures which allow individuals and small groups to take considerable responsibility for their own learning, with the teacher serving as a guide and source of help when it is needed.

Another approach is to develop interesting large-group or en masse instructional techniques which combine specific skill practice with playlike combinations of component parts of the game and with a limited amount of full play. Thus, in tennis, for instance, there may be en masse drill on specific strokes, stroking against a wall, which combines component parts into an interesting playlike situation, and occasional opportunity for full play on a court.

Another approach, a questionable one which is not highly recommended but which may be useful in some situations, is to introduce a sport without planning to give opportunity for full use during class time. Following this procedure a unit in golf might provide for (1) instruction in rules and etiquette, (2) mass instruction and practice in swinging clubs, and (3) attempts to stimulate interests in playing outside of school. If such a procedure results in play by a large number of boys and girls, it is worthwhile. The difficulty lies in the fact that such limited experiences are not likely to develop sufficient skill and interest to motivate students to play.

GENERAL SUGGESTION CONCERNING METHODS

The steps underlying method in the teaching of individual games are those that have been presented earlier, and adapted to team games in the previous section. They are concept of the whole, early performance of the whole activity, practice on parts as needed, performance of the whole, part practice as needed, whole performances, and so on, with analysis of performance throughout all whole play and part practice. The teacher of individual games can select specific methods by deciding the extent to which the specific method carries the learner through the steps in the most economical and interesting ways. Effectiveness of teaching individual games, like that of teaching all other motor skills, is determined by the extent to which the teacher helps the student to (1) create and modify concepts, (2) engage in meaningful and purposeful practice, and (3) analyze.

Generally speaking, individual games are learned most effectively by a method that places emphasis upon playing the whole game. Two aspects of individual games make emphasis upon whole play particularly advisable. One is that a learner can grasp a fairly adequate whole concept of these games rather rapidly. The other is that the playing of individual games provides a good deal of practice in the component movements. The situation is quite different from that in team games whose complexity requires considerable breaking into parts or whole-parts which are smaller than the whole game. It was pointed out in the discussion of the teaching of team games that playing a whole team game frequently provides insufficient opportunity for repetition of practice of movements in which skill needs to be developed. But in individual games considerable practice of the component skills usually occurs as the whole game is played. While playing tennis, for instance, the player repeats strokes and foot movements frequently.

The above statement should not be interpreted to imply that part practice is to be avoided. The rapidity with which full game play is introduced and the amount of time devoted to full play will depend upon the ability of players, facilities available, and class organization as well as upon teacher opinion concerning relative effectiveness of a whole method of teaching and learning. The key basis for decision concerning prescription of playing, or of specific part practice, is the answer to the question, "Is John or Mary learning satisfactorily during play? If not, what specific practice is needed?" When practice of isolated skills is arranged, teachers should be as certain as possible that it is meaningful and purposeful. Students should see the need for this practice; teachers should help them feel that practice of specific part skills represents an opportunity to improve their game.

Level of skill sought should be high enough to stimulate interest in the game and desire to play. Class instruction should seek continuous improvement for each student but does not need to aim at high levels of skill such as those sought by coaches and players intending to compete in tournaments and meets.

SPECIFIC SUGGESTIONS CONCERNING METHODS OF SELECTED ACTIVITIES

Suggestions for methods of organizing and teaching are made for each of several individual sports. Teachers who want information concerning techniques, tactics, rules, or equipment will, of course, consult sources which deal with the sport in question in some detail.

Archery A wholesome and interesting recreational activity, archery may be enjoyed by youngsters and older persons of both sexes. It is one of the sports which require only a small amount of instruction and practice to develop sufficient skill for enjoyment. Yet it challenges the most experienced and expert toward further improvement over a long period of years.

Teachers of archery can and should encourage continued participation outside of school by helping students see the opportunities for shooting at home, on vacant lots, in tournaments, and in hunting. If proper safety precautions prevail, targets and other shooting areas can be arranged in basements, attics, yards, and vacant lots. It is possible to adapt archery to almost any available space. If the space is small, reduction in the size of the target serves much the same purpose as shooting from regulation distances at standard-sized targets. Most available spaces can be utilized by construction of backstops of sufficient size behind the targets.

Some teachers favor grouping students homogeneously with respect to archery ability. Others feel that results are better when beginning archers have the example and advice of experienced performers in their own groups. It has been found very helpful to enlist the aid of advanced archers for helping beginners. Probably it is best to arrange practice groups of similar ability with the exception that one advanced archer be asked to join each beginning group and assist in the teaching when class composition makes it possible. For competitive shooting, relatively homogeneous grouping is advisable.

There should be enough targets so that all can keep active. A minimum of one target for every three archers is generally recommended. As is the case with most individual sports, it frequently is desirable to combine archery with other activities when equipment and facilities are not adequate for the accommodation of the entire class.

Movies, slides, charts, diagrams, and demonstrations by competent archers are excellent teaching aids. Brief lectures are in order for beginners. Information concerning the care of equipment as well as shooting technique should be given. Because of the possibility of accident, safety should be stressed. Students should be taught to make absolutely sure that no one is in a possible line of arrow flight.

School instruction should seek the development of interest in continued shooting in out-of-school situations. It has been pointed out that fundamental skills sufficient for enjoyment of archery can be taught rather quickly. The question of the appropriate length for an instructional unit arises. Many specialists in individual sports have recommended a unit of about 16 lessons. Although 16-lesson units are desirable, an 8- or 10-lesson presentation might be worthwhile when time is at a premium.

Interest may be stimulated through competing in rounds and ladder tournaments, through flight shooting (shooting for distance), clout shooting (target on ground), archery golf, and recreational archery with mixed doubles, and through keeping weekly scores. School archery clubs have created the desire for class instruction. Interest can be heightened by calling attention to private and community archery clubs, to hunting with bow and arrow, to shoots and meets sponsored by clubs or associations, and to the possibilities for home and neighborhood shooting.

Badminton The minimum skills necessary for enjoying the playing of badminton can be learned in a short time. The game also permits the development of expert skill that comes only with years of play. It is a recreational game that may be enjoyed in a social setting by everyone. Although the game may be learned outside of school, school instruction increases both the quantity and the quality of play in a community.

The extent to which badminton becomes a widespread sport depends to a considerable degree upon the acceptance or rejection of outdoor play. Opportunities for indoor play are limited, whereas almost everyone who so desires can engage in outdoor play because of the small amount of space and inexpensive equipment required. Encouragement of outdoor play is an important function of the badminton teacher who wishes to help make the game available to all. Highly skilled competitive play may require indoor facilities so that all wind interference will be eliminated, but outdoor recreational play using the heavier shuttlecock can be quite satisfactory. Teachers who themselves may prefer indoor play should be careful not to create general prejudice against outdoor play.

The extent to which group instruction is employed depends upon the availability of courts to accommodate all, as well as upon beliefs of the teacher concerning appropriate method. With sufficient courts available, giving most of the instruction as play progresses or during appropriate interludes constitutes one desirable method. The teacher circulates from court to court giving instruction as needed. With more players than courts will accommodate, certain mass techniques prove satisfactory. A continuous net may be stretched across a grassed or indoor area. Rows of players with partners facing on either side of the net practice proper grip, wrist exercises, watching the shuttle, footwork, basic strokes, and the like. Modified games can be devised for this arrangement, and it also proves valuable for learning short-placement skills and long volleying.

Stroking the shuttle against a wall is recommended highly by many badminton teachers. It provides practice that develops stroking, sharpens ability to follow the shuttle with the eye, and improves footwork. Such practice is especially appropriate when there are not enough courts to accommodate all players. It makes for frequent and rapid repetition of stroking movements.

While there is considerable reason to favor the whole method approach, the teacher should not neglect needed part practice. One of the dangers of continual competitive play rests on the tendency of players to avoid their weak strokes instead of working to improve them. A weak stroke should be practiced as a drill, with careful correction of basic faults.

In deciding relative emphasis upon playing and specific-part practice a basic consideration is interest of the player. Part practice that is needed, interesting, purposeful, and related to use produces good results. Part practice which is not well accepted by the learner is ineffective even though the teacher may believe it to be necessary.

Bowling Bowling is North America's most popular participant sport. What import does this fact have concerning school sponsorship and instruction? Some believe that such popularity demands school instruction to help more people receive greater satisfaction from bowling. Others feel that people will bowl without the impetus of school instruction, and therefore physical education programs might better concentrate their attention on less popular sports which have merits that are in more need of expansion. In determining whether or not bowling should be given a place in class instruction in individual schools, it is necessary to consider time available, facilities, and student interests. Although it may be sound judgment either to include or to exclude bowling from class programs in individual schools, it would seem that school sponsorship of this sport as an extraclass activity in the form of clubs or leagues is always appropriate.

Available time and facilities need to be considered. Some may consider it worthwhile to teach bowling in makeshift alleys in a gymnasium, using either regular balls or mock bowling balls. Others may believe that putting time and effort into other activities would be more valuable than bowling under makeshift conditions.

Some of the fundamentals of bowling may be taught in a gymnasium or out of doors without alley facilities. The steps and swing may be practiced, scoring and etiquette may be explained and demonstrated, and films may be shown. Although part practice without participation in the full activity generally is not advisable in the teaching of sports, it may be that such a limited introduction to bowling is worthwhile because a substantial number of students may follow with full participation on their own initiative. A satisfactory unit in bowling may be taught through the medium of group instruction at the school during regular class periods followed by school-sponsored alley bowling during extraclass time.

Since a minimum of about forty minutes is needed for bowling and since many schools must depend upon alleys some distance away, the problem of arranging sufficient time during the school day presents difficulties. Yet it is during regular school time that commercial alleys are more available for rental at favorable rates. Schools which have their own alleys, either in units designed specifically for bowling or laid out in gymnasiums, of course, do not face these difficulties.

Casting Bait and fly casting merit consideration. School sponsorship may increase the frequency as well as the intelligence and satisfaction with which one fishes and (or) casts at targets. Instruction may lead to participation in skish (casting at targets) tournaments or events sponsored by municipal recreation departments, clubs, or other organizations. Casting enriches a school program if it can be offered without impoverishing other worthwhile activities.

The ease with which arrangements for casting can be made on lawns or other relatively small open areas is one good reason for school sponsorship. Interests and skills developed in school may lead to home recreation for the entire family. Bicycle tires or barrel hoops make good targets; automobile tires will do. Rod, reel, line, and plug, either bait or fly, complete the equipment needed.

Organization for school sponsorship may be on the basis of extraclass recreational or club casting or instruction in classes or both. As is the case with many popular recreational activities, extraclass school sponsorship may lead to class instruction, which, of course, increases the number who participate. Casting may be organized as a sport in which all members of the class participate at one time or as one of several activities which progress simultaneously. Interests of the group as well as facilities and supplies available are bases for determining which procedure is advisable in specific situations.

When all members of a class work on casting, several groups may be formed with some casting while others practice grips and wrist action and consider applications to fishing. Bait casting may be practiced either indoors or outdoors. Fly casting seldom is appropriate for indoor instruction because a minimum of 80 feet is needed. The middle of an open area the size of a football field supplies a safe area for fly casting. Since bait casting requires only about one-half as much space as fly casting, indoor practice, especially in the beginning stages, may be appropriate. However, the sport seems better suited to out of doors.

Demonstrations and brief explanations should be followed immediately by student casting. More specific practice in parts such as grips and wrist action should be provided as needed. Competition against casters of similar ability as well as records of weekly scores add zest and motivation. Movies, pictures, and diagrams are useful aids. As in other sports, experienced students should be encouraged to help beginners.

Golf Should golf be included in the required school physical education program? Many will say yes, many no. Although golf can no longer be considered a rich man's game, it is still more costly both in money and time than most games. Local school program planners may be on sound ground when they decide to either include or exclude golf from the required program. However, golf always can be considered appropriate as an extraclass recreational, intramural, or interscholastic activity in schools which have needed resources. There is question, however, concerning cost to the student. In a public school, items for which students have to spend money should be held to a minimum. Probably all agree that students should not be required to purchase golf clubs in order to satisfy their physical education requirement. Less agreement exists, however, when the game is sponsored on an elective basis. Schools and teachers should seek to prevent pressures which create unhappiness and discontent among students whose parents cannot afford extra expenditures.

Group instruction methods prove particularly adaptable to golf. A good deal of practice in the several strokes is necessary to the development of skill in golf. However, since school facilities usually do not permit large numbers to hit long balls repeatedly, with attendant uncertainty of direction, it becomes necessary to depend upon practice in less natural situations which lack the advantages of practice in real gamelike settings. Procedures that have been used with success may be categorized as follows: (1) en masse practice of strokes or swings without balls or with cotton or plastic balls which do not go far, (2) en masse practice with regular golf balls, (3) division of the class into several groups which practice various skills, (4) combinations of the above three procedures, and (5) combinations as in step 4 with the addition of the opportunity to play on a course or partial course.

En masse practice of swings without the use of balls, with teacher suggestions addressed to the group and to individuals, helps develop the ability to swing properly. Musical accompaniment is an aid to the development of rhythmical swinging. Also, the occasional use of music for group practice provides a variation which students welcome. En masse swinging without balls has a place in group instruction if it is purposeful and meaningful to the class members. A distant advantage is that a large group can be handled in a small space.

Whole-group practice in hitting cotton or plastic balls is considered superior to swinging without balls because it more closely approximates the playing situation. Use of cotton or plastic balls requires more space than does practicing swings with no ball. However, such balls may be hit against a wall, so it is possible for two lines of students near the center of the long axis of a gymnasium to direct balls toward opposite walls. Also, two lines may be used with players hitting balls to opposite lines.

For practicing swings on floor surfaces either with or without balls, protection for floor and clubs is needed. Cocomats or doormats and small platforms built up to the level of the mats serve the purpose very well.

En masse practice with hard balls may be used on an outdoor field of sufficient size. Hard balls may be hit in a gymnasium if space is sufficient and if there is a flexible surface for the balls to hit. A canvas suspended from the ceiling or held in position by uprights is satisfactory. Driving cages are available from sporting goods dealers. Some schools fashion canvas driving cages which are quite satisfactory; the cost is small although considerable time and effort may be required. A substantial amount of practice hitting real balls is highly recommended when facilities permit this without waste of time while waiting for turns.

The division of a class into several groups which practice various skills is probably superior to en masse practice when the locale is a gymnasium or a small outdoor space. One group may drive, another chip, and a third putt. The availability of cages adds to practice possibilities for indoor classes. For example, part of the class can engage in putting, part swing at cotton balls, and the remainder hit hard balls in cages. Rotation is practical with use of any scheme of subgroups.

Some combination of the above three procedures—en masse practice of swings without balls and (or) with cotton or plastic balls, en masse practice with hard balls, and division of the class into groups—proves superior to exclusive use of any one of the three. A combination of formal methods, which emphasize form, and informal methods, which are more natural and emphasize end results, gives best results.

It is, of course, highly desirable to provide opportunity to play on a course or a partial course. Very successful units in golf have been taught in schools which have a few iron shot holes. Group instruction and division into subgroups with one group of from six to twelve playing the short course while others practice elsewhere has been found quite satisfactory. A three-hole course can be set up on a football or soccer field or similar area.

Handball Because it provides for the use of both hands and therefore both sides of the body, handball has advantages over racket games from the standpoint of development and use of musculature. As with other individual games, the intensity and tempo of play can be adjusted to the needs and desires of players. The repeated starting, running, stopping, and hitting movements develop attributes of agility, speed, and balance.

The game can be and is played both indoors and outdoors. Regulation four-wall courts are expensive and are not commonly found in schools. However, the one-wall game is very satisfactory, and one-wall courts may be installed in many gymnasiums simply by painting lines on the floor. Frequently a small gymnasium will accommodate four courts. This is not always the case because a smooth wall is required. Outdoor courts may be installed on any smooth cement- or asphalt-type surface by erecting a backboard or using the wall of a building and painting lines. One firm backboard that is smooth on both sides will accommodate two courts. Short side walls or partial side walls about 3 feet high and 3 to 6 feet long attached to the backboard add the interesting corner shot to the outdoor one-wall game.

Appropriate class organization for handball will vary according to the size of the class and available facilities. If there is one court for every four players, emphasis upon the whole method, learning the game as it is being played, is recommended. The teacher moves from court to court giving instruction and taking occasional turns at playing as needed. While playing, the teacher may direct his shots so that players get practice on the strokes most in need of improvement. Because the help of experienced players is valuable to beginners, student leaders are helpful.

Two different procedures work well when there are not sufficient courts to permit all to play at one time. One is to have the whole class work on handball, with some playing while others work on skills by stroking a ball against a wall or backboard. The other is to make handball one of several class activities. In many gymnasiums, a combination of handball with apparatus and tumbling stunts works out very well. One large high school which has only one handball court reports considerable success in developing carry-over interest in handball by simply giving a brief explanation of the game at the start of the year, displaying rules and suggestions for play, assigning four boys each period throughout the year to the handball court through use of a rotation scheme, giving some teacher help as handball is played, and encouraging boys to help one another. Each boy plays handball approximately ten or twelve times a year in this situation, and almost all the boys look forward with pleasure to their turn in the court.

Whatever method is chosen, the teacher will find students receptive if there is reasonable opportunity to play with others of near equal ability.

Tennis Though it was formerly a game for the economically favored few, many of modest means now enjoy tennis. Municipal and school courts, as well as reasonably priced rackets and balls, provide opportunities for extensive play. Because the game can be most vigorous or quite mild from the standpoint of exercise, it is adaptable to the energy status of individual players. Equally suitable for men and women, boys and girls, tennis ranks high as a carry-over sport. However, the development of skill sufficient to play with satisfaction requires more instruction and practice than is the case with badminton or handball.

If teachers, perhaps favoring a whole method, permit novices to play the full game, what happens is that there will be precious little practice because most of the time will be spent retrieving errant balls. Indeed the whole method is effective, but the largest whole most beginners in tennis can handle without undue confusion and waste of time is the very whole act of guiding and controlling the ball as it travels rather short distances. So early practice should be directed toward development of ball-control ability.

Through what practice procedures may beginners learn ball control effectively? Some of them are (1) bounce a ball on the floor with a racket, (2) bounce it into the air, (3) alternate steps 1 and 2, and (4) backboard practice, or volleying a ball against a wall. The latter is highly recommended for use both indoors and out. Practice is speeded up; a player hits the ball much more frequently than he would while playing a game because a wall always returns the ball. Approval by the United States Lawn Tennis Association of the use of boards for the development of playing skill indicates that tennis experts believe this practice effective for experienced players as well as novices.

Teaching of ball control should emphasize hitting the ball with the center of the racket. Of course practicing ball control should not be made monotonous. Interest-developing procedures include such things as counting how many bounces were made onto the floor, into the air, or against a wall without a miss, establishing goals such as 50 bounces on the floor or 25 against a wall, and competition among individuals or groups with those most successful at controlling the ball winning such competition.

After students have developed a reasonable ability to control the ball over short flight distances, consider having them play the game. Some teachers favor teaching strokes, including serving, as youngsters play, after they can control the ball reasonably well. Others believe that the various strokes should be practiced separately to a point of rather good performance before play under game conditions. Early play, with interpolation of specific practice as need is indicated, is recommended.

As with other individual sports, tennis may be taught to a whole class or to a group within a class. It is possible to teach tennis to all members of a large class by having students practice footwork, ball bouncing, racket swings, and the like. Among the skills possible to teach to a large group of as many as 60 students in an area the size of a tennis court are (1) grip, (2) ball tossing for service, (3) positions for body balance, (4) movements from one position to another, (5) footwork for forehand and backhand strokes, (6) swings without hitting a ball. The amount of time spent, or the emphasis placed upon large-group instruction indicated above, depends very much upon local situations. Decisions concerning allocation of time to such practice should be made with recognition of the fact that a primary objective of school tennis instruction is to develop interests which will lead to continued playing of the game. It is axiomatic that students who do not like tennis as it is taught are not likely to develop interests leading to continued play. Teachers eager to work for perfection should remember that although they are teaching required classes in tennis they are not training players for championship play, but rather attempting to develop activating interests.

Table tennis Suited to almost all ages, abilities, and capacities as well as to both sexes, table tennis ranks high as a recreational game. Tables are found in homes and recreation centers. Opportunities to play are many. Schools which give students an opportunity to learn and play this game encourage a wholesome leisure activity and help young people to enjoy themselves.

Almost all high schools have one or more tables for encouragement of recreational play. It no doubt is true that most people who play this game have learned by watching others play, by listening to a description of the main rules, including scoring, and then by playing with someone who knows how to play. Why, then, is this game appropriate for inclusion in a class program? First, it seems worthwhile to see that more young people learn the game, and second, to realize high-level skill possibilities, instruction is necessary.

Although some United States players have become top-notch competitors recognized internationally, many who play are hardly aware of the possibilities for expertness. It is true that playing the game without help from a teacher will improve skills. It also is true that instruction and practice are necessary for high-level development.

Demonstration matches by good players or films of championship play serve to increase the challenge of the game. The next steps in teaching may well be (1) to have students play after a brief description, (2) to help students who seem to need help most, and (3) to have all students practice various shots—serve, half-volley, push shot, chop stroke—followed by prescription of further specific practice for some and playing for others, according to need.

For practice on ball control and on basic strokes, backboards are helpful. Half tables can be placed against or near a smooth wall, and strokes can be practiced in a fashion similar to backboard practice in tennis.

As is the case with other individual games, table tennis may be taught in conjunction with other activities, and usually is. In some school situations it is good teaching procedure to detach a small number of students from other activities for the purpose of learning and playing table tennis. If this is done, a possible teacher tendency to let youngsters play without instruction should be avoided. Enough teaching to clear the path toward development of good playing ability is needed.

Wrestling The virile combat and contact sport of wrestling has many advantages as an activity for boys. It does a good deal to satisfy the need of many boys for matching their strength and skill directly with that of others. It develops attributes of strength, balance, speed, and agility, and may also develop courage and allay fears. An added advantage is that boys can be matched according to weight and age. The small boy has a chance, as frequently is not the case in football, another common school sport of a direct-contact nature.

Contact sports develop physical ruggedness. In our "triple A, T" civilization, automobiles, airplanes, automation, and tension, with its many softening influences, there is need for such sports. Wrestling is one of the few which can be recommended. Combative contests and football are others. Football is geared largely for participation by a few boys of superior strength, size, and ability. Boxing, a sport which is approved by a few physical educators, is a highly questionable activity. It is the only one of our sports which accepts the infliction of punishment upon a partner or an opponent as an objective. Because of the danger of brain injury, because the sport is not appropriate for participation unless conditions are rigidly controlled, and because surrounding influences frequently are not wholesome, boxing is not recommended as a school sport or physical education activity. Wrestling, then, commands attention as one of the few acceptable sports of a body-contact nature.

Group instruction can be interesting and effective when occasional opportunities for competition are provided. Because of limited facilities it usually is necessary to use large-group procedures if wrestling is taught to all members of a class at the same time. Members of the class should be paired with partners of approximately equal weight and height. Although height is of secondary importance, it should be considered for instructional purposes because fairly equal height, arm length, and leg breakdowns, reverses and escapes, pinning combinations, and counters to length are of value in the teaching and learning of some maneuvers.

Starting with the referee's position on the mat, it is possible to teach a large number of boys in a fairly small space. In this situation it is advisable to have wrestlers practice maneuvers against opponents in unison. Performance should be either by numbers, on count, or all should start in the same direction. Although some may object to this much rigidity or formal control of movement, such procedure has the advantage of permitting many to practice safely, without being kicked, elbowed, or rolled on by a classmate.

Starting with the referee's position, of course, eliminates the on guard and standing referee's positions, as well as takedowns. Is it desirable to teach a unit in wrestling without teaching these? Would not failure to teach them give a student an objectionably incomplete experience? It is true that some physical educators, including wrestling coaches who do not teach physical education classes, feel that skills from the upright position should be taught. Most persons who teach wrestling to large groups in physical education classes find it satisfactory to eliminate the upright position. Time is saved, many more students can actively participate, and safety is enhanced. Boys seem happy with that plan, when they spend a good deal of their practice time performing various maneuvers in unison, if they are permitted some competition wrestling and some combative contests to help maintain interest.

What kind of competitive experiences are best? Short bouts, starting from the referee's position on the mat; a coin flip should determine which wrestler gets the top position. What kind of combative contests are most interesting? The United States Navy [2] recommends modified combative games adapted from wrestling techniques. Among these contests or games are collar and elbow wrestling, sidehold wrestling, Indian, ring, leg, and stick wrestling, and rooster fighting.

SUMMARY

Underlying principles and techniques of method must be adapted to each of the separate activities commonly found in physical education programs. Each physical activity presents unique teaching problems, and effective teaching depends upon the ability to translate basic principles of method into procedures practical for individual activities.

Major considerations in teaching team games which consist of a number of separate skills and other learning elements include creating concept of the whole, providing for early performance of the whole activity, providing for drill in smaller parts as needed, providing for student participation in planning, organizing, and managing, and providing for recreational play of the activity.

Individual sports help to satisfy immediate needs for recreation for high school students, as well as to provide learning which is likely to carry over into adult life.

To solve difficulties presented by facility limitations in offering individual sports in secondary schools, several activities can be offered at one time with the class divided among different types of activities. Individual sports may be combined with others which accommodate large numbers, or group instruction techniques can be introduced with modified play situations.

Generally speaking, individual games are learned most effectively by methods which place emphasis upon playing the whole game. Tennis is an exception; putting novices on courts to play before they can control a ball reasonably well is a waste of time. Wrestling also is an exception; in this sport each maneuver is in itself a unified whole.

Questions and problems for discussion

1. Identify several desirable objectives in the area of social development, and propose teaching procedures designed to assure achievement of each through the medium of team games.

[2] Clifford P. Keen, Charles M. Speidel, and Raymond H. Schwarz, *Championship Wrestling*, 4th ed. written for the *V-Five Association of America*, rev. by Raymond H. Schwarz, United States, Naval Institute, Annapolis, Maryland, 1964, pp. 203–205.

2. What bases would you use in determining whether to advise or prescribe (a) drill on individual skills or (b) practice through play for a student participating in a volleyball unit? Do the same for a student participating in a badminton unit.

3. List probable detrimental results of overemphasis upon the use of competition as a motivator in physical education activities.

4. Propose a plan for introducing casting into a high school program which never has sponsored this activity. Select and describe the school for which your plan is proposed.

5. List problems occasioned by a teaching procedure which calls for simultaneous participation in several different types of activities by members of a given class. Propose a solution for each problem identified.

6. Prepare a wrestling unit for a class of 36 sophomore boys, 30 of whom participated in a 12-lesson wrestling unit as freshmen. Select your own length of unit and of period, or, if you prefer, plan for a 15-lesson unit and 55-minute periods. Twelve hundred square feet of mats are available.

Selected references

Ainsworth, Dorothy S., et al.: *Individual Sports for Women,* 4th ed., W. B. Saunders Company, Philadelphia, 1963.

American Association for Health, Physical Education, and Recreation: Skills Test Manuals: *Football for Boys, Softball for Boys, Basketball for Boys,* National Education Association, Washington, D.C., 1966.

Barnes, Mildred J., Margaret G. Fox, M. Glody Scott, and Pauline Loeffler: *Sports Activities for Girls and Women,* Appleton-Century-Crofts, Inc., New York, 1966.

Menke, Frank G.: *The New Encyclopedia of Sports,* 3d ed., A. S. Barnes and Co., Inc., New York, 1963.

Meyer, Margaret H., and Marguerite M. Schwartz: *Team Sports for Women,* 4th ed., W. B. Saunders Company, Philadelphia, 1965.

Mitchell, Elmer D. (ed.): *Sports for Recreation and How to Play Them,* A. S. Barnes and Co., Inc., New York, 1952.

Seaton, Don Cash, et al.: *Physical Education Handbook,* Prentice-Hall, Inc., Englewood Cliffs, N.J., 1965.

Shaw, John H., et al.: *Team Sports for Men,* Wm. C. Brown Company, Publishers, Dubuque, Iowa, 1964.

Shaw, John H., Carl A. Troester, and Milton A. Gabrielson: *Individual Sports for Men,* Wm. C. Brown Company, Publishers, Dubuque, Iowa, 1964.

Stanley, D. K., and I. F. Waglow: *Physical Education Activities Handbook,* Allyn and Bacon, Inc., Englewood Cliffs, N.J., 1966.

chapter 9

TECHNIQUES FOR ACTIVITIES OTHER THAN GAMES

INTRODUCTION

This chapter discusses procedures applicable to teaching activities other than team and individual games and sports. Not all possible activities are included. The authors chose to discuss apparatus and tumbling, basic movement, combative contests, conditioning activities, group games and relays, posture, rhythms and dance, rope jumping, swimming, and track and field athletics, because they are used frequently in high school programs and because each presents a different teaching problem.

A general characterization of the value of each activity is followed by suggestions for teaching. As in the previous chapter dealing with games, there will be no detailed treatment of the activities as such. Readers wishing to study subject matter aspects of the several activities should consult sources dealing with them in depth. Several will be found at the end of this chapter.

APPARATUS AND TUMBLING

Apparatus activities develop upper-body musculature more than do many of our games, sports, and other running activities. The necessary localized strengthening of arms and shoulders may be achieved through hanging, climbing, swinging, and other activities which require support of body weight with hand grips.

Tumbling is especially valuable for the development of the integration of skills in body manipulation. Since he is agile and flexible and possesses excellent powers of balance, the tumbler is able to execute movements which require a relation to other movements in sequence and timing, and which require integration of many body movements.

The interest of American youth in apparatus and tumbling activities is somewhat spotty. These sports are so popular in many high schools that qualified teachers, especially those qualified to coach interscholastic teams, are in short supply. Some schools include neither gymnastics nor tumbling in their program, and others provide rather meager opportunities for students. It seems unmistakably true that boys and girls develop interests when schools give good instruction and generous opportunities for participation.

In the teaching of both apparatus and tumbling, success for all in simple stunts and progression to more advanced work for those showing aptitude should be goals. Many interesting and challenging maneuvers may be performed on bars, rings, horses, bucks, trampolines, and mats.

The setting of a good model by demonstration and (or) pictures is especially important because a verbal description of body positions and movements is difficult to comprehend. Ability to demonstrate, to show how, is an asset for teaching gymnastics and tumbling. One lacking such ability can compensate by using movies, loop films, or pictures, or by having students or invited guests demonstrate by asking questions which lead students toward a concept of the performance.

Teaching method should assure ample practice for all. Waste of time while waiting turns should be avoided. Generally speaking, not more than five students should be assigned to a given piece of apparatus or to one mat station at one time, and assigning more than ten almost always results in waste of time. However, it sometimes is desirable for large groups to watch demonstrations, view movies, and listen to explanations for the purpose of gaining information and building concepts of movements to be performed.

Work at several locations should progress simultaneously. Squad organization with student leaders and with a considerable amount of student responsibility for their own activity is effective for teaching gymnastics. The teacher moves from group to group, making suggestions, giving approval, criticizing, and demonstrating as he deems advisable.

Interest may be motivated by (1) helping individuals set attainable goals, (2) helping students see their progress, (3) encouraging progression to more difficult and challenging stunts as ability develops, and (4) arranging competition for individuals and groups. Interest wanes rapidly for those who feel that they are not succeeding. Hence it is important to start with easy stunts and to help some feel that they have achieved a worthwhile goal when they have mastered a movement which might seem very elementary to the teacher and to some of the students.

It usually is necessary to provide for a wide range of individual abilities in gymnastics and in tumbling. Class members lose interest when asked to repeat many times stunts that they feel they have mastered. Progression to more challenging movements is indicated as ability develops. Since some will learn much more rapidly than others, the teacher should not only permit but also encourage various members of the class to work on different stunts rather than require all to perform the same activity. It is helpful to present units which specify and describe a minimum number of relatively easy stunts which all are expected to learn and in addition describe a large number of optional stunts which will challenge superior performers.

Competition with others, as well as with one's own previous performance, adds interest. Opportunities to compete, individually and in groups, add interest and speed up learning. A unit can include plans for an intrasquad gymnastics meet or two. In some cases it might be possible to arrange a meet between two classes as a culminating activity.

BASIC MOVEMENT

What is basic movement? Women readers will have more answers than will men. Some regard basic movement as an area, a group of activities which should be taught as such in courses, classes, or units with basic movement as *the* subject matter; they also feel that problem solving and mechanics should be emphasized.

The importance of problem solving, of discovery, in the learning of movements can hardly be overemphasized. When one discovers for himself, when he gets an idea and a feel which for him represent creativity, the learning is highly meaningful and satisfying. Retention of such learning is good. It is likely to stay with one forever. Better yet, it provides a base for further learning and, in one sense, it may be said that retention is 100 percent plus as additional skills pyramid.

It is true, of course, that learning by discovery seems to take much time. The question is does it take an extravagant amount of time or is it time saving because of the eventual results. There is a similarity between the time required for such discovery learning and the time needed for solving problems through a democratic process of group problem solving. There are times for learning movement through discovery and times for shortcuts toward skills needed, as, for instance, in learning the game of softball.

Some feel that it is important to teach basic positions and movements which are common to almost all physical skill performance, but that instead of teaching basic movement as an entity in itself it is better to make it a part of teaching games, sports, gymnastics, rhythms, aquatics, dance, and conditioning activities.

One succinct definition of basic movement as an area in itself is given by Souder and Hill: [1] it ". . . provides a developmental sequences of activities basic to the more complex and coordinated activities of sports, games, and dance." In their book, which followed some years of experimental and televised teaching of basic movement, they classified basic movement into several categories including (1) exploration of basic skeletal framework, (2) flexing, extending, and hyperextending movements, (3) abducting, adducting, and lateral flexing movements, (4) movement sequences, (5) muscle awareness, (6) muscles in activity, (7) muscles in relaxation, (8) gravity and balance, (9) motion and force, and (10) manipulation of objects.

Those who approach teaching basic position and movement as part of an activity would be quite concerned with several of the above ten categories but might well be unaware of, or unconcerned with, others. Gravity and balance would be given high priority; motion and force would be emphasized, at least in some activities; muscle awareness, muscles in activity, and manipulation of objects would get attention.

Broer [2] studied the effect of instruction in general basic skills upon skills of volleyball, basketball, and softball, emphasizing problem solving and understanding of mechanics. Two seventh-grade classes were taught experimental basic skills; three seventh-grade classes served as control groups. After instruction in basic skills, and with less instruction than the control groups in the sports themselves, the experimental subjects scored significantly higher than the control groups in the skill tests of all three sports—volleyball, basketball, and softball.

Broer found that the experimental groups worked diligently when given problems to solve and that they shared their conclusions with members of other groups within the class. She also found lively discussion and rarely needed to give specific methods or reasons because the girls solved the movement problems themselves.

In another study Broer found basic skills instruction effective in the

[1] Marjorie A. Souder and Phyllis J. Hill, *Basic Movement, Foundations of Physical Education,* The Ronald Press Company, New York, 1963, preface.

[2] Marion R. Broer, "Effectiveness of a General Basic Skills Curriculum for Junior High School Girls," *Research Quarterly,* the American Association for Health, Physical Education, and Recreation, 29:379–388, December, 1958.

case of college freshmen women of low motor ability.[3] Compared to a matched or control group, the experimental group in basic skills instruction improved general motor ability, attitude toward physical education, and skill and knowledge in various activities.

Among the persons who have made basic position and movement a part of teaching other activities is Walter Verson, Associate Professor of Physical Education, University of Illinois, Chicago Circle. At clinics and convention programs he has presented a plan for teaching sports of all kinds which includes the same basic position and basic first movements for each and every sport. The position he finds basic has been given different names and descriptions. Mr. Verson calls it the "basic" position and the "hit" position. It has been described as similar to the on-guard position in wrestling; some refer to it as balanced, ready to move in any direction, others as coiled, ready to strike. Whatever it is called, it is true that from this basic position the body may move in any direction.

Coaches and teachers of almost all sports, perhaps especially those working with basketball and the racket sports, have taught a balanced-and-ready-to-move position for many years and have insisted upon practice of starts in various directions. Running has been taught as a basic skill for all sports.

Have teachers and coaches, then, been teaching basic movement for many years? To some extent, yes. However, if the reader accepts the Souder and Hill definition literally, the answer is no. Although for years teachers have been working for ease and control of movement, it is true that rather recently United States women physical educators have developed basic movement to a greater degree. They have approached it with greater analysis; they have studied movements basic to physical education activities, gone into more detail, and taught basic movement as a subject or a unit rather than only as part of instruction in other activities.

What teaching procedures are appropriate for basic movement? If it is taught in connection with other activities, it follows that such instruction should be worked into teaching methods such as those described for team and individual games in the previous chapter, and those described for various other activities later in this chapter.

Three teaching procedures may be recommended for teaching basic movement to a class. The first is to teach the whole class as a group, with at least some en masse instruction in which each and every student would respond to teacher questions or directions. It seems wise to start with this approach. There must be a considerable teaching of knowledge;

[3] Marion R. Broer, "Evaluation of a Basic Skills Curriculum for Women Students of Low Motor Ability at the University of Washington," *Research Quarterly*, 26:15–24, March, 1955.

the instructor must give more information and ask more questions than would be the case when leading calisthenics. One teaches what the skeletal framework will permit and also the principles of flexing, extending, abducting, adducting, movement sequences, balance, relaxation, force, manipulation, anatomy, kinesiology. These concepts should be taught during student tryout of various positions and movements.

A second method is to teach basic movement to groups within a class. After some half dozen class days of whole-class same activity, groups might be formed on the basis of need. Some may have progressed rapidly, others slowly; some may need more detailed instruction in certain categories; others may be quite advanced. The third procedure recommended is to combine the above two. There might be whole-class work or group work for part of a period, or it might be better in some situations to have whole-class work and work in smaller groups on alternate days. Whichever procedure is selected should include attention to individuals who are doing very well and who therefore can provide a sort of model, and to others who may need additional help from the teacher.

COMBATIVE CONTESTS

Hand wrestling, rooster fighting, hand pulling, shoulder pushing, drake fighting, neck pulling, Indian wrestling, and a host of other relatively simple contests are fun activities, particularly for boys. The physical attributes of strength, coordination, and balance are developed as friendly antagonists vie in pushing, pulling, feinting, dodging, and balancing. Combative contests offer appealing personal-combat competition in simple and easily organized form and require little or no equipment. Every member of a large group may secure a substantial amount of pleasant exercise in a short time.

Teaching procedure may either allow students to select their own partners or arrange partners by having a class line up according to height, and then open order. If the open-order scheme is used, a few adjustments usually are needed to compensate for inequities in weight, strength, and ability. A given number of rounds for each bout should be set. The selection of an odd number of rounds, usually three, five, or seven, facilitates the determination of a winner.

Both formal and informal procedures are appropriate. When the formal procedure is used, all members of the group start a bout at the same time. The teacher signals "ready" and "start" by word, whistle, or gesture. The informal method calls for students to signal "ready" and "start." When it is used, there should be groups of three rather than pairs. One of the three serves as starter or signal giver while the other two compete. Rotation permits all to participate in the contests.

Because of the large amount of strenuous exercise and because high interest is not likely to be maintained over a long period of time, it usually is advisable to devote only a part of a given class period to combative contests. Eight to twelve minutes is suggested. These contests are particularly appropriate when combined with activities which demand only mild exercise.

CONDITIONING ACTIVITIES

An element of body conditioning is present in all vigorous physical education activities. Hence it is not possible to segregate conditioning activities as such with anything like complete accuracy. No attempt to do so is made here. Neither is there an attempt to discuss all the activities which might place dominant emphasis upon conditioning of the body. Rather, there is a discussion of representative types of activities commonly engaged in for the principal purpose of developing body flexibility, balance, strength, and endurance; this conditioning permits one to pursue arduous physical tasks with a minimum of effort and fatigue.

CALISTHENICS

Calisthenics probably are used more than any other conditioning activity. Frequently employed as warmup movements, they may be mild or strenuous, depending upon the speed and duration of the performance and upon the exercises selected. Calisthenics become purposeful self-activity when participants see a need to perform them in order to achieve a goal regarded as worthwhile. The teacher should help students see a relationship between the exercises and the desired goal of a well-conditioned body.

Teaching procedure should ensure a good model. Snappy demonstration and a minimum of description by the teacher are advisable. Occasional leadership by students increases interest and quality of response. Because musical accompaniment contributes to pleasant rhythmical movement, teachers should give serious consideration to piano or record accompaniment.

An exercise new to the students should be demonstrated, named, and briefly described. Naming alone or naming with a once-through performance by the leader suffices to set the stage for an exercise already known to the class. Rather than remain in front of the class at all times, the leader should move about among the performers part of the time, giving cues and help as needed. Although the leader should perform with the class at times, it is not necessary for him to do so throughout.

Calisthenics may be presented formally with the leader counting or with music setting the rhythm as the class responds in unison. They may be presented informally by having the class members perform at their own volition. Informal methods are particularly appropriate for performance of a prescribed series of exercises which have previously been learned. It is believed that informal performance increases the probability that students will use the exercises as conditioners during out-of-school time and as adults.

Exercises such as pushups should be prescribed according to individual differences. For some members of a class, 20 pushups may produce no overload and therefore provide no development and no contribution to strength or endurance. For some class members 10 pushups might be an overload and 20 would be impossible. Hence, if included among calisthenic exercises such exercises should be adjusted to individuals rather than taught on the basis of a common prescription such as 20 repetitions for all.

CIRCUIT TRAINING

A well-balanced workout for a physical education class may be arranged by having students participate in rapid succession in a group of activities which comprise a circuit. An obstacle course can provide a circuit. The teacher should select alternating exercises so that completion of a circuit provides hard work for a group of muscles and then rest for this group as other muscle groups are taxed. For instance, a circuit providing a quite balanced workout and requiring a minimum of equipment might include the following:

1. Agility exercises such as heel-click, jump-over-leg, and hopping.
2. Balance activities such as squat balance, handstand, and headstand.
3. Activities providing circulatory and respiratory load or overload such as running, jumping rope, hopping, or other movements which exercise the whole body.
4. Flexibility activities including arm circles, leg circles, wrestlers bridge, touching toes, and touching forehead with toes.
5. Muscle-endurance exercises such as pushups, situps, half-levers, and hyperextensions.

GRASS DRILL

The grass drill, probably originated by the late Frank Cavanaugh as a conditioner for his football teams, provides a fast-moving and vigorous workout which is interesting to boys and girls alike. It is a position-changing drill. As the instructor calls a body position, class members move to it as rapidly as possible. Good selection of a variety of positions and movements from one to another among them ensure exercises for various muscle groups.

Among appropriate positions are the following: (1) stand, (2) front (front support or front-leaning rest–support on hands and toes), (3) back (lying on back), (4) sit, (5) prone, (6) squat, and (7) up (running in place). Moving from back to sit provides a situp, from prone to front a pushup, and from stand to half squat and return a knee bend. Movements from prone or front to back, and vice versa, are lengthwise, not a mere rolling over. In making these movements, the performer comes to a near-sitting position and supports his weight on his hands as he moves his legs between his arms on the way to the new position.

The stimulation of group, rather than individual, performance seems to add zest to grass drills. Although the name of the activity might imply limitation to outdoor use, the grass drill may be used either indoors or out. The teacher or leader may either call out the names of the desired positions or perform the movements as signals to the class. Any open-order formation in which there are three paces in each direction between performers is adequate. A circle formation seems best when space permits. Care should be exercised to avoid overstrenuousness. A five-minute drill provides a strenuous workout.

Student leaders are recommended because of added enthusiasm and variation which usually results. Students may lead either the whole class or several smaller groups. Since the movements are learned quickly, little or no special training for leaders is required.

INTERVAL TRAINING

Used a good deal by track coaches, this form of exercise conditions the body largely through running, which may be the best exercise. Teacher and student decide upon a beginning interval running distance and pace schedule. For instance, a starting schedule for a high school sophomore might be as follows: distance, 150 yards; number of repetitions, six to eight; rest interval between each 150-yard run, 90 seconds. The target, or predicted, time for each of the 150-yard runs might be set before or after the first session of interval running. Repeated sessions of running, with rest intervals, increases endurance and ability to run. Revision of distances, number of repetitions, and length of rest intervals may be made as teacher and runner believe desirable.

ASTRONAUT ACTIVITIES

Astronaut activities, sometimes called ranger or commando, are effective for body conditioning, for development of endurance, coordination, and balance. A variety of movements such as walking, running, walking with knees in half-bent position, elephant walking, hopping, skipping, jumping for height, jumping for distance, walking on toes, and leapfrog jumping are performed at commands or signals from the leader. Continuously moving circles or rectangles of performers, with about three paces between each, constitute proper formations for these activities. Teacher or student may lead from the center or from the lead position in the formation.

When the center position is used for leading, commands may be given or performance of the movement may be the signal to start. When the leapfrog movement or others such as crawling between legs or dashing around a partner are employed, it is necessary to have the class numbered or counted off. For these movements a whistle is an excellent signal. In the leapfrog movement, for instance, at the first signal odd numbers squat and even numbers jump. At each succeeding signal odd numbers and even numbers exchange movements. When the leader takes a position in the formation, signals for new movements are given by simply performing. The class acts in follow-the-leader style. Leadership from a position in the formation is satisfactory for movements like hopping and bear walking but may not be used for leapfrog or other movements requiring teamwork.

RESISTIVE EXERCISES

Three forms of resistive exercises are:

1. Isotonic—weights are lifted repeatedly at a moderate rate of speed; they are added as strength increases. This is usually called weight training.
2. Isometric—muscle contraction without movement; the muscle holds or builds up tension without shortening or lengthening.
3. Speed method—muscle groups are contracted rapidly using relatively light weights, or only against the resistance of the body itself.

A program of only resistive exercise does not develop all-around fitness. Cardiorespiratory endurance is not developed; neither are the favorable body responses which accompany significant improvement in circulatory function.

Isotonic resistive exercise, or weight training as it commonly is called, not only is a popular curricular activity in secondary schools but also attracts many students when sponsored as an extracurricular activity. Further, weight training ranks high among physical education activities which carry over into out-of-school life.

Excerpts from a description and outline of an Oak Park and River Forest, Illinois, high school, weight-training program will show characteristics of an isotonic exercise program and imply suggestions for teaching. A ten-page description of this program, prepared by Robert J. Wehrli, outlines a three-level program, gives suggestions, instruction, and directions to students. An outline of the main headings and a brief description of what is included follows.

Introduction, which deals with elements of physical ability, overload, warmup, exercises to correlate with weight-training, and general nature of the program.

Rules and Regulations, which deals with necessary routine procedures.

Routine of Program, sets a general pattern for a workout.

Safety Suggestions.

Calisthenics for Weight Training.

Three Levels of Weight Training, describes the basic, power, and advanced levels; names and describes exercises for the basic level and conditions for advancement to the power level; proceeds to describe the eight exercises of the power level; indicates conditions for entry into the advanced level; and describes the dozen exercises which are included in the advanced level.

Three Individual Record Forms, one for each level, which provide for daily entries showing accomplishment; also individual record forms with entries for name, age, year in school, height, weight, and measurements of neck, chest, arms, legs, etc.

Teaching methods for weight training should assure that students know their exercises, including order, amount of weight, and number of repetitions, know how to record their performances on their own record cards, recognize the need for compliance with safety precautions, and be able to care for equipment. Students should take primary responsibility for their own workouts. Teachers should help as needed, lend encouragement, use motivating procedures including recognition and approval of progress, see that students are using their time well, and prevent misbehavior. Displays of instructions, diagrams, posters, etc., in easy-to-see places represent excellent visual aids. Some resourceful teachers display the whole basic program in letters large enough to be easily read from any location in the teaching station.

The isometric exercise, contraction without movement, in which the muscle holds or builds up tension without shortening or lengthening, became popular in the United States shortly after reports of work done by E. A. Müller and his associate Th. Hettinger at the Max Planck Institut für Arbeitsphysiologie in Dortmund, Germany. A report that German scientists had learned that one maximum contraction per day held for six seconds will develop strength as fast as strength can be developed stirred interest. One might say that isometrics took the country by storm. Articles appeared in magazines of wide circulation; proponents were given radio and television time; books were published; devices and equipment such as straps and bands were marketed; coaches of various sports and physical educators introduced programs for strength-developing purposes; professional baseball and football players embraced isometrics; and some professional teams employed a person to prescribe exercises which emphasized isometrics.

Before dealing directly with the value of isometrics, let us view the developments which undergirded the great interest. This may be done through selected words of Arthur H. Steinhaus, who served as a subject for the experiments conducted by Müller and Hettinger. Readers may wonder why a teaching book gives considerable space to this. It is because of the conflicting opinions and feelings regarding isometrics.

Steinhaus, writing on the subject of overload, says:

> And in 1953 E. A. Müller of Germany surprised us with his discovery that as little as six seconds of static contraction once per day is enough to increase strength, provided that it is of appropriate intensity.[4]

Dealing with the subject of training for strength Steinhaus remarks:

> For more than a decade Erich A. Müller of the Max Planck Institute für Arbeitsphysiologie experimented in Dortmund, Germany, to discover the fastest way to increase muscle strength and the essential factors necessary to produce hypertrophy. Success came when, toward the end of this period, he began to work with one of his students, Th. Hettinger, on static contractions in which intensity and duration were easily measured.[5]

Then, after describing the experimental procedures used, Steinhaus continues:

> A number of significant findings emerged:
>
> 1. Muscle strength increases an average of five percent per week when the training load is as little as one-third of maximal strength.
> 2. Muscle strength increases more rapidly with increasing intensity of training load up to about two-thirds of maximal strength. Beyond this, increase in training load has no further effect.
> 3. One practice period per day in which the tension is held for six seconds results in as much increase in strength as longer periods (up to full exhaustion in 45 seconds) and more frequent periods (up to seven per day).[6]

[4] Arthur H. Steinhaus, *Toward an Understanding of Health and Physical Education*, Wm. C. Brown Company, Publishers, Dubuque, Iowa, 1963, p. 43.
[5] *Ibid.*, p. 135.
[6] *Ibid.*, p. 135.

Six other findings are not quoted. They deal with cause for increase in strength, correlations, and a ceiling on development of strength. In addition, Steinhaus summarizes later findings communicated to him by a letter from Müller dated June 6, 1954, which dealt with the amount of exercise needed to maintain strength after it has been developed.

Steinhaus, under the heading Training for Strength in Sports, Overload Not Isometrics, comments concerning the excitement about isometrics:

> Now that strength magazines have begun to talk isometric contraction and *Sports Illustrated* calls it I.C., everyone is getting excited, as though there were some special virtue in contraction without movement.[7]
>
> There is no special magic in I.C. or isometric contraction. Popular magazines have confused the issue. A muscle will grow in strength whenever it is overloaded whether in concentric, eccentric or isometric contraction.[8]
>
> Müller and Hettinger used isometric contractions in their now famous experiments because it is easy to measure, graduate and control this kind of exercise. It was their purpose to discover just how much is overload, i.e., how much was needed to make a muscle grow stronger.[9]

Steinhaus shows that the reports of Müller's and Hettinger's research should be accepted not as definitive but as reports of progress in research. In a note added to a 1954 paper before publication in his collected works, Steinhaus says:

> *Note:* Since this paper was written the Dortmund workers . . . have made further findings as follows:
>
> 1. Oxygen deficit is not the stimulus for muscular growth as originally reported. The actual stimulus is unknown but in some way related to tension.
> 2. There is no magic in the "six second" holding rule. They now believe the contraction should be held for a period that is about ten percent of the maximum time it can be held. A maximal contraction that usually can be held just under ten seconds need be held only one second once a day to induce maximal increase in strength.[10]

To say the least, the last quote from Steinhaus should cause people who are "sold" on isometrics with six-second contractions to stop, look, and listen. Of course we should appreciate ongoing research, but we also

[7] *Ibid.*, p. 322.
[8] *Ibid.*, p. 323.
[9] *Ibid.*, p. 323.
[10] *Ibid.*, p. 136.

should be a bit careful about it. We should stay "on board" rather than go overboard.

Are isometrics valuable? Yes, they will develop strength. So will any exercise which produces overload or which taxes muscles harder than their customary work. Isometrics will develop only strength. They do little or nothing for endurance; they do nothing at all for circulatory efficiency; and they have no effect upon cardiovascular development.

If one chooses to use isometrics for rehabilitation or for specific muscular strengthening it is necessary to individualize, to diagnose, and prescribe. To do this effectively and without danger of affecting the wrong muscles, one needs to know kinesiology well. After prescription and direction to the student, the teacher needs to supervise or to check occasionally.

Isometrics may be taught to a full-class group for brief periods for the purpose of generally strengthening various muscular groups. En masse teaching utilizing a response-to-command method serves in such a situation.

Speed resistive exercises help to develop both strength and muscular endurance. Light weights may be used, or only the body and gravity may provide the resistance. Teaching procedures recommended for calisthenics are equally appropriate for the speed method of resistive exercise.

A considerable number of studies concerning isometric and isotonic exercises have been reported in United States physical education literature. Rather than to review them it seems appropriate for a text on teaching to review only one comprehensive study which comments about others. McCraw and others studied the effectiveness of the three methods of resistive exercises for developing strength and endurance. The investigators summarized in part by saying: "The findings of this study relative to strength seemingly are similar to those of other investigations. In most instances where the isotonic and isometric methods have been compared, no significant differences were found and strength was improved by both programs." [11]

After pointing out conflicting results of previous studies concerning the development of endurance the report of the study says:

It is well known that as the muscle increases in strength it can move the same load longer and more readily. Thus it would appear that strength and endurance are closely related. . . . While the contention may hold in contractions against a constant load, it does not appear to be true for repeated contractions

[11] Lynn W. McCraw, principal investigator, and Stan Burnham, associate director, *Resistive Exercises in the Development of Muscular Strength and Endurance*, Cooperative Research Project No. 1979, The University of Texas, Austin, 1963, p. 83.

against a resistance that is related to the strength of the muscle. . . . Furthermore, the isometric program produced considerable improvement in strength, whereas there was a decrease in scores for the endurance tests. On the other hand the isotonic and speed groups . . . exhibited substantial improvement in endurance.[12]

McCraw and his associates do not criticize isometrics as the authors of this text did above. They look with favor upon the use of isometrics for strength development. After a discussion of the low cost of isometric equipment in comparison to the higher cost of weights for isotonics, they say: "On the basis of the findings of this study and in view of the above considerations, it would seem that a combination of isometric and speed exercises would be best for a practical classroom situation." [13]

RUNNING AND HIKING

For running, gradually increasing distances and speeds may be employed as individuals develop condition. Running tracks, laps around a gymnasium, or courses of the cross-country type may be used. Novelties, such as changing directions, zigzagging, and running to or around markers, add interest. Leadership of the follow-the-leader type is excellent when the same "dosage" for all members of a given group is desired. The whole class may form a group. However, in order to adjust to individual differences, it usually is advisable to arrange several groups according to ability and condition. Either the teacher or selected students may lead. Leadership of the type used by track coaches, with the teacher observing and making suggestions for improvement in style, usually produces better analyses and more instruction. A combination of the follow-the-leader and track-coach types of leadership seems best.

Hiking is an excellent conditioner for occasional use. A difficulty arises because physical education class periods usually are too short to permit hikes of sufficient length to contribute significantly to body condition. Occasional class hikes may be useful both for the quite immediate effect upon condition and for the development of student interest in taking hikes during out-of-class time. However, probably the most effective use of hiking in physical education classes is found in alternating it with running.

TEST-TYPE ACTIVITIES

It has been said with considerable truthfulness that tests such as the AAHPER-sponsored battery are valuable not only as measures of physical fitness but also as desirable activities which develop fitness.

[12] *Ibid.*, p. 87.
[13] *Ibid.*, p. 90.

For use as a conditioning drill, selected test-type activities may be performed by a large group in response to count or rhythm. They also may be performed informally by students who either perform each movement a specified number of times or regulate their own dosage. One good method is for the teacher to ask each class member to do each of several movements about three-fourths as many times or three-fourths as fast as he could in an "all out" performance. Another method, highly recommended, is for the teacher and individual student to agree upon an advisable selection of activities and dosage. Thus, various students would work on the basis of the movements and dosage appropriate for them. One student, or more likely one subgroup, might emphasize test-type movements designed to strengthen the arms, another work to strengthen abdominal musculature, another to increase speed, and so on.

GROUP GAMES AND RELAYS

Group games, games of low organization, are an important part of all elementary school programs. They also have a place in secondary schools. They prove useful as warmup activities, leadup activities, as mixers at parties, and for drill-type practice of skills of more complex sports.

Organization for the teaching of group games should ensure vigorous activity for all. Little time should be taken for explanation. The focus of explanation should be on end results; for example, in the case of dodge ball, the teacher might say, "The idea for this team is to hit members of that team with the ball, and the idea for that team is to dodge so that they will not be hit." The details can be learned as play progresses. Groups should be formed quickly; new games should be compared to those already known.

Relays, especially, find favor for use with secondary school students. They add zest to practice drills and can introduce important elements of speed and competition for practice of game skills. The following questions suggest important points in the effective conduct of relays:

1. Are there sufficient teams and supplies; do all students receive sufficient activity?
2. Are the teams equated; are winning and losing distributed?
3. Does every student participate in every relay?
4. Are distances long enough to demand effort?
5. Are important skills being practiced correctly?
6. Are the relays holding student interest?
7. Do the relays have real purpose in the skill-learning sequence?

POSTURE

Good posture helps one look good and feel good. It also lessens the probability of backache, sore feet, excessive protuberance of the abdomen, round shoulders, and curvature of the spine. How does one teach good posture? Not by arranging to present it as a separate unit and let it go at that. Although teaching the values and concepts of posture as a discrete subject matter in itself might be effective for the establishment of a basic reference, little is gained unless good posture is encouraged consistently. All activities and all units of instruction are likely to affect student perception of the value of good posture.

Physical educators should teach posture, should encourage it, by example and precept. It is true, of course, that appropriate postures for different activities and functions vary. It also is true that there are several elements of good posture applicable to almost any waking activity and that teachers consistently should encourage these. They are (1) sit or stand tall, reach upward; (2) abdomen in, hips tilted forward; and (3) when walking use a heel-and-toe, weight-inclined-toward-the-outside foot action.

Frequent and consistent teacher attention to good posture may prevent physical ills including backache, sore feet, and feelings of fatigue. More important is the possible psychological benefit to the student. Posture may have a considerable causal effect upon optimistic outlooks or upon pessimistic and debilitating attitudes.

RHYTHMIC ACTIVITIES

Dancing and other rhythmic activities contribute to physical as well as to social, emotional, and recreational development. These activities require a good deal of strength and endurance for extensive performance. Folk and social dancing, with their social setting and recreational popularity, are activities through which schools can influence young people toward social amalgamation and wholesome recreation. Through creative rhythmical movements there may be imaginative and dramatic expressions of feelings and thoughts. Rhythmical movements may release tensions, bring relaxation, relieve self-consciousness, enhance joy in movement, improve gracefulness, and increase agility.

A good program of rhythm and dance in the elementary school considerably enhances the effectiveness of the secondary school dance program. For kindergarten and primary school children, singing games, folk dances, and fundamental rhythms in walking, running, skipping, galloping, and hopping are appropriate rhythmical activities. There should be opportunity for individual creative expression. However, formal or semiformal procedure of the follow-the-leader type may well be used in presenting fundamental rhythms in walking, running, skipping, galloping, and hopping. Rhythm records as well as dance records provide splendid aids.

In the intermediate grades, folk dancing and fundamental rhythms should be continued and expanded to include increasingly advanced movements as children's abilities develop. Exercises of the calisthenic type may be performed in rhythm with musical accompaniment or with counting or time beating. Because of student interests there should be more emphasis upon dance for girls than for boys in these grades, but it should not be discontinued for boys.

Social dancing, an excellent corecreation activity, may be introduced in the intermediate grades, but there is no unanimity among physical educators nor among citizens of communities concerning its desirability at this level. Many believe that ideally the teaching of social dancing should begin in the grade school. Many of the fundamental steps, such as the waltz and the basic two-step, are used in folk dances, and in schools where pupils have experiences in folk dancing the transition to social dancing is natural and easy if it is delayed until later.

In junior and senior high schools fundamental rhythms and folk, social, and modern dancing are valuable activities. Because of boys' greater needs for rugged sports and because of greater interests in dancing among girls, more time should be allotted to dancing for girls than for boys. However, boys should have opportunities to dance not only to develop rhythm but also to improve adjustment between boys and girls, lessen self-consciousness, and gain social and recreational skills.

Among physical educators there is considerable confusion and controversy concerning modern dancing which emphasizes creative self-expression of emotions and thoughts, deals with dynamic movements of a wide range, and teaches dance as expression rather than ready-made dances. Most teachers who lack interest or who belittle the activity are those who do not understand the art form of modern dancing and its contributions to culture. It should be remembered that successful teaching of modern dance requires a teacher whose preparation and experience has led to interest in and understanding of the art of dancing and one who knows other arts so that he understands artistic expression.

The teacher of dance and rhythms of all kinds must, of course, know subject matter which is not considered here. It will be helpful for beginning teachers to consider the following items concerning teaching procedure:

1. Demonstration by the teacher or by students is an important step in helping get a picture of rhythmic movements. When predetermined

steps are to be learned, demonstration sets a pattern; when variety of creative expression is the goal, illustrative demonstration stimulates imagination. For creative rhythms, however, emphasis is placed on moving to inward responses to stimuli rather than imitation of outward forms.

2. Preliminary explanation should be brief. Interesting information about history and use provides worthwhile motivation.
3. The class should be permitted to perform immediately after brief demonstration and explanation.
4. Analysis of performance indicates what further demonstrations and explanations are needed.
5. Students should feel that they are performing and achieving—that they are dancing rather than preparing for dancing at a later time.
6. Opportunities for individual practice of steps should be provided; self-conscious students need extra help.
7. Diagrams, illustrations, and other information placed on bulletin boards or chalkboards help. Providing written material is a good aid.
8. Listening to the music and to the beating or stamping of the rhythm, seeing a diagram of the rhythm, and clapping or stamping the beat help students appreciate tempo, accent, and phrasing.
9. For beginners in partner dancing, short dances and mixers should ensure frequent changing of partners.
10. Correlation of dancing with other schoolwork such as geography, social studies, sewing, music, and art is beneficial for multiple school areas because it enriches the experiences of students.
11. Dance instruction should be correlated with extraclass opportunities to dance at school parties, at home, at community events, and the like.
12. Rhythmical accompaniment is important. Counting or clapping or stamping may be employed successfully for fundamental rhythms and for early introduction to dances. Music of good quality is superior for most rhythmical work.

ROPE JUMPING

Both boys and girls like to jump rope. There is a challenge to the beginner and to the expert. Progress in the ability to perform the single jump, in which the rope is jumped with each swing, satisfies the beginner. Backward swings, crossed arms, double jumps, skipping, hopping, partner jumps, and other variations offer a continued challenge as ability develops. Cardiorespiratory development and endurance can be improved. Coordination, agility, and balance can be developed. Student satisfaction and enjoyment are likely.

Ropes are inexpensive. Ordinary clothesline rope, cut in 8- to 12-foot lengths, is reasonably satisfactory. Sash cord is better because added weight permits more accurate control. Jumping ropes may be purchased from almost any sporting-goods dealer. Storage presents little or no problem because ropes can be hung on hooks, bars, poles, or hangers.

Sound teaching procedure sets a pattern by demonstration and very brief explanation, followed quickly by practice of the whole act for all students. As practice progresses, the teacher should give help and encouragement to individuals as needed. New patterns should be introduced as mastery develops. Counting of consecutive successful jumps motivates learning. Informal competition among group members stimulates interest. Competition may be for the greatest number of consecutive jumps or for the greatest number of jumps in a given length of time.

Musical accompaniment is recommended. A rope-jumping period of about five minutes with piano accompaniment is employed by some basketball and wrestling coaches for the dual purpose of improving condition and developing foot and leg agility. Physical education teachers find that students respond enthusiastically to brief periods with the ropes.

SWIMMING

Only swimming, rather than aquatics including lifesaving, synchronized swimming, and canoeing, is discussed here. A teaching book needs to treat swimming; those likely to teach advanced water activities will be in a position to apply principles of learning to them because of specialized experiences and preparation.

Because ability to swim enables one to enjoy a wholesome and healthful recreational sport and because it serves as a safety skill which may save lives, school sponsorship of swimming instruction is appropriate. Many young people learn to swim under the guidance of parents and other interested persons and in programs sponsored by organizations such as community recreation divisions, the Red Cross, and the YMCA. It has been estimated, however, that more than 25 percent of adults in the United States are unable to swim. Schools which include swimming in their programs serve a needed service; they help youngsters prepare for living.

Because of wide differences in previous experiences and because of administrative difficulties encountered in attempting to assign students to classes according to ability, many school swimming classes include students whose abilities vary widely. Subgrouping according to ability almost always is necessary. The common classification into three groups —beginning, intermediate, and advanced—is quite satisfactory. Although such grouping produces some homogeneity, it must be remembered that individual attention is necessary because of differences in ability, body build, and feelings of confidence or insecurity.

In teaching beginners, the first step is to help the learner to feel at home in the water and to develop confidence. Student activities likely to accomplish this include (1) getting into shallow water and moving about at will, (2) counting fingers or recognizing objects while the face is under water, (3) pushing off from the bottom of the pool, (4) practicing floating, (5) practicing kicking while holding on to the side of the pool, (6) kicking while grasping a flutterboard or similar device, (7) kicking while the instructor or an assistant pulls the learner through the water by the hands, (8) using leg and arm strokes while being supported by the instructor or an assistant, and (9) attempting to swim a few strokes with a helper nearby.

The teaching of strokes, breathing, and diving begins after the learner feels at home in the water. Brief explanation and (or) demonstration should be followed by student tryout and practice. The teacher notes student successes and problems and teaches according to the help needed by the various class members.

The day a nonswimmer becomes a swimmer is a big day. It seems impossible to find anyone who is not thrilled with his first success in swimming. Teachers should work hard to help a nonswimmer learn to propel himself through water a short distance, perhaps 35 feet, the width of a medium-sized pool. After that is accomplished, stroke improvement is taught.

How can one teacher handle several different groups in an activity which requires close supervision and strict attention to safety precautions? One way is to organize so that each group works in designated areas of the pool with the instructor frequently viewing the whole pool as he moves from group to group helping those who seem most in need. Another is the *buddy system* which calls for students to work in pairs. A third is through a student-leader organization. Leaders usually are chosen from among class members; in some schools experienced swimmers, not necessarily members of the class involved, serve as leaders or assistants to the teacher. The latter arrangement works well and seems appropriate if such leaders are willing and can afford the extra time without detrimental effect upon their studies or other activities.

How can a large group be taught effectively in a small pool? Successful solutions to that problem include (1) having each of several groups work crosswise in designated areas of the pool; (2) having students enter the water in "waves" with about 10 to 15 feet between swimmers; after swimming a length students climb out, walk back to the starting point, and get ready to swim another length; (3) having students enter the water in "waves" with intervals of 10 to 15 feet, swim a length in the lane they entered, turn and swim a length in the opposite direction in a designated adjacent lane, turn and swim another length in the original lane, and so on. Sometimes called a circle formation, the latter arrangement permits continuous swimming. Beginners must be confined to shallow water; they can work lengthwise only in shallow pools, not in pools which have the usual deep end.

Interest in swimming may be maintained and increased through relay races, water games, recreational swimming, and occasional competition within a class. Knowledge of progress, of course, motivates; although students usually are quite aware of their progress or lack of it, occasional tests of form, speed, and endurance provide highlights and help students see their progress more clearly. Relay races seldom fail to provide enjoyable activity and increase interest if teams are reasonably equal in ability.

Water games such as polo, soccer, and basketball add interest but, of course, are appropriate only for those who can swim fairly well. Recreational swimming periods, either short ones near the end of a period or occasional full class periods, provide not only opportunity to put swimming skills to use but also fun and relief from monotonous practice. Occasional competition of the swimming-meet type between two or more groups within a class motivates learning for experienced groups. Such competition may be extended to extraclass meets between two or more classes with interest-renewing results. Selection of appropriate methods for increasing interest are likely to vary from class to class because of differences in individuals and in group composition.

TRACK AND FIELD ATHLETICS

Ancient and almost universal, track and field athletics consist of basic and fundamental sports involving running, jumping, and throwing. Participation leads to the development of strength, endurance, and agility. Because of the variety of events, individuals have opportunities to select those for which they are best suited. Progress in performance ability can be measured accurately. Although not everyone can become a champion, each person can attain satisfaction in improving his own performance.

Class track and field units should be designed to introduce all members to a variety of events. Opportunities for specialization should be provided for secondary school students, but teachers should remember that specialization should follow, rather than precede, exploratory experiences in a variety of running, jumping, and throwing events. Some specialization may well form a part of classwork for older boys and girls. Further specialization is appropriate in intramurals and, for boys at least, in interscholastics.

Demonstration and brief explanation should be followed quickly by tryout opportunities for students. Loop films, movies, pictures, diagrams, and charts help students build concepts of the techniques of good performance. Groups or squads within a class are particularly appropriate for track and field. When several events are in progress simultaneously, there usually is sufficient activity for all and a minimum of waiting for turns. Student leaders are valuable, especially in large classes. The teacher should move from group to group, giving help as needed.

Information about records and outstanding athletes adds interest, as does the knowledge of average performances for various ages and classifications. As in all learning, knowledge of progress motivates. Students like to check their performance in competition with others, as well as with their own progress in time and distance. Relays, all-around or decathlon-type events, group competition, and track-meet type events add interest to class units and should be considered as methods for teaching track and field in physical education classes. However, highly pitched competition with emphasis upon individual winning, appropriate for interscholastic teams, does not fit a class situation since it tends to discourage below-average performers. Group competition, giving each student an opportunity to contribute to a group effort, is appropriate for class instruction.

SUMMARY

Major considerations in teaching apparatus and tumbling include setting adequate models, allowing for initial success by providing successful experience for each student, and assuring ample practice. The squad system of organization is effective for this activity.

All agree that basic movements are important. Not all agree that basic movement should be taught as such, as discrete subject matter. The importance of problem solving, of discovery, in the learning of movements can scarcely be overemphasized. Basic movement, as a subject or unit in itself, emphasizes movements which are basic to more complex and coordinated activities involved in playing games and dancing.

Combative contests offers personal-combat competition especially appealing to boys. Because high interest is not likely to be maintained for long periods it is advisable to devote only a part of any one class period to these contests.

Conditioning activities seek to develop body flexibility, balance, strength, and endurance which permit one to perform arduous physical tasks with a minimum of effort and fatigue. Although conditioning may occur as one participates in various sports, games, gymnastics, rhythmic activities, and aquatics, some activities for the specific purpose of conditioning are needed. Among them are calisthenics, circuit training, grass drills, interval training, astronaut activities, resistence exercise, running and hiking, and test-type activities.

Group games and relays may be secondary school activities for recreation, for leadup activities to teach skills, and for warmup purposes. They should be organized to ensure vigorous and continuous activity as well as practice of skills.

Posture is important and its teaching should be distributed; i.e., it should be taught and encouraged almost continuously regardless of the principal thrust of a particular unit.

A good program of rhythmic activities, including dance, in the elementary school enhances the effectiveness of secondary school programs. Creative response and self-expression should be emphasized.

Rope jumping provides interesting rhythmic activity which can satisfy beginners as well as challenge experienced jumpers.

Swimming instruction at the elementary school level would be desirable. Secondary school swimming classes require ability grouping. With beginners, teachers should first help students feel at home in the water, then help them to swim some, to propel themselves through water. After that is accomplished, practice and improvement of stroke technique is in order.

Track and field-type activities represent the almost universal and basic movements of running, jumping, and throwing. They are interesting and satisfying to secondary school youth because performance can be measured accurately and competition can be against others or against one's own previous performance. Classes should introduce students to several events. Specialization may be pursued after exploration of various types of activities.

Questions and problems for discussion

1. Defend or criticize the practice of requiring participation in calisthenics during every physical education class period.
2. Prepare a plan for teaching basic movement to boys or girls in a high school of your selection. Support your reasons for planning to teach this as a special subject or unit or for teaching it as a part of various units.
3. How do you account for the wide difference among physical educators, as well as among others, concerning isometrics? Defend or criticize isometrics as an appropriate activity in a high school physical education program.
4. Debate with some colleague, or as one of several debaters against another

team, the following question: Resolved, that schools should neither sponsor nor teach social dancing below the eighth grade.

5. Propose a program of track and field activities for a physical education program in a junior high school of your choice. Do this either for boys or for girls.

Selected references

American Association for Health, Physical Education, and Recreation: *Physical Education for High School Students,* Washington, D.C., 1960.

Andrews, Emily Russell, et al.: *Physical Education for Girls and Women,* Prentice-Hall, Inc., Englewood Cliffs, N.J., 1963.

Bender, Jay, and Edward J. Shea: *Physical Fitness: Tests and Exercises,* The Ronald Press Company, New York, 1964.

Broer, Marion Ruth, and E. F. Martin: *Efficiency of Human Movement,* 2d ed., W. B. Saunders Company, Philadelphia, 1966.

Casady, Donald R., Donald F. Mapes, and Louis E. Alley: *Handbook of Physical Fitness Activities,* The Macmillan Company, New York, 1965.

Fait, Hollis F.: *Special Physical Education: Adapted, Corrective, Developmental,* W. B. Saunders Company, Philadelphia, 1966.

McCraw, Lynn W., and Stan Burnham: *Resistive Exercises in the Development of Muscular Strength and Endurance,* Cooperative Research Project No. 1979, The University of Texas, Austin, 1963.

Scott, Glody M.: *Analysis of Human Motion, A Textbook of Kinesiology,* 2d ed., Appleton-Century-Crofts, Inc., New York, 1963.

Souder, Marjorie A., and Phyllis J. Hill: *Basic Movement, Foundations of Physical Education,* The Ronald Press Company, New York, 1963.

Wessel, Janet A.: *Movement Fundamentals; Figure, Form, Fun,* Prentice-Hall, Inc., Englewood Cliffs, N.J., 1961.

chapter 10

USE OF AUDIO-VISUAL MATERIALS

INTRODUCTION

The Dictionary of Education[1] defines audio-visual instruction as "that branch of pedagogy which treats the production, selection and utilization of materials of instruction that do not depend solely upon the printed word." Use of audio-visual materials can represent a teaching method as well as an aid to more effective use of other types of method. For example, a poster can be used to illustrate a lecture, or it may be the only method used to present some kinds of learning such as a reminder to walk, not run, on the pool deck. Television can be used to supplement a lesson, or it can be used to teach an entire course over a period of many weeks. Whether used as a method or a teaching aid, audio-visual materials serve to make learning more meaningful. This chapter considers the scope, value, criteria for selection, basic steps in use, and suggestions concerning selected types of audio-visual materials as they relate specifically to physical education.

[1] Carter V. Good (ed.), *The Dictionary of Education,* 2d ed., McGraw-Hill Book Company, 1959, p. 290.

SCOPE OF AUDIO-VISUAL MATERIALS

Audio-visual media include a wide range of instructional materials and devices designed to provide realistic imagery and substitute experience to enrich curricular experiences of many kinds. The types which have the most use in teaching physical education include chalkboards, bulletin boards, and magnetic and flannel boards; pictures of all kinds; school-made photographs; graphic devices such as posters, cartoons, maps, diagrams, sketches, drawings, and charts; illustrated textbooks; models and specimens; projected devices such as film loops, filmstrips, lantern slides, stereoscopic pictures, overhead and opaque projector materials, and motion pictures; disc and tape recordings; and television and video tape.

There are many new instructional media which are mainly electronic in nature. These include regular and closed-circuit television; programmed learning devices of many types, both simple and complex; and learning laboratories which permit listening to and (or) viewing various materials. By use of computers and closed-circuit television, a teacher or student may dial a code number and have the desired material flash on the screen. This could be a page from a rulebook, a skilled performer demonstrating a motor skill, or any other type of stored learning material. We now have satellites capable of transmitting simultaneously 27 color programs. With the development of satellite transmission systems a student will be able to sit at home or in the classroom and tune in to a wide variety of scheduled educational broadcasts. Although physical education teachers now find limited application of these new media, the future will surely see greatly extended use.

VALUE OF AUDIO-VISUAL MATERIALS

The purposes and general values of using audio-visual materials in teaching include the following:

1. *They help the teacher clarify and illustrate, thus making abstract material more concrete.* Explaining something with which the students lack previous experience is difficult. For example, if one were to try to explain an unfamiliar game such as jai alai, he likely would do so in terms of an already familiar game. Even if he explained that jai alai is a dual game which resembles handball and is played on a long indoor court using basketlike rackets and a hard ball, his explanation would leave the students with various mental pictures of the game. A film, pictures, or other visual materials would aid students in getting a clearer concept.
2. *They create interest.* The entertainment industry depends largely upon audio-visual media such as radio, television, illustrated publica-

tions, and the like. Use of these same types of devices for educational purposes can make learning attractive.

3. *They extend the scope of experience.* Through such media as television and motion pictures, students can go far afield without even leaving the classroom.
4. *They permit students to come in contact with expert teachers and specialists.* A comparatively small number of children would ever have an opportunity to see a national champion of golf give a series of lessons. Yet with a film this experience can be brought to many students.
5. *They can effectively show interrelationships among complex wholes.* A diagram of a football play can show where each of the 22 players is at a certain time. This would be almost impossible to do verbally, short of a lengthy statement, and then it would be difficult for the average person to retain more than a portion of that verbalization. Likewise, in illustrating human interrelationships, a film showing the effect one student's behavior problem has on an entire classroom can be dramatically presented with good acting in a cleverly constructed story.
6. *They aid retention of factual knowledge.* Students tend to remember more of what they learn through use of audio-visual materials because they have a clear picture of the whole. Their learning very often has emotionalized overtones of some kind, and the interest created by the device tends to reinforce their interaction with the learning experience.
7. *They provide variety in a teaching strategy.* The criteria for selecting teaching methods, presented on pages 277–280, refer to the importance of variety in teaching. Audio-visual materials enable teachers to approach a subject in a number of different ways, maintaining or recapturing student attention, creating new interest, and allowing for individual differences in rate and pattern of learning.
8. *They enable processes which would not normally be available for class study to be capsulated.* A class could not directly follow an athlete through an extensive training period, but a film taken at regular intervals over a season would illustrate the stages of progress. A football game which takes three hours to watch can be cut to actual playing time, or cut even more if huddle time is eliminated.

TEACHING MOTOR SKILLS WITH AUDIO-VISUAL MATERIALS

Most of the research directed toward ascertaining the value of audio-visual materials in teaching relates to cognitive and affective learnings, although perceptual-motor skill learning is receiving increasing attention.

Research summarized in the *Encyclopedia of Educational Research* [2] reveals that there is little doubt about the general effectiveness of the use of audio-visual materials in teaching. However, research is specific to time, place, and type of device, and a proven effective technique used in an inept way may produce negative results. This simply means that almost any device, if used effectively, will enhance a learning experience, but the most effective device used poorly is no guarantee of good educational results. As has been reiterated from time to time in this text, *there is no best method,* and similarly, *there is no best audio-visual aid.* Circumstances of use determine value. It can be concluded, in any event, that since audio-visual materials do create interest and increase perception and conception, they can be of major value in teaching motor skills.

One of the problems in using films and other audio-visual materials in teaching motor skills is how to introduce them into the teaching sequence. When their purpose is solely to create interest in an activity or to give a concept of the whole game and the like, students can view a film or use other audio-visual materials in an adjacent classroom. For these and other such purposes immediate participation is unnecessary. When the purpose is to replace the demonstration phase of teaching motor skills, it is important that students have a chance to practice the skill immediately after viewing the model. A long delay may nullify much of the advantage in most cases, though not necessarily in all.

Since most gymnasiums are poorly equipped for showing films with ordinary projectors, films of the automatic type such as loop films and slide films, which require no threading, are especially helpful. Still pictures may be feasible and helpful for developing concepts and stirring interest. Playbacks of video tapes are valuable since both the teacher and the student see the student's performance. Although school facilities for video taping of class performances are not extensive at this writing, they are used some, and increased use is likely when easily portable and less costly equipment becomes more available.

CRITERIA FOR SELECTING AUDIO-VISUAL MATERIALS

The following criteria suggest pertinent points for consideration in selecting various types of audio-visual materials, and in determining how, why, when, and where they should be used.

Audio-visual materials should be considered as a teaching method or technique rather than a product or subject. They serve as a means to stimulate and aid learning. They should be selected as a means to aid

[2] *Encyclopedia of Educational Research,* the Macmillan Company, New York, 1961, pp. 115–137.

learning and never as an end in themselves. They should be selected only if in the judgment of the teacher, they are likely to contribute significantly toward achievement of the precise purposes of the lesson.

They should be timely. An audio-visual device should not only be pertinent to the focal point of the lesson, but should also be used in the learning sequence at a time when it will make the greatest contribution. It serves little purpose, for example, to show a motivational film on a sport after the season is about over; nor would it be desirable to show a film demonstrating skill at the end of a period, when students would have little opportunity to practice until much later. It would be best, for example, to show a motivation film on ice hockey at the beginning of the winter season, rather than late in the season when good skating is about past. Likewise, a film or device for illustrating skill or form should be shown at the first of the period when students can practice immediately following, rather than at the end of the period when there may be considerable lapse between seeing the film and practicing.

They should be accurate. Research reveals that on the whole students retain more of what they see than what they hear. If any aspect of a visual device is inaccurate, students are more likely to recall the wrong picture than they are to remember a teacher's explanation of what is wrong about the observed picture. Negative teaching has its pitfalls. When a student is shown the wrong way to do something, there is no guarantee that he has learned the correct alternative. Occasionally an audio-visual device, such as a film, may be old. Rules change yearly in some sports, and an old film which uses an out-of-date rule may only confuse beginners. Also, although many posed newspaper and magazine pictures have some points of interest, they may also contain glaring errors in form. Teachers should ascertain that all elements of materials used are accurate.

Devices should be technically excellent. Commercial use of audio-visual devices of all kinds has set high technical standards. Television shows and motion pictures shown in public theaters represent maximum technical perfection. Students are used to this perfection. When shown an old film or one that is poorly lighted or clumsily acted, they very often laugh or deride the presentation, rather than closely observe the message, no matter how accurately it is presented. This does not imply that inexpensive devices cannot be used effectively but rather that teachers must ascertain that the form of the device contributes to and does not detract from its effectiveness.

Use of the audio-visual device should be administratively feasible. Administrative feasibility includes several factors. The first of these is economy of time. The basic purpose in using teaching aids of any kind is to increase teaching efficiency in terms of both time consumed and quality of the resulting learnings. Some audio-visual devices, such as a complicated tableau, can consume more teaching time than they are worth. A prearranged model or a picture or a chalk drawing might be just as effective and take a fraction of the time. Any device used should be evaluated according to the proportion of the total teaching time it will take.

Administrative feasibility also refers to cost. Funds for education are limited. The best possible use must always be made of the money available. This represents a relative judgment. For example, a teacher must decide if it would be better to spend seventy dollars for a basketball film or to rent the film for three dollars, make limited use of it, and spend the remainder of the money for additional equipment.

Another aspect of administrative feasibility relates to the adaptability of the device to the setting of a particular lesson. A teacher can hardly show pictures or slides on a windy playground, whereas a sandbox model might be quite practical. Each different device presents its own problems and possibilities in this regard.

The final factor in administrative feasibility concerns the skill needed to utilize the device. Some audio-visual devices require technical skill to use. For example, an individual who takes motion pictures of an activity so that the films may be used later for instructional purposes must be expert in camera techniques and understand the important points of the activity he is filming. A highly skilled amateur or a professional photographer is important. Posture pictures, when taken, should be technically well done for best use. Unless devices are made and used skillfully, much of their value will be lost and both time and money wasted. When skill is lacking for best use of a device, its use should be postponed until it can be developed.

A variety of audio-visual devices should be selected. Exclusive use of one or two types of devices not only limits possibilities to realize potentials of those particular devices, but the medium may lose some of its effectiveness by overuse. In addition, very often a combination of two or more devices increases the value of both. For example, if still pictures for posting accompany a motion picture or filmstrip, students may be aided in retaining and using information from a film viewed only once or twice.

The audio-visual material should be free from objectionable commercial features. Some schools have regulations which prevent the use of any materials which contain advertising in any form, but most do not. Before use, each item should be carefully evaluated. The National Education Association recommends the following criteria for judging the worth of commercial materials in their bulletin *Consumer Education Study.*[3]

[3] National Association of Secondary School Principals, *Consumer Education Study,* National Educational Association, Washington, D.C., 1950.

The content of commercial supplementary teaching materials must be:

1. Sound, in terms of the educational philosophy and program that the school has adopted.
2. Significant, in the sense that it promotes the educational program better at the time than any ordinary pedagogic material that is available.
3. Timely, contributing information too recent to be included in available textbooks, thus helping the curriculum to keep up with current life as it develops. Each contribution should be dated.
4. Well-balanced, articulating with the adopted educational program without disturbing the relative values that education assigns to details.
5. Accurate in facts, without concealment or exaggeration.
6. Fair in the presentation of a point of view in a controversial matter.
7. Concerned with principles or products in general rather than with specific brands only.
8. Adapted to the needs, the interests, the maturity level, the economic level, and the locality of the students who will use it.
9. Truthful, presenting not only what is in itself true, but as far as possible, insuring against conclusions or attitudes not in accord with the whole truth. Misleading statements or suppression of important relevant information should invalidate any material.
10. Objective in presentation, without making or influencing interpretations that promote sales rather than the learner's education.
11. Responsible. Since even with the best intentions of objectivity and impartiality, a writer may manifest, by statement or by omission, prejudice in favor of the product or the point of view that he presents, the source of every commercial supplementary teaching material should be clearly, but not obtrusively and repetitiously, stated.

BASIC STEPS IN USING AUDIO-VISUAL MATERIALS

Before presenting some of the uses of selected types of audio-visual materials in teaching physical education, basic steps which apply to the use of any of these devices are outlined.

The first step in effective use of audio-visual materials relates to proper selection of an appropriate device. The criteria listed above for selecting materials can be used as guides for making appropriate choices. In order to apply these criteria properly, it is necessary for a teacher to be thoroughly familiar with the device under consideration and have his lesson objectives clearly in mind. If use of a film seems appropriate for a particular lesson or event, a teacher must carefully review available films and ascertain if any of them will be appropriate. It serves little purpose to use a device well if in the long run the original selection was unsound.

After an apt selection has been made, the next step in effective use concerns preparation. Materials must be gathered, equipment put in order, the room arranged, time scheduled, and the like. In addition to all administrative factors, the teacher or leader using the device must carefully analyze its full teaching potential. In the case of a film, he must see it through as many times as necessary to familiarize himself with all pertinent points. He must make a list of his comments, thoroughly study the suggested teaching guide, if any, and finally make his own teaching guide to fit his own setting. Similar analysis must be made of any device used, no matter how small a part it plays. Even such a simple device as use of a poster during a lecture requires preplanning in order that such factors as visibility and ease of use do not detract from the central thoughts.

The third step deals with presentation. Each different device will dictate a different pattern of presentation, but all require that students be prepared for their use. The purpose may be explained to students, or very often the selection and use of a device may be the direct result of student participation in planning. In this instance, orientation will center primarily on a discussion of the focal purposes of the device and how it will be used.

The fourth step encompasses follow-up procedures. While audio-visual materials aid in creating clearer concepts, it does not necessarily follow that resulting impressions will be correct. A discussion of what was seen, questions and comments, and written checks on information acquired are a few means of finding out if results have been satisfactory. Very often, as in the case of films, it will be necessary to reshow them, perhaps several times. Other devices, particularly models, diagrams, and the like, may be left in sight for periodic referral while practice proceeds. Provisions for practicing or applying learning resulting from these devices should follow closely. This is particularly true in motor skills, since the chief purpose in this case is to set a model to aid students in gaining a concept of the complex coordinations involved.

The final step involves evaluation by both teachers and students. Evaluation should be based upon the effectiveness of the device in contributing to the specific objective of the occasion. Interest alone is not enough, although often the resulting interest does lead to better learning, and also some devices are designed for this purpose alone. Students very often are the best judges of whether the device is an effective one, but their comments prove of most worth when they understand the purpose of the device in relation to an equally clear lesson purpose. For example, students may respond favorably to an interesting skiing film, while in reality the film has no pertinency to the immediate school physical education goals. On the other hand, if there were a valid purpose for showing a skiing film, the fact that they liked it would be important. In addition to qualitative evaluation of devices used, teachers and students alike can decide whether results from use of a device have been concrete. It is possible to measure change in attitude, improvement in skill, and increased knowledge. Efforts should be made to evaluate the worth of a device used on every occasion, because, owing to the inherent attractiveness of audio-visual devices, sometimes they are accepted at face value, with their worth assumed and not proved.

SUGGESTED USES OF SELECTED AUDIO-VISUAL MATERIALS

Because physical education is concerned with development of attitudes and appreciation and with acquisition of knowledge and understanding as well as learning of motor skills, all available audio-visual devices would conceivably have some use in the program. The following section treats selected devices which have major pertinency for physical education teaching, with special reference to problems which are peculiar to physical education. The suggestions should be viewed as provocative and not inclusive, since the potentialities are inexhaustible.

CHALKBOARDS

Chalkboards aptly reveal the truth that audio-visual materials are not an innovation in education. Chalkboards offer an inexpensive and effective means of producing information or material which all students can view at the same time. Chalkboards can be used for diagramming plays, showing boundaries of fields and courts, introducing new rules or vocabulary, keeping score, drawing music-rhythm patterns or floor patterns for dance, listing squad leaders and squad activities for the period, giving simple announcements, advising of lost-and-found equipment, and displaying other notices of all kinds.

Perhaps maximum use has not been made of chalkboards in the gymnasium, because few are equipped with them. It is desirable, of course, to have as much clear wall space as possible in a gymnasium for use in volleying activities of many kinds. Also, wall projections may constitute a hazard. Nevertheless a chalkboard does have many uses. In some instances, it is possible to place them in a bleacher area. In gymnasiums used for dance as well, wall mirrors, which fold inward for protection, can be backed with a chalkboard, thus making double use of this space. When it is not possible to place the chalkboard on a gymnasium wall, it is desirable to have a permanent one in the corridor or space adjacent to the gymnasium or have an adequately sized movable one which can be easily brought into the gymnasium on occasion and removed for safety reasons.

Writing on the chalkboard should be done in advance whenever possible. A teacher should not waste class time while he draws and labels an entire field or court. If the drawing or diagram is intricate, the teacher can put key lines in faint outline, then quickly retrace them in front of the class while illustrating the point.

A practical device is to have permanently marked chalkboards with outlines of major areas traced upon them. Thus one portable board may have a football field painted or scored on it, and plays can be quickly superimposed upon the area. Another board for dance can similarly contain a permanent musical score for quick drawing of musical passages.

A grided chalkboard is also valuable for drawing illustrations. The teacher can superimpose a transparent guide over the original drawing and quickly copy it square by square.

Material should be presented as attractively as possible. Legibility is particularly important, since a chalkboard in a gymnasium is seldom in a focal location. The teacher should always check the legibility of his chalkboard material by viewing it from the vantage point of the class. Colored chalk finds particular use to attract attention and to indicate differences among teams or positions and for related purposes.

Students should be encouraged to use chalkboards. Paper and pencil are seldom available in a gymnasium. A chalkboard can be used by students to diagram plays, figure out rotation systems, list their squad members, and the like. This does not imply that students should engage in classroomlike activities during an activity period at the expense of lessened participation. It does suggest that with optimum use of chalkboards, much time can be saved for actual participation by expediting verbalizations which must accompany activity teaching.

BULLETIN BOARDS

Bulletin boards are essential equipment for a physical education program. The large numbers participating in all phases of physical education, the diversity of activities and programs, and the general level of activity and movement around a physical education plant necessitates having a medium of communication such as provided by bulletin boards. They serve a multitude of purposes. They are appropriate for making available such diverse information as routine messages, general administrative policies and procedures, intramural schedules, tournament dates, tournament charts, playing schedules, permanent squad lists, notices of club activities, playing or ground rules, pictures of all kinds, lists of available books, sport guides, and other materials, publicity clippings of the program and other pertinent newspaper clippings, motivational messages, e.g., rules of good sportsmanship, and achievement standards.

Location of bulletin boards presents some of the same problems as with chalkboards. Wall space within the gymnasium should be free when possible. In addition, papers on bulletin boards are easily torn or destroyed when hit by balls or brushed frequently by players. The best solution for the location of bulletin boards suggests that more than one be made available. One protected board within the gymnasium is desirable for posting of instructional materials such as playing rules, instructional pictures, and other information needed during actual participation. Another board just outside the gymnasium entrance to include such information as daily squad lists, playing schedules, and the like places this type of information where it can be referred to on entrance to or exit from the playing area. Another board should be located in a place accessible to the main entrance where students can see it on approaching the dressing room or gymnasium; it is also convenient for those who wish to drop in between classes to check on available information. A portable bulletin board may also prove worthwhile for use during a single class period for the presentation of instructional pictures, diagrams, and other materials for that class period only. All bulletin boards should be located in well-lighted spots, where normal traffic allows for maximum viewing.

Bulletin-board use should be a carefully planned endeavor. A tentative schedule for the year should be worked out, and maximum use made of all available space. The purpose of each board should be determined, and if more than one is used, consistency of function should be maintained. This means that students will always look in the same place for the same type of information and are less likely to overlook important materials. When but one board is used, it helps to have it divided into sections, and the same consistency of function maintained.

The bulletin board should be neat and attractive. An overcrowded, untidy board attracts only casual attention. Use of attractive materials, such as colored backing cards for typed sheets, colored mats for pictures, and colored thumbtacks and tape, all assist to make the board a decorative as well as informative asset.

The material should be varied. If old material remains on the board, students lose interest in daily or regular reading of contents.

The board should also be used for presenting information which supplements specific teaching purposes. For example, if the library obtains an interesting new book on fencing, even though fencing is not a part of the regular program, the posting of its dust jacket on the bulletin board will interest some students in reading the book. Similarly, stories of good sportsmanship, cartoons, or other suitable materials should be posted.

Students should share in the responsibility for maintaining bulletin boards. This responsibility may grow out of class, club, or any other unit of organization. Intramural managers may have the responsibility of maintaining a bulletin board, or section of a board, devoted to that activity. A letter group may accept responsibility for the motivational or newspaper-clipping section of the board. Placing responsibility for design and maintenance on students both increases interest and serves as a worthwhile educational activity.

A file of suitable material should be maintained. An outstanding picture or display may well be repeated another year or for another class. Careful filing of reusable material will provide an excellent source for future use.

The attention of students should be directed to vital information. It can never be assumed that mere placing of material on bulletin boards will assure its effectiveness. Information relative to classwork can be pointed out in class; school papers and homeroom announcements can call attention to special information.

MAGNETIC AND FLANNEL BOARDS

Magnetic and flannel boards are types of bulletin boards whose special properties give them unique functions.

Magnetic boards are made of sheet metal and come equipped with magnetized metal markers. They prove particularly valuable for teaching formations, plays, or any other kind of movement in series. For example, a football coach marks a football field on the magnetic board. Each player is represented by a metal disk, which can be colored, marked with a number, or attached to a miniature figure of a football player. In explaining a play, the disks can be moved about with ease, but the magnetic force holds them in place on the board when contact is made. Because of their solid construction, boards of this kind can be taken out of doors to the playing fields, formations set up, and the boards used for ease of teaching new plays or drill formations. The magnetized disk can be attached to any kinds of figures or symbols to add realism to the scene.

Magnetic boards can be used also to teach dance formations, mass drill formations, field markings, position of testing stations, referee positions, and the like. Generally one or both sides of the magnetic board is coated in such a way that it can be used as a chalkboard. Sometimes one side of the board has a permanent marking, such as a football field or basketball court. Magnetic boards are sold commercially and can also be made in the school shop. Magnetized disks are readily available.

Flannel boards are constructed of any of several different kinds of long-fibered material, such as flannel, felt, velvet, or suede. A sheet of plywood, fiberboard, or heavy cardboard is covered with this material. Cutouts of the same material or others backed with strips of sandpaper will cling to the board providing a highly versatile teaching device. The flannel board can be used for many of the same purposes as the magnetic board, but its one added advantage is that it can be made into a most decorative and eye-catching display.

PICTURES

Each physical education teacher should have a growing collection of pictures. These may include pictures of athletes in various poses illustrating different form, newsworthy events, suitable activity costumes, events of historic importance, dance costumes, dance forms of all kinds, and works of art related to any phase of physical activity, including sculpture, painting, and the like. Current magazines, newspapers, books, and art-picture outlets provide rich sources of pictures.

Pictures are important to good teaching since they are an easily procured and handled effective visual device. Research has shown that retention is greater when narration is accompanied by use of pictures. They are particularly valuable in physical education teaching because superior form can be illustrated much more accurately than is usually available firsthand. While motion pictures are even better for this purpose, still pictures are of significant usefulness.

Use of pictures is particularly worthwhile in teaching dance. Authentic costuming can be illustrated in this way. The *National Geographic* and folk-dance books are particularly good sources for pictures of this kind. Modern dance, which emphasizes creative art form, can be considerably enhanced by a good collection of pictures.

Pictures can contribute to artistic and aesthetic development. Some of the world's greatest art relates closely to the subject matter of physical education. The physical education program has a responsibility for bringing this phase of art to the attention of students. Current pictures of dance forms also serve this end.

Pictures serve to evoke emotional responses which can promote the development of desirable attitudes. Few individuals can view a picture of Lou Gehrig receiving his last great tribute at Yankee Stadium without being moved and reminded of the concept of American sportsmanship which this great athlete epitomized.

Students learn more from pictures if their viewing is directed or the content of the picture or its meaning is explained or discussed. When using pictures of form, for example, teachers should indicate the important points and assist students to understand the major factors. For some pictures, a written explanatory statement or suggestions for further reading may prove worthwhile; but even with this device, attention should be drawn to the picture.

When pictures are used during a teaching sequence, they should be clearly visible to all. It is generally desirable to focus attention and discussion on one picture at a time. The practice of passing pictures about a class while a lecture or discussion has proceeded to another topic serves only to detract attention from the immediate point. When it is desirable for all to view a picture at the same time and its size does not permit clear viewing, some use should be made of a projective device (see pages 253–254).

A filing system as mentioned in connection with bulletin boards applies equally to pictures. Students can assist materially in increasing the file of suitable pictures if a teacher enlists their interest. They can be encouraged in connection with some courses to collect appropriate pictures and make scrapbooks of major topics, both to keep themselves or to pass on to other groups.

PHOTOGRAPHY

The motivational value of taking and posting pictures of squad leaders, teams, individual honor winners, and the like is quite obvious. In fact, in sports or activities for which there is little external status or recognition, posting the achiever's picture on the bulletin board may provide him with great satisfaction. For example, the student who makes the most improvement over a semester in his physical fitness score, despite the fact that his total score is still far from illustrious, may be spurred to even greater effort by the simple recognition of his picture being posted. Schoolmade photographs can also be used to illustrate high quality performance which will serve as a model for other learners. The layup form of the high school basketball star may be equally as good for teaching purposes as that of a professional. The fact that it is another student who can achieve that level of skill may encourage students who might become discouraged at trying to reach the perfection of the super athlete.

Photographs are particularly useful in the dance program. It is one way to preserve some elements of superior creative dance efforts and costume design for recognition and future reference.

Photographs can be especially useful in helping both the student and teacher diagnose weaknesses. A high jumper may suddenly find himself retrogressing or not progressing as expected. Camera shots of his form may reveal some minor deviation which the eye of the coach did not catch. Obviously a motion picture might be more useful, but extensive movie taking is often not feasible. The Polaroid camera which provides a finished picture in ten seconds is especially valuable in this regard.

The new Polaroid sequential frame camera gives promise of being an effective device for on-the-spot diagnosis of form. It operates on the same principle as the regular Polaroid camera but has a special shutter system which produces a final picture of 12 still frames in sequence. It takes three seconds to complete its cycle, so it can capture a basic skill movement such as a golf swing showing sequential stages of the movement.

Another useful Polaroid device is one that permits making a slide in three minutes. A regular camera is used, but special film and an additional copier outfit are required. The uses of this device in physical education programs are unlimited. As one example, a coach could work out a play or defense strategy, quickly reproduce it on a slide, and have it ready for projection when the team assembles for "skull practice" after a workout. Considerable chalkboard time can be saved by this device; and materials can be preserved for later reference. Materials from many other sources can be reproduced in this way. (See Slides, pp. 253–254.)

GRAPHIC DEVICES

Graphic pictorial devices include such media as posters, cartoons, maps, diagrams, sketches, and drawings. Their value and potential are basically similar to that just discussed for pictures, and in addition they allow for greater scope, more timeliness, and pertinency to the immediate school situation. For use in the physical education program, these devices can be both commercially prepared and individually made. Charts showing refereeing positions and signals exemplify a commercially available type of chart useful for a physical education program. Diagrams of fields and playing areas of all kinds generally accompany rulebooks. Achievement standards, if of standardized test items, may be available in chart form, or handmade charts of local achievement standards may be constructed. Tournaments of all types are usually charted, and playing schedules for large groups become more readable if posted on a large chart. It is helpful to students if diagrams of dance steps, floor patterns, plays in football and basketball, and the like are made and posted for quick reference.

The basic purpose of a poster is to put across an idea. Good posters limit themselves to one major point and utilize wording, color, design, or picture to attract and hold a viewer's attention. Posters are widely used to publicize events and to spot-teach, particularly in the habit or attitude area.

A considerable amount of time is generally spent in preparing graphic devices. To be effective, they must be attractive, readable, and carefully constructed. Lettering must be neat and legible and the vocabulary within the range of the students. A chart should present information more clearly than a less time-consuming way. If extensive explanation is needed to explain the chart itself, little is accomplished. Materials used should be sturdy enough so that they will withstand use. Some charts and posters very often are suitable for but one occasion, but generally, because of the work which goes into a graphic device, this time should be spent only on materials which can be used many times. Chalkboards will suffice for chartings or diagrams which cannot be reused.

ILLUSTRATED TEXTBOOKS

Reference was made in Chapter 6 to the increased availability and use of textbooks for teaching physical education in secondary schools. Fortunately, most of the new books are filled with pictures and illustrations. Many of the sports books written by national champions for public consumption are also suitable for high school students. These, too, generally contain many fine pictures of good form. Books written for coaches generally are replete with diagrams, pictures, and other illustrations. Many of the folk and square dance books for teachers have fine pictures or colorplates of costumes, and the illustrated step patterns and descriptions of dance steps may assist some students to master formations more readily.

Using pictures or illustrations from this source involves the same practices as recommended previously in relation to other types of pictures and graphic devices. A glass-enclosed bulletin board or showcase is helpful, for books can be left open there to appropriate pages to show a particular picture at the right time.

In appraising the worth of a book with illustrations, one should look for accuracy and clearness of pictures and diagrams and for ample explanation of the illustration or diagram in the text itself.

Teachers must avoid violation of copyright laws in reproducing diagrams, music, or other material from books, but projectors (see page 253) provide one means of using book material during a class period so that all may see the same material at the same time.

In selecting books to be used as texts, teacher references, or library additions, the effectiveness of the illustrations should be one of the major criteria in making choices. Good illustrations considerably improve the value of physical education texts.

MODELS AND SPECIMENS

Replica models and specimens are useful in several ways. A model of a gymnasium with all equipment is useful in laying out teaching or testing stations and planning for rotation of groups, demonstrations, or mass activity of any other kind. Models of the playground are useful for similar purposes, and if these are carefully made to scale—which is important for all types of models—track and field events, markings for special events, and the like can be planned more readily.

Model figures are valuable for use in posture work, particularly those that are jointed and can be manipulated to show various principles of movement. Model figures illustrating such things as team formations and costumes can be both instructional and interesting. Models of body cross sections, muscle groups, and the like are useful in teaching conditioning, health, and other classroom learnings.

Specimens are particularly valuable in teaching about the selection and care of athletic equipment. Such displays as those showing the many operations involved in making a badminton shuttle, a crosscut section of a basketball, and the thread count in various kinds of athletic clothing can be used in teaching about equipment.

PROJECTED PICTORIAL DEVICES

Projected pictorial devices include opaque and overhead projector materials, lantern slides, filmslides, filmstrips, film loops, stereoscopic pictures, and motion pictures.

Opaque and *overhead projectors* permit projection of a flat picture or graphic device on a wall or screen. The opaque projector projects opaque materials by reflected light. The advantage of this machine is that any flat material can be projected without processing, but its disadvantage is that it requires a darkened room. The overhead projector is similar to the opaque projector, except that the material to be shown is transferred to a transparency either by photographic means or by handtyping, writing, or drawing. There is a dirth of commercial material for the overhead projector for use in physical education, and one of its major advantages is the ease of preparing material. The overhead projector can accommodate any material which would normally be put on a chalkboard. Added advantages are that a teacher may face the class while writing or explaining the material; much of the material can be prepared beforehand to save writing time during the class session; and complicated drawings and diagrams or any material which might be reused can be stored for later use. The retractable screen needed for projecting is suitable for gymnasium use. Good visibility is provided even in a normally lighted room. Recent technical developments with this machine offer a process whereby animation or motion can be added. A simple overlay process and masks allow the addition of motion effects in meaningful sequences. This technique has considerable potential in developing materials for teaching physical education.

Lantern slides, filmslides, and *filmstrips* all serve the same general purpose but utilize different mechanical media. Lantern slides usually are drawn on clear or etched glass or plastic, then mounted. Filmslides are photographed lantern-type slides. Filmstrips are made on 35mm film, the same as motion-picture film, with side-sprocketed holes. The pictures usually are in a continuous series and can be shown one at a time. Some filmstrips are accompanied by recordings which give directions or explanation.

Projected still pictures have definite advantages. They are significantly less expensive to produce than motion pictures, and for some subjects they can be adequately made by teachers or students. A considerable number of physical education-activity filmstrips are available. They are superior for some teaching. Many items can better be shown by still than motion pictures. For example, in showing field markings, a still picture is superior to a motion picture. Filmstrips are useful in teaching form in physical education because various sequences of movements can be adequately shown. A series of pictures of a golf swing can, for example, show relative positions of elbows on the backswing, at contact with the ball, and on the follow-through.

Slides and *filmstrips* permit adjustment of the length each item will be viewed and permit selection of only those items from a series which are pertinent to the lesson. Another advantage is their portability and ease of storage. The simplicity of the machinery used makes it feasible for students to use equipment and to assist with showing materials while the teacher comments on the picture or works with students; the picture can remain on the screen as a model.

Filmstrips have a prearranged sequence since all pictures are attached. Other types of slides, which are shown one at a time, can be used in any order. Ease of manipulation, of course, makes it possible to find quickly a single picture from a filmstrip for reshowing. Single slides have greater flexibility, but if an automatic magazine changer is not used, the teacher must exercise care not to mix up the sequence in the dark or insert the slides upside down.

Loop films are closely akin to filmstrips, but because of their design find particular use in the physical education program. The filmed sequence is placed in a cartridge, which is easily slipped into the projector and never needs rewinding. The projector and screen are small, lightweight, and completely portable. Equipment is available for showing to large groups, small groups, or individuals. Simplicity of operation permits use by students with a minimum of initial instruction and no supervision. The equipment can be set up in any part of the gymnasium or at any teaching station. The student can play and replay the sequence, practice the skill, and recheck the film. Because of its adaptability for motor skill teaching a considerable number of expertly made loop films are now available.

Stereoscopes are devices which project a picture in three dimensions, thus giving more of a sense of reality than obtained from flat pictures. All such devices require individual use, those for group viewing still being in the experimental stage and unavailable for general school use. Stereoscopes prove valuable for individual study. For example, a set of dance-costume or dance-form pictures for use with a stereoscope would be of interest and value to students.

Motion pictures have become well entrenched as an acceptable and desirable instructional aid in modern schools. Their advantage lies in the versatility and expertness of experience they can provide, their inherent interest to students, and their value in influencing learning of all kinds.

The fact that the *Sports Film Guide* published by the Athletic Institute lists more than two thousand 16mm films shows widespread availability of physical education and sports films. Commercial firms sell films, and various film libraries rent them. Health and physical education films also are provided free or at nominal cost by voluntary agencies, industries, and public or governmental units. Teachers should check local or nearby sources, including universities and state libraries, and secure catalogues of available films. Most large school districts have audio-visual aids departments; of course, a teacher should be thoroughly familiar with the services available in his own school.

Too often motion pictures are thought of only as a medium of entertainment. While this purpose may be valid on some occasions in schools, a motion picture becomes an instructional film only when it is used as one. In using a film for instructional purposes, the same basic steps outlined on pages 243–245, which include preview, planning, presentation, follow-up, and evaluation, apply. Some specific additional factors are suggested.

Some films, especially those used for motivational rather than instructional purposes, will be shown but once; others should be run two or more times. Sometimes the subsequent showing takes place on later days. This proves good practice for films which present expert performers. These may be run many times throughout a season or unit to set a model for students.

When a sound film is used, the teacher must remain quiet during the showing. Often it proves desirable on a second showing to turn off the sound and supplement the showing with comments and explanations. Also, on second showings, it is sometimes worthwhile to stop the film, rewind quickly, and reshow a brief portion.

When the film is shown as an instructional technique and not as entertainment, students should be expected to see a film through as many times as is necessary to improve learning and should approach viewing with an attitude conducive to receiving instruction.

A teacher should keep his own written evaluation of every film used and seek student suggestions about it. Very often student reactions to some aspect of a film will be unexpectedly negative thus undoing potential good. Unless these reactions are revealed, time will be wasted showing it to a second group who may react similarly.

A film should never be used to replace the function of a teacher. Instead, it should be used as an adjunct to his abilities. Films prove of most worth for instructional purposes when they are preceded by explanation and followed by discussion. Initial and undiscussed reaction to a single film may produce a wide variety of responses in a group of students. The very speed at which events move and the scope of detail covered indicate the essentialness of teacher direction in their use.

Advantages of motion pictures cannot be questioned. They illustrate movement, which is basic to physical education teaching; they create interest; and they offer unlimited potential for presenting many phases of the program. On the other hand, their limitations should not be overlooked. They are expensive and can consume a disproportionate share of budget funds; they are time-consuming in that care must be exercised in setting up equipment and handling film; they must be shown in darkness, a requisite which is often difficult, if not impossible, in gymnasiums. All these disadvantages, however, cannot detract from the considerable contribution motion pictures can make to effective teaching of physical education.

Schoolmade films, as well as video tapes, warrant consideration. Filming and (or) video taping of performances in interscholastic athletics or of public demonstrations of physical education activities are rather common. It would be most helpful to make movies of beginning performances of various motor skills so that students could analyze their own performances as they see themselves in action.

DISK AND TAPE RECORDINGS

A good library of disk records or magnetic tapes can be a valuable asset to a physical education program. Recordings are particularly useful in a dance program. Even assuming that a satisfactory accompanist would be available at all times, a dance program can be enriched by use of recordings. If other types of accompaniment are lacking, recordings provide a means to carry on a satisfactory dance program. They can be used to provide music for classwork in all forms of dance, for noon-hour and other recreational social, square, and folk dancing, and for students to practice any type of dance on their own time. In addition to uses in connection with dance, recordings can also be used to provide background and marching music for pageants, demonstrations, and festivals, to provide patriotic music preliminary to athletic contests, to provide music for synchronized swimming and water carnivals, and for general recreational purposes in physical education–sponsored recreational programs.

In selecting recordings for any phase of the program, several general criteria should be considered.

1. The quality of the music should always be such that it contributes to the musical taste and growth of pupils. Songs with objectionable

words or with music that is not expressive and that is trite in style, should be avoided.

2. The recording should be of music expressly designed for the use to which it will be put. For example, for square dancing, folk songs which have been traditionally used for the dances should be selected.
3. The arrangement of the song should be one that is suitable. For example, a vocal arrangement of square dance music may not be adequate for dancing. An arrangement especially designed for dancing should be selected.
4. The tempo of the recording should be proper. Many times music is recorded at a tempo faster or slower than it should be.
5. In songs for dancing or marching, the rhythm should be the most prominent element. Music with florid melodies often proves unsuitable for rhythmic activities of all kinds.
6. The technical quality of the recording should be superior. Qualities of recordings vary from company to company and even within pressings of the same recording.

In using recordings for any occasion, the teacher should be thoroughly familiar with the record and have carefully analyzed its potential for use in the selected situation. Teachers should strive for variety in recordings. For example, although "Turkey in the Straw" can be used for many square dances, using a variety of material makes for much more interesting and enriched experiences.

Teachers should encourage students to use recordings and recording equipment, developing concurrently their responsibility for its care. If they have access to records and equipment, they can conduct their own recreational dance sessions and use the equipment at the beginning of the period when assembling for activity and at other free times. The more they can hear and respond to music, the better the results. If the record library contains high-quality music and a wide variety of selections, the musicality of students will improve.

Availability of a good record collection and adequate equipment represent one aspect of satisfactory use of music in a physical education program. Maximum use should be made of music in other forms as well.

TELEVISION

Almost everyone agrees that television represents potentially the most profound educational medium yet invented. One of the realities of the present day is that educational television is playing an increasingly prominent role. There are two types of educational television systems: broadcast television and closed-circuit television. Broadcast television consists of programs sent out by either commercial or educational television stations. Closed-circuit television can be received only by sets connected directly to the transmitting unit. This system is widely used within a school or college and requires no licensing. Some states have their own statewide educational television systems, and the number of educational and regular network shows being piped into the classroom cannot but be considered as a significant influence on our schools.

Use of a television show for a single period is synonymous with use of educational films or other audio-visual techniques discussed in this chapter. On the other hand, in many instances, whole units or whole courses extending over many weeks are being taught by means of television. Thus television teaching is emerging as a method in itself, and might well have been included as a topic in Chapter 6, Basic Types of Method. It is included in this chapter, however, since for purposes of physical education, television is likely to find its major use as an audio-visual technique rather than as a basic teaching method.

It is unlikely that physical education will be taught by television to any major extent in the near future. However, teachers of physical education cannot ignore the considerable impact on students of today's entertainment television. A significant percentage of commercial television is devoted to sporting events. Teachers should help students increase their sports appreciation and also improve their understanding of various games through television. The precise effect of television on improving extent or degree of sports appreciation is hard to determine. Obviously, however, students viewing a major-league baseball game would realize the same or greater potential effects as seeing a movie of major-league teams. Teachers can improve the possibilities of students gaining in understanding and appreciation if they make some effort to guide their viewing.

A teacher can suggest to students certain points to observe. If it is baseball, he can suggest that they watch particularly the batting stances of certain players, or how the second baseman backs up the first on certain plays, or any other technical aspect of the game.

A teacher can give lecture-viewings of given games. For example, either on a class or volunteer basis, students can watch a televised contest, and with the sound turned off the teacher can explain what is going on, emphasizing selected learnings. While commercial sports announcers do an expert job of announcing, too often the focus is upon score rather than upon appreciation of the technical performance level. Physical education teachers should help students to learn to appreciate the fine points of a game.

No doubt television can serve a useful purpose in helping student performers gain an insight into skills to be learned. For example, a rookie center on a high school basketball team astounded his coach and teammates by turning in a superb game in which he scored twenty-five points, mostly on a pivot play to the left. When asked about it after the game, he said, "I know the coach has been trying to teach me that shot all season, but I was watching television over the week end and saw the Celtic's center work that shot perfectly. I realized what I was doing wrong, and the shot just suddenly clicked for me." This story merely illustrates that a concept must be gained of the motor skill to be performed, and television served in this instance to set the model. The effectiveness of television for this purpose depends upon the concurrent practice opportunities.

Video taping is another form of television being used in today's schools. It has been discussed in the section Teaching Motor Skills with Audio-Visual Materials on pages 239–240 and mentioned in connection with the use of motion pictures on page 255.

SUMMARY

Audio-visual materials provide realistic imagery and substitute experiences to enrich curricular experiences for students. Their value lies in assisting the learner to grasp a concept of the precise nature of desired outcomes, in creating interest, in enlarging the scope of experiences that can be brought to the classroom, in helping to show interrelationships among complex wholes, in introducing the element of variety, and in promoting retention of desired learnings.

In using visual materials for teaching motor skills, opportunity for practice of the skill should be provided immediately after the visual model is set. Oftentimes visual materials other than motion pictures prove more feasible for use in teaching activities in a gymnasium. Audio-visual materials find use for teaching many kinds of physical education learnings in addition to motor skills.

Criteria for selecting audio-visual materials require attention to their use as a method rather than as a product, pertinency to the occasion, timeliness, accuracy, technical excellence, administrative feasibility, variety, and freedom from objectionable commercial features.

Steps in using audio-visual materials include analysis and selection of the best available device for the stated purpose, preparation by thorough study of the contents and arrangement of all administrative factors for use, presentation which includes student orientation to the device, follow-up procedures which encompass discussion of what was seen and re-showing if necessary, and evaluation of achievement of outcomes from use of the device with notations for possible future use.

The types of audio-visual materials which are most useful in teaching physical education include chalkboards; bulletin boards; magnetic and flannel boards; pictures of all kinds including schoolmade photographs; graphic devices, such as posters, cartoons, maps, diagrams, sketches, drawings, and charts; models and specimens; projected devices such as film loops, filmstrips, filmslides, lantern slides, stereoscopic pictures, opaque and overhead projector materials, and motion pictures; tape and disk recordings; and television and video tape.

Questions and problems for discussion

1. What specific considerations should be given to use of audio-visual materials in the yearly program plan, the unit lesson plan, and the daily lesson plan?
2. Describe opportunities for use of physical education films in addition to regular class periods.
3. Make a list of criteria for judging the effectiveness of technical aspects of performance in physical education–activity films.
4. Prepare a one-semester plan for the maintenance of a glass-enclosed bulletin board in the main corridor of a high school, which has been assigned to the physical education department. Include educational objectives for use of the board as well as kinds of materials and frequency of change.
5. Prepare an instructional guide for teachers for any appropriate physical education film or filmstrip.
6. How can a supervisor of physical education promote more extensive and effective use of audio-visual materials of all kinds in his schools?
7. One school suspends all afternoon physical education classes during the World Series so students can watch the games. Do you approve of this practice? Give your reasons.
8. How may field trips be used in teaching physical education? Describe ways for making such trips of maximum educational value.
9. Many teacher-education institutions offer courses in audio-visual education. Would you recommend such courses to physical education majors? Give your reasons.
10. Indicate ways in which you can prepare physical education facilities for ease of use of all kinds of audio-visual materials.

Selected references

The Athletic Institute: *Sports Film Guide,* Chicago, 1966.

Brown, James Wilson, Richard B. Lewis, and Fred F. Hardwood: *A-V Instruction: Materials and Methods,* 2d ed., McGraw-Hill Book Company, New York, 1964.

Cross, A. J. Foy, and Irene F. Cypher: *Audio-Visual Education,* Thomas Y. Crowell Company, New York, 1961.

De Fieffer, Robert E.: *Audio-Visual Instruction,* Center for Applied Research in Education, New York, 1965.

Educational Media Council: *Educational Media Index,* McGraw-Hill Book Company, New York, 1964.

Erickson, Carlton W.: *Fundamentals of Teaching with Audio-Visual Technology,* The Macmillan Company, New York, 1965.

Monlarn, John E.: *Preparation of Inexpensive Teaching Materials,* Chandler Publishing Company, San Francisco, 1963.

Riefsvold, Margaret Incore: *Guides to New Educational Media,* American Library Association in cooperation with the U.S. Department of Health, Education, and Welfare, Office of Education, Washington, D.C., 1961.

Schultz, Monten J.: *The Teacher and Overhead Projection,* Prentice-Hall, Inc., Englewood Cliffs, N.J., 1965.

Trow, William Clark: *Teacher and Technology: New Design for Learning,* Appleton-Century-Crofts, Inc., New York, 1963.

part 4

PLANNING AND GUIDING LEARNING EXPERIENCES

INTRODUCTION

The preceding part presented basic concepts of method and varying kinds of patterns, procedures, and techniques which apply to different kinds of learnings and activities in the physical education program. The value of understanding underlying principles is realized as a teacher has the ability to adapt them to the specific problems he encounters in organizing and conducting various aspects of the physical education program. The purpose of this part centers on planning for instruction and organizing and guiding learning in all phases of the physical education program.

Chapter 11 discusses instructional planning, the process through which methods are selected. It considers teacher-student planning as an instructional method, describes steps in preparing daily and unit lesson plans, and presents criteria for selecting methods.

Chapter 12 deals with the class instruction program. It describes factors of organization and management in the conduct of class physical education which impinge upon methodology. Chapters 13 and 14 serve a similar purpose for extraclass instruction, by considering problems of organization and management for intramural, recreation, and interscholastic programs.

chapter 11

PLANNING INSTRUCTION

INTRODUCTION

Planning of units and lessons, short-term planning, is important subject matter for a text on methods. As one makes such short-term plans he decides how he is going to organize and proceed to teach whatever is to be taught. In other words, during the planning of units and lessons he selects his methods.

In professional preparation for physical education, long-term planning is appropriate subject matter for a course dealing with curriculm or program rather than for a course dealing with methods, for which this text is designed. It is unmistakably true that long-term planning—for one, four, six, or even twelve years—affects student experiences; hence teacher skill in this area is required. While Chapter 5, Programs for Secondary Schools, dealt with this in a general and introductory way, the authors intentionally avoid the kind of depth coverage needed in a text on curriculum.

Attention is called to the fact that responsibilities and opportunities for long-term planning given to teachers vary considerably from school to school. As noted in Chapter 5, it is quite common for a physical education faculty, a committee of the faculty, or the director to prepare a written program showing the activities for each of the weeks of all the school years. This means that not all teachers will have direct and primary responsibility and opportunity for long-term planning.

Professional teachers, however, make their own short-term plans, select their own methods, make their own lesson plans and units. If volleyball, for instance, is required of all sophomores for three weeks in March, the teacher teaches volleyball. How he will teach it is usually up to him. In preparing a unit he delineates fairly specific objectives, exact activities, and methods of teaching. In making lesson plans growing out of the unit, he selects still closer-range objectives, activities, and methods.

UNIT PLANNING

A unit is a planned sequence of learning activities or experiences which make up a meaningful whole involving purpose for the student and achievement of significant goals. Physical education, with its variety of activities appealing to young people and its ready adaptability to procedures which use a large amount of student participation in planning and managing, is well fitted for unit organization. Units vary in type and in length. Generally speaking, physical education units vary in length from six to twenty-four lessons depending upon the subject matter involved as well as upon students and objectives. A unit in bowling might be short, having for its main purpose introducing students to that activity. A unit in basketball for freshmen who have had little experience with that game might be quite long in number of lessons, whereas a unit in that sport for seniors might be short to provide additional experiences with the game.

The two most widely used types of units are *resource* and *teaching*. A third type, *diary* or *log* unit, is used extensively by some teachers. The first may be used in many different situations; the second is for "*these* students in *this* situation"; the third summarizes what has been done.

RESOURCE UNIT

A resource unit gathers together various information and ideas useful in teaching a given subject or activity. Its purpose as its name indicates is to provide resources needed for teaching and for preparing teaching units. Assume that you are preparing to teach a unit in volleyball. You probably would review literature on the subject and the teaching of it: read one or more books, review your college notebook, study the rules, search for and read magazine articles. You might review tests, find out what others have said about such things as objectives, interest development, teaching procedures, introduction, and practice of various skills, and search for ideas about evaluation. That is, you probably would make such preparation if you did not have a resource unit available. A resource unit would give the information and ideas, the background needed to prepare a teaching unit. If you are preparing to teach your first unit in volleyball without having a previously prepared resource unit, then by all means you should make one as you read, study, investigate, and review literature as described above; you then would have a resource unit for future reference, and the next time you prepared to teach volleyball you would not have to consult source after source but use only your resource unit for the information and review needed to set about preparing a teaching unit for a specific group of students.

Resource units may be arranged in various ways; no one best organization can be recommended. It may be helpful, however, to suggest content categories. One such unit [1] uses 13 main categories as follows:

1. Objectives: the game and its skills with effects upon students are related to more general objectives of physical education
2. Ways of appraising needs, interests, and abilities of students
3. Ways of increasing interest: some 20 suggestions are made
4. Facilities and equipment: suggestions about balls and courts needed and their use and adaptation are made
5. Safety precautions: several suggestions are included
6. Lead-up games: a number are suggested for young players
7. Simplified or modified volleyball: gives suggestions concerning teaching beginning players
8. Teaching the game and its skills: points about procedures are presented
9. Suggested culminating activities: activities for providing a climax, something to end up with, are mentioned
10. Rules: sources are given
11. Coeducational volleyball: comments concerning procedures are made
12. Suggestions for evaluation: approaches include observation, judgment, skill and knowledge tests
13. Bibliography: books, periodicals, and films are mentioned

TEACHING UNITS

A resource unit may serve equally well in many situations. A teaching unit is specific to time and place; it is made for a specific group of students in a specific situation; it is tailor-made. It is true, of course, that some parts of one teaching unit may become parts of another; what is appropriate for one may be effective for others as a doctor's prescription may serve several patients equally well. The teacher, the architect of the teaching units, uses some of the same subject matter and procedures for more than

[1] See Clyde Knapp and Ann E. Jewett, *Physical Education Student Teaching Guide*, Stipes Publishing Company, Champaign, Illinois, 1962, pp. 61–70.

one class if they are equally appropriate and effective for the different students and situations.

There are two kinds of teaching units. One is called either a traditional unit or, as we will call it, a subject matter unit. The other is called an experience or an experience-oriented unit. A subject matter unit arranges the subject matter to be taught in whatever way the maker feels it is logical to present it. Neither the students nor the situation is considered. The teaching job is viewed as presenting the subject matter and not as being concerned with the students involved. The teacher's job is to present; the student's job to take it or leave it. Whether they learn well is not the teacher's concern.

An experience unit centers about the experiences needed for achievement of the desired objectives and is organized psychologically around objectives which are meaningful to students or can be made so. What kinds of experiences do these students need to develop health, strength, vigor, recreational skills, and cooperative and competitive abilities? What approaches and activities will best accomplish the ends sought?

These two teaching units seem to be poles apart, and they are if viewed as units which are concerned only with subject matter, on the one hand, and only with experiences, on the other. Actually it is hardly possible to have a unit that is all one or the other. Rather, some characteristics of each type exist in all teaching units. If one starts with subject matter he will get to experiences and vice versa. It is unmistakably true, however, that units will reflect emphasis upon one or the other. If the teacher making the plan feels that presenting subject matter represents almost the whole responsibility of a teacher, he will emphasize subject matter. If one feels that it is important to consider the needs, attitudes, abilities, and previous knowledge and skill and to build motivation, he will emphasize experiences for students.

The finished product of a written teaching unit may be narrative or outline in style, or some combination of the two may be preferred. Units leaning heavily toward experience center on the students and tend to emphasize teacher-student cooperation in planning and in handling the procedures needed as the unit plan is carried out. Persons interested in examining sample units, one using the subject matter style and one using an experience-oriented approach, may read those presented by Knapp and Jewett.[2] They use the same class, the same students, for both units so that differences between the two types readily appear; the subject matter approach deals with the students as a group which assume common characteristics, whereas the experience-oriented unit studies the students individually, indicates probable needs, and plans activities and experiences accordingly.

[2] *Ibid.*, pp. 70–73, 76–84.

To guide the reader in preparing teaching units, the authors list the following steps. They suggest a student-centered approach; student participation in planning and operation may be incorporated in all, any, or none of the steps, depending upon the situation and upon the preference of the person making the unit plan. The sequence of steps remains the same whether a subject matter or an experience-oriented approach is used, or whether the teacher alone or with student participation prepares the unit.

1. Study the students, their needs, interests, and abilities.
2. Prepare proposed objectives, ends, or outcomes. State goals in terms of student behaviors, conducts, attitudes, achievement in skilled performances, expanded interests, physical development, and adjustment to living in social, emotional, and recreational areas.
3. Consider limitations imposed by time, equipment, and facilities available as well as by characteristics and ability of the teacher.
4. Consider various subject matter, activities, and experiences which might contribute significantly to achievement of unit purposes.
5. Select from step (4) activities, experiences, and subject matter which will be practical and manageable and which will lead to progress toward the objectives.
6. Plan the introduction or orientation, including ways to help students understand what the unit involves, to help them create concepts of what may be accomplished.
7. Make sure that students know their role, their opportunities, responsibilities, and regulations during the progress of the unit.
8. Plan for evaluation.
9. Consider culminating activities such as exhibits, assembly programs, all-star games, competition with other classes, and outings. (While not always necessary, they prove very useful as interest developers in some cases.)
10. Plan for writing a log or summary as the unit progresses, which will show strengths and weaknesses of the unit thus becoming useful in planning future units.

The following ten criteria are suggested for evaluating unit plans:

1. Does the unit grow out of valid, useful, and significant needs and interests of students?
2. Do the experiences take place in a lifelike context which has meaning and values to students?
3. Does the unit provide experiences which lead naturally toward new adventures and serve as motivation for additional learning?
4. Do the levels of difficulty challenge the most able students and allow

purposeful participation and satisfying achievement for the less able?

5. Does the plan provide the best possible use of time and effort of all concerned as objectives in the areas of skills, knowledge, understanding, interests, and attitudes are pursued?
6. Are the experiences of value in integrating learning from other units or areas of the class and from the physical education program as a whole?
7. Does the unit provide for cooperation, competition, student planning or responsibility, or other activities which allow for realization of social values inherent in group activity?
8. Are there ample opportunities to apply what is learned in out-of-class situations?
9. Is the unit practical? Are the proposed objectives achievable with these students considering the time, equipment, and facilities available?
10. Does the unit provide for optimal use of exploratory activity, problem solving, discovery?

LESSON PLANNING

The best of long-term and unit planning falls on barren soil if the day-by-day experiences that constitute lessons are not intelligently planned and carried out. As used here, the basic concept of a lesson is the work of one day or one activity period. However, a lesson may cover more or less than one day or period, and, of course, continuity from day to day and from period to period must pursue the objectives of units or other longer-term plans.

Unitary organization of learning requires related and purposeful activities for students. Few class experiences of one day are or should be complete in themselves. The most ardent enthusiast, however, for units which provide for experiences projected over a relatively long period of time finds day-by-day planning and checking necessary. Such planning is continuous; it goes on as teachers and students make suggestions for next steps. The teacher who guides individual learners as they engage in learning experiences counsels and plans with them as they participate in class activities. Planning of this sort necessitates anticipation of the next steps not only for the class as a whole but also for individuals and groups within the class.

Written lesson plans help the teacher to organize his thinking. They afford protection against forgetting, tend to ensure availability of needed materials, lessen waste motion, provide a record of progress along the way, aid in the making of future plans, and serve as one basis for evaluation. They help the teacher to feel secure and assured because needed teacher procedures are likely to be more clearly understood and remembered.

Lesson plans should be made shortly before use. Fixed subject matter lesson plans, originating in the intent of the teacher to require all students to achieve fixed standards, can be prepared for use in the quite distant future. If adhered to strictly, they are worse than useless because fast learners become bored, slow learners become confused, interest falls to a low ebb, and disciplinary problems arise and multiply. Plans for a day's activity that are made shortly before they are put to use can reflect adequately the situation and the immediate needs of the various students. Unit and long-term plans project procedures into a somewhat distant future. Lessons are the steps along the way.

Lesson plans are more specific and detailed than are plans covering a longer period. Objectives, procedures, and activities should be quite specific since both the teacher and the student know better where the student is in terms of progress toward larger goals; hence there are bases for immediate decisions concerning what the needs are. One appropriate objective for a unit in volleyball may be stated as *to help each student develop playing skills up toward the upper limits of his capacity*. But such an objective is relatively meaningless for a lesson plan where needed specificity makes such objectives as *to help every member of the class to understand the rotation scheme, to help Mary develop ability to serve the ball over the net,* and *to help Sue understand why cooperative play is necessary,* appropriate. Planning for specificity and detail becomes a quite complicated procedure. It is as complicated as are the needs of the individual students involved.

Lesson planning must take cognizance of individual differences. In a unit on soccer, it may be appropriate, on a given day, for some boys or girls to concentrate on rather advanced team play, while others may need to work on simple skills needed for satisfactory participation in advanced team play. Again, some may badly need help in developing ability to cooperate in team play or group work, while others may need only practice in specialized skills.

In considering the need for adjustment to individual differences in lesson plans, let us point to situations common in swimming classes. There are likely to be students who swim quite well, others who can stay afloat, and others who cannot swim at all. Swimming needs of individuals are quite obvious. No teacher would ask a boy who cannot stay afloat to dive off the deep end of the pool and swim a length. The teacher is forced to pay attention to individual differences. It is likely that ability differences in soccer or any other complicated activity are as marked as they are in swimming. But they are not so obvious; hence some teachers are inclined to pay too little attention to them.

Lesson plans may be written in detail, they may be outlined with attention called to key points, or they may be planned mentally without writing. The inexperienced teacher needs to write plans in some detail to be prepared to lead effectively. The more experienced and resourceful the teacher, the less the need for full preparation in writing. All teachers need plans that will let them thoroughly understand what needs to be accomplished and how attacks are to be made. Such plans will help the teacher to be resourceful.

Some teachers erroneously believe that little attention needs to be given to advance planning because it is desirable to adjust to circumstances as they arise. The exact opposite is true. It is desirable and necessary to adjust to circumstances as they arise. The teacher who does not plan well in advance cannot adjust effectively because he has poor concepts of the larger whole into which circumstantial adjustments must fit. The thorough planner can be more flexible because his fuller knowledge of what is to be accomplished permits him to make intelligent adjustments that will make for student progress toward recognized ends.

ESSENTIAL INGREDIENTS OF A LESSON PLAN

There is no one best form for lesson plans. Insistence upon particular forms frequently makes for stereotyped plans that neither encourage sufficient attention to the particular group and the individuals at hand nor permit adequate teacher-student planning. However, there are essential ingredients for all lesson plans. They are:

1. A statement of goals or objectives appropriate for the group and for each individual that are, or can be made, meaningful to the students
2. A statement of experiences and activities proposed for the various class members with key instructional points listed
3. A list of materials needed
4. A description of methods and procedures to be used
5. Provisions for linking with previous and future plans, assuring continuity
6. Provisions for evaluation
7. Provisions for comments by the teacher after the lesson has been taught for the purpose of helping in preparation of future lessons

TEACHER–STUDENT PLANNING

Student participation in planning and managing has value for several reasons. First, in almost all cases student interest and motivation is increased. Second, goals, purposes, and procedures will be understood better; because of this, learning is likely to be more rapid. Third, class morale is likely to be better. Fourth, through the democratic, responsibility-sharing group process of having something to say about plans which affect them and their activities, students may acquire valuable practice in working with others and develop knowledge and skills which will serve well in many situations.

From a theoretical standpoint, the case for student participation in planning is clear-cut. However, there are problems which present considerable difficulty. Some teachers have little skill or ability in group planning. The nature of physical education programs, with emphasis on physical activity and the universal problem of restricted time, makes extensive use of full-scale group planning more difficult than it is in some other curricular areas. However, as will be pointed out, physical education makes some participation in planning easy. The following discussion attempts to deal with some of the practical problems which face a physical education teacher who uses teacher-student planning as a basic method.

RECONCILING TEACHER OBJECTIVES AND STUDENT OBJECTIVES

Frequent seeming differences between teacher and student objectives need not bother the teacher as he plans with students. Ends sought by the teacher and those sought by students need to be compatible; they do not need to be synonymous. Teachers need not be concerned about students having differing objectives if end results are likely to be the same or similar. For example, for a unit on speedball a teacher might have contribution to student strength and enduranceas a major goal. A student's goal might be pleasure and satisfaction playing the game rather than developing strength and endurance. But the teacher's goal may be reached more effectively than it would if teacher and student objective agreed.

To develop desirable cooperative and competitive attitudes among students might be an important teacher objective for a unit in basketball. A student, hardly conscious of this teacher goal, might set for himself a goal of becoming more popular with his teammates and opponents. Achievement of the student purpose would contribute to attainment of the teacher goal although the two had different ends in mind. An important function of a teacher is to help students set goals for themselves. Frequently the best results are achieved by encouraging students to accept goals which in themselves are unlike teacher objectives but which, nevertheless, bring progress toward teacher goals as well as toward worthwhile student objectives.

STUDENT SELECTION AND A BALANCED PROGRAM

Some physical educators believe that permitting students to have a part in selection of activities would endanger a balanced program. They feel that it is necessary for the teacher to do all of the selecting to assure a variety of student experiences. All agree that every boy and girl should learn a substantial number of activities. A core program which assures that all have basic experiences in selected activities seems very desirable. However, this does not preclude student sharing in selection.

Consider the case of a high school class during a fall season. Assume that the teacher, or a curriculum committee with student representatives, has decided that an outdoor team game should be the central activity for 20 class days. There are objectives concerning physical development as well as development in the social, emotional, citizenship, and leisure-time areas. In the case of boys, it is likely that touch football or soccer or speedball would meet the fundamental objectives. For girls field hockey or soccer or speedball might very well do the job. In such cases, student voice in selection proves not only appropriate but also highly desirable. But a word of caution is in order. Complete student selection without teacher leadership in expanding the interests and abilities of boys and girls toward substantial experience in several team games can impoverish a program. This results from a tendency on the part of students to choose games they already know and like. Games new to them might later become more enjoyable than the game that is now their favorite. But before this happens, knowledge of and skill in the new game must be developed. This calls for teacher guidance; it means that students should not always be allowed to select with entire freedom. Rather, they should be permitted and encouraged to choose within limits.

STUDENTS MAY SHARE IN PLANNING WITHOUT SELECTING THE CENTRAL ACTIVITY

Whether or not students select the central activity, they may have a part in planning. For example, they can have a part in dividing the class into groups or teams, in organizing for practice, in arranging for student leadership both in skill practice and administration of games, in checking attendance, distributing and collecting supplies, and seeing that dressing rooms are kept safe and clean.

Suppose that a teacher selects a 20-lesson soccer unit and that he plans learning experiences before he introduces the unit to his students. In this case he would have determined the objectives he wanted students to achieve; he would have considered the facilities and supplies available, studied the physical abilities, and he would have learned considerably about the social and adjustment problems of various students. He would have planned social and emotional experiences he hopes each student will have during the soccer unit. He would have considered how John, a bully at times, or Mary, a frequent withdrawer, or Irene, an unpredictable vacillator, and other students probably will be affected by various projected learning experiences.

In this case the teacher has selected soccer as the central subject matter. He has projected various learning experiences. Does this sort of teacher planning rule out teacher-student planning of this unit? Not by any means.

A considerable amount of teacher-student planning may be injected into this soccer unit even though the class members had no voice in the selection of the main subject matter. Teacher preplanning has selected major areas; it has provided for skill practice and drill as well as for games and gamelike activity. It has not, however, provided rigid and detailed controls such as five minutes for trapping practice, seven minutes for heading practice, and eight minutes for dribbling practice on each of ten days during the 20 lessons.

In introducing this unit it would be good procedure to invite student suggestions concerning the division of the class into groups or teams. Students might decide that they would like to elect captains and that the captains should choose teams. This might be done at the outset of the unit or after preliminary practicing and playing experiences. The boys or girls might decide that they would like to have teams assigned by the teacher, or that groups should be assigned according to height-weight-age classifications; or they might prefer to pursue the unit by grouping and regrouping from day to day.

Student suggestions concerning leadership should be sought. Would they like student leaders or captains? What responsibilities and prerogatives would they like their captains to have? The leaders might be assistant teachers who would lead in the learning of skills, in the selection and assignment of players to positions, in the development of team play, and in the selection of officials. On the other hand, the class might decide that their leader should be only their representative in competitive games, acting as a captain would in an interscholastic game.

Students may be given opportunities to make suggestions concening skill drills. They might suggest drills that are as sound fundamentally as those the teacher might select. If drills suggested by students are selected, there is likely to be wholehearted response because class members will feel not only pride in the selections but also responsibility for success of something that is their own.

The class members may well be invited to make suggestions concerning the distribution of time between practicing and playing. Some teachers hesitate to permit this because they feel that the students will want to play the game too much of the time and avoid needed skill drill. This feeling may have validity, but it is true that when a teacher invites suggestions, there will be opportunities to discuss the need for skill drill and to point out that it is necessary for efficient learning. Students thus may be led to relate the drilling to their end purpose of playing the game with the satisfaction that comes from playing well.

Suggestions for arranging competition may be sought. Would the students prefer four teams of equal strength and a round robin schedule during the latter part of the unit? Would they like two teams of approximately even ability selected from among the better players in the class and two more teams made up from the less able players and a world series of games? Or would they suggest a tournament arrangement of games?

Other things in connection with this hypothetical unit on soccer about which student suggestions might well be sought include (1) selecting and training of officials, (2) distributing and caring for supplies, (3) keeping and posting records of team standings, (4) checking attendance, (5) supervising dressing rooms, and (6) reporting to the school paper.

There are several methods of securing student suggestions which a teacher may use in a situation such as the one described in this soccer unit. One approach is to ask the class for suggestions and follow with a discussion and disposition of the proposals. Another is to invite the class to select representatives to meet with the teacher for the purpose of planning. Still another is to encourage students to make suggestions to the teacher either orally or in writing.

INITIATING STUDENT–TEACHER PLANNING PROCEDURES

Effective student participation in planning requires that students acquire skill in the techniques and have interest in the process. In schools in which other areas of the curriculum utilize student planning, little trouble exists in carrying out similar procedures in physical education. When students are unfamiliar with basic techniques and lack orientation to the process and their responsibilities thereto, a physical education teacher may find his task more difficult. Since method must always play a secondary role to ends sought, a teacher must guard against utilizing a disproportionate amount of his class time in planning. If students are inept at planning, he should introduce the method slowly, giving opportunity to plan for small projects, and gradually increase responsibility. An appropriate place to develop both skill and interest in student planning is in the extraclass program. Placing major responsibility for program planning and leadership directly on participants through homeroom groups or other organizational units and extraclass clubs is feasible administratively. Until students become responsible and proficient, teacher controls must be more rigid, but the advisory capacity of the teacher in this respect can become increasingly nondirective.

FINDING TIME FOR PLANNING

Finding time to plan presents a problem in physical education programs. There is a natural and sound desire to make maximum use of the available time for activity. There is no major problem in the extraclass program where time is more flexible. For yearly or vertical program planning, representatives are often elected from either the student body as a whole or from basic class or homeroom units. Since this planning must take place at the times teachers themselves are free, which means nonclass hours, it does not lessen instructional time. Several suggestions are offered, however, for appropriate times to plan on the unit and daily lesson levels.

At the beginning of the term, general school administrative factors, such as short periods, registration, orientation assemblies, and school locker assignments, usually prevent dressing for the first physical education class period. If routines involved in physical education such as locker assignments, towel fees, and directions for purchase of clothing are handled with high efficiency there may be time left for planning. Mimeographed directions and preassigned lockers, for example, are two ways of saving time often dissipated in these routines.

Teachers can request information from principals in advance about days which will result in short periods because of special events. These days may be used for planning sessions. Also, elected or volunteer student leaders might meet during free times. Homeroom time may be available if good relationships exist between the physical education and other departments.

Proper planning procedure requires time to discuss issues. A teacher's asking a class to vote on whether they would rather play volleyball or basketball hardly constitutes effective planning. If only a few moments are available during the class period, the issues may be presented to students at a previous meeting and provisions made for them to discuss them in their homeroom groups, in club periods, or informally before or after class. Under these conditions, a few class moments might be taken for final discussion and voting or consensus reaching. Similarly, having a class assemble dressed for activity, only to spend a majority of the period in a planning session, represents a misuse of time. If a major portion of a period is to be devoted to planning, students should meet in a classroom prepared for discussion. Although a teacher must exercise prudence in utilizing limited class and facility time for planning, he will find that the method, if properly used, makes major contributions to achieving many objectives of physical education.

CRITERIA FOR SELECTING METHODS

When one plans instruction, he decides how he will teach; he selects methods. Checking methods which are considered for use against a set of criteria helps a teacher think through the probable effects of using those methods. The following criteria, in the form of questions, are presented.

Is the method selected compatible with goals sought? The basic guide to selecting methods is examination of desired outcomes. Means determine ends, and therefore ends must determine means. For example, favorable attitudes toward a sport as a recreational pursuit require presentation of that game so students will both enjoy it and have sufficient skills to pursue it recreationally. In teaching beginning badminton, for instance, for use in the noon-hour recreation program, early practice should be given in a whole game with sufficient playing rules and elementary strokes presented so students could begin participation without supervision. If a strictly drill approach were used, with single strokes taken up in order, and playing rules were introduced only after a number of basic skills were mastered, participation might be long delayed, and the initial interest might be lost. On the other hand, an intermediate badminton class, selected by students with an initial interest in badminton, may well be devoted to extensive practice on basic strokes, with emphasis on skill-developing routines. The purpose, assuming that it is accepted by students, dictates the best method for a given class period. This principle applies particularly to the area of attitudes since the methods used to present learnings will condition a student's future feelings about the activity.

Are the methods used the best possible means of achieving the goals sought? Very often methods which are successful do not necessarily represent the best choice. Other possible methods might lead to even fuller values. Actually, the chief problem in relation to this criterion lies in a limited concept of goals. Teachers should keep in mind the breadth of goals sought in physical education. A method which may lead to the greatest achievement of a motor fitness objective may offer little progress toward objectives related to social and emotional development. A satisfactory method is not always the best possible choice.

Are the methods used adaptable to the types of activities involved? Each activity in physical education presents unique problems for methods. The nature of the activity should be analyzed to determine the most appropriate methods. Square dancing, for example, lends itself to large-group procedures, but wrestling and archery, particularly in their beginning phases, require groups small enough to give close individual attention and maintain optimum safety controls. Strokes in swimming and track and field-type activities lend themselves to use of the whole method, whereas the nature of team sports suggests the advantages of the whole-part-whole method.

Are the methods selected feasible in relation to time available, space, equipment, and teacher load? Very often the method which appears most appropriate on first analysis of both purpose and type of activity cannot be used because of limiting aspects of the physical environment. When this occurs, efforts should be made to adapt method to existing conditions. For example, in a beginning swimming class, it probably would be desirable to give individual instruction. Since it is seldom possible to assign a single student to a teacher, teachers devise methods for individualizing instruction within groups. Teachers with one basketball court and more than ten students devise modified games making use of supplemental baskets on the sides of the floor to approximate gamelike conditions and to allow for maximum participation. In a case like this, the teacher asks, "Is it better to have 24 boys playing a modified one-basket game with teams of three men each, or to play the regulation game, using the full court, but requiring that 14 boys sit idle waiting for their turn?" Both methods might be used at different stages of play and under varying circumstances, but the creative teacher finds ways to make the best use of the physical environment.

Does the teacher have skill in using the selected method? Teachers must acquire adeptness at using certain kinds of methods just as they learn any other skill. Chapter 15, Method and Supervision, suggests ways for teachers to improve their skill at various kinds of methods. When immediate plans call for a method in which the teacher is unskilled, he should give special attention to use of supplemental methods and not base the entire project upon his success with a new method. Also, he should try out new methods on experimental groups and on one class at a time. This should be interpreted only as a precautionary procedure because actually teachers should be continually experimenting with new methods—for better ways of organizing learning. It is suggested that when teachers are unfamiliar with a method proposed for use, they proceed with care, taking every precaution to provide a satisfactory learning experience for the group with which the new method is being tried.

Are the methods inherently interesting to students? It has been pointed out that interest is requisite to effective learning, that students learn only after they have been sufficiently aroused to participate actively. Initial interest in an activity can be stifled by inappropriate methods. The same students who eagerly await the noon hour or school's closing to engage in their favorite sport show little interest in a class program devoted to the same activity when inept methods are used. Few students enjoy overemphasis on drill or highly formalized technique in which rigid disciplines are imposed. Care, too, should be exercised to provide for maximum participation since waiting in line for one's turn is both uninteresting and frustrating. Methods, also, should be within the range of ability of students since oversimplified drills, for example, are as destructive of interest as complicated organizational patterns which are beyond the skill level of participants. In addition, with adolescents, group activity very often provides interest in itself. For example, a drill practice of volleying a volleyball against a wall may be uninteresting to an individual but become of interest when undertaken as a team drill.

Do students have sufficient understanding of the purposes of the methods to profit by their use? If not, are provisions made for proper orientation to the methods? A procedure which appears desirable in terms of goals, the activity, and the setting may be beyond the comprehension or ability of the students. This problem is quite likely to appear in connection with teacher-student planning. One cannot take an untutored group of youngsters who have no skills in group planning and expect that they will suddenly learn through mere exposure to that method. It becomes necessary to help students understand how the method will lead them to goals they seek and to teach them the skills involved. Often understanding alone changes an unsuccessful method to a successful one. A coach may find his players grumbling and "dogging it" on prescrimmage practice warmup drills. A discussion of the value of the drills and of their purpose in relation to the conditioning program may change their attitude and lead to enthusiastic participation in this phase of the total learning experience. A teacher who uses the buddy system in swimming classes obtains best results from this method when he impresses upon students the reason for using it and enlists their cooperation.

Are methods considered a means to an end and never an end in themselves? Teaching methods represent the most efficient way to organize a learning experience so the best results will accrue. Occasionally, one finds that teachers become so interested or sold on a type of method that outcomes take a secondary role to the method itself. A good example of this is the teacher who gives formal calisthenics at the beginning of each period. When asked his purpose, he replies that it is good discipline. Discipline for what? one may ask. The other extreme is the teacher who is enamored of the group process. As long as students are busy planning their own games and programs and leading and refereeing their own activities, he is confident that he has a good program. Democratic group activity is a means of stimulating certain kinds of learnings, but it does not guarantee good results. Ends must be held primary, and unless the methods used lead to significant progress toward these goals, they may be judged inadequate. Methods have only relative values; they are good methods if they lead to goals sought.

Do the methods used stimulate creativity and independent thinking and allow for individual differences? Learning is an individual endeavor, and unless methods selected are sufficiently flexible to allow for individual variance within groups, many will make unnecessarily slow progress. Also, in learning of all types, including motor skills, the learner must be able to adapt suggestions to his own peculiar traits. Unless students are given opportunity to think independently and to experiment to find the best solutions to their own learning problems, learning may be impeded. An extreme example finds a left-handed student required to perform a mimetic drill in a right-handed position to achieve a uniform class effect.

Fortunately, such obvious lack of individualization has all but disappeared, but less revealed differences may be neglected unless students are encouraged and given opportunities to seek the best solutions to their own learning problems. Different body builds require different approaches to stunts and tumbling; leg length determines takeoff points in hurdling; dance realizes its best educational contributions when there is creativity in performance. Activities realize their educative potentials best if introduced through appropriate methods.

Has the method been used excessively to the exclusion of other methods of equal or greater value and at the expense of the potential value of variety? A fine method may lose its effectiveness through overuse. Excessive exposure to one method may produce monotony and deprive the class of stimulation which comes through variety. Further, since different methods emphasize different kinds of learning, goals and programs may be narrow in scope unless students are exposed to a variety of methods. Some programs are organized entirely on a squad and squad leader basis. This system gives opportunity for only one type of leadership and is not always useful in all kinds of activities. Additional patterns of class organization are needed. There is no best method; variety leads to more satisfactory all-around results.

SUMMARY

As units and lessons are planned, methods are selected. Not all teachers will have opportunities to plan a whole-school program, but all will make their unit and lesson plans and thus select their own methods.

Physical education lends itself readily to the unit plan of organization. A unit represents a planned sequence of learning experiences which centers about a meaningful whole, such as a central problem, an activity, or a subject matter area.

Degree of emphasis distinguishes the difference between subject matter and experience units. The subject matter unit is organized logically and centers primarily around the acquisition of predetermined standards of knowledge or skill. The experience unit is organized psychologically and centers primarily on the intention of the learner to achieve a purpose.

The major value of the unit plan rests upon the implication that it is a planned endeavor which gives attention to all factors surrounding the student and the learning environment.

Daily lesson plans prove essential to good teaching. They help a teacher to organize his thinking, to use available time efficiently, and to feel secure and assured.

Unit and daily lesson plans require attention to precise selection of methods for use in carrying out the plans. A teacher should list acceptable criteria for selecting methods and consistently apply them in making unit and daily lesson plans.

Student participation in planning is of value because it serves to create interest, increase insight into goals or purposes, heighten class morale, and teach techniques of democratic participation in group work.

Teacher objectives for students and student objectives for themselves need to be compatible but not necessarily synonymous. Students generally focus on immediate and tangible goals, whereas teachers may have more remote values in mind.

Effective student participation in planning requires skill in techniques and interest in the process of planning. Extraclass activities provide an excellent laboratory for initiating teacher-student planning procedures.

Questions and problems for discussion

1. Explain why a unit plan should not be constructed as a series of daily lesson plans.

2. Construct a teaching unit plan for a class about whom sufficient facts are known, or construct a resource unit for a hypothetical group.

3. How much attention should be given to instructional materials and supplies in the unit lesson plan? In the daily lesson plan?

4. Indicate procedures for individualizing instruction which would be a part of unit planning and those further provisions for individual differences which would be included in daily lesson planning.

5. For a group of high school students with whom you are familiar, develop an experience unit plan which would center around use of some natural community resource.

6. Draw up a skeleton form for a daily lesson plan which would provide for all essential points and would facilitate your preparation of daily lesson plans.

7. Analyze any physical education classwork which can be observed over a period of weeks. Is instruction organized on a unit plan? Is there any evidence of a written plan for the class? Is the class organized on a subject matter or an experience basis? Is there any evidence of sound daily planning? Is the work properly sequential?

8. To what extent should teachers reuse for subsequent classes (a) resource units, (b) teaching units, and (c) daily lesson plans?

Selected references

Darron, Helen Fisher: *Independent Activities for Creative Learning,* Bureau of Publications, Teachers College, Columbia University, New York, 1961.

Davis, Elwood Craig, and Earl L. Wallis: *Toward Better Teaching in Physical Education,* Prentice-Hall, Inc., Englewood Cliffs, N.J., 1962.

Davis, Robert Alexander: *Planning Learning Programs in Secondary Schools* George Peabody College for Teachers, Nashville, 1963.

Department of Classroom Teachers: *Innovations for Time to Teach; Project: Time to Teach,* National Education Association, Washington, D.C., 1966.

Hass, Glen, and Kimball Wiles: *Readings in Curriculum,* Allyn and Bacon, Inc., Englewood Cliffs, N.J., 1965.

Lee, Florence Henny: *Principles and Practices of Teaching in Secondary Schools,* David McKay Company, New York, 1965.

Norr, Gertrude: *Teaching and Learning, The Democratic Way,* Prentice-Hall, Inc., Englewood Cliffs, N.J., 1963.

Richey, Robert W.: *Planning for Teaching,* 3d ed., McGraw-Hill Book Company, New York, 1963.

Steeves, Frank L.: *Fundamentals of Teaching in Secondary Schools,* The Odyssey Press, Inc., New York, 1962.

Wiles, Kimball: *Teaching for Better Schools,* Prentice-Hall, Inc., Englewood Cliffs, N.J., 1959.

chapter 12

ORGANIZING AND MANAGING CLASS PROGRAMS

INTRODUCTION

Required classes are scheduled during the regular school day and exclude after-school activities such as intramural, recreational, girls' athletic association, club, extramural, and interscholastic activities. This chapter deals with organizational matters in preparation for class meetings and with managerial problems during the progress of classes. The line of demarcation between details of organization and management, as thus conceived, is not clearly established in unmistakable terms. For the purpose of discussion, organization gives direction to management, and management carries out the plans projected by organization.

Of course, in a very real sense, planning, organizing, and managing all represent teaching. Learning effectiveness will be enhanced and teaching will proceed more smoothly if organization provides for efficient ways of accomplishing what needs to be done. Management should see that values made possible by organization are realized.

Organization differs from administration. In this chapter, organization and management mean things the teacher does, things over which the teacher has control, and things directly related to teaching a class. Chapter 16, Method and Administration, considers matters such as scheduling of classes, time allotment, policy concerning atypical students, supplies, and facilities. Although teachers are concerned with these things, school administrative officers play the key roles; this is not the case with organization and management as discussed here.

ORGANIZATION OF ROUTINES

Whatever needs to be repeated frequently should be routinized because (1) time will be saved, (2) students are likely to be at ease because order and knowledge of how to behave will prevail, (3) class morale and cooperation will increase, (4) fewer disciplinary problems will arise, (5) teacher words will be saved, (6) students' minds can better be occupied with subject matter or with approaching activity since attention to little procedural details is not necessary, and (7) learning effectiveness will increase as values mentioned in the above six points are realized.

What things need to be routinized? Some of them relate to procedures for dressing and bathing, uniforms and towels, checking attendance, the handling of temporary exemptions, getting teaching stations ready to use, distribution of supplies, safety, and record keeping.

How does one establish a routine? He does so by announcing it to his class and then insisting upon conformance. Can one expect complete conformance immediately? No, but he can establish unfailing compliance, usually after about a dozen class days, if he insists upon conformance, calls attention to every violation, and if the requirement represents a reasonable regulation in the opinion of the students. For illustrative purposes descriptions of several routine procedures which have been readily accepted in secondary schools follow.

One school faced an irritating problem due to noise, running, and occasional ball tossing by students as they went up two flights of stairs from their dressing room to the gymnasium. First, the teacher told the students that if they could not go from the dressing room to the gymnasium without noise, which disturbed others, without running, and without ball tossing, which might cause injury as well as inconvenience to other people using the stairs, then they would have to march as a group. Since that kind of talk proved effective for only a few days, the teacher carried out the alternative—the students marched. This they disliked because everyone had to wait for the slowest dresser before going to the gymnasium. After some time it was decided that students could go by themselves and that four regulations would be imposed: (1) walk; do not run; (2) walk one step at a time; (3) supplies such as balls, nets, and rackets must be in a bag or other container; and (4) talking in conversational tones is permitted; no loud talk. The teacher was a bit surprised when these regulations became routine with multiple classes in about two weeks. Other teachers and classes followed suit. For several years this routine was followed, and teachers were gratified that as school years started and as new students appeared there was little need to reestablish the routine. Somehow, it carried over.

Many readers likely have been in gymnasiums where no one violates a "no street shoes" regulation; many have been in others where that regulation exists but is violated with the result that teachers frequently have to tell youngsters to get off the floor. The difference between success and failure in establishing a reasonable routine regulation such as this is consistency, or lack of it. The difference is between never failing to insist on the one hand, and on the other hand announcing the regulation but neglecting the necessary insistence upon complete compliance for whatever length of time it takes for the regulation to become established so that students comply routinely without constant reminders.

One more example of a helpful routine procedure: At the sound of a teacher's whistle all supplies in use, such as balls, rackets, and bats, are placed wherever they belong by whatever students have them or are closest to them. When this routine is established, early arrivals may start an activity needing such supplies, but there will be no problem or delay bringing the class to order when the teacher wants their attention. Teachers who do not see fit to establish this routine sometimes refuse to permit early arrivals to use equipment because of a problem in getting the supplies gathered and the class assembled. When this is the case early arrivals are left with idle time on their hands until all have arrived. Is that making good use of student time? Further, when arriving at a gymnasium, students' minds are likely to be on the approaching physical activity; the youngsters are ready. Where will their minds go during idle time?

The above examples illustrate how to establish routines and indicate several values of routines. Let us proceed to consider several class operations which should be routinized.

DRESSING AND BATHING

What regulations are needed to assure orderliness, cleanliness, convenience, safety for valuables, and economy of time during those minutes in which students are in the locker room? It is fair to say that it depends upon the situation since lockers and dressing space vary from school to school. While the most satisfactory locker facility may be a large dressing room locker for each student, few schools provide these. Need for economy leads to use of smaller lockers or baskets. Two rather commonly used facilities are (1) combinations of one large locker and some six to nine small ones, and (2) enough large lockers to accommodate the largest single class, and baskets. In both cases the large lockers are used for storage of school clothes while the student wears physical education clothing.

The smaller storage areas, whether small lockers or baskets, store physical education clothing. Locks are needed in either case, and, of course, the same lock serves both to secure physical education clothing during storage and to protect school clothing in the large locker occupied during the class period.

Combination locks with master key attachments seem quite satisfactory. When they are used it is relatively easy for a teacher to help a boy who may be having trouble with his lock. When combination locks without key attachments are used it is necessary for a teacher to take time to consult the list of combinations in the physical education office in order to open a lock.

Loss of money, watches, and other items occurs too frequently. Arrangement for the safekeeping of valuables which belong to students who want to check them should be provided. Some physical education departments provide a checking service which issues a tag, ticket, or other claim check. Others provide a container, frequently a desk drawer which can be locked and which is in the teacher's office, and depend upon recognition by owner and teacher for identification. The teacher must use a plan he believes appropriate and safe in the situation or follow directions coming from the department or its administrator.

Boys' showers, appropriately, are of the open type. There is no unanimity concerning the relative merits of individual control or central control of water supply and temperature. Some individual controls permit users to adjust the water temperature. The push-button individual control tends to conserve water but does not permit the user to control temperature. Central control permits the instructor to regulate temperature and duration. It provides warm, medium, and cool water as users move along the shower line. Central control, or gang, showers save time and prevent usurping of shower time by some class members, which sometimes occurs with individual controls. They are not satisfactory, however, when there is need for showers by a small number. For this reason, when a central control plan is used, there should be some individually controlled showers for use during extraclass activities.

Generally speaking, girls' showers may be of the same type as those for boys. However, there still is some objection to open showers for girls. Although formerly popular plans of private and semiprivate showers and dressing booths for all girls no longer are necessary or desirable, it may be advisable to provide a few semiprivate booths for girls who object to dressing in view of other girls. Many favorable reports and few unfavorable ones have come from women teachers and girls who use open showers.

A fixed amount of maximum time for dressing should become a routine. How much time? Usually five minutes at the start of the period and ten minutes at the end is allotted for boys and a minute or two more for girls. This is satisfactory when there is sufficient space and enough shower heads. If bottleneck conditions are inevitable, additional time may be needed. Time allowed should be enough to avoid rushing, with attendant inevitable cases of tardiness, but not enought to waste time. Routinely classes should start and end at appointed times. Fluctuating time schedules invite students to dally or to rush, neither of which is desirable.

UNIFORMS AND TOWELS

Maintenance of cleanliness and sanitation requires organization of procedural routines. A complete concept of free public education implies provision for free uniforms and towels as well as free textbooks and supplies. However, only a few schools provide uniforms. Hence it usually is necessary to place major responsibility for cleanliness of uniforms upon students and their families. It is strongly recommended that towel service, whether cost is borne by the school or the student or shared by both, be provided in order to eliminate the need for students' carrying and storing damp and dirty towels.

If uniforms are supplied, paid attendants are necessary. Towels may be handled by paid attendants, students, teachers, or by a joint effort of two or more of these. Whatever plan is used should assure continuity of routine, avoid confusion, conserve time, and prevent loss. A highly recommended plan is to have each student (1) take a towel from a conveniently located supply at a shower exit, (2) use the towel in a drying area, and (3) deposit the towel in a receptacle in or near the drying area before going to his locker and dressing area. This procedure eliminates the need for an attendant to handle each towel, permits easy checking to assure no loss of towels, and keeps dressing areas dry.

CHECKING ATTENDANCE

Required and accepted student accounting practices as well as the need for records of physical education experiences make it necessary to check attendance in most physical education classes. There is no one scheme that can be recommended for universal use. Whatever procedure is used should ensure accurate accounting and be economical of time.

Several appropriate plans find use. One is *covering numbers;* students stand on numbers on a floor or place hands over numbers on a wall. One can note numbers and record those not covered easily and quickly. Another plan is *squad leader check;* a squad leader, or another student responsible for attendance check, reports names of absentees to the teacher, either verbally or written on a form provided for that purpose. After the first several class meetings, this plan takes little time. Teachers using a student leader plan find it accurate. As a matter of fact, some find students more accurate than teachers. It is true, however, that some teachers feel that accuracy is not assured when students check attendance. In that case, of course, such a plan should not be used for two reasons. First, and sufficient, a teacher feeling uneasy about probable accuracy of students' taking attendance should adopt some other plan. Second, if such a teacher still arranged for students to check the roll, the results probably would not be accurate. Why? Because students tend to live up to teacher expectations; a teacher fully expecting accuracy will get it, whereas a teacher fearful of sloppy work by students is very likely to receive just that.

Another attendance-taking procedure may be called *teacher checks roll during dressing period.* When feasible this is an excellent scheme. It is not satisfactory if members of more than one class use the same dressing area; it is quite desirable when one class has one dressing room or area not used by others. Since the teacher needs to be in the dressing room to check cleanliness, encourage attention to business, give incidental instruction, and promote class morale, this plan of checking attendance may be thought of as taking no time. It has been found that teachers who know class members well can record attendance of classes numbering up to 40 without lessening the effectiveness of other activity during a five-minute dressing period.

Teacher calling roll sometimes is used. The authors do not recommend it for routine use because it takes too much time. However, it is quite worthwhile to use this method until the teacher recognizes his students by name.

One procedure which is used rather commonly in connection with taking roll seems highly objectionable. It is the practice of insisting upon quiet, perhaps standing at attention, after students arrive at the gymnasium, or other teaching station, but before physical activity is allowed. This requires students to do something unnatural. When youngsters get into a gymnasium, what do they want to do? Run, shoot baskets, volley a ball over a net, play handball, something physically active; that is what is natural for them to want. And that is what teachers want to encourage. Such activity is physical education, isn't it? So what happens when adolescents, ready and anxious for physical activity are required to be sedentary, to be quiet, perhaps stand at attention. They "cool off" psychologically, and their readiness for physical activity wanes. When teachers insist that youngsters stand still and be quiet when they naturally want to be active and run off some pent-up energy, a still worse thing happens. It is contentiousness between teacher and students. If teachers say such things as, "Be quiet," "You are wasting time," "We will wait until all are quiet," or "If you are not quiet we may be here all period," what happens? Rapport between teacher and students may be damaged, eagerness for physical activity dulls, and students may react negatively.

Unnecessarily produced needs to use disciplinary procedures are likely to appear.

Why do some teachers surround roll-taking with such undesirable insistence upon unnatural quietness and refuse to permit their students to get into physical activity immediately upon arrival? They may answer, "This is good disciplinary training." Discipline for what? A concentration camp? They may say, "Our school requires that absence reports be ready five minutes after the last bell." That may be true, but so are two other factors true: (1) another form of roll check could assure that the absence report would meet the deadline, and (2) almost all schools would grant a request for extra time for submitting physical education absence reports. Either of these solutions would permit students to get into activity without delay, thus eliminating several possible detrimental developments as well as increasing learning opportunities.

TEMPORARY EXEMPTIONS FROM VIGOROUS PHYSICAL ACTIVITY

Temporary periods of lowered vitality or incapacity resulting from recent illnesses, headaches, colds, menstruation, or injuries call for adjustment of physical activity to the temporary needs of individuals. Present school practice ranges from excusing those temporarily handicapped to providing completely for individual differences including bed rest and varying modifications of full activity. Good practice demands activities appropriate for the individuals concerned. Programs should provide opportunities for mild physical activity as well as vigorous movement.

A complete physical education emphasizes helping boys and girls to meet their own problems. Periods of temporary disability represent times when persons need added help. Some may wish to engage in strenuous activity when their condition makes this inadvisable. Others, disliking the activity involved, may plead disability when none exists. Some belittle minor difficulties; others magnify them. A physical education teacher, frequently seeking medical advice and sometimes encouraging students to secure medical help, is in a position to help those who are, or think they are, suffering temporary physical debility.

The question of appropriate activity during menstrual periods confronts physical education teachers. Fears and false beliefs among girls may cause exaggeration of the idea of sickness rather than acceptance of a normal function. Because menstruation has different effects upon various girls, the question of appropriate activity during menstrual periods must be approached on an individual basis. Generally speaking, medical opinion agrees that much of the feeling of incapacity accompanying menstruation is due to emotional reactions and that the pursuit of usual activities is advisable in most cases.

Procedures for dealing with requests for temporary adjustment should be clearly understood by everyone involved. Some schools ask that all recommendations for reduced activity or exemption come from a doctor or nurse. Such a policy is unnecessary for brief adjustments involving only a day, or two, or three. Of course, medical recommendation should be required and followed in cases involving prolonged adaptation of program. Teacher and student, together, can make intelligent decisions concerning temporary exemption. Boys and girls who frequently are temporarily indisposed, as well as youngsters who react abnormally to exercise, should be referred for medical attention.

Some schools require an excuse from home to cover a short period, one to three days usually, and a statement from a doctor for a longer period. The authors see no value in the practice requiring an excuse from home. Why? Although it is true that parents may know more about the physical condition of their sons or daughters than teachers do, it also is true that a physical education teacher knows more than most parents about the effects of exercise. If there is a good relationship between students and teacher, questions concerning substitutes for vigorous activity can be decided by the teacher after a brief discussion with the student who requests exemption or substitution.

A chief objection to a practice of requiring excuses from home for temporary exemption lies in damage to image, to public relations. A youngster who wishes, unnecessarily, to avoid activity may find a yielding parent writing an excuse; a student may find an unyielding parent refusing to write an excuse when the youngster does have lowered vitality which would make vigorous activity inadvisable. In either case, physical education causes a problem in the home itself or in connection with it. What is this likely to do concerning the formation of public opinion relative to physical education?

GETTING TEACHING STATIONS READY TO USE

For orderly operation and economy of time, teaching stations should be ready ahead of class time. Courts, diamonds, areas for games and relays, wrestling or tumbling mats, apparatus facilities, etc., should be ready so that classes may use them without waste of time. Lines and boundaries should be marked, volleyball standards set up, and nets arranged so that little or no time is lost getting started. In some schools janitors or caretakers get teaching stations ready for use. In most situations the teacher and students, working together, do whatever arranging is necessary. Besides accomplishing the immediate purpose, the latter method may have the advantage of encouraging students to become involved in organizing and managing their own affairs.

DISTRIBUTION OF SUPPLIES

Balls, bats, rackets, measuring tapes, and the like, which are needed for class use, should be distributed and collected without waste of time and without loss. Several schemes for accomplishing this are equally effective. Kinds of supplies needed, storage facilities, and student acceptance of responsibility must be considered. The scheme of permitting the first student ready to take supplies from their storage place and return them at the end of the period works well when only a few items are needed and when students can be depended upon. Some teachers like to have one member of the class serve as supply manager. Another effective procedure is to have one member of each squad or class group responsible for the supplies his or her group use. Many boys and girls like the responsibility of managing supplies, and may find increased feelings of worth as they do so.

Accessible storage facilities help with distribution and collection. Going to out-of-the-way supply rooms before and after class not only uses time but also may lead to irritation and carelessness. When storerooms are not easily accessible, boxes, baskets, shelves, hooks, or hangers should be placed in gymnasiums, dressing rooms, or at nearby locations so that temporary storage is convenient. When supplies are to be carried some distance, such as up flights of stairs, to fields not adjacent to dressing rooms, or to classrooms or audio-visual projection rooms, suitable containers should be used.

Pride in good supplies should be developed. Use of things such as ripped balls, torn nets, dirty mats, and shaky standards leads to carelessness and destructiveness. When supplies needing cleaning or repair are removed from service until they have been renovated, students are likely to take better care of the adequate supplies they use.

It seems highly desirable to encourage all students, early arrivals and others, to use supplies immediately upon reaching the gymnasium or other teaching station. Reference was made to this idea in one of the three illustrations of how to establish a routine, the one concerning placing of all supplies in use wherever they belong immediately at the sound of the teacher's whistle (page 287). Further reference occurs as part of the discussion of checking attendance (page 290), in the context of criticizing the practice of requiring students to be inactive and quiet until after roll check is completed. It seems necessary here to emphasize only that, whatever method of distributing and collecting supplies is selected, early availability of enough supplies such as balls, rackets, shuttlecocks should be assured in order to permit physical activity, and all supplies which can be used *safely* should be appropriate for use upon arrival.

SAFETY

Participation in attractive and even daring activities with a minimum of accidents requires the establishment of routine conformance with safety measures. Students should know that running, pushing, or horseplay in dressing and shower rooms causes accidents and hence cannot be tolerated. Running on dangerously slippery surfaces is to be avoided. Routine use of mats and spotters with high apparatus is necessary. Although development of attitudes of overcautiousness should be prevented, youngsters must understand that activities which may be perfectly safe in some surroundings are not safe in others.

Instructors should be sure that equipment is safe. Periodic inspection of apparatus such as ropes, rings, bars, and ladders is a must. Gymnasiums and play areas are to be free from unnecessary obstacles. Ground surfaces require continual attention in order to prevent and correct dangerous conditions such as holes and rocks. Unsafe equipment is to be removed quickly and repaired; dangerous conditions should be remedied immediately.

Since there will be some accidents in connection with physical education it is *essential that there be a well-understood procedure to follow in the event of injury requiring more than just removal from activity and first aid.* Whatever procedure is adopted should ensure (1) teachers' knowing exactly what they are to do, (2) immediate and temporary care (first aid), (3) notification of proper school authority and parent, (4) securing of medical service, and (5) the making of a report, at least one copy for filing in the central office and one for the physical education office.

School practice concerning the securing of medical aid and notification of parent varies. When they are available, school doctors or nurses should take over upon notification from a teacher. In some schools the principal or an assistant principal follows through. School records should include the name of the family physician so that the proper person may be called in the event that a parent is not immediately available. Orderly, predetermined procedure that eliminates indecision and leads to calm action is essential. Reports should state (1) nature of the injury, (2) circumstances that led to the accident, (3) name or names of eyewitnesses, and (4) the procedure followed.

RECORD KEEPING AND REPORTING

Organization for keeping and reporting information should provide simplicity and ease of operation. It must, however, assure accuracy and ease of location. Record plans vary a good deal from school to school and from teacher to teacher. The brief discussion here classifies physical education records roughly into three categories: (1) central-office records, (2) physical education–office records, and (3) teacher's records.

Results of medical examinations and recommendations by physicians constitute a record of primary importance.[1] They should be kept in central locations accessible to all teachers. It is important that physical education offices and individual teachers keep accurate records of all students whose medical examinations show deviations which indicate a need for adapted or modified activity.

Central offices of public schools keep records of attendance and of achievement. Attendance reports customarily are made during each class hour. Besides reporting absences to the central office on a form provided for that purpose, teachers should record absences in class record books. Records of achievement, required by central offices periodically, may include any one or more of the following: letter or numerical grades; ratings on traits such as industry, cooperation, resourcefulness, initiative, and dependability; paragraph-style description of the progress of the student; listing or description of physical education activities engaged in by the student; physical fitness or motor ability test scores; and anecdotal records.

Physical education offices should have more detailed records than do central school offices. In addition to the record items mentioned above, physical education offices should keep copies of such things as program plans, units, lesson plans, instructional guides and aids, height and weight records, minutes or summaries of staff and committee deliberations, inventories of equipment and supplies, catalogs, schedules of teachers, copies of reports of injuries and accidents, annual reports, and schedules of teachers.

Besides keeping the information that has been mentioned in the above two paragraphs, individual teachers should keep additional records which aid in understanding and helping boys and girls. Such records include temporary excuses, descriptions of significant behavior, records of tests taken and inventories or rating scales used, day-by-day or week-by-week progress, squads or groups or teams, and records of intraclass competition. In schools which have only one man and one woman physical education teacher, the records of the physical education office and those of the teacher are synonymous, except that some information may be discarded at the end of a semester or a year rather than filed for long periods of time.

[1] Recommended forms may be found in Joint Committee of the National Education Association and the American Medical Association, *Health Education*, 5th ed., National Education Association, Washington, D.C., 1961.

SQUAD ORGANIZATION

The probable advantages of organizing physical education classes into squads or subgroups are as follows:

1. Squads provide excellent opportunities for a student-leader plan to work well. A leader may serve each squad and take whatever responsibility the teacher wishes to assign. Several student leaders may serve various functions: one might serve as captain or assistant teacher; another may manage supplies; another may check attendance, while another serves as a recorder when written records are needed.
2. Working in squads is likely to increase student acceptance of responsibility. Working in groups such as squads tends to promote a feeling among students that the affairs and ventures are their own. This develops pride. Heightened morale is a probable result.
3. Class operation will be smoother, easier, and more orderly. Although teachers will deal with all students, for many things they can work with leaders who will help to get things done.
4. More homogeneous groupings can be arranged. Squads may be relatively permanent or may change for each unit or activity. Changing groups for each main activity may produce considerable homogeneity.
5. A teacher is likely to be in a better position to pay genuine attention to individual differences. He will spend a relatively small amount of his time in formal work with the whole class so he can pay more attention to individuals.
6. Facilities are likely to be used well; maximum efficiency in using space, equipment, and facilities may be approached because several squads can be assigned to various areas and activities.
7. Squads provide a convenient and effective organization for intraclass competition. A squad may be a team.

How should squad membership be decided? Different methods are found desirable. Some frequently used and found effective are listed below.

1. Choosing by student leaders is a popular and effective method of arranging squads. A high degree of group cohesion, loyalty, and pride usually is a result. The leaders who do the choosing may be selected by the teacher or by vote of class members. The practice of choosing while all class members are present is not recommended. Embarrassment on the part of those chosen last is avoided when

leaders choose from a list of names and then list the names of squad members alphabetically.

2. Teachers may select members of the several squads. Subjective judgments concerning abilities, needs, interests, and social status should be considered. Not infrequently students prefer to have teachers make selections. Results usually are quite satisfactory when teachers know the students and when class members have a high degree of confidence in the judgment of the teacher.
3. Skill tests may serve to determine squad membership. Standardized or locally prepared tests in sports such as basketball, volleyball, and badminton may be used. Performance tests in activities such as tumbling and dancing, with teacher and students serving as judges, have been found useful. When teams or other competitive units are desired, it may be wise to distribute class members so that team or unit strength is equated, rather than to place superior performers in one group, less experienced students in another group, and so on. Further discussion of this point appears in the team-sports section of Chapter 8, Techniques for Team and Individual Sports.
4. Height-weight-age coefficients have been found useful for classifying boys in elementary and secondary schools and for classifying girls in elementary and junior high schools. They are not generally recommended for senior high school girls because performance of girls above junior high has not been found to be affected significantly by factors of height, weight, and age. These coefficients are particularly useful for testing and for classification for contact sports such as wrestling. They are of value when relative homogeneity is desired for equating groups for participation in a wide variety of activities. Thus, a teacher who wishes to establish relatively permanent groups for participation in several activities, such as soccer, field hockey, badminton, gymnastics, and volleyball, may find this satisfactory. One wanting to change squads frequently would not select this scheme.
5. Groups or squads within a class may be formed according to the results of physical fitness tests. This plan may be helpful for conducting a program suitable to individual needs. It has been suggested that tests such as the one sponsored by AAHPER [2] be used for this purpose. Boys scoring low might be taking a conditioning program only until test scores improved; boys making average scores could combine emphasis upon conditioning with skill development and recreational activities, whereas boys scoring high might appropriately be assigned

[2] American Association of Health, Physical Education, and Recreation, *Youth Fitness Test Manual,* rev. ed., National Education Association, Washington, D.C., 1965.

to a program which provides exercise through skill development and recreational activities.

ORGANIZING TO PERMIT STUDENT SELECTION

Subject to the limitation that all should participate in a minimum core of required activities, opportunities for student selection broaden and improve a physical education program. Almost all physical educators agree that high school juniors and seniors should have a chance to select activities if the required variety of activities is satisfactory. Student selection of activities within a class is a popular, growing, and sound practice, and, as noted above, can well be handled through a squad scheme of organization. Election of extraclass activities is universal, although in too many high schools students have only meager opportunities to select activities of their own first or second preference.

During the later years of the secondary school, after all have had experiences with several types of activities, it is appropriate that students be allowed to select classes which permit specialization. Small schools find it impractical to organize such classes. Some large schools offer several alternatives such as courses in conditioning, swimming and diving, team sports, and individual sports. Others, pursuing greater specialization, offer selection from among activities such as advanced tumbling and gymnastics, lifesaving, tennis and badminton, and soccer and volleyball. In schools whose schedules make choice of classes by advanced students practical, opportunities for class selection should be encouraged for boys and girls who have participated in a satisfactory variety of physical education activities during earlier years.

CHOICE OF ACTIVITIES WITHIN A CLASS

It is sound procedure to permit students to select from among several activities within one class. One group might work with tumbling, another with dancing, another with track and field. For advanced students considerable election is desirable. For younger boys and girls limitation of choice usually is necessary to ensure participation by all in the various games, sports, gymnastics, rhythms, swimming, and conditioning activities which make up a well-rounded education in physical activities: a required core.

CHOICE OF EXTRACLASS ACTIVITIES

Intramurals, club activities, extraclass recreational activities, and interscholastic sports are based upon a principle of voluntary or elective participation. One function of a school is to provide opportunities for self-expression and achievement in pursuits which students desire. A chief justifiable criticism is that not enough students have realistic opportunities to participate significantly in these activities. Although it is true that many boys and girls do take part in extraclass activities, it also is true that many more would if opportunities were greater and that those who do take part would do so more often if they could.

Organizing time, facilities, and personnel to permit widespread participation in extraclass intramural and recreational activities requires very resourceful planning in most schools. Compromises are required. The interscholastic program needs time, facilities, and coaches, and may tend to get them at the expense of intramural and recreational programs. Everyone may want the hours immediately after school. Some may have to settle for insufficient time and less favorable hours. Interscholastic athletics provide significant experiences indeed for those who participate. Certainly, opportunities for development and expression of superior ability should be provided; so should genuine opportunities for physical recreation for all boys and girls, for good, medium, and poor performers. Few, if any, high schools will have resources permitting what many would regard as an ideal program of extraclass activities. Resourceful teachers, coaches, and planners organize to make the most of what is available.

TEACHER-STUDENT SHARING IN PLANNING AND MANAGING

Student participation in planning was discussed in Chapter 5 (pages 111–112). Here emphasis is upon organizing and managing, that is, upon what teachers may do before and during class to facilitate student participation in planning and (or) managing.

Teachers may involve students by using one or more of the following levels of teacher-student cooperation in planning and managing.

1. Students participate in planning by making suggestions which receive consideration by the teacher. When a class is organized and managed or conducted so that students feel free to make either oral or written suggestions, students become involved. When such suggestions are given due consideration, a substantial amount of sharing is likely to develop. Long before the present verbal and written emphasis upon teacher-student sharing in education, physical education teachers commonly invited youngsters to make suggestions and frequently followed them. When this procedure is used, an atmosphere and understanding of responsibility should be developed. Although students should be encouraged to make sound and sensible suggestions, they should understand that proposals based upon whim or passing fancy are out of order.
2. A second level occurs when, instead of only conducting a class so

that students feel free to make suggestions as on the first level described just above, a teacher encourages and asks students to make suggestions. This provides more structure and gives more positive encouragement. Industry makes use of this scheme of encouraging suggestions by providing suggestion boxes for deposit of written proposals and by offering monetary rewards for suggestions which find use.

3. Representatives from a class, or several classes, may meet with the teacher during out-of-class time to plan for organizing and managing. This plan is particularly appropriate when a squad-leader type of class organization is used because elected or appointed leaders quite naturally function as representatives of their squad or group. Groups of representatives are more wieldy than the larger groups described below. Less student time is required and the risk of domination of a whole class by a few aggressive members is lessened.
4. A teacher and a whole class may plan together. This procedure can be and has been very successful in some situations. It will not be successful, however, unless the teacher and the students previously have developed some skill in group work. Students with little or no experience should be introduced to cooperative planning through one of the simpler levels.

   In this plan a teacher leads class discussions of proposals and suggestions for procedure. He can start by giving a résumé of his or her concept of the purposes of physical education, proceed to comment about possibilities and limitations in the existing situation, and then invite suggestions and discussion. Some questions, such as a choice between soccer and field hockey, can well be decided by majority vote. In other cases plans or activities for groups or individuals might be arranged. It is generally considered wise for the teacher to reserve the right of veto, which, however, should be used judiciously.
5. A combination of the class-representative plan and the whole-group plan may be used. In this case the whole group can decide on policy and large issues while the representative groups make detailed plans. One approach to this combination scheme is to have the whole group initiate procedure and refer appropriate matters to small groups. Another approach is the reverse; i.e., representative groups make plans and present them to the whole group for approval, rejection, or modification. Usually both of these approaches are utilized.

With all levels of student participation in organizing and managing, one of the better ways to promote student involvement is through student leaders who may be elected or appointed to leadership positions or who may naturally emerge as leaders from time to time. Realistic sharing of joint undertakings not only facilitates class operation and learning of specific skills but also provides maturing experience for young people. Thus, a leader who procures and delivers a needed film may learn something about films and the handling of them as well as perform a useful and needed service for the class. One who helps draw up a schedule and a set of regulations for an intraclass round-robin schedule may learn how to manage athletic events, improve his or her ability to work with a group, and help get a needed job done. One who handles equipment and supplies may grow in self-responsibility and in ability to deal with others. All who perform these and other student-leader functions may find their feelings of personal worth and their satisfactions from recognition and accomplishment enhanced.

When handling formal student-leader organizations, teachers should also encourage groups and subgroups to work together. In a group of about eight students the specified leader should not be the only member who accepts responsibility for success of the group. A situation in which one student continually leads in all things while the rest follow is undesirable. Rather than leader and followers, what should be encouraged is leader and group members.

A formally selected leader indeed fills an important position and may serve with satisfaction to himself, his squad mates, and his teacher. However, as a project or an activity develops, other members of the group may emerge as leaders in some phases of the work. During a game someone other than the selected leader may emerge as the natural and effective leader around whom other members of the group tend to rally. As a unit in tumbling and gymnastic unfolds, several members of the group may become leaders in various stunts because of demonstrated abilities which are recognized and respected by their peers. A creative-dance unit is likely to produce a number of leaders.

If formally organized student leaders are to do effective work, they must be trained and encouraged. If a teacher or class decides to have squad leaders, assistant leaders, referees, equipment managers, towel distributors, and the like, the teacher must work with the leaders if the procedure is to function well. Extraclass meetings for the purpose of preparing leaders for their roles are needed. During such meetings attention is given to clarifying the responsibilities and functions of the leaders as well as to consideration of methods and procedures to be used by the leaders. If student leaders are to serve as assistant teachers who instruct or lead others in the performance of activities, it is necessary that these leaders learn the technique and purposes of the activity involved. Students will not accept realistically the leadership of persons who have not demonstrated ability to lead even though they may have the title of leader. If a teacher does not have the time or inclination to help leaders prepare, it is far better to avoid any formal student-leader organization. Leadership classes for juniors who will become leaders as seniors provide excellent preparation.

Capitalizing upon leadership ability as it emerges during the progress of a class or venture, with or without formal organization of leaders, has at least two aspects. One is the utilization of leadership ability for the benefit of members of the group other than the person who becomes a leader at a particular time. The other is concerned with the educational experiences involved in functioning as a leader. In physical education situations it is likely that boys and girls learn more from each other than they do from the teacher. A function of the teacher is to arrange and encourage an environment in which learning can take place. A part of the creation of such an environment is the providing of opportunities for the expression of emerging leadership abilities. Students take their cues from those recognized as worthy of following; hence members of a group benefit from leadership by one of their peers who has recognized ability. In all probability the more important of the two aspects of student leading is the effect upon the person doing the leading.

PROVIDING FOR INDIVIDUAL DIFFERENCES

Need for adjusting instruction to individual differences has been established, perhaps even overemphasized. The types of class subgroups or squads and the reasons for them have been discussed. What remains to be considered here is the management of classes as it concerns individual differences.

Groups or squads within a class need to be flexible enough to permit changes or regrouping from time to time in order to meet needs of individuals. Temporary disabilities may present a need for regrouping. A sprained ankle may make it inadvisable for a member of a group working on tumbling to continue with that group. However, this student might be quite able to work on horizontal or parallel bars and might profit from temporary change from a tumbling group to a squad working on an activity which does not require the participant to bear weight on his feet.

Rapid or slow student progress may indicate desirability of regrouping. For instance, a member of a volleyball group which is playing the whole game may have difficulty serving. In such a situation specific practice of serving might be indicated for one student whereas continued playing of the game might be best for the rest of the group. The student needing practice in serving might well join another group which is emphasizing specific practice rather than playing the whole game.

Whether one teaches a full class as one group or as several subgroups within a class, there always will be differences among individuals. Individual differences in ability to perform physical skills are quite obvious to the physical education teacher. There are also individual differences in personality, temperament, and emotion which affect learning, although these may not be so obvious. The effective teacher recognizes and assesses these differences and gears his teaching accordingly.

In one case a person might teach best if he helps a placid person develop motivation. In another case superior and artistic teaching might be achieved if the teacher reduces tension, if he helps an excitable youngster to learn how to develop calmness. Some students may need help in developing confidence in their own abilities, whereas others may need to realize that there is room for improvement although their present ability is above the average.

A master teacher assesses what problems and conditions facilitate or hamper learning and knows that although some of these apply to many or all students, others apply to only a few, or solely to one. How can a teacher learn all these things about all of his students? Does he need to be a psychologist, psychiatrist, medical practitioner, and sociologist? Certainly not, although the exhortation of educators that teachers must understand the abilities, needs, capacities, interests, purposes, home backgrounds, school activities, and leisure pursuits of each student in order to know how to teach is sometimes so interpreted.

Teaching may be viewed as tremendously complicated, as may any pursuit in which one deals with organisms as complicated as human beings. It also may be viewed as quite simple because any method or approach that works is good. An important characteristic of a good teacher is the ability and disposition to try multiple approaches with various individuals and to select those that work best.

Many students are glad to follow detailed teacher orders because for them the specificity of orders produces a feeling of security. With such boys and girls a prime function of the teacher is to help develop initiative and self-responsibility. Some students have a tendency to rebel at compulsion of any kind. Although such persons may irritate teachers to no end, they frequently turn out all right and not infrequently become outstanding leaders. The successful teacher works to guide individuality into useful channels.

Some students react badly to criticism of any kind. Almost all resent open negative criticism. Yet, rather severe criticism may release energy and move students to desirable action. Although it is true that teachers should stress the positive and the giving of approval to worthwhile accomplishment, it also is true that disapproval may stir some to needed action. The placid person accomplishes little; tension which the individual desires to relieve is necessary for effective learning. But since overtension produces confusion and frustration, the teacher should help each student develop a pattern of adjustment that produces essential equilibrium as well as tensions that drive to action in order to restore equilibrium.

Tensions created by needs facilitate learning, provided they can be relieved by action which leads to learning. They interfere if relief is not within reach of the individual. For this reason teachers should help each student set goals which are high enough to require best efforts but low enough to make success possible. Thus a girl who feels that she can achieve no success in dancing needs help in stirring to action which will make it possible for her to realize that success is possible. A girl who really possesses only ordinary dancing ability but who feels that her ability justifies her desire for a career as a professional dancer needs help in bringing her goals down to reality.

Rapport between the teacher and the student is essential for the adaptation of instruction to individual differences. It is based upon mutual confidence and respect. Without satisfactory rapport the student tends toward antagonism and rebelliousness which leads to slow and spasmodic learning. One must not, however, assume that antagonism and rebelliousness always retard progress. Motivation of the "I'll show the teacher" type may lead to significant learning. But continual existence of antagonism is an ineffective base for learning and adjustment. The existence of a dominant pattern of pleasant and cooperative rapport is the best base for an effective teaching-learning situation. Generous approval whenever possible, with sparing use of well-justified disapproval, produces the best motivation.

Mutual confidence, respect, and liking may be achieved differently with various students. Timid youngsters who regard themselves as lacking genuine ability and attempt to adjust by withdrawal need encouragement and reassurance. Students who feel inferior and who adopt aggressive behavior as a mechanism of adjustment also need encouragement and reassurance rather than blame for aggressive behavior. Generally, young people are quick to recognize unwarranted praise or blame as insincere or unfair. They lose confidence in a teacher who uses either indiscriminately. But those who have high aspirations may be nettled by approval which has the same foundation as that which is gladly received by those who have lower aspirations.

Personalities are important in the establishment of teacher relationships with students. Some react excellently to considerable levity, joking, and even kidding, whereas others may rankle at rather small amounts of this sort of thing. Some appreciate detailed instruction; others are quickly bored with any talk after they have grasped the "big idea."

Student perception of and confidence in a teacher depends largely upon whether or not students regard the teacher as one who essentially is fair and helpful. Youngsters will overlook what they regard as occasional unfair treatment, even mistakes, by a teacher if, overall, students think the teacher has their interest at heart. Neither youngsters nor adults expect whatever they regard as perfection from any teacher or any person. Teachers, like all persons, are judged by their overall tendencies, abilities, and actions. No one should feel that he can or should please everyone at all times; one who attempts to do so must be a weakling who has few convictions or little courage.

MANAGING STUDENTS WHO HAVE SPECIAL AND IMMEDIATE PROBLEMS

In most cases, problems which are special and immediate will be related to temporary exemption or adaptation which was discussed earlier in this chapter, with emphasis upon organization, policy formation, and decision making before classes start. Let us now consider efficient management during a class period.

First, a teacher should make sure that students who want to make a request know what to do and when and where to do it. Requests by students for adjustment should be presented in the morning before school if convenient and never later than immediately at the start of the physical education period. Requests made following the dressing period when activity is about to be started almost always cause delay and, not infrequently, cause irritation which results in poor decisions and unnecessary cross words.

Because of shortness of time it usually is necessary to decide rather quickly. If rapid decision is required it is prudent for a teacher to tend toward the safe side in questionable cases. It seems better to permit restricted activity, even for a student who would profit from vigorous exercise, than it would be to require heavy activity for a youngster who might be adversely affected.

In cases of restricted activity, there usually will be need for special attention by the teacher. After the student gets started, and after class activities get underway, the teacher should check to see whether a handicapped student is getting along all right and give help as needed. Youngsters playing games such as shuffleboard or quoits may need help; further exploration of the physical condition of a student may be advisable. If students have been assigned tasks such as scorekeeping, timing, recording, or caring for supplies, they are likely to need help.

If exemption from school is deemed advisable the teacher should make sure that the student knows exactly what to do. If there is a question of the student's ability to do whatever his school requires, the teacher must see that help is provided. Among the procedures used by various high schools are referral to the central office with recommendation by the referring teacher, or referral to a school nurse, to a school doctor, or to a counselor. In any event the home will be notified if it is possible to do so. After a teacher refers, he depends upon others to take over, but he will want to get further information before the student returns to class.

Some schools send reading and (or) writing assignments for temporarily disabled students to a physical education library or study room, some to an all-school library, others to a supervised study hall. When transferring a student from the supervision of one teacher to another it is customary to account for the change of location and teacher. Signature on a form which shows the date and hour of the transfer is customary. It is recommended, however, that referral to a teacher outside the physical education department be avoided when feasible.

Student appearance without physical education clothing is a problem. As is true in all cases of a temporary nature, it is highly important to have a procedure, regulations, which students know and which teachers use consistently. Clothing may be lent from a supply kept for that purpose, or some participation in school clothes may be the policy. Penalties such as detention or makeup classes for appearance without proper clothing are imposed by many schools, and may be necessary in order to avoid excessive occurrence. However, one should try to avoid the need for penalties by teaching interest and motivation because excessive use of penalties may lessen morale and cause negative attitudes.

MANAGING FOR MAXIMUM STUDENT ACTIVITY

A physical education class should be managed so that every student is physically active a great deal of the time because (1) learning is purposeful self-activity; (2) there can be no teaching unless there is learning; (3) what a teacher says or does is important only if it leads to student activity; (4) physical education should be active; it is movement; (5) time almost always is at a premium; and (6) overload is necessary to develop strength and endurance. This does not mean, however, that highly pitched physical and (or) mental activity should prevail every minute. Relaxation and rest are appropriate between periods of strenuous exercise and between periods of mental concentration.

PHYSICAL ACTIVITY

Physical activity is the heart of physical education. Students learn as they perform, so class management should see that all available time is used. Time is valuable, particularly so because of the short time usually available and because of the need for physical activity and for education in a variety of activities.

Activity should start promptly and continue with the least loss of time possible. Waiting for turns and watching others perform should be held to a minimum. Tennis should not be selected for a whole-class activity when only a few can perform at one time nor should handball or squash or wrestling or any other activity unless a good deal of physical activity is possible. When there is work on ball skills, there should be enough balls so that there is little waiting in line. A general rule is that there should be at least one ball for each team or group and that there never should be less than one ball for every eleven students.

Watching others perform does have some value in learning motor skills. Concepts of techniques may be gained or modified. Observation of good performances, demonstrations, pictures, movies may be quite worthwhile. Such activity is to be encouraged with principal emphasis upon participation by all. The thing to be condemned is management which permits inactivity because of poor selection of activity or method.

MENTAL ACTIVITY

Learning physical skills and activities requires mental activity because motor learning is almost always perceptual, cognitive, and rational. Most of it should go on as the physical activity progresses. Still, there is a need for the devotion of some time to purely mental aspects. For instance, learning strategy and team play in highly organized team games may require considerable explanation, listening, observing, and reading, as well as performing and playing. Learning about the effects of exercise and the rudiments of anatomy, physiology, and kinesiology requires mental attention and study. Teachers of physical education should consider the directed-study method of teaching explained in Chapter 6; in other words outside-of-class reading assignments may be used to teach knowledge.

It seems quite certain that beginning physical education teachers tend to talk too much. So do many veterans. Demonstrations (show-how), gestures, and other visual aids should be used liberally. Competent teachers communicate with their physically active students by gesture, sign, or one- or two-word statements while the students continue activity. For instance, a great deal of volleyball and basketball can be taught through these means without ever breaking the continuity of practice or play. Games which require larger spaces, such as soccer, speedball, and baseball, are not so easy to teach without breaking the continuity of play. Short periods of sedentary or dominantly mental learning should be sandwiched between periods of vigorous muscular activity.

RELAXATION AND REST

Physical education should teach relaxation. As Arthur H. Steinhaus [3] has indicated, if muscles are relaxed there can be no tension. The ability to relax helps to ensure against physical and mental fatigue, distress, and

[3] Arthur H. Steinhaus: *Toward an Understanding of Health and Physical Education,* Wm. C. Brown Company, Publishers. Dubuque, Iowa, 1963, p. 308.

illnesses stemming from hypertension. Vigorous physical movement itself provides relaxation from tensions produced by sedentary pursuit. It also relieves tensions produced by secretions of internal glands. It may mitigate fears, angers, jealousies, and anxieties. Class management which assures abundant activity for all serves to provide this kind of relaxation.

Easy rhythmical movements help to relax muscular tension. Teachers who recognize signs of hypertension can help students who need to reduce muscular tension by teaching specific methods of muscular relaxation. Although relaxation exercises have a place in class or group instruction, they also may be taught selectively to individual students who need to relax. The teacher who recognizes such individual needs and manages his class so that these needs can be met adds to the value of physical education for his students, perhaps in significant, new vista experiences.

Rest periods become necessary occasionally during physical education classes. Periods of rest or comparative rest are inherent in some activities. Playing volleyball, for instance, does not require continual exertion of muscular force. There are periods of comparative rest for the player between brief periods of rapid movement and strenuous exertion; hence breaks for rest seldom are necessary. Every effort should be made to teach as students engage in these activities. Other activities, such as running a 220-yard dash or a half mile, which demand peak effort need to be followed by rest periods, which may provide opportune times for teaching knowledge, for giving information.

MANAGERIAL EFFICIENCY

Considered here are a few tasks or functions which must be performed during class periods. Although they represent necessary procedures, they have little direct bearing upon actual learning. They should be handled with dispatch so that a minimum amount of time is needed for them. Thorough organization, as discussed earlier in the chapter, facilitates the performance of these tasks. It also is necessary to manage well in order to realize the timesaving possibilities inherent in the organizational structure.

CHECKING ATTENDANCE

After a suitable scheme for checking attendance has been organized, it is necessary to do the checking and attendant bookkeeping day by day. If the teacher checks roll, it is customary and efficient to record absences in a class record book or similar permanent record immediately. If student leaders check and report orally to the teacher, the same immediate permanent recording is advisable. In the event that student leaders check and report in writing, it usually is best to defer permanent recording until later. In any case, if hourly reports are required by central offices, as they frequently are in secondary schools, they will need to be made during the class period. This requires the writing of names of absentees. The teacher is responsible for the accuracy of the report. He may write the names himself, or that responsibility may be delegated to a student.

SIGNALS FOR FREQUENT OPERATIONS

Signals for such things as falling in to some predetermined formation, covering numbers, becoming quiet to listen, moving from one location or activity to another, and dismissal save time and words. The customary whistle signal, sometimes combined with word cues, seems satisfactory. The important thing in establishing routine response to such signals is consistent and never-failing insistence upon the correct response. Difficulties presented by student action, such as wanting one more shot at the basket after the whistle, grow rapidly if exceptions are permitted. When correct responses is asked for unfailingly, class members quite rapidly accept the routine if they see a reason for it.

MOVING CLASS TO VARIOUS LOCATIONS

When class members know what activity they are going to participate in, moving the class usually presents little or no problem. Generally speaking, the best plan is to have the class assemble at the place of the activity. Groups or individuals can be assigned to fields or courts or stations prior to class time. This may be done by announcement in a previous class or by posting assignments on a bulletin board.

Moving the class may present a problem if it is necessary to go some distance to a playground, to cross a busy street, or to go through halls or up stairways. The simplest scheme is to make each student responsible for appearance at the appointed place. Although this may represent the best plan for older boys and girls, it is usually necessary for teachers to accompany younger children if they are to go very far in a group. If busy streets are to be crossed, it seems best to go in class groups throughout the secondary school as well as in the elementary school.

For activities such as calisthenics, grass drills, ranger activities, combative contests, and partner-type tests, it may be convenient and timesaving to use marching tactics. Particularly appropriate for secondary school boys, rudimentary marching maneuvers, including extending order, facilitate class movement. Informal scattering may be used for activities requiring that a large number of students be located in a relatively small space so that they can swing arms and legs without interfering with a neighbor. But the objection made by some to all types of marching tactics on the basis that it is militaristic regimentation seems to have no validity.

RECORDS

In addition to attendance records, discussed above, teachers need at times to record during class periods information pertaining to tardiness, temporary exemptions, temporary adaptations of program, lack of appropriate clothing, test results, and notations concerning achievement. Much of this information can and should be recorded in class record books, or similar records. Symbols should be used. A number or a letter is an excellent symbol for categorical items such as absence, tardiness, temporary exemption, and lack of appropriate clothing.

Test results take time to record. If the teacher does the recording, there usually is less bookkeeping required during out-of-class time. If students record, less class time may be required, and the teacher is more free to teach. Each teacher must decide which plan to use. When tests of the endurance type are given, the recording may be done during necessary rest periods. Teachers should manage testing so that no more than one-sixth of the class time is required for recording.

SUPERVISING DRESSING ROOMS, LOCKER ROOMS, SHOWERS, AND SUPPLIES

Classtime teacher attention to use of dressing rooms, bathing facilities, and supplies is necessary in order to assure proper behavior, prevent accidents, and protect property. Even though youngsters may have developed considerable self-responsibility, they are likely to engage in towel snapping, water throwing, foul talk, and other antics that lead to trouble if not under direct teacher supervision a good deal of the time. Continual teacher presence in dressing and locker rooms is not necessary, but continual absence leads to problems. Police-type supervision should be avoided. While in dressing rooms teachers should learn more about their students through observing and visiting; they should give individual instruction as opportune situations arise and help to develop favorable attitudes toward cleanliness and health.

Organization for the distribution and care of towels has been discussed. If attendants are employed, there may be little or no teacher responsibility for distribution and collection. When students handle towels, the teacher must be available for help when it is needed. Complete student responsibility for towels, without teacher guidance and supervision, usually means excessive loss. Periodic inventory, or towel count, seems necessary to prevent loss. If complete accounting is desired, it is necessary to record the number of towels in stock each period. Whether or not a complete check is worthwhile will depend upon the experience the school has had with loss. Daily or occasional spot checks, rather than records for every class period, usually suffice when good attitudes toward protection of property have been developed.

Equipment such as horizontal and parallel bars, horses, bucks, teeterboards, and volleyball or badminton standards that needs to be brought from storage places and put into place for class use presents a problem. Because of the tremendous differences in arrangements and facilities from school to school, it is impossible to make detailed specific suggestions. There are, however, two principles that should be considered. One is that, whenever it is possible, the program should be synchronized so that several classes, perhaps all that meet during a half day or a day or a week, may use equipment which requires some time for setting up. The other is that students should be taught how to set up and remove the equipment and that squads or groups be assigned responsibility for specific pieces of equipment.

Mats which are stored on trucks or hung on pegs or hooks can be put into place quickly and back into storage with dispatch, provided students know what is to be done and who is to do it. The teacher who has not taken time to instruct students in mat transportation and care finds poor cooperation. There will be delay and frequent need for instruction as the task is being performed. Comments such as, "Don't sweep the floor with the mat; pick it up," or, "We need more help here," will be common if students have not been taught the proper procedures. The teacher who prepares the students by instruction and assignment finds that mat transportation is accomplished easily.

CORRELATING CLASSWORK WITH EXTRACLASS ACTIVITIES

All parts of physical education supplement and complement one another. The extent to which successful interrelationships are achieved depends to a considerable extent upon organization and management. Class instruction which develops skills and interest in various sports increases interest in extraclass participation in those sports; at the same time, extraclass activities stimulate toward increased intensity in classwork. For instance, if boys and girls learn and play volleyball in their classes, they are likely to request opportunities to play that game during extraclass periods. When volleyball is a highly respected intramural sport, more zestful skill practice and play in classes is a result. Carrying the example one step further, when volleyball is included in a school interscholastic program, interest in both class and intramural volleyball is heightened.

Many men physical education teachers complain, "All the boys want to do is play basketball, so it is difficult to have a well-balanced program." Organization of "gear meshing" class and extraclass programs is one excellent step toward developing interests in a variety of activities. Schools and communities which place tremendous emphasis upon interscholastic basketball are likely to find that it is difficult to develop interest in a broad program of physical education. Schools which sponsor a wide variety of interscholastic and intramural sports, with each sport in reasonable perspective, are likely to find boys anxious to learn and play many sports.

Should boys who play on interscholastic teams, or who are regularly practicing members of a team or squad, be required to take physical education, to attend a class in addition to practicing with the team? This problem faces men teachers and those who make policy for boys' physical education programs. There is no unanimity among physical educators concerning these questions. Further, it seems unmistakably true that opinions tend toward polarity and that frequently more heat than light exists.

Those who favor required physical education classwork for team members point out that physical education is much more than a few games and that boys who do not take part in classes miss many essential and valuable experiences. Men who favor excusing squad members maintain that these boys do not need additional physical activity, that additional strenuous exercise may overburden the boys, that they have significant physical education experiences as squad members, and that they get more than their share of instruction and use of facilities.

In deciding whether or not team members should be members of physical education classes, it seems helpful to eliminate use of the word "excuse" and decide the issue on the basis of appropriate student selection of physical education activities. It was stated above that almost all physical educators agree that high school juniors and seniors should have a chance to select activities if requirements of a minimum core have been satisfied. If it is agreed that student selection is appropriate for those who have completed the core and that interscholastic sports are physical education activities, then the questions become, "Has this boy completed the core?" and, "If he has not completed the core, will he be able to do so before graduation without participating in both team practice and class physical education, or will it be necessary for this student to double up to complete the core?"

If athletes attend a class only during part of a semester, it is necessary to both organize and manage differently than would be the case with continuous attendance. Some teachers regard such changes in class membership as a disturbance; consequently they object. There are three effective means of adjusting to this kind of fluctuating attendance. One is to synchronize classwork with sport seasons so that activities or projects are terminated when athletes leave the class for a season of interscholastic participation; new activities will be started when boys rejoin a class following a sports season. Another means is to make one or more class groups composed only of these athletes; such groups or squads might engage in the same activities which occupy the rest of the class, and they might work on something quite different. A third way is to assign athletes to only one class hour. This procedure is feasible in large schools, and popular among them. Of course, it produces the need for class reorganization only during one period, usually the last in the afternoon. In some cases all athletes are assigned to only one class when their sport is not in season.

Regardless of which plan is used to remove athletes from a class and (or) to reinstate them, records must account for the students. All should be assigned to a class and their names carried on the roster. If interscholastic participation is substituted for classwork, the record shows when the athlete starts team participation and when he will rejoin his class after the close of the sport season.

SUMMARY

Organizing and managing are teacher functions. A teacher organizes before class and manages during class. Management carries out plans projected through organization.

Effective organization and management of routine procedures saves time, helps put students at ease, improves morale and cooperation, prevents disciplinary problems, saves teacher words, and tends to let students concentrate on the subject matter of the day. Whatever needs to be repeated daily, or with great frequency, should be routinized. Procedures dealing with dressing and bathing, uniforms and towels, attendance, temporary exemptions, supplies, safety, and records need to be accomplished routinely.

Organization of a class into squads facilitates operation of a student-leader plan, increases acceptance of responsibility, tends to make classes operate more smoothly, facilitates homogeneous grouping, increases teacher opportunity to teach individuals, promotes maximum use of facilities, and provides organization for intraclass competition. Squad membership may be decided by student choice, teacher selection, tests, or height-weight-age measures.

High school juniors and seniors should have the opportunity to select activities provided there is assurance of experiences in a variety of activities. There should always be the opportunity to select extraclass activities and to select activities within a class.

Students may share in organizing and managing in one or more ways; they may make suggestions, serve on representative committees, or participate in class-group planning. Group involvement is desirable; it is better to have leaders and group members than leaders and followers.

Providing for individual differences within a class presents a persistent teaching problem. Individual needs can be met through procedures which allow for flexible grouping and through optimum student participation in management which allows teachers to work with individuals or small groups.

Necessary tasks or functions which may have little direct effect upon learning should be accomplished quickly and easily. Checking attendance, getting students where they need to be, recording, handling supplies, and supervising dressing rooms are such necessary functions.

Class and extraclass programs should supplement and complement each other. Class instruction that develops skills and interests in various activities increases interest in extraclass participation in those activities; at the same time, extraclass activities stimulate students to increased intensity in their classwork.

Questions and problems for discussion

1. What are some of the advantages of having students assist with the formulation and conduct of class-management procedures? Indicate some of the kinds of managerial problems for which student cooperation is especially advantageous.

2. What learnings are involved in the entire dressing problem for physical education? Prepare a list of general principles to govern desirable practices in regard to dressing. Include attention to types of costumes.

3. Should the same degree of student responsibility be expected of first-year high school students as fourth-year? Describe some of the ways in which practices would be differentiated among varying age groups.

4. Describe ten techniques physical education teachers can use to provide for individual differences in group teaching.

5. How do you account for the lack of unanimity of opinion on the best method of homogeneous grouping? Describe grouping practices you prefer for teaching class swimming, recreational dance, and varsity competition.

6. In terms of physical education objectives, how important is it to teach students about the selection and care of physical education equipment? What specific procedures do you suggest for promoting necessary learnings in this regard? What is the relationship, if any, between students' attitudes toward care of school equipment and a teacher's attitude and managerial procedures?

7. What are the issues involved in the problem of making up absences from physical education classes? What procedures in this regard are most in keeping with sound educational practice?

8. What worthwhile activities can be provided for youngsters temporarily excused from a physical education class for (a) limiting health reason preventing active participation and (b) lack of proper equipment?

9. It is generally recognized that one of the pressing needs of adolescence is a sense of belonging to a group. Discuss ways in which a teacher can help to serve this need through apt selection of methods and class routines.

10. One of the principal emphases in good class management should be to make

optimum use of instructional time. Using this statement as a criterion, observe several physical education classes and evaluate their management procedures.

Selected references

American Association for Health, Physical Education, and Recreation: *Physical Education for High School Students,* Washington, D.C., 1960.

Bookwalter, Karl Wibbes: *Physical Education in the Secondary Schools,* Center for Applied Research in Education, Washington, D.C., 1964.

Davis, Elwood Craig, and Earl S. Wallis: *Toward Better Teaching in Physical Education,* Prentice-Hall, Inc., Englewood Cliffs, N.J., 1962.

Gnagey, William J.: *Controlling Classroom Misbehavior: What Research Says to the Teacher,* Bulletin No. 32, Department of Classroom Teachers and the American Educational Research Association, Washington, D.C., 1963.

Kozman, Hilda C., Rosalind Cassidy, and Chester O. Jackson: *Methods in Physical Education,* 3d ed., W. B. Saunders Company, Philadelphia, 1957.

McIntosh, P. C.: *Sport in Society,* C. A. Watts & Co., Ltd., London, 1963.

Seaton, Don Cash, et al.: *Physical Education Handbook,* Prentice-Hall, Inc., Englewood Cliffs, N.J., 1965.

Stanley, Dennis K., and I. F. Waglow: *Physical Education Activities Handbook,* Allyn and Bacon, Inc., Englewood Cliffs, N.J., 1966.

Vannier, Maryhelen, and Hollis F. Fait: *Teaching Physical Education in Secondary Schools,* W. B. Saunders Company, Philadelphia, 1964.

chapter 13

ORGANIZING AND MANAGING INTRAMURAL AND RECREATIONAL PROGRAMS

INTRODUCTION

As commonly used, the term intramural sports denotes competitive activities, whereas the term physical recreation activities denotes noncompetitive activities such as dancing, hiking, free play, skating, riding, recreational swimming, and the playing of competitive games in an informal way without organization into leagues or tournaments for which records are kept and continuity planned.[1] However, the two have much in common and belong in the same category for school sponsorship. Both are recreational and provide physical activity. Both are voluntary; students choose to participate for pleasure or for the satisfaction of felt needs or urges. Intramurals may be thought of as recreational play in organized leagues and tournaments, whereas nonintramural physical recreation may be thought of as including all recreational activities which demand a considerable amount of physical performance but which are not organized for continuity of competition against others. Both have a place in secondary schools. Since both are integral parts of a physical education program, it is appropriate to combine them. Many

[1] The word "intramural" sometimes is used broadly to include both competitive and noncompetitive activities. See Pat Mueller and Elmer D. Mitchell, *Intramural Sports*, 3d ed., The Ronald Press Company, New York, 1960.

institutions refer to them as the intramural and recreational program. Because it indicates two closely related types of physical recreation, the name seems quite appropriate.

The name, however, must not be accepted literally because it certainly is not intended to include all recreational and voluntary activities sponsored by a school. It is universal in the United States for secondary schools to offer voluntary extraclass activities of a recreational nature in physical education, music, and dramatics. It also is true that leisure-time pursuits may be associated with and grow out of any and all school areas and subjects.

Are recreational activities of a quiet nature properly included in a program of intramural and recreational activities? A negative answer seems proper since physical education departments seek to promote physical activity. However, in some situations it may be appropriate for physical education to accept some responsibility for recreation which is sedentary. For instance, physical education teachers or departments in some schools organize and manage noon recreation, designed for the dual purpose of keeping youngsters busy when they might otherwise get into mischief and providing wholesome developmental recreation. Such a program might include activities requiring mild exercise, such as table tennis, loop tennis, tetherball, darts, horseshoes, quoits, free throwing, shooting baskets, archery, softball, volleyball, and dancing—all physical education activities. It might also include sedentary recreation such as checkers, chess, and cards, as well as hobbylike activities in libraries, shops, art, music, and dramatics if a school has a long lunch period. For such a program some person or department must take primary responsibility, and physical education personnel rather frequently do so. It is true, of course, that to operate such a program cooperation of other school departments is necessary.

All physical education activities can be used for intramural or recreational purposes. Dance and sports clubs find increasing popularity among boys and girls. Weekend recreational leadership also may be in the province of physical education. Gymnasium and playground programs, hikes, climbs, skiing trips, excursions, sports days, play days, and outings demand attention, time, and development.

PURPOSES

The underlying purpose of an intramural and recreational program is to provide opportunities for athletic competition and physical recreation for all students. What percentage of students is likely to accept such opportunities? Why do almost all boys and girls in one high school participate whereas in another school only a small percentage show interest? Although it is true that extensiveness of offerings may produce interest, it also is true that active promotion of interest brings results. Providing opportunities by simply announcing them is not enough; it is necessary to build attractiveness in order to make the opportunities genuine and widespread.

How does one go about stirring interests in these activities? Since a section on developing interests appears near the end of this chapter, just a few points directly related to providing opportunities will suffice here. One is that adolescents will accept activities which have high value in the eyes of their peers. Another is that it is relatively easy to attract those whose athletic ability is average or above and not so easy to develop interest among those who do not perform well. Two things are certain: first, youngsters want to feel adequate, and they tend to avoid activities which they fear will make them feel inadequate; second, adolescents value status with their peers highly.

While the prospect of doing something which will give satisfaction, fun, and pleasure moves students to action, schools and physical educators have other purposes in sponsoring physical recreation. In addition to providing wholesome and pleasant recreation for students, intramural and recreational activities may contribute to (1) better physical and mental health, (2) physical fitness and improvement of skills, (3) improved social living, (4) development of permanent interests in sports participation, (5) group spirit and solidarity, (6) wise use of leisure time, (7) better cooperation and self-control, and (8) balanced living which relieves tensions and strains. Also, the development of athletes for interschool teams may be accepted as a purpose of intramural sports. When this purpose is paramount or emphasized, the fundamental purpose of providing recreational opportunities for all may be defeated. As an incidental purpose, however, this objective proves acceptable. A boy who discovers, through intramurals, abilities and interests which lead to later interscholastic competition may have had a significant experience in self-discovery and self-expression.

Attention to objectives or purposes gives direction to programs by establishing goals toward which the program should be aimed and bases upon which decisions can be made. With a view toward desirable goals and outcomes, the most important single consideration would seem to be the promotion of recreation for all, recreation which has concomitants that enable participants to live better.

TEACHER RESPONSIBILITIES

Leadership of intramural and recreational activities and programs involves arranging times and places of play, handling supplies and equipment, organizing teams and groups, organizing and training student managers and officials, developing and enforcing rules and regulations, making schedules, and supervising the conduct of activities. Since the smooth operation of extraclass activities depends to a large extent upon satisfactory performance by student leaders, managers, and officials, the leader must be a good organizer who works well with people. He must deal effectively with student groups, consider their suggestions, discuss with them their proposals and requests, delegate responsibility, and help youngsters perform the services required to make the activities operate efficiently.

The conduct of intramural and recreational programs emphasizes free participation in activities which students have learned in physical education classes or elsewhere. However, there are opportunities for direct teaching, sometimes demands for it. Rather frequently, for instance, practice sessions for teams will be scheduled shortly before competition is to start. A teacher may organize and conduct such practices, or he may make himself available upon request from a team captain.

Working with sports clubs is likely to require teaching. Examples of this include (1) preparing a dance group for a recital, (2) preparing a swimming club for a demonstration of synchronized swimming, (3) planning for a hike or other outing which may involve a half day or more, and (4) teaching a group of team captains their responsibilities and (or) rules, regulations, and techniques of a sport.

SELECTION OF ACTIVITIES

Any wholesome physical activity which attracts, or can be made to attract, student interest is appropriate for an intramural and recreational program. Activities frequently sponsored in high schools include the following:

Fall: touch football, soccer, speedball, cross country, table tennis, tennis, golf, bowling, paddleball, badminton.

Winter: basketball and similar games such as 21, clock basketball, and free throwing, volleyball, swimming, indoor track, wrestling, handball, gymnastics, dancing.

Spring: softball, track and field, tennis, golf, horseshoes, archery.

Since student interest is one of the criteria for selection, student opinion should be sought and student requests for organization of new activities should be encouraged. When there is considerable student interest in an activity not currently offered, that activity should be added if facilities, time, and personnel permit integration into the program.

Although it is important to have close correlation with class physical education, there is no reason why intramural and recreational activities should be strictly limited to those taught in class. It is true that extra-class programs should give students opportunities to use skills learned in classes. It also is true that young people should be encouraged to expand the horizon of their participation to enter into activities which appeal to them, especially if they take considerable responsibility for organizing and managing. Hiking, fishing, skating, ice hockey, skiing, bowling, baseball, and other activities may be impractical for class instruction yet quite appropriate for intramural or recreational sponsorship during longer periods of time and under different conditions.

By and large, intramural programs for boys have tended to emphasize the popular team sports which parallel interscholastics. Those sports are excellent intramural activities, and modifications of them or informal playing provides excellent recreation. However, in most high schools there is a need to broaden recreational opportunities, to expand programs. Individual sports such as archery, badminton, bowling, casting, golf, handball, horseshoes, paddle tennis, sidewalk tennis, table tennis, and tennis merit encouragement and expansion not only because of their possibilities for pleasant immediate recreation for boys and girls, but also because of the probability that they may become lasting recreations for many. Recreational activities not involving competition, such as bicycling, boating, dancing, hiking, hunting and fishing, riding, swimming, and winter sports, seem to demand increased attention if all or most of the students are to have realistic and rich opportunities.

Intramural and recreational programs should be fluid enough to permit revision by adding or dropping activities according to student interests and changing recreational patterns; they should not be static and inelastic, with the implication that students must accept what is now offered as the only activities which can become available. This should not be interpreted as a recommendation for changing in response to mere whims and fancies. It does recommend alertness in recognizing the signs of real student interests as well as a program which permits relatively easy change.

ORGANIZATION

Lodging of responsibility for organization and policy formation is necessary for a successful intramural and recreational program, just as it is for successful operation of any other school activity. It is common and appropriate for students to accept a good deal of responsibility. Their sharing in the making of policies and regulations promotes interest, gives experience in democratic procedures of planning, and ensures the adoption of plans which are likely to be accepted by students. Their sharing in administration and management gives experience which may be valuable in the development of the young person, and it may lessen the amount of work required of staff members.

DIRECTOR

A responsible head is a necessity. Schools which have competent directors who are ego-involved almost always have excellent programs, whereas schools which attach little importance to the position of director, or which have different persons in charge during various seasons, almost always have lackluster programs which attract relatively little student interest. Duties of a director center about planning programs, preparing and administering budgets, devising schedules, selecting time and facilities for events, keeping records, caring for facilities and supplies, making and enforcing rules and regulations, securing adequate and appropriate publicity, selecting and training officials, achieving integration with all school activities, and generally supervising the program.

What type of person should be selected as head or director? It is generally agreed that a physical education teacher should have charge of intramural and recreational sports in secondary schools, and also that a woman physical education teacher should direct the high school program for girls. The director of boys' programs in high schools may be a man who teaches physical education classes but who does not coach an interscholastic team; he may be an interscholastic coach; or he may be one who has teaching responsibilities in an academic area.

A physical education teacher is an appropriate director for a high school intramural program provided his class load is such that he has adequate time to do justice both to his classes and to intramural and recreational sports. Too frequently directorship of these activities is added to an already heavy load and a meager program results.

Although some athletic coaches do direct excellent programs, it often happens that intramural and recreational activities suffer with a coach in charge because of concentrated attention upon the team coached. It is quite possible, however, for the head of a physical education department who also coaches interscholastics to serve effectively as an administrative director of recreational sports provided there are staff assistants to whom much of the day-to-day responsibilities may be delegated.

Men who teach in academic areas may be good choices for directors if they understand and have enthusiasm for many sports, and if they have a knowledge of physical education in its broad aspects and time for the work. When academic teachers direct intramural and recreational sports, they serve as part-time members of the physical education staff. In order to achieve integration they must be well acquainted with the whole physical education program. In small high schools which employ only one man physical education specialist, it proves advantageous to have academic teachers either coach interscholastic teams or direct intramural and recreational sports so that some staff member has time to work with sports for all.

PRACTICAL AIDS FOR THE DIRECTOR

Bulletins, announcements, records of events held, written notations concerning difficulties encountered, and written suggestions for future improvement should be filed. They provide guides for future action as well as a record from which a season's or a year's program can readily be summarized. Immediate availability of such records eases the work from year to year. Procedures previously used and materials previously prepared may be used again either as they are or as a basis for revision.

Mimeographed or printed forms for operations, which are frequently duplicated, save time and work by helping to reduce necessary writing to a minimum. Filing is facilitated if such forms fit the filing cabinets. Among forms frequently used are entry blanks, score sheets or cards for various sports, blanks for reports by officials, cards for judges and timers, dummy forms for tournaments and round robin schedules, "check out" forms for use in distributing and collecting supplies, record blanks for point systems, and award certificates.

FACULTY ASSISTANTS

Multiple activities sponsored at one time require considerable adult leadership. In large high schools, faculty assistants to the director are needed. The number needed depends upon the extensiveness of the program and upon the location and type of facilities used. It also depends upon the effectiveness of student leadership and responsibility. Assistants may well be either full-time physical educators or qualified persons who also teach in other areas.

STUDENT MANAGERS

A good deal of the work involved in contacting teams and individuals, handling details in connection with publicity, record keeping, bulletin board displays and announcements, scorekeeping and timekeeping, officiating, and distribution and care of supplies may be done by students who serve without pay because of interest in the program. When students have pride in their own program, many aspire to assistant or manager assignments. Successful plans for organizing student managers or assistants include the following: one student manager of all intramural and recreational sports, with appropriate assistant managers for various activities; a student manager of each activity, with assistant managers if needed, who is responsible to the director or a faculty assistant rather than to a student manager of all sports; class or grade managers; homeroom managers; and schemes of managers and assistant managers available for assignment to responsibilities at the discretion of the director or a faculty assistant.

Illustrative of the "one student manager with appropriate assistants" plan combined with the "homeroom manager plan" is the student-manager organization for the boys' intramural and recreational program at New Trier East High School, a large suburban school.[2] The student head has the title of Student Director. Additional students serve in capacities which are, generally speaking, indicated by their titles: (1) Head of Team Sports, (2) Assistant Head of Team Sports, (3) Head of Individual Sports, (4) Assistant Head of Individual Sports, (5) Head of Special Events (halloween party, open house, bowling, ice hockey), (6) Head of Points, (7) Head of Awards, (8) Head of Communications, (9) Office Administrator, (10) Head of Display, (11) some 40 student staff members who serve as tournament managers, game supervisors, point and award staff, and publicity staff, and (12) some 50 boys who serve as "adviser room" managers.

The director and his faculty assistants work a good deal with the student heads and assistants and with student managers. They train managers, officials, scorekeepers, timekeepers, equipment and supply managers, etc. They supervise the work of student managers, give assistance when it is needed, commend and encourage, and lend the stability of adult presence.

POLICY BODY

An overall committee or board or council, charged with the responsibility of making general policies for the guidance of persons responsible for carrying them out, gives a broad base for consideration of varying interests, points of view, and knowledge. Schools, governmental agencies, and various welfare agencies find such bodies helpful in planning overall programs. They have been used extensively in interscholastic athletics. There is a question concerning the advisability of having such an organization which functions only in the area of intramural and recreational sports. Theoretically, at least, overlapping is lessened, correlation improved, and desirable relative emphasis upon each phase of the program more nearly achieved when one such policy body deals with physical education in its entirety. Thus, one board or council concerned with class physical education, intramural and recreational sports, and interscholastic athletics may produce better results than two or three bodies dealing with

[2] New Trier East High School, Winnetka, Illinois, Mr. Wayne Wiemer, Faculty Director of Intramural Sports. Mr. F. A. Barney, former Faculty Director, laid bases for a student manager plan which Mr. Wiemer has continued to develop.

parts of the physical education program. Similarly, one organization which encompasses all school extraclass activities might achieve desirable correlation better than several councils or committees, each of which is interested in a specialized area such as intramurals, interscholastics, music, or dramatics, and each of which may be inclined to overemphasize the particular area of its immediate interest. On the other hand, a group interested in only one specialized area may have greater interest and more drive, thus more energetic promotion which may lead to improvement of the program.

Advice from representatives of several interested groups can help. Whether or not a given school should have a council or committee specifically for intramural and recreational sports should be decided among faculty members of that school. Conditions likely to affect this decision center upon the leadership abilities available and upon the relationships among various groups including faculty members, faculty and students, community and school, and professional groups and school.

Representatives of interested groups and perhaps some interested individuals should serve on a policy body dealing with intramural and recreational sports. Groups and individuals likely to be interested include:

1. The students. Since the program is for them and belongs to them, they surely should be represented.
2. The physical education department. Intramural and recreational sports are an important part of physical education. In almost all cases this department, or one of its members, directs the program in secondary schools.
3. The faculty. Teachers are interested in extraclass activities. Since they know the problems of students and of the school, their help in policy formation is likely to be of real value.
4. The school health coordinator or a doctor or nurse. Representatives of the health sciences are in a position to give counsel that will help the program contribute to good health.
5. The guidance director or a representative of guidance services.
6. The head of the school or his representative.
7. The parents. Equipped with an interest in youngsters and knowledge of their home behavior, they may have suggestions that would be overlooked without their representation.
8. The director of municipal recreation or his representative. His suggestions may improve correlation between school and other community recreation.
9. Private and voluntary agencies interested in recreation. Their help may contribute to more integrated recreation for the community.

STUDENT BOARDS

Whether or not there is a policy body, committee, or board with adult representation, student intramural-recreational boards or councils composed of representatives of various groups of students serve useful functions. If no group with adult representation exists, a student group, with the advice and guidance of faculty personnel, may take responsibility for the program and for formation of broad general policies as well as for putting them into operation. If there is a policy body with adult representation, a student group still may plan activities and procedures within the framework of policies set by the former group. The making of proposals by student groups which are subject to acceptance, rejection, or modification by the all-school group or by the director represents sound procedure.

Any one of several plans of representation may result in successful student boards or councils. Each sport or activity may be represented; classes or grades may select one or more representatives each; homerooms may elect delegates; physical education classes may form the basis; homeroom managers may serve; or some combination of two or more of these schemes may be employed. It is important that a wide range of interests be represented. Boards made up only of representatives from each sport or activity now in the program may be inclined to be ambitious for the sport they represent but slow to sense needs for the addition of activities not presently sponsored. More complete representation of interests is likely to result from grade, homeroom, physical education class, or some other basis which reflects a wide range of student interests.

BASES FOR COMPETITION

Intraschool competition between teams is possible only when teams represent some unit within the school, only when identifiable units or groups form and operate teams. Whatever base or unit is selected should satisfy three criteria:

1. Athletic ability should be distributed. Reasonable evenness of team strength produces interesting competition and tends to distribute winning and losing among a number of teams over a period of years instead of permitting one or a few teams to win most of the time while others lose continuously.
2. The base or unit should have or be able to develop group solidarity or loyalty. Feelings of pride add zest. Identification with a group gives a feeling of belonging. Players who feel "This is our team" work and play together well.

3. The unit should be able to manage its teams. Selection of units which have structure, such as homerooms with advisers and student officers or leaders, leads toward formation of teams which can be depended upon. Absence of ability to manage without excessive outside help leads toward confusion and disappointment.

Among units for competition which have been found successful are physical education classes, school grades or classes such as ninth or tenth, homerooms, specially organized groups formed by students, and students of the same geographical residence. The considerable variety of units in use indicates that selection must be made in local schools after a study of school characteristics and circumstances. Specific units which satisfy the three criteria for selection in one school may not do so in another.

The physical education class as a base for units of competition has the distinct advantage of ensuring correlation between class and intramural-recreational aspects of physical education. In classes students may develop condition, learn games and activities, organize teams, and experience competitive play. Competition carried on in classes may be extended quite naturally to extraclass competition. When a teacher of physical education also works with the intramural-recreational program, he finds that this unit provides a most favorable medium for contacting students, disseminating information about the extraclass program, and developing interest. When an academic teacher directs the extraclass program, the physical education–class unit of competition helps substantially to integrate the class and extraclass activities.

School class or grade (as tenth grade) is a popular unit in smaller schools. It may have the advantage of utilizing existing classifications into groups which already have solidarity and pride in their identification. One disadvantage lies in the probability that groups will be unequal in competitive strength, another in the limited number of units. Further breakdown is almost always indicated when this unit is used in large schools. Small schools also find that it produces unequal competition, particularly in the junior high grades and for girls in the high school. However, small high schools frequently find this unit quite satisfactory for boys because the elimination of interscholastic squad members from intramural play tends to equalize team strength and because almost all boys can find places on class teams.

The homeroom unit provides an excellent base in many schools. Team or group strength usually is quite equal. Homeroom population is small enough to permit almost all members to participate in team or group competitive events. Announcements and plans may be made conveniently during periodic sessions of the groups. Already existent unity and pride of students in their own group may be enhanced through common interests in intramurals which tend to develop attitudes of pride and cooperation.

Independent groups may be organized for the specific purpose of forming intramural teams. Students who wish to form a team may do so and enter competition. This scheme usually produces groups who wish to play with one another, who wish to belong to the group. However, there may be disadvantages. Democracy from the standpoint of equal opportunity for all may break down because boys and girls who wish to play may receive no invitation to do so. Unless some control, such as preparation of a list of superior players and enforcement of regulations such as, "No more than two of these on any one team," is exercised, unit strength is likely to be unbalanced.

Geographical-residence-area units sometimes are used with good results. Maps of the city may be used for division. While such units may stimulate interest, it is probable that the risk of excessive rivalry which might tend to divide students rather than to amalgamate them is greater than the potential benefits.

SELECTION OF TIME AND FACILITIES

A most difficult problem in the promotion of intramural and recreational sports is finding time and facilities for the activities. In almost all schools many more boys and girls would like to participate regularly than time and facilities permit.

AFTERNOON HOURS

Late afternoon is the time favored by most participants and potential participants. It is the time which overtaxes gymnasiums, swimming pools, and playfields. In many situations interscholastic teams use the bulk of the facilities during these hours. Although the concept that each student is entitled to equal opportunity in the use of time and facilities seems sound, there can be little doubt that interscholastic squad members usually are favored. Quite frequently, the minority who participate in interscholastics use most of the facilities during the late-afternoon hours four days a week while the remaining majority of the boys, and all the girls, get one afternoon a week.

The ideal solution may lie in the provision of facilities sufficient to accommodate all during these hours. However, this is not likely to occur, and probably expenditure of money for the purpose would be difficult to justify. Practical considerations require continual efforts to find time and facilities for intramural and recreational sports. A practice favorable to intramurals during the late-afternoon hours is to reserve the facilities for these activities during the first hour after school and delay the start of practice for interscholastic teams until that time.

NOON HOUR

In schools which have a relatively long break at noon, a considerable number of intramural and recreational activities may be offered at that time. While immediately after lunch may not be best for strenuous sports, it is favorable for dancing, table tennis, shuffleboard, free-throw contests, clock golf, darts, loop tennis, horseshoes, and basket shooting. Also, volleyball and softball may be played if time permits. The extent to which the noon hour may be effectively utilized depends, of course, upon the local school situation. If a lunch period of thirty minutes or less is provided, no noon program is indicated. If the break is forty-five minutes or longer, organized recreation serves to keep students busy during a time when destructive mischief may arise and to provide recreational opportunities with positive educational concomitants.

EARLY-MORNING HOURS

Early-morning hours may not be popular with either students or faculty members when first considered. Nevertheless, they should be considered seriously because of the availability of facilities at that time. Attractive schedules of events and activities become quite popular if a pattern of continuity is established. Junior high school boys and girls frequently embrace a morning program wholeheartedly. Senior high students are attracted to well-organized programs during these hours. In schools where there is competition for time and facilities, utilization of early-morning hours helps to solve a difficult problem. Often school bus schedules increase the feasibility of using morning hours.

WEEKEND

Cessation of school intramural and recreational activities from Fridays to Mondays causes waste through idle facilities. Can we afford this? Expansion of weekend activities is needed. It is true that not all students are free to participate during weekend periods. It is also true that many can profit from participation in a voluntary program at that time. Some acutely need wholesome and interesting activities to occupy their time. Saturdays may be utilized for team-game competition in some cases. However, since not all are free, individual competition and recreational periods during which the participant may select an activity of his choice may be preferable. Hikes, excursions, skating, skiing, fishing, short camping trips, bicycle trips, and kiteflying, activities which require more time than physical education classes provide, prove particularly appropriate.

If extensive weekend recreation is to be provided, teacher time must be available. A director or staff assistant who already has a heavy load of responsibilities can hardly be expected to contribute long weekend hours. Cooperation between schools and municipal recreation departments may solve the personnel problem and increase the use of facilities during weekends.

EVENING HOURS

Are evening hours appropriate for intramurals and school recreation? Opinions are sharply divided. A chief objection is found in the belief that young people should be at home nights and that the school should not encourage youngsters to do anything that will take them away from home in the evening. However, others feel that young people will spend evenings away from home whether or not school activities are available at that time. They believe that it is important for the school to provide interesting activities in wholesome surroundings in order to counteract questionable influences found elsewhere. Objections to evening school recreation programs for students sometimes are based upon the feeling that evening hours should be reserved for adults, for occasional interscholastic events, a few dramatic and musical productions, and periodic school parties or dances. The decision concerning evening intramural-recreational programs must rest upon an analysis of local situations.

REGULAR SCHOOL HOURS

Providing intramural-recreational–type activities within a generous allotment of time to regular physical education classes has the tremendous advantage of drawing all or almost all the students into the activities. When daily class periods of sixty minutes or more are available, it seems wise to include a substantial amount of recreational play. However, a program limited to only class time fails to take advantage of many opportunities to help students use their leisure time advantageously.

Some schools schedule club periods for which each student may select one of several activities. Physical recreation activities may well be scheduled during such times. However, the problem of facilities becomes acute under such a plan because, customarily, all students have their club period at the same hour. Available facilities usually will not accommodate all who wish to participate. Activities sponsored during such periods serve well as one of several approaches to the intramural-recreational problem, but limitation to the club period only is likely to result in a meager program. Probably the best use of club periods for intramural-recreational programs is to utilize that time for working with leaders' clubs composed of student officials and managers.

SUMMER PROGRAMS

It seems clear that secondary schools which offer a program of classes during summer months should offer, or at least seriously consider, an intramural-recreational program. Should school facilities be available for such activities when classes are not offered? There is considerable reason for recreational use of school property, tax-supported and owned by the public, during school-vacation time; but there are objections.

In some instances the expenditure of money for school-sponsored recreation is legally questionable. The problems connected with the use of school property by nonschool agencies such as municipal recreation departments can be serious. Because school boards are responsible for school property, reluctance to permit use by other agencies and nonschool personnel is understandable. Efforts to provide recreational programs during the summer and other school vacation periods definitely should be encouraged. Problems related to cooperation with other public agencies are by no means insoluble.

DEVELOPING AND MAINTAINING INTEREST

In this chapter there are comments about developing interest in intramural activities related to the *central purpose* of providing opportunities (page 319). These comments concerned adolescent needs and desires for peer approval, for achievement, and for avoidance of activities which they think will show weaknesses. Here, attention is given to procedures, to things which might be done, steps which might be taken, to develop and maintain interest. Publicity, awards, point systems, and periodic recognition events are considered.

PUBLICITY

Publicity affects interests by giving information and building an image or opinions concerning value. It attracts boosters and improves cooperative efforts among students and others. What kind of publicity is appropriate for intramural and recreational programs? Dissemination of information always is appropriate; it is absolutely necessary for participants, and it is useful for interested persons. Information concerning opportunities may create interests which turn nonparticipants into participants. Publicity which exaggerates, propagandizes, or leads to false impression is in bad taste and unworthy of any educational program.

What media are appropriate? Newspapers and radio and television, both student and other, handbooks describing program and rules, yearbooks, bulletin board displays including artistic designs and photographs as well as announcements, daily all-school bulletins, and bulletins from the director. It is helpful to have student assistants; a student publicity chairman and a committee can perform useful work while securing writing experience and knowledge about publicity.

AWARDS

The practice of presenting awards in recognition of achievement in intramural and recreational activities is widespread. Considerable disagreement exists concerning its desirability. Some persons feel that all motivation should come from interest in the activity itself. Others believe that awards are not only appropriate symbols but that they supply motivation and interest which lead to desirable behavior. It may be that proponents of awards are very largely persons who work directly with secondary school students, whereas opponents most frequently are theorizers who write and speak. Some of the opponents make no attempt to hide honor keys or their watch chains or service-club insignias in their lapels as they speak of the evils of awards.

Whether or not awards should be made is a question for local decision. The ideal situation would be one in which all boys and girls participated consistently, with satisfaction, fun, and the concomitants in health and social living, with no awards other than those inherent in the activity. But it may be advisable to use awards for the purpose of supplying satisfactions and feelings of self-enhancement and worthwhileness on the part of young people as well as to motivate interest and participation in activities which will be of benefit.

It is recognized that everyone wants recognition. The extent to which it can or should be supplied by intramural and recreational awards is open to question. If awards supply desirable goals and subgoals more effectively than does the enjoyment of activity alone, then they are useful. A purpose of awards is to stimulate interest in participation. An extrinsically aroused interest in sports may be the starting point for the development of complete intrinsic motivation.

An award is a symbol of achievement, not a reward for accomplishment. Inexpensive symbols serve the purpose well; emblems, letters, ribbons, certificates, and medallions are acceptable as individual awards. Group awards tend to emphasize the importance of a group or team. Team trophies or plaques which can be displayed in central locations such as a trophy case or in a homeroom may add interest and increase feelings of pride.

POINT SYSTEMS

Various schemes of awarding points are used in intramural and recreational programs. Almost all of them award points for participation and additional points for winning or for playing on a winning team. Many of them award points for healthful living, leadership, sportsmanship, and service. Recognition, usually in the form of an award, is given for the earning of a specified number of points. Gradations commonly give opportunity to earn several recognitions or awards, such as one insignia for 100 points, another for 200 points, and a third for 300 points. Some schemes are designed especially for individual schools; others serve several schools in one school district, and some are statewide in scope.

A chief purpose of point systems is to stimulate participation. Limitations on the number of points which may be earned in one activity tend to encourage a spread of recreational pursuits. Awarding points for healthful practices and sportsmanship is designed to improve behavior in these areas. Points for service and leadership have the purpose of motivating students toward activity which is desirable to their development and in which they can provide adequate student help.

As in the case of awards, there are conflicting opinions concerning the desirability of point systems. Proponents and opponents use the same reasoning and arguments as they do for or against awards. This, of course, is logical because a point system is a device for determining who is to receive awards or recognition.

PERIODIC RECOGNITION EVENTS

Annual banquets, occasional school assemblies devoted to presenting awards, and periodic gatherings are events which recognize achievement. Only a small minority of schools sponsor annual banquets in honor of achievement in intramural and recreation activities. However, the schools which do have developed a tradition which attracts favorable attention and which youngsters and their parents enjoy in anticipation and retrospect, as well as during the banquet. Since such an event attracts attention it gets publicity and affects opinions concerning values.

The quite common practice of presenting awards at periodic school assemblies steers student and teacher attention toward recipients, toward those who are honored. It also increases the awareness of opportunities for participation and may be responsible for the growth in popularity of various activities in the program.

Among periodic gatherings are box-lunch gymnasium events which honor achievers or simply provide an opportunity for people with similar interests to get together, outings or picnics, and group attendance at a public event such as a baseball game, track meet, or stage show. It certainly is not necessary for a school to have periodic recognition events in order to achieve excellence in its intramural and recreational program. Such events may add interest and attractiveness, and they are worth considering. Whether or not they are worth the effort required is another question. Annual banquets and other periodic gatherings to honor achievers do require a lot of work. Occasional school assemblies, however, require little effort or preparation; what they do require is student time to attend.

SUMMARY

The term intramural sports indicates competitive sports, i.e., playing games or otherwise competing against others. The term recreational sports applies to all noncompetitive physical recreation as well as to informal competitive play with no officials, no records, no schedules. The basic purpose of a program of these activities is to provide participatory experiences for all who wish to engage in them.

Teachers who have responsibilities for intramurals and recreation usually are called directors or assistant directors. Their work involves organizing, scheduling, supervising, and enforcing regulations. A good deal of their work is with student leaders or managers.

Any wholesome physical education activity which attracts student interest is appropriate for intramurals and recreation. A program may include some activities not in the class physical education program.

To have a good program, a high school needs a responsible head, a director who is ego-involved. The faculty assistants needed depend upon the size of the program and the location of facilities. Students should accept a good deal of responsibility. Student-manager plans include a head manager with assistants, a manager for each sport, homeroom managers, director assignment of managers from time to time, and combinations of these. Teams should represent units or groups which (1) have unity and loyalty, or can develop it, (2) provide equitable distribution of athletic ability, evenness of teams, and (3) demonstrate ability to manage their teams.

An overall committee, board, or council which considers and recommends general policies may be worthwhile in many secondary schools. It should be made up of students, faculty, a school health director or a doctor, guidance personnel, parents, municipal recreation, and representatives from other agencies interested in recreation.

Finding sufficient time and facilities is a problem. Late-afternoon hours are popular. Other times including early morning, noon, evening, and weekends should be considered seriously.

Intramural and recreational sports may be very popular or lackadaisical in a given secondary school. Interest may be developed through an attractive program, enthusiastic leadership, publicity, awards, and point systems.

Questions and problems for discussion

1. Draw up a prospectus for a program of intramural and recreational activities for a selected high school. Consider time, facilities, and personnel available, as well as correlation with class and extramural physical education.

2. Suggest an appropriate intramural-recreational policy-body organization for a high school of 400 students located in a farming center community, which also has a few small factories. Show what contributions you would expect from the representatives you select.

3. Propose an intramural student-manager organization for a school which you select and describe. Indicate duties of the managers as well as a plan for training them.

4. What principles would you consider in preparing a recommendation concerning the advisability of evening-hour intramural activities?

5. Assume that you are a physical education teacher in a school of your choice. Defend or oppose a proposal to institute an intramural point system.

6. Assume that you are an intramural director for boys or for girls in a high school whose students have little interest in intramural and recreational activities. Describe the school, and propose a plan for developing student interest.

Selected references

American Association for Health, Physical Education, and Recreation, Division for Girls' and Women's Sports: *Standards in Sports for Girls and Women: Guiding Principles in the Organization and Administration of a Sports Program; A Project,* rev. ed., Washington, D.C., 1961.

Baines, Mildred J., Margaret G. Fox, M. Gladys Scott, and Pauline Loeffler: *Sports Activities for Girls and Women,* Appleton-Century-Crofts, Inc., New York, 1966.

Kleindienst, Viola K., and Arthur Weston: *Intramural and Recreation Programs for Schools and Colleges,* Appleton-Century-Crofts, Inc., New York, 1964.

Leavitt, Norma, and Hartley D. Price: *Intramural and Recreational Sports for School and College,* 2d ed., The Ronald Press Company, New York, 1958.

McIntosh, Peter Charles: *Sport in Society,* C. A. Watts & Co., Ltd., London, 1963.

Means, Louis E.: *Intramurals: Their Organization and Administration,* Prentice-Hall, Inc., Englewood Cliffs, N.J., 1963.

Mueller, Pat, and Elmer D. Mitchell: *Intramural Sports,* 3d ed., The Ronald Press Company, New York, 1960.

Nash, Jay Boyan: *Recreation: Pertinent Readings,* Wm. C. Brown Company, Publishers, Dubuque, Iowa, 1965.

National Conference on Intramurals, Michigan State University, 1964, *Intramurals for the Junior High School,* The Athletic Institute, Chicago, 1964.

National Conference on Intramurals, Michigan State University, 1964, *Intramurals for the Senior High School,* The Athletic Institute, Chicago, 1964.

chapter 14

ORGANIZING AND MANAGING INTERSCHOLASTIC PROGRAMS

INTRODUCTION

Interscholastic athletics are an important part of secondary school physical education programs. School teams are in the limelight; students and adults pay attention; sometimes a great deal of the recreational and social life of communities centers around high school teams. Almost every high school sponsors boys' athletic teams: some have only team games such as football, basketball, and baseball; others sponsor interschool competition in individual and dual sports such as wrestling, tennis, and golf. In most sections of the United States, highly organized interscholastic competition for girls no longer exists, but planned competitive experiences, called extramurals, in the nature of field days, sports days, and invitational games play an important part in girls' physical education programs.

The controversy surrounding interscholastic athletics centers around three areas: (1) whether or not junior high schools should have interscholastic athletics, (2) whether or not either junior or senior high schools should have them for girls and (3) disagreement about emphases upon and methods of conducting interscholastics for high school boys. These areas will be discussed after the purpose, nature and scope, and teaching or coaching of interscholastic athletics are dealt with. It is hoped that readers will keep an open mind, will read with minds rather than emotions and with light instead of heat, as they examine these parts of interscholastics which some extoll and some condemn. (Perhaps that is too much to hope.) The last part of the chapter considers management and public relations.

PURPOSES

During the relatively short period of their existence, interscholastic athletics for high school boys have become a part of American culture. Along with music, art, and dramatics, they are a medium through which both performers and spectators express living interests. For performers they provide opportunities for the expression of natural desires to match strength, speed, skill, and cunning with that of performers from other schools. For spectators there is opportunity not only for recreation but also for identification with a community activity through vicarious participation. A school provides desirable opportunities for self-expression by both performers and spectators when it conducts interscholastics in wholesome and socially approved surroundings.

Introduced into our schools in response to demands by students, interscholastics were, during the early period of their existence, organized and managed largely by students with the aid of interested adults who were not, as a rule, members of school faculties. At that time faculties frowned upon games between schools. As the movement gained momentum, school officials tended to accept the addition reluctantly, perhaps with the thought that since boys insisted upon playing, athletics would have to be tolerated. During the early 1900s, the growing interest of school people in the educational experiences which were involved in interscholastic contests led to school acceptance, to faculty sponsorship, and to the setting up of organizations for the purpose of controlling athletics and guiding them toward sound educational ends.

As secondary schools became institutions for a majority of our youth rather than for a selective minority, as emphasis upon preparation for college became less pervasive, as attention to learning to live through satisfying living in the present increased, and as emphasis upon meeting the present needs of students grew, athletics became more and more an integral part of the school program. The welfare of participants has been the principal guidepost of a host of schoolmen who have worked to guide and develop interscholastic athletics. Attention to opportunities for physical, social, emotional, and recreational development of the player has been stressed.

Although welfare of participants is the primary consideration, the effect of athletics upon spectators and interested students and adults is important. Zest is added to school living. Cooperative enterprise in athletics may help to unify school populations, enhance pride in the institution, and improve morale. Watching sports, reading and talking about them, and watching television or listening to radio broadcasts may provide interesting and wholesome leisure pursuits. It is apparent that sports serve as a public-relations medium providing the most direct contact between school and community for many adults.

NATURE AND SCOPE

Any sport which is wholesome in nature and free from undue risk of injury may be considered for inclusion in an interscholastic program. Almost all team and individual sports commonly played in the United States fall into this category.

Within the limits of the ability of a given high school to provide satisfactory conditions, it is wise to sponsor a variety of sports and multiple teams in order to give many boys opportunities to play. What determines the ability of a school to provide satisfactory conditions? Key factors are (1) existing, or at least potential, player interest, (2) enough boys so that teams may be manned without overtaxing a few, (3) time and facilities for practice and contests, (4) availability of coaching personnel, (5) ability to supply equipment, and (6) ability to provide travel and contest expense.

When there is substantial student interest in playing other schools, officials should consider the advisability of providing an outlet for this interest through interscholastic competition. Generally speaking, instigation of school teams should be based upon already existing student desires. However, potential interest should be considered when it seems desirable to expand interest in a given sport. Thus, if a school wishes to promote sports such as volleyball or tennis or gymnastics, the organization of interscholastic competition for the purpose of developing interests which will result in more widespread play should be undertaken.

Since one purpose of an interscholastic program should be to spread opportunities to play rather than merely to enhance school pride through representative teams, it follows that sports should not be sponsored unless there are enough boys to make teams without calling upon boys to compete in more than one sport during a given season. Thus, a school should not attempt to have track, baseball, and tennis teams if sponsorship of such teams results in a few boys' competing in two or all three of the sports during the same season.

Similarly, a school should not attempt to sponsor eleven-man football if such sponsorship overtaxes participants by creating a situation in which boys are led to feel that they have a responsibility to play in order that the school may have a team. Generally speaking, schools with fewer than

100 boys should have six-man football, soccer, or speedball as a fall sport rather than eleven-man football.

Because of the necessity of time and facilities for successful operation of an interscholastic sport, a school should be careful not to overload its program. For instance, it is unwise to sponsor teams in basketball, gymnastics, wrestling, and volleyball if the same gymnasium must be used for all and if sufficient separate practice and contest time cannot be arranged for each. It is important to consider needs for intramurals as well as for interscholastics. School teams should serve to round out opportunities for widespread sports participation rather than to provide intensive participation for the gifted at the expense of others.

Since it is necessary to have coaches to help boys develop toward the upper limits of their potentialities as well as to care for them during practices, contests, and trips, it follows that schools should avoid sponsoring school teams which overtax available faculty leadership. As a general rule, one man should not be asked to handle more than twenty boys at a time in interscholastic sports. Also, it usually is unwise for one man to coach more than one sport at a time.

If a school sponsors an interscholastic sport, it must accept responsibility for seeing that appropriate equipment is supplied. Football requires an adequate supply of protective equipment; track and field requires hurdles, standards, rings, poles, and throwing implements; and most sports require clothing, balls, and other implements. If boys participate, they should have equipment which protects them and gives good opportunity for development of skills. It is not at all necessary, however, to have gaudy or expensive equipment merely for show purposes. Although there is no unanimity of opinion concerning the appropriateness of asking performers to supply their own equipment, it is important for schools to guard against a situation which places any boy at a disadvantage because of inability to purchase equipment necessary for team membership without hardship.

Since expense for travel and for operating home contests almost always is incurred, it becomes a responsibility of a school which sponsors a sport to see that needed money is available. It follows, of course, that one of the factors which determine ability of a school to provide satisfactory conditions for a sport is ability to arrange for such expenses. Concerning the advisability of asking participants to pay all or part of expenses involved, such as for travel, the situation is similar to asking students to supply their own equipment.

TEACHING OR COACHING

One often hears the remark, "The best teaching in physical education is found in the interscholastic program." Among reasons why this appears to be true are :

1. Ego-involvement of coaches is high. They work hard, with determination to do their best. Their teams take examinations as they play games in public; the success of players reflects credit upon the coaches.
2. A coach works with athletically gifted students.
3. Students are highly motivated. The prestige, desire to achieve, stimulation of competition for positions, and desire to win lead toward optimum effort.
4. Ideal teaching loads generally prevail, with squads kept to feasible size for effective work.
5. The coach-teacher knows and understands each player better than the teacher knows each member of his several classes because of the smaller number of students and greater length of time per practice.
6. Facilities, equipment, and supplies for interscholastic teams are generally superior.
7. Objectives, goals, both short-term and long-term targets, usually are well defined for both coach-teacher and student, making for effective concentration of effort.
8. Coaches plan carefully both for the season as a whole and for each week and each day.
9. Teaching time generally is more adequate; practice periods usually are long and frequent in comparison with time for classes.

If all parts of physical education programs could enjoy equally advantageous circumstances, student achievement of objectives in other areas would be equally great. The favored position of interscholastic athletics presents no argument for deemphasis. Rather it suggests a need for improving the conditions for learning in classes and intramurals.

The basic teaching procedures for teaching team and individual games and component skills apply to teaching or coaching interscholastic athletics. There are, however, some teaching principles which apply particularly to preparing teams for highly pitched competition. The level of skill sought must be high, greater, of course, than that appropriate for emphasis in classes. Development of strength and endurance differs in degree; training-rule requirements may be set for interscholastic teams which could not be used for classes; and motivational procedures differ because of the high motivation already present in interscholastic athletics.

From a teaching procedure, or methodological standpoint, the greatest opportunity presented to and the greatest problem facing a coach-teacher is to teach and foster social and personal learning and development of his players. Teaching methods used, examples set, precepts conveyed, and personal relationships between coach and player do help to build student attitudes. Coaches have great opportunities to affect the lives of their players. Further, because athletes tend to be peer-group leaders, they may have widespread social influence within the school and community.

The general administrative structure surrounding athletics affects attitudes. For instance, lack of genuine opportunity for all who want to participate to do so is a basic problem in most high schools. Too frequently boys from affluent homes are favored because of enjoying more free time, more money to buy equipment, greater sense of belonging, and more social acceptance. A school which sponsors multiple teams and supplies all needed supplies, equipment, and transportation provides greater opportunities for those who would like to play on teams and who would develop favorably while doing so.

INTERSCHOLASTICS FOR JUNIOR HIGH SCHOOLS

The question of whether or not junior high schools should sponsor interscholastic athletics is highly controversial. The great difference of opinion among educators and physical educators is shown by the fact that many writers, speakers, and leaders in the field, as well as national committees and organizations, oppose interscholastics below the ninth grade, although a great many schools sponsor such competition. Most leaders in the fields of physical education, education, and medicine who have expressed themselves formally object to interscholastics at this level and advocate class physical education, intramural competition, and recreational play for prepubescents.

Inability to agree made it impossible for a subcommittee composed of representatives of three national organizations to formulate a statement concerning junior high interscholastics which included specific recommendations. Louis A. Alley,[1] reporting for the AAHPER Subcommittee and the Joint Committee of the National Association of Secondary School Principals and the National Federation of State High School Athletic Associations on Junior High School Athletics for Boys, reported that four years of work made it apparent that it was not possible to formulate a statement concerning interscholastic athletics for junior high schools which included specific regulations. What was acceptable to some parts of the country and to some groups did not agree with what seemed suitable in other sections of the United States and to other members of the subcommittee. Accordingly the subcommittee developed a statement of basic principles and regulations including the points which are paraphrased as follows:

[1] In National Conference on Secondary School Athletic Administration, *Administration of High School Athletics, A Report,* American Association for Health, Physical Education, and Recreation, Washington, D.C., 1962, pp. 16–19.

The first duty is to provide opportunity for all. Because of limited space, facilities, and personnel, opportunities for all can best be provided in the junior high school through:

1. A required class physical education program for all.
2. An intramural program.
3. A recreational program.

If the above three programs adequately provide opportunities for all, an interscholastic program is appropriate if it is a limited program. Such an interscholastic program should be organized and conducted in accordance with four principles:

1. Educational objectives should be accomplished.
2. The program should supplement rather than substitute for class physical education, intramurals, and recreation.
3. Properly trained personnel should conduct the program.
4. Physical welfare of the boys should be protected and fostered.

It seems apparent that persons who deal with this problem in a theoretical way are more opposed to school teams below the ninth grade than are those who work directly with boys of that age. There are at least three reasons for this situation. One is that it is natural for boys of superior physical ability in any given school to want to match their skill and strength against boys from other schools. Although this group may represent only a small proportion of the total school population, they are influential with their peers and their desires are presented forcefully. Teachers who work directly with the boys feel the problems presented by this situation more acutely than do those who are further removed. Perhaps the immediate and practical problem serves to hide the broader implications.

A second reason for reluctance to forgo interscholastic competition is found in the inadequacy of intramural programs. Intramural schedules which provide opportunities for many to participate in continuing and frequent game and practice experiences satisfy desirable and natural urges to compete that are found among junior high school boys. But "continuing" and "frequent" are the imprecise words in the preceding sentence. Not many intramural programs permit sufficient games and practices to satisfy needs. Limitations of time and facilities and the numbers of students attracted to sports programs make it well-nigh impossible to schedule frequent sessions for all participants.

What is an adequate intramural program which gives all students opportunities to compete? In one city with about 100 junior high schools, an overwhelming majority of the junior high physical educators reported that hardly enough boys to make school teams were interested in voluntary after-school programs. However, teachers in a small minority of the junior high schools in that city reported that almost all the boys in their schools wanted to play after school; these men suggested that boys in all or most of the schools would be attracted to intramural programs which gave all genuine opportunities to compete against others of similar ability.

When one examines details of a junior high school intramural program which enjoys a reputation for being quite good, he is likely to find that many students participate but that they do so only once a week or less even though the facilities and personnel are used to capacity. Participating once a week or less hardly qualifies as providing genuine opportunity to satisfy athletically inclined boys or to develop in many students the kind of skills and inclinations which may make sports abiding and long-lived interests. Partial solution to the problem lies in improving intramural and recreational programs by getting more time and using facilities toward the upper limits of their capacities. More substantial solution lies in adequate time for physical education classes and better integration between classes and voluntary extraclass programs.

Desires of athletic directors, coaches, and others interested in developing material for winning high school teams present a third reason why many junior high school teams are sponsored. In and of itself, of course, development of senior high school athletes is an entirely unjustifiable reason for the conduct of junior high school interscholastics. Decisions concerning appropriate programs at any level must be based upon sound answers to the question, "What practices will best serve the school population directly concerned?"

A junior high school intramural program which reaches all or most of the students not only serves physical, social, and emotional needs of boys and girls but also develops abilities and interests that may lead to membership on high school teams. The authors feel that junior high school interscholastic competition generally is not advisable because (1) emotional surroundings become tense, unnatural overstimulation and overexcitement may occur, and boys tend to push themselves too far physically and emotionally; (2) exploration rather than a high degree of specialization is appropriate at this age; (3) interscholastics tend to deprive boys of opportunities to explore abilities and interests in a rich variety of sports; (4) facilities, time, and teacher services are likely to be more equally shared by all boys and girls when emphases are upon class, intramural, and recreational programs; (5) although interschool competition under well-controlled conditions may be wholesome for boys of this age, programs which start with satisfactory controls have a way of getting out of hand through emulation of high school and college sports practices;

and (6) a satisfactory time allotment for physical education classes plus well-conceived intramural and recreational programs which will meet the needs and desires for competition will require all the facilities, time, and personnel available.

INTERSCHOLASTICS FOR GIRLS

Interscholastic competition for girls in team sports is not as widespread as it was several decades ago. Generally it is not recommended. Although competition in individual sports is looked upon with more favor than team-sport competition, it is frowned upon by many.

Play days, in which teams of girls made up of students from more than one school play for recreation and without determination of school championships, and sports days, in which each of several schools brings two or more groups of players for competition in one or more sports, have been found to meet competitive needs and urges of girls quite well. These events serve to broaden social horizons as well as to provide stimulating, healthful, wholesome, and satisfying play. To indicate type of activity and competition involved, these events are called extramural, rather than interscholastic, athletics.

The Division of Girls' and Women's Sports of AAHPER approves extramural competition but not interscholastics with full schedules of games with other schools. As extramural competition, the DGWS approves sports days, play days, telegraphic meets, and informal extramural competition.[2]

Recommendations made by DGWS do represent considered opinion, and they are rather generally accepted. There is, however, much controversy concerning interscholastics for girls. In some states high schools sponsor girls' basketball teams. Driving through one state, as he approaches certain towns one can see signs proclaiming "__________, Home of the 19__ Girls' State Champions." Especially since the ascendancy of the U.S.S.R. women's Olympic track and field teams, there has been increased interest in competition for girls and women in the U.S., especially in the development of track and field athletics.

Although controversy concerning interscholastics for girls has been less heated than that surrounding interscholastics for junior high schools, it has been persistent. Katherine Ley, speaking about interscholastics for girls to a National Conference on Secondary School Athletic Administration, commented that it would be difficult to clear up in a short time a subject about which there had been confusion for fifty years.[3] Miss Ley quoted from a report concerning policies and procedures for competition

[2] Division for Girls' and Women's Sports, *Standards in Sports for Girls and Women,* American Association for Health, Physical Education, and Recreation, Washington, D.C., 1961, pp. 47–48.

[3] *Administration of High School Athletics, A Report, op. cit.,* pp. 20–29.

in girls' and women's sports published in the September, 1962, issue of the Journal of the American Association for Health, Physical Education, and Recreation as follows, "A school may consider arranging interschool competition provided the rest of the program is not jeopardized. . . ."[4] So the basic agreement concerning interscholastics for high school girls is the same as that for boys in junior high schools: If schools provide opportunities for all in class physical education, intramurals, and recreation, then interscholastics may be of value.

KEEPING ATHLETICS EDUCATIONALLY SOUND

All, or almost all, agree that interscholastic athletics for boys are desirable, or at least have desirable inherent qualities. There is controversy about proper emphasis and about methods of conducting the activities. Aspects of interscholastics which have been seriously criticized include (1) overemphasis upon competition; (2) a tendency toward encouraging vicarious, rather than active, participation; (3) overemphasis upon winning; (4) commercialism; (5) interference with other school activities; (6) early overspecialization in one or two sports; (7) anti-intellectualism; (8) copying of methods and techniques used by colleges, and even professional teams, which produces practices unwarranted with high school boys; (9) interscholastic athletics which are undesirably affected by influences coming from sources other than the school faculty; and (10) public games which encourage rioting, fighting, property damage, looting, and delinquency. Each of these ten points is discussed below.

OVEREMPHASIS UPON COMPETITION

Some educators, believing that there is far too much competition and too little cooperation in American life, feel that interscholastics and other highly competitive sports are questionable because they are likely to develop attitudes which place too much emphasis upon competition against others and too little upon respect for the value of cooperation. This viewpoint may represent a valid objection to some programs which emphasize winning so much that questionable and even unfair and dishonest practices are condoned. It is not a valid objection to programs which urge participants to do their best in an attempt to win over friendly rivals. Competition and cooperation are not inimical human characteristics; rather they are complementary, and development in both is part of the education of young people. John E. Anderson[5] has found a positive correlation between competition and cooperation in children: the more cooperative children are more competitive, whereas children who are not competitive are not cooperative.

[4] *Ibid.*, p. 22.

[5] John E. Anderson, *The Psychology of Development and Personal Adjustment,* Holt, Rinehart and Winston, Inc., New York, 1949, p. 360.

Interscholastic team games demand cooperation with teammates. They also are surrounded with cooperative efforts on the part of students who are not team members who pool their efforts in supporting teams, cheering and cheerleading, playing and marching in bands, decorating fields and gymnasiums, entertaining visitors, and planning social activities which are identified with games.

Cooperation should be stressed. Competition, a normal and natural expression among humans, also needs to be learned. Even if schools could eliminate all competition in athletics, grades, honors, and other avenues through which students seek satisfaction, it seems clear that students would compete in out-of-school situations. Rather than attempt to eliminate competition, schools should seek to help young people learn to compete without rancor in friendly situations. It is interesting to note that some educators who condemn the competitive aspects of school activities enjoy playing golf or bridge and receive satisfaction from membership in honor societies.

VICARIOUS AND ACTIVE PARTICIPATION

Rather frequently critics have presented the theory that interscholastic sports tend to encourage vicarious rather than active participation. But the existence of highly developed competition in a given sport is not likely to make for fewer participants in that sport; rather, it is likely to make for more. This contention is supported by the popularity of football and basketball or modifications of these games as intramural and recreational sports. It also is supported by the popularity of soccer (football) as a recreational sport in countries where that game is played a great deal by school, industrial, club, and professional teams.

It probably is true that interscholastic emphasis upon a few so-called major sports tends to attract our young people to participation in these games and make for less play in other sports which do not have as much momentum supplied by public attention. A school whose interscholastic program includes a wide variety of sports without undue emphasis upon one or two or three will find its students interested in playing a variety of games.

Probably all physical educators agree that it is better for young people to play games than to watch others play them. Spectator interests in sports, however, are wholesome just as is spectator or vicarious participation in music, art, or dramatics. It is only natural for people to be interested in outstanding performance. Whether it is a fine art or sports or any other field of endeavor, appreciation of the arts and abilities of others is likely to lead to more rather than less active participation.

Because of spectator appeal to students and other members of a community, interscholastic athletics can become a unifying force, a point of common interest about which groups express themselves in unison. School teams add zest to school life; they provide a rallying point, a center, an activity, a group focus upon which student groups can center feelings of unity, loyalty, and common cause. High school principals have noted that when a student body gets together in proudly supporting school teams, the quality of school citizenship increases and disciplinary problems sometimes lessen.

OVEREMPHASIS UPON WINNING

Undue emphasis upon winning causes abuses and criticisms. What emphasis upon winning is appropriate? The concept that players should do their best is sound. One of the values of athletics lies in the participant's experience in learning what he can accomplish when he throws himself wholeheartedly into a project or into an attack upon a problem which requires careful preparation individually on the part of each player and collectively on the part of the group or team. But recognition of the rights and abilities of opponents is essential. Since there must be a loser for every winner, it follows that consistent winning can be achieved only at the expense of others. Schedule makers should attempt to arrange games and meets between teams of similar strength so that competition over a period of years is likely to provide experiences in winning and in losing for all participants and schools.

Undue emphasis upon winning may be likened to forms of ruthless business competition associated with the rugged individualism stereotype. A businessman who does not care to serve society, who is interested only in personal gain, is not likely to be fully accepted by his colleagues who believe in fair competition. Those in charge of interscholastic athletics should be interested in the broad effects upon all who play and watch games, not just in the results in one school. An urge to compete is held to be a natural form of self-expression, but there can be no interscholastic competition without cooperation between at least two schools who agree to play. The all-important concept of fair play necessitates not only competition but also cooperation for the general good.

What causes overemphasis upon winning? What produces a situation which includes cheating and winning whether or not the game is played according to the spirit of the rule? One thing is certain. There would be less of this if games were played in private with neither spectators nor publicity. When outside attention builds up, when reputations of coaches and pride in school stir up emotions, underhanded practices may occur. To a large extent boys will play games hard but fairly if they are not overurged by adults.

Coaches, faculties, counselors, administrators, and school boards who demand fair play, adherence to the golden rule, will have well-behaved teams and crowds. Consistently carrying out these demands certainly is not easy. It takes attention and effort; it requires communication with students, parents, and representatives of media of mass communication; and it requires setting good examples. Further, it is necessary to do what is required to prevent overemphasis while at the same time fostering among players and others a keen desire and determination to win, if it is at all possible to do so fairly and squarely. Some of the difficulties, the forces working against such development, include adult examples of cheating which affect youngsters' feelings about fairness or at least about the importance of it. What develops sportsmanship and fair play in a given high school is consistent, everlasting insistence upon gentlemanly behavior.

COMMERCIALISM

Criticism of athletics as commercial ventures is more applicable to large colleges and universities than it is to either smaller colleges or high schools. It must be recognized, however, that commercial aspects have invaded high school programs, most of which depend upon gate receipts for financing at least a part of their cost. When gate receipts are needed for support of the program, there is a tendency to arrange "money" games, to play an excessive number of games, to place undue emphasis upon winning because winning teams attract large crowds, to advertise extensively, and to heed pressures from outside-of-school groups whose dominant interest is in winning.

Decisions concerning the conduct of interscholastic athletics should be made on the basis of welfare of the athletes and the students. Incidental gate receipts are not objectionable; it is clear, however, that educational and recreational considerations, not financial returns, should determine policy. If income considerations clearly affect decisions, players and fans can be expected to regard interscholastics as commercialized, to feel that the school is in the entertainment business. When this is the case, the existence of athletics as an integral part of the educational program is threatened.

Financing from the general education budget does much to eliminate overemphasis upon winning, scheduling of games for the purpose of attracting gate receipts, and other undesirable practices connected with commercialization of sports. If interscholastics contribute significantly to educational aims, if they are education—and why else should they be sponsored by schools?—they are entitled to and should receive financial support from funds appropriated for education. It seems certain that most educators would like athletics to be financed through general education funds.

Why, then, are interscholastics generally expected to earn at least a part of their expenses? No doubt precedent is a large factor. When athletics came into schools in the form of student projects outside the educational program, school funds were not available for their support, so independent means of raising money were developed. Another factor, of course, is that interscholastics, like school musical and dramatic events, can and do earn money. People pay to attend these events but do not pay to visit a science class. School boards are reluctant to add to the tax burden by passing up this available source of income. The high cost of interscholastics, when figured on per capita player expenditure, is another reason why school boards may be hesitant to appropriate all the money needed.

INTERFERENCE WITH OTHER SCHOOL ACTIVITIES

The allegation that overemphasis upon athletics interferes with other school activities may be valid in occasional cases. It already has been pointed out that intramural and recreational sports suffer when interscholastics preempt facilities. It is possible for demands upon athletes to prohibit participation in other desirable activities. An anecdote will provide a case in point. A high school principal, one who has been president of the National Association of High School Principals, told one of the coaches that some boys had said that training rules prevented going to the junior prom, and asked if there was any truth in that report. After the coach said it was indeed true, the principal asked if the coach would like to relax that rule to permit the boys to go to the prom. The coach said, "No, sir." The principal, with levity and sting, said (paraphrased), "In that case I will be just a trifle undemocratic. I will inform the boys that they may go to the prom and will urge them to go."

EARLY OVERSPECIALIZATION IN ONE OR TWO SPORTS

There is justifiable criticism if a coach demands complete dedication to one or two sports. Happily, practices justifying such criticism are not widespread. Some swimming coaches may insist that if a boy wants to be on a team he must swim almost all through the school year and during the summer. They may seek to justify this by arguing that if a boy wants to become a champion swimmer and is willing to pay the price, the coach is helping the boy by giving him an opportunity to excel. That argument would have substance if the boys involved already had tried their hands at various sports and had good reason to decide to specialize. When applied to early adolescents, say freshmen, the argument hardly has substance, and criticism is needed. Another occasional demand is that a boy participate in cross country and not in football in order to be a member of a basketball squad. Sometimes one coach, say a football coach, demands that during the winter and spring, boys participate in a conditioning program instead of other sports if they want to play football the following fall.

ANTI-INTELLECTUALISM

Is there truth to the charge that high school athletics are anti-intellectual? Do players and other students in some high schools regard athletics as the important thing and become absorbed in them to such an extent that studies are regarded as not so important? Does it become fashionable in some high schools to center on athletics and just try to get by with a "gentleman's C" in their courses and no more? If this is so in an occasional school, athletics are out of reasonable perspective. Athletics should satisfy the needs of adolescents, provide wholesome recreation, contribute to fitness, and complement rather than depress scholastic effort. Athletes, generally, are average or above as scholars, as multiple studies have shown.

COPYING METHODS OF COLLEGES AND PROFESSIONAL TEAMS IS UNWARRANTED

The authors agree that this criticism may have some validity. It is possible to adapt some techniques and tactics used by older players for high school boys and make them satisfactory. It is not possible to copy techniques which fit older players, who have more experience and who have much longer practice seasons available, and apply them to high school boys without the probability of undue pressure and harmful effects. If coaches do not teach on the basis of their answer to the question, "What is appropriate for these youngsters?" criticism is valid. Do some high school coaches put undue pressure on boys by demanding the unreasonable?

INTERSCHOLASTICS ARE UNDESIRABLY AFFECTED BY INFLUENCES FROM SOURCES OTHER THAN THE SCHOOL

Does nonschool influence affect policy and practice? One way to answer this question is to ask, "What about the booster clubs?" The organization and growth of booster clubs seemed, at least in most cases, to be a desirable approach to encouraging public interest in a school activity. No doubt many of them do encourage wholesome interest and support. But they present a problem. Usually they meet on nonschool property. They view game films, hear a coach narrate, and listen to scouting reports or other information relative to the approaching game. That is well and good. Some members also think they know more than the coaches, become critical, and spread criticism and dissatisfaction. Not infrequently attendants drink, smoke, and play cards in connection with booster club meetings. Without condemning those activities as such, one can suggest that they seem out of place in association with high school athletics.

Other outside sources which sometimes affect athletics unfavorably include gamblers. If they do influence athletics in a high school, they do so indirectly but in ways which may produce undesirable undercurrents.

Influential citizens, not infrequently some who are entirely rational and use good judgment in most situations, may get excited about high school athletics and either try to apply pressure to win or set poor examples, or both. Tact and a velvet-glove approach to putting a damper on such things may be needed. On the other hand, "telling off" in unmistakable terms may be required. The important thing is to use precaution to prevent the development of objectionable behavior by individuals, groups, or booster clubs and to do something quickly to correct such situations if they come into existence.

GAMES CAUSE UNDESIRABLE CROWD BEHAVIOR

The most fervent enthusiasts for interscholastic athletics will not deny the possibility of misbehavior by spectators. People attending games have fought, rioted, and looted. They have damaged property, injured people and engaged in various kinds of delinquent behavior. Although criticism of interscholastic games because of this is vociferous, it is not widespread. What precautions and controls are needed?

Some schools, mostly in large cities, have decided to hold all games during daylight hours to prevent, or at least to lessen the chance of rowdyism, destructive behavior, and damage. Some have permitted only students and teachers from the schools involved to attend. Few, if any, cases of crowd misbehavior have occurred under these circumstances. All schools, or almost all, routinely provide police protection in the event of public gatherings. Some have greatly increased such protection after experiencing crowd misbehavior or seeing indications that trouble might develop.

Continuous or periodic attention to sportsmanship and citizenship education, including exemplary behavior by adults involved, aids in the development and maintenance of positive attitudes which underlie good citizenship and acceptable behavior at athletic events. Approaches to teaching, or influencing, students to be good spectators include (a) frequent verbal reference, short and not sermonlike, by students, coaches, or principals during gatherings such as pep assemblies and honor-award functions, (b) short statements in game programs, (c) pictorial displays, including cartoons or other humorous approaches, (d) student committees studying problems and making recommendations, (e) establishment of a code of ethics which either covers all behavior or applies particularly to athletics, and (f) the example set by coaches and players, probably the most influential among the multiple procedures.

MANAGING INTERSCHOLASTIC ATHLETICS

Management procedures affect teaching or coaching as well as student and public interests and attitudes toward school programs of athletics. Some management problems may be solved by each school according to local preference. Others, involving rules or regulations of league, stage, or national organizations, require a local school to comply but, of course, permit local determination of methods, of detailed procedures through which an end, required of all schools, may best be achieved. The management problems discussed below are (a) lodging of responsibility, (b) making schedules, (c) managing equipment and supplies, (d) handling eligibility regulations, (e) medical examinations and insurance, (f) managing home contests, (g) managing trips, and (h) securing officials.

LODGING OF RESPONSIBILITY

Effective organization for managing interscholastic activities in a given school requires that each person involved is certain of his responsibilities and that everything needing attention is assigned. It is relatively unimportant how delegation is accomplished. What is important is that someone does his job without fail. Allocations of responsibilities vary from school to school. Larger schools delegate much of the necessary work to faculty managers and (or) athletic directors. In smaller schools the superintendent, principal, or coach frequently must take responsibility for considerable detail. Although it is important that duties be clearly and unmistakably delegated, the question of who performs a given task is less important than is the assurance that someone may be depended upon to see that needed functions are performed.

Formulation of policy is necessary. Although many high schools carry out reasonably effective programs through an internal organization in which almost sole authority resides with the principal and is delegated by him to various staff members, it seems desirable to lodge responsibility for policy formation with a board or committee representing various interests. Appropriate makeup and functions of such bodies were discussed in the previous chapter in relation to intramural and recreational activities.

It has been suggested that boards which determine policy should have members representing various interested groups. Students, of course, represent a primary interested group. In general, the extent to which students assume responsibility for interscholastic athletics in a given school is indicative of the extent to which athletics are geared to student interests and reflect their opinions and desires.

MAKING SCHEDULES

The number of games played and the opponents selected are important determinants of the quality and satisfaction of interscholastic athletics. Schedules which permit participation with teams of approximately equal strength and with schools which have similar athletic programs and ideals are desirable because they enhance interest and promote good sportsmanship. They also tend to produce similar won-and-lost records over a period of years for the several schools involved, thus providing educational growth attendant to both winning and losing.

For schools which operate independently, without league affiliation, the making of schedules presents a difficult problem which requires much correspondence with other schools. Membership in a league or conference, which most schools hold, facilitates the scheduling of games through arrangement of schedules projected for several years. It also provides opportunities for periodic mutual consideration of problems such as selecting or approving officials, establishing fees for their services, promotion of sportsmanship, admission prices, determining length of sport seasons, awarding of championships, and keeping permanent league records.

MANAGING EQUIPMENT AND SUPPLIES

Each interscholastic sport requires equipment and supplies. Uniforms are needed. Equipment such as mechanical blocking and tackling practice aids for football, screens and nets for baseball, goals for soccer, standards and implements for throwing for track and field, etc., must be supplied. It is important that everything needed is anticipated and requisitioned.

Budgets must be prepared and presented for approval. Authorized purchases must be made, either after bids from several firms have been received or as the athletic director or purchasing agent sees fit, depending upon local organization. After equipment and supplies have been received, plans for storage, care, distribution, and return must be made and carried out.

Inventory and safeguarding of school property need attention. Equipment should be marked both for easy identification and for security. Forms which provide records of the equipment and supplies loaned to each student should be provided, signed, and filed. When purchasing equipment, the following things should be considered: (1) design and material, (2) probable durability and cost of maintenance, (3) availability and dependability of merchandiser, (4) quality, (5) safety factors, and (6) price.

Equipment and supplies should be kept in good condition. Balls, nets, standards, helmets, shoes, etc., which need repair should be withdrawn from service and restored to good condition promptly. At the end of a sport season, all equipment and supplies should be inspected. What is in good condition should be inventoried and stored carefully. What needs cleaning and repair should be scheduled for renovation and stored after the necessary work has been done.

HANDLING ELIGIBILITY REGULATIONS

The making and enforcing of participant eligibility regulations serve as one means of control against practices associated with overemphasis.

State associations have standardized regulations. Although rules differ from state to state, there is considerable commonality. Generally speaking, all states follow the minimum eligibility requirements recommended by the National Federation of State High School Athletic Associations which have been widely publicized in state-association publications and in professional periodicals. They include (1) twenty-year age limitation, (2) eight-semester limitation, (3) scholarship and consecutive-semester-attendance regulations, (4) amateur requirement, (5) independent-team-participation rule, (6) school-transfer regulation, (7) recruiting and "undue influence" rule, (8) enrollment rule (not later than the eleventh day of school), (9) limitation of value of awards, (10) grade rule prohibiting playing on high school teams by students below the ninth grade, and (11) physician's certificate rule.

Although the above eligibility requirements are commonly enforced by state associations and although they have been approved by national organizations and by the Joint Committee of the National Federation of State High School Athletic Associations, the National Association of Secondary School Principals, and the American Association for Health, Physical Education, and Recreation, criticism of the scholarship requirement continues. Some believe that no student acceptable for school attendance should be denied opportunities to participate in a school activity.

Scholastic-eligibility requirements remain, however, partly because of precedent, but also because a substantial majority of schoolmen believe that such requirements have a favorable effect upon athletics. Prevailing opinion holds that the elimination of these requirements would create a situation in which boys who are interested in playing on school teams but not interested in doing other acceptable schoolwork would be team members. Such a situation, the reasoning goes, would make athletics incompatible with desirable ends rather than an integral part of a school program designed to promote education.

Another reason for support of scholastic eligibility lies in its use as a motivating force toward acceptable scholarship. Boys uninterested in applying themselves to schoolwork may do so in order to remain eligible to do something they want to do. Also, school authorities are interested in the effect of scholastic-eligibility requirements upon students who are not team members. Boys who have aspirations to become athletes may dedicate themselves more fully to schoolwork. And the pattern of the requirement may emphasize to all students the need for acceptable scholastic achievement.

Ideally, perhaps all will agree, each school activity or subject should provide its own motivation without need for dependency upon outside sources, such as a desire to be eligible for athletics. If and when the curriculum is realistically fitted to the individual, motivation for schoolwork may become intrinsic to the degree that such pressures as scholastic athletic requirements and fear of failure are unnecessary. That millennium may be here for some students and around the corner for others, but it is hardly on the horizon for most.

Faculty managers or athletic directors must see that eligibility regulations are enforced. The first thing to do is examine the record of scholastic achievement and age of each boy whose name is submitted by a coach. Next, eligibility lists must be prepared, using forms supplied by the state association involved. These lists must be sent to the competing school for a specified length of time, as required by the state association involved; five days is the requirement in many states. Acceptable scholastic standing from week to week must be certified; if a student fails more than one subject his name must be deleted from the school's eligibility list until he brings his work up to acceptable standards. Each school determines its own procedure for collecting information about scholarship from week to week; some circulate forms among teachers requesting a report on the grade to date of each athlete; others request teachers to report the name of any student-athlete whose work is less than satisfactory. Eligibility regulations which cannot be determined by an examination of the school record and by information supplied by teachers are the amateur requirement and the independent-team-participation rule. Some schools ask athletes to sign statements certifying that they have not violated such rules; others see that athletes know these rules and depend upon them to avoid playing for money and playing on independent teams. The physician's certificate rule is discussed as part of the next topic.

MEDICAL EXAMINATIONS AND INSURANCE

Physician's certification of freedom from defects or conditions which would make athletic participation medically inadvisable is a requirement of all of the state associations. Forms approved and supplied by the state association are used. Procedures used are determined by local schools. Some require their athletes to be examined and certified by their family physician; others have school doctors examine and certify. In some cases volunteer physicians do the work upon request of the county medical association. Reexamination after injury commonly is required; in most cases the same procedure as for the original examination and certification is followed.

Accident insurance always is suggested and sometimes is required. Accident benefit plans are operated by some state associations—Wisconsin, New York, Michigan. In these states enrollment of athletes in the plan is required. Forms which must be completed include one for listing the athletes enrolled and specifying the individual and total fees, one for reporting of accident, and one for claiming indemnity. Various commercial firms offer insurance plans. It is customary for a school to adopt one after examining several, just as group insurance plans are adopted by businesses, industries, or employee groups. An athletic director or principal must see that forms are completed, records are kept, and fees or premiums are collected and accounted for. He does this himself or sees to it that responsibility is delegated and accepted and that all necessary procedures are carried out.

MANAGING HOME CONTESTS

Needed preparation for home contests centers around satisfying the state-association regulations, seeing that facilities and equipment are ready, extending courtesies to visiting teams and officials, and accommodating spectators. Principals, faculty managers, athletic directors, coaches, teachers, student managers, players, cheerleaders, and others are likely to have tasks to perform. In the brief discussion which follows, no attempt is made to recommend specific duties for specific persons because of the wide variation of acceptable practices among various schools.

Since state-association regulations vary from state to state, it is important for responsible school athletic officials to keep posted concerning regulations in their state. A required exchange of eligibility lists has been mentioned. Many states require that sanction, or state-association approval, be secured at a specified time prior to contests involving more than two schools. In those states whose associations require regularly approved officials, it is necessary to employ only officials who have satisfied the requirements. Some state associations have regulations designed to increase safety, and some have variations from regulation game rules which must be respected.

Necessary facilities and equipment must be ready for service. Football fields may require rolling or draining; they need to be lined; yard markers and a down box must be supplied; stop watches, extra horns, whistles, and balls should be on hand. Basketball gymnasiums need cleaning and airing; their temperature should be controlled; balls, timers, and score-books must be ready for gymnastic meets; apparatus and mats must be in place. Wrestling meets require mats and watches. Facilities and equipment must be in order for tennis, golf, swimming, and volleyball contests. Tracks require rolling and lining. Jumping pits and runways must be in good condition. The equipment needed for a track meet includes guns and cartridges, watches, yarn, batons, standards, crossbars, hurdles, event-and-score sheets, measuring tapes, spades and rakes, whistles, and starting blocks. First-aid supplies should be available at all contests.

Extending courtesies to visiting teams and officials is a mark of a good host. The exact information concerning the time and place of contests should be supplied. It is only courteous for home schools to offer help in arranging for food and lodging. Guides may be provided. Dressing rooms should be clean and safe for storage of clothing and supplies; either guards or keys may be provided. Towels and soap should be readily available. Offers to supply any item of equipment which visitors need may be made. Ready access to a telephone is likely to be a convenience for visitors. Officiating fees and visiting-team guarantees should be paid promptly.

For comfortable accommodation of spectators, there must be enough ticket sellers and takers (if admission is charged) and ushers. The presence of police officers is necessary if crowds are large. Easily readable scoreboards and time clocks contribute to spectator enjoyment. Public address systems are helpful, provided the announcer uses good judgment. Programs should be available. Convenient toilet facilities will be needed. In many instances, parking arrangements should be made. Sports reporters should be accommodated. If games are to be broadcast, preparations for radio or television personnel and equipment should ensure favorable broadcast conditions.

One of the principal functions of managers of contests is to encourage good sportsmanship on the part of spectators. Examples by coaches and players probably influence crowd behavior more than does any other one thing. Cheerleaders can be of great help. Continual interpretation of the purpose of athletics to students and to the general public promotes good sportsmanship. Assembly programs which give information about sports and rules and develop appreciation of good performance by home and visiting teams help. Those which continually emphasize winning and supporting the team to victory are likely to contribute to poor sportsmanship. School newspapers should support sportsmanship, and school officials should encourage the commercial press to do so.

MANAGING TRIPS

Besides arranging for transportation, food, and lodging (if needed), trip management involves the responsibility for seeing that all necessary equipment is carried and for supervising trip personnel. Transportation by public carrier is recommended. If private cars are used, the school should make sure that public-liability laws are satisfied, that insurance coverage is adequate, and that drivers are mature and responsible. Expense money should be withdrawn in advance and accounted for by receipts.

Trip personnel, starting time and location, and probable time of return should be determined well in advance and publicized. The personal equipment of players may be cared for by individual players or by student managers. The care of equipment such as balls, training and first-aid supplies, blankets, towels, paper cups, and extra clothing is a proper responsibility for student managers.

Players should know what standards of appearance and behavior are expected and know that they are likely to be judged as reflecting the tone of the institution which they represent. Acceptance of responsibility for their own behavior is desirable, but supervision is needed. When unpopular regulations and unnecessary restrictions are demanded, the joy of a trip is lessened, and violations, with attendant need for disciplinary action, are likely to occur.

The safety and protection of the boys is of paramount importance. Responsibility for taking boys to a neighboring school unmistakably implies responsibility for their safe return. Players should return with the team in all cases except those in which custody is transferred to parents or guardians.

SECURING OFFICIALS

Competent officials enhance the educational and recreational values of interscholastic athletics. State associations have improved and tended to standardize officiating through education and certification. They have required registration and certification, sponsored rules-interpretation meetings, and required examinations on rules; they also invite schools to report on officials and officials to report on schools.

Employment of officials is a home-school responsibility unless leagues, district organizations, or state associations assign them in specific cases. Since officials should be satisfactory to both (or all) competing schools, approval prior to employment is proper procedure. Leagues or conferences frequently compile lists of approved major officials for football, basketball, and baseball. In such cases home schools may employ any approved man. In some cases officials are assigned by a secretary or officer of the organization involved. Payment, however, is a home-school responsibility. In any event, names of officials should be sent to visiting schools.

Competent so-called minor officials such as timekeepers and scorekeepers are important, but not ordinarily subject to the approval of visiting schools. The commonly used procedure of assigning faculty members to these roles seems satisfactory. Desirable uniformity and needed competence usually are achieved best when able persons are selected, rules and duties are studied, and the same persons perform the tasks frequently or throughout a season's schedule.

Since numerous officials are needed for track and for swimming and since all except the starter and referee customarily serve without pay, the problem of arranging for officials for these sports is quite different from that for football or basketball. Invitations or requests to serve should be sent well in advance. Particular care should be taken to select competent officials for key positions such as head finish judge, head timer, and head field judge. It is a source of amazement to some athletic officials to view a group of men whose time is valuable spending an afternoon serving gratuitously as officials. It need not be. The men like the sport and are glad to provide needed help for a community project in which they have a share. Their serving is a manifestation of amateur sports appreciation at its best.

PUBLIC RELATIONS

Any organization, institution, or program which attracts public attention, as do interscholastic athletics, should consider ways and means of educating the public and interpreting the purposes and characteristics of programs and practices. The need for interpretation of the purposes is indicated by the tendency on the part of a considerable number of people to be overinterested in the spectacular aspects of sports such as the winning of games and the outstanding performances by a few individuals. In order to establish and maintain public interest in interscholastics as educational and recreational ventures of young people, it is desirable for administrators and coaches to call attention frequently to the purposes of sports such as provision for healthful recreation for participants and spectators, development of physical prowess and skill, development of abilities and tendencies to cooperate and compete, provision of opportunities for boys to express natural desires for competition in socially approved surroundings, establishment of friendly rivalries, and the development of good sportsmanship by players and spectators.

An important aspect of public relations lies in the manner in which schools conduct their sports. Coaches and other school officials who demonstrate interest in the welfare of boys, in worthy performances of home and visiting athletes, and in good sportsmanship by performers and spectators find that the public tends to be interested in these ends. On the other hand, coaches and other representatives of the school who seem to show dominant interest only in winning, who alibi, criticize opponents and officials, and fail to give credit where it is due tend to lead the public toward overemphasis upon winning and lack of respect for friendly rivalry and good sportsmanship.

Other media through which school officials may interpret interscholastics to the public include reports to boards of education, annual school reports, parent-teacher association discussions, speeches before representative groups, school assemblies, school newspapers, and public media of communication. Reports, discussions, and speeches give opportunities to deal with actual and desired accomplishments of interscholastics as educational and recreational activities. Faculty leadership of school assemblies and newspapers can and should guide student groups toward appreciation of the fundamental values of school teams and good sportsmanship.

Public media of communication (press, radio, and television) have a responsibility to present news to the people. Athletic contests provide news which is of interest to many people, and it is a reporter's job to collect and write such news. Since attitudes of and statements by coaches and others connected with the management of athletics are news, it follows that emphases given by these people are reflected in news stories and in radio and television reports of or concerning contests.

Mutual responsibility exists between reporters, on the one hand, and school athletic officials, on the other. In pursuing his job of collecting news, the reporter needs reliable sources, and school representatives have the responsibility to serve as sources of information. Mutual understandings between school officials and sports writers help both parties and, more important, help in the interpretation of athletic programs to the public. It is desirable for coaches and athletic directors to discuss problems with sports writers and to invite them to meetings at which plans and programs are discussed. The broader understandings which result tend toward publicity which reflects educational ends rather than that which emphasizes and magnifies the spectacular incidents apparent at games.

Because coaches deal with sports writers more than do other school officials, it is important for them to establish and maintain satisfactory relationships with representatives of the press. Most newspapermen are equally interested in mutual understanding with coaches of the problems involved.

Coaches or other athletic officials should see that the information needed by newsmen is supplied. The necessary basic information includes accurate team rosters with the full name of each player and information concerning his age, height, weight, year in school, position, and previous letter awards; and schedules, with dates, time, and location of events, and names of officials. Biographical material relative to coaches and players is useful to newsmen and harmless to the individuals concerned.

Publicity releases should be given at appropriate times and should go to all newsmen, including representatives of newspapers, radio, and television. When an athletic director, coach, or any other school official submits news such as a season's schedule, squad roster, or change in time of game, it must be submitted to all competing newsmen, without fail. On the other hand, if a reporter receives information as a result of a visit or call by him, individual initiative should be respected and competing newsmen need not be notified.

One of the complaints reporters have against high school coaches is that they are never available. Since coaches are busy teaching classes and performing other duties and since they may not have offices with secretaries, this is understandable. The situation can be handled satisfactorily if coaches agree to be available at a given place at a fixed time each day and so notify sports reporters.

Newsmen need accommodations at contests in order to do their work without handicap. Complimentary newsmen's cards, in the quantities requested, should be sent to each news media representative who wishes to report a public event. Satisfactory seats and working places should be supplied. Convenient arrangements should be made for radio and television stations which are to report events. Programs should be supplied for reporters.

When school athletic officials seek a mutual understanding with the representatives of the mass media and see that the necessary information and accommodations are supplied, they may expect, and almost always receive, their cooperation. Although an occasional reporter may refuse to cooperate, the great majority of them are interested in interscholastic athletics and are willing to respect the opinions of athletic directors and coaches concerning the outlooks of school sports.

SUMMARY

Interscholastic athletics are an important and visible part of a high school physical education program. Controversial aspects include the questions of whether interscholastics for girls and for junior high school boys are desirable, and the methods of conducting athletics for high school boys.

The welfare of participants is the primary consideration; the effects of athletics upon students and adults, upon the community, also is important. Any sport may be included in a high school program if it is wholesome in nature, free from undue risk, and fits into the program.

The best physical education teaching may be done in the interscholastic program because of favorable conditions. Rather than implying that interscholastics should be deemphasized, this suggests the need for improving conditions for classes and intramural-recreational programs.

To keep interscholastic athletics educationally sound it is necessary to conduct them intelligently. Criticism, sometimes valid, has been directed toward (1) overemphasis upon competition, (2) vicarious participation, (3) overemphasis upon winning, (4) commercialism, (5) interference with other activities, (6) overspecialization, (7) anti-intellectualism, (8) improper methods, (9) out-of-school influences, and (10) misbehavior of spectators.

How athletics are managed affects coaching or teaching as well as the attitudes of interested persons. It is necessary to lodge responsibility, determine policy and carry it out, make schedules, manage equipment and supplies, see that eligibility regulations are carefully managed, arrange for medical examinations and insurance, manage home contests and trips so that all concerned are assured of reasonable comfort, and arrange for game officials.

Attention to public relations is necessary because many citizens are interested, and because they may be overinterested in the more spectacular aspects and uninterested in the more fundamental purposes of interscholastic athletics. Athletic directors and (or) coaches or other school officials should cooperate with the newsmen who represent the media of communication including newspapers, radio, and television.

Questions and problems for discussion

1. With one or several classmates, debate the question: Resolved, that elective physical education programs for seventh and eighth grades should be limited to intramural and recreational activities.

2. Propose a plan for an extramural program for girls in a school you know. Indicate activities to be included and time to be allotted to each.

3. Assume that football and basketball spectators at a given school rather frequently boo officials and attempt to distract opposing players. Propose a plan for improving crowd behavior at games.

4. Propose a plan for managing home contests in a given sport at a school of your choice. Consider sale and distribution of tickets; gate, door, or ticket-booth attendants; ushers; provisions for police protection; arrangement for officials including all needed timekeepers, scorekeepers, judges, and inspectors; dressing-room arrangements for visiting teams; accommodation of reporters; parking; and anything else you think needs attention.

5. Prepare an itemized list of things needing consideration in the purchase, storage, distribution and collection, and care of equipment necessary for a sport of your choice.

6. What underlying principles should be considered in preparing a plan for interpretation to the public of an extramural program for girls or an interscholastic program for boys?

Selected references

American Association for Health, Physical Education, and Recreation, Division of Men's Athletics: *Athletics in Education, A Platform Statement,* Washington, D.C., 1963.

Bucher, Charles A., and Ralph K. Dupee, Jr.: *Athletics in Schools and Colleges,* Center for Applied Research in Education, New York, 1965.

Coleman, James S.: "Athletics in High School," *The Annals of the American Academy of Political and Social Science,* vol. 338, pp. 33–43, November, 1961; reprinted in *Student, School and Society: Crosscurrents in Secondary Education,* Chandler Publishing Company, San Francisco, 1964.

Educational Policies Commission: *School Athletics; Problems and Policies,* National Education Association, Washington, D.C., 1956.

Forsythe, Charles Edward: *Administration of High School Athletics*, 4th ed., Prentice-Hall, Inc., Englewood Cliffs, N.J., 1962.

George, Jack F., and Harry A. Lehman: *School Athletic Administration: A Textbook for Professional Students and a Guide for Local Athletic Directors*, Harper & Row, Publishers, Incorporated, New York, 1966.

Grieve, Andrez W.: *Directing High School Athletics*, Prentice-Hall, Inc., Englewood Cliffs, N.J., 1963.

Healey, William A.: *The Administration of High School Athletic Events*, Interstate, Danville, Illinois, 1961.

National Conference on Secondary School Athletic Administration, *Administration of High School Athletics, A Report*, American Association for Health, Physical Education, and Recreation, Washington, D.C., 1963.

part 5
RELATION OF METHOD TO SUPERVISION, ADMINISTRATION, AND EVALUATION

INTRODUCTION

The functions of curriculum, instruction, supervision, administration, and evaluation cannot be separated in school operation. Optimum coordination is necessary for the best results. Teacher education programs usually separate the areas for purposes of depth study not only because specialists teach the courses, but also to allow the functions and technical aspects to be studied intensively.

Chapter 11, Planning Instruction, clarified the relation of method to curriculum. This part presents a similar analysis of other major working areas, dealing in turn with supervision, administration, and evaluation. Each chapter follows a similar pattern. Each presents a brief description of the functions and purposes of the area involved, explains the interrelationships of method and the area, and describes the major functions which have the greatest pertinence for methods. The central focus throughout remains on method.

chapter 15

METHOD AND SUPERVISION

INTRODUCTION

The basic function of supervision is to improve the design and process of instruction. It aims to improve both what is taught and how it is taught. To achieve these ends supervision directs study and analysis to the physical and social setting for learning, the nature of the curriculum, and the general problem of personnel improvement.

Supervisory practices as they exist in schools today follow several different patterns, each type representing roughly a chronological development of supervision. The earliest form, *inspectional*, focuses attention on the methods of the teacher, adheres to strict and rigid forms, and recognizes the supervisor as a superior officer. The second supervisory type is characterized by a *guidance* approach. With increasing interest and understanding of democratic human relationships and recognition of the general lack of effectiveness of authoritarian methods, the guidance approach, while still clinging to the superiority of the supervisory officer, emphasizes encouraging a teacher toward self-improvement and makes extensive use of cooperative participation in in-service education projects of various kinds. The third basic type of supervisory practice conceives of supervision as *democratic professional leadership*. This philosophy of supervision directs attention to all factors in the teaching-learning environment.

It attempts to improve learning conditions by understanding underlying factors. It provides for teacher participation in policy making and planning. The supervisory officers have a peer relationship with teachers, and leadership is shared. Authority and policies are derived by group action.

In addition to these three types of supervisory practice it should be noted that some schools neglect their supervisory functions. If they are not provided for administratively, a laissez-faire attitude exists with little done to improve instruction.

The above discussion may suggest that in order to have the benefit of adequate supervision it is necessary for a school to have one or more persons whose title is supervisor. This is not so. What is important is that the function of supervision is performed, in other words that there is provision for improvement of instruction. What personnel, then, can contribute to this function? Those key persons who devote full time to working for better teaching in various schools possess such titles as supervisor, consultant, curriculum coordinator, research director, and personnel officer.

Any and all faculty personnel, and students, may devote part of their time to major efforts to improve instruction, thus participating in supervision. Among school officials who do so a good deal of the time are administrators, department heads, guidance and counseling specialists, and head teachers in team teaching or cooperative instruction situations. The teacher, a most important officer in supervisory function, is the focus of this chapter. The text that follows considers the aspects of supervision which relate most directly to the improvement of method. All involve the teacher. Some find the teacher performing functions which a supervisor does full time; some find him actively participating with others in attempts to improve instruction; others find him receiving the benefits of supervision without either performing the function himself or participating in the work of supervising directly.

RELATION OF METHOD TO SUPERVISION

Supervision, it has been indicated, aims to improve the design and process of instruction. Design, in this definition, refers to curriculum, to what will be taught, whereas process refers to how selected learnings will be taught. Earlier chapters have described the inseparability of curriculum and instruction. Any supervisory effort which affects the nature of learning experiences inevitably affects methods as well.

Supervision specifically relates to method in three basic ways: (1) it strives for the overall professional growth of teachers, aiming toward general improvement in the teacher and his understanding of what is taught; (2) it provides direct experiences whereby teachers learn particular teaching skills; (3) participation of students in supervisory activities serves as a method of providing selected types of learning for students.

Continued professional growth of teachers is fundamental to successful teaching. Even if a teacher-preparation program were strong in every respect, a beginning teacher still enters his profession with much to learn. Just as lawyers, doctors, and other professional men and women expect to study continually to improve and keep up with advances in their fields, so must teachers seek continued improvement in their professional competencies. It is never possible in a professional preparation program to turn out finished products. A professional person who expected to get by on just what he learned in college would soon find himself hopelessly outclassed by his more professionally minded colleagues. Supervision aims to encourage this continued professional growth of teachers. Techniques described later suggest ways in which this may be accomplished.

This text has emphasized throughout a student-centered approach to method in which a teacher's role is that of democratic leader and understanding guide and counselor. Many teachers are ill-equipped to play this role because they have been taught by strictly conventional methods and have had little chance to practice democratic-leadership skills. Supervision faces a primary task of reeducating teachers not only in their concepts of method but in the actual skills of teaching.

The development of skill in selected teaching techniques remains a basic job of supervision. One of the chief causes of limited scope of activities in physical education programs rests on teachers' lack of ability or confidence to introduce new activities. Almost anywhere one finds some unusual activity extremely popular in a school, he usually finds that a teacher favors that activity and transfers his enthusiasm to students. To a less extreme extent, teachers are most likely to select activities for their programs on the basis of their interests and competencies in teaching those activities. Almost every woman physical education teacher would agree that modern dance represents a highly desirable activity. Many of these same teachers give little attention to it in their programs because of their lack of skill in teaching it. Supervision must provide opportunities and encourage teachers to improve their teaching competencies in all basic activities.

The supervisory program can also use students in its teacher-in-service education activities in such a way that the experiences will be mutually beneficial to both teachers and students. For example, a group of students may be taken on a field trip to a nearby city to present a demonstration at a teachers' institute or meeting. Participating in such an event offers opportunities for valuable learning experiences for students as well as for teachers. When students are used in supervisory activities such as demonstrations, intervisitations, and research, the welfare of the students should be held paramount. Too often demonstration lessons are overpracticed, seeking a performance perfection and using time which might better be used for other activities. Also, there is some tendency to select only the better performers and to neglect less apt students as the teacher works with the group which is preparing for an appearance at some workshop, clinic, or conference.

GROUP TECHNIQUES

Through participation in groups teachers not only can help to solve specific problems but also can improve their own democratic leadership skills. Thus, experience in a faculty or community group is likely to improve a teacher's ability to work with student committees, student leaders, and other groups. The supervisory program, then, should use committees for some of its activities and concurrently study the process of committee or group work in order to give teachers the necessary training in such work.

A few words about group techniques in general are offered prior to the discussion of various group techniques of supervision. Work in groups, of course, should accomplish desired ends. Although it is highly desirable for one to increase his knowledge of and ability in group work, the techniques of the process should not become ends in themselves. For example, an expert in group methods tells the story of how a professional-organization chairman asked him to run a section meeting at a forthcoming conference. When asked the purpose of the section meeting, the chairman said he had not decided on any special purpose; he just wanted to use the group process. The group-dynamics expert had some little difficulty convincing the section chairman that a specific purpose for the meeting must be ascertained before the types of techniques to be used at the meeting could be selected. That is to say, if the purpose of the meeting were to plan for future activities of the section, one kind of technique would be indicated, but if the purpose were to resolve a professional problem or present information on a new teaching technique or study current development in the area, different group-action techniques would be employed. Unless some purpose clear to participants dominates group action, methods used become largely meaningless.

Focusing on a meaningful goal does not preclude study of processes used concurrently with moving toward the goal. A group at work on a project, such as planning a fall physical education program for the two high schools of a system, should examine their methods of working on the curriculum problem as well as work directly on the problem at hand. Conversely, if a supervisor feels that the teachers with whom he works lack skill in working together, the best way to improve skills suggests that for initial cooperative effort the group select a problem which lends itself to feasible solution and while resolving the problem study their methods of working on the problem as well.

The growing science of group dynamics offers many suggestions for making group work more effective. The selected references at the end of the chapter list recent publications which describe principles and practices of effective group action. Description of several group supervisory techniques follow.

COOPERATIVE STUDY OF CURRICULUM, INSTRUCTION, AND ADMINISTRATION PROBLEMS

Cooperative study of various problems in the conduct of educational programs has several direct salutary effects on teacher growth, in addition to very often providing a sounder solution to the problem involved than would result from one person's consideration. When teachers participate in solving school problems, they grow in understanding of the factors of the problem and see valid reasons for operating in line with decisions as made. In regard to curriculum planning, earlier concepts of supervisory function usually resulted in the supervisory staff's writing the course of study. Each teacher was literally handed a printed copy of the document and expected to follow the sequence prescribed. Obviously a program stereotyped in this way cannot meet the shifting needs of boys and girls, and also in many cases teachers lacked understanding of the objectives of such a program, did not believe in certain prescribed activities, and felt a lack of responsibility for what went on in their own classrooms. Under modern concepts of curriculum planning, teachers participate in selecting program content, with methods suggested and never prescribed since methods must be unique to individual teachers. Through planning, teachers grow in understanding of the purposes of selected experiences. Through discussing relative values of various practices, they gain new insight. A teacher who may have been opposed to an activity or practice becomes willing to give it a try, particularly if he has had a part in selecting overall program objectives and recognizes possible contributions of new activities to them.

If a teacher has had a part in developing a program, he feels responsibility for its success and tackles his teaching responsibilities with keener enthusiasm, insight, and confidence. The considerable attention given throughout this text to the importance of students' understanding of the purposes of their learning and having a desire to learn the tasks at hand applies equally to teachers. They must believe in what they teach, have understanding of its importance, have enthusiasm for its value, and have the skills to guide learning effectively. Teacher participation in program development, general instructional planning, and setting of administrative policy represents one of the best ways to stimulate desired teacher growth and responsibility.

Curriculum committee work can produce significant improvement in teaching, and hence falls in the area of supervision as well as curriculum and evaluation. One or more curriculum committees in a given school may work toward better practices. Several levels of such work include (1) the level of evaluating what is being done, discussing ideas for improvement, and making preliminary suggestions for innovations, changes, additions, or deletions; (2) the level of developing the preliminary suggestions, refining, drawing together, seeking opinions of others, and stating general characteristics of changes proposed; (3) the level of doing whatever final detailed work is needed to get new ideas, activities, materials, and techniques ready for use in gymnasiums, playgrounds, or classrooms. If considerable change is involved after completion of the work of these three levels, it is desirable to have a "pilot run" to try out the newly proposed activities and techniques in a few classes before schoolwide adoption. A good procedure is to have tryout units in classes taught by members of the curriculum committees which developed the revisions or additions. If extensive revision or innovation is planned, such tryout or demonstration or pilot procedure is likely to take a year or so, after which general adoption may be in order.

Principles of good group action should be followed. The group should be kept to a size feasible for the kind of problem under study. Large group meetings should be devoted to general policy, approval of subgroup action, orientation to problems, and final disposition of overall planning proposals. Meeting places should be conducive to achieving the purpose of the meeting. For discussion, chairs should be flexibly arranged so that all participants can see each other. A formal seating arrangement, in which a leader faces a group seated in rows, prevents best interaction among group members. The leader for any specific meeting should be adept at his job and be able to help the members organize themselves as a group; he should clarify purposes, define working arrangements, and maintain objectivity that subjugates personal issues; he must have skill in releasing individual group potential, stimulating contributions from all members of the group, and establishing means of evaluating group progress.

COOPERATIVE COMMUNITY GROUPS

Community recreation services and opportunities which should supplement and complement school physical education exist in almost all communities. The supervisory program should facilitate bringing physical education teachers and personnel interested in nonschool physical recreation programs together for mutual discussion of common problems. Such discussion should produce improved coordination and mutual support among institutions, organizations, and persons affiliated with several programs which work with young people and which have at least some goals in common.

Programs sponsored by various agencies, including the YMCA and YWCA, churches, service clubs, and boy and girl scouts, may relate to physical education so that coordination between them and schools may be worthwhile. Coordination with government-sponsored recreation, however, should be given priority. It is desirable that maximum use be made of community facilities, that needless duplication be eliminated, and that facts and opinions concerning appropriate activities and programs be exchanged.

In cities and counties which have joint administration of school physical education and community recreation, a direct basis for coordination is built directly into the organization. The school-park concept is favorable for mutually supportive operation of school physical education and governmental recreation. Teachers working in such schools are likely to find themselves cooperating with community groups whether or not the school supervisory program takes direct steps to bring physical education teachers and nonschool personnel together for discussion of mutual problems.

INTEREST STUDY GROUPS

Many instructional problems facing teachers are of interest only to a relatively small group. The teachers responsible for swimming clubs may wish to study the latest materials on synchronized swimming, whereas football coaches may desire to study the latest rule changes or ways to reduce injuries. Volunteer teacher groups to study shared instructional problems represent one of the better means of in-service education of teachers. The supervisory program can stimulate the organization of such groups by providing time to get together, making study materials available, securing resource people for special occasions, and indicating possibilities for such small study groups.

Football and basketball officials have poignant interests in rules interpretation and officiating procedures. They attend interest study group meetings of two types. One is a large group meeting during which an official interpreter selected by a conference or a state association informs and interprets rules, especially new ones; an examination may follow such a meeting. The other type of officials' meeting typifies interest study groups. It is a series of periodic meetings of small groups of officials for the purpose of discussing matters concerning officiating.

Sometimes a need for a small study group arises out of a larger problem. For example, as the result of a serious football injury, a small but vocal minority in one community started a movement to abolish football in the high school. The matter came to extensive public debate, and although football was continued, it was agreed that serious study should be given to reducing the high overall accident rate in the sport. The coaches requested that several interested persons, including the school safety instructor, the school physician, a community member working with the American Red Cross who was trained in safety, and an insurance company executive, work with them to ascertain factors in the football program causing injury and to make suggestions for the correction of any poor practices. An analysis of past accidents and a careful reexamination and redirection of many minor practices did succeed in a marked reduction of football accidents.

CLINICS AND WORKSHOPS

Clinics and workshops provide one of the better means of in-service education for physical education teachers. Since actual physical skill is involved in much of the teaching of physical education, teachers need the opportunity to see and preferably practice the skills involved. Particularly when a new activity or a new technique is being considered, in-service procedures of clinics or workshops are of value.

Coaches attend clinics quite regularly. Many state coaches' associations sponsor clinics in various sports. Problems are studied, and expert advice is given. Some of these clinics emphasize participation on the part of the coaches attending; others depend upon talks, discussions, and demonstrations.

Most of the literature on the organization and conduct of workshops deals with those concerned with intellectual problems, but the basic idea of the workshop is equally applicable to physical activities. Workshops can be of one day's duration or can continue over a period of days or weeks. The principal idea of a workshop is that participants bring their own problems and, with the aid of resource leaders, work in groups on those problems. A workshop may have a major problem and subproblems. For instance, a workshop on modern dance may find one group interested in working on basic techniques, another on music, and another on stimulating creativity. After work by each of the several groups, the entire workshop membership would meet to share experiences, summarize, and evaluate.

The supervisory program can promote both workshops and clinics on a local level, or in smaller communities they may wish to organize them on a county or larger-unit level. Professional organizations and regular college programs also conduct workshops, and local supervisory officers may wish to publicize these among teachers and assist them to make the necessary arrangements to attend.

SUPERVISORY BULLETINS

Publication and distribution of instructional materials and other types of supervisory bulletins serve as excellent means of disseminating certain types of information and stimulating teacher improvement. Most large systems have some kind of routine bulletin which contains announcements of forthcoming events and other day-to-day information which every teacher should have. In addition, many school systems have an annual bulletin which lists pertinent information of a more enduring nature, such as the yearly school schedule, the names, addresses, and telephone numbers of staff, any basic school policies needing emphasis, procedures in case of accident or fire drill, procedures for obtaining equipment and supplies, and report-card dates. Routine bulletins of this kind may well emanate from the central administrative office.

The supervisory program also will be interested in the preparation and distribution of instructional materials, suggestions to teachers, reading lists, and other written material which contains either information or suggestions helpful to teachers. Formerly the course of study represented the basic type of supervisory bulletin used in schools. The present trend favors a less rigid form, one preferably in looseleaf form, to which new materials, resource teaching units, reading lists, and the like can be continuously added.

RESEARCH

Research can be either a group or individual project. Present trends favor group research in addition to and not to the exclusion of individual research. The term *action research* has arisen to describe cooperative group research in which solutions to local school problems are approached scientifically. Research of this nature seems particularly essential in the area of teaching methods. This text should make clear that there is a dearth of research in the area of teaching methods in physical education. Much of the learning research, from which empirical practice has been derived, is actually too limited in scope to assure logical conclusions when applied to more complex or even slightly varying learning-teaching conditions. Well-structured research projects on teaching methods pertinent to local conditions seem of paramount importance if physical education teaching is to cope effectively with the multiplicity of problems which surround the field. Some of the areas which need special attention include ages at which selected activities should be taught for the first time; methods of handling group instruction in both team and individual activities; improved means of evaluating form, attitudes, and other instructional outcomes; uses of modified equipment; effects of reducing ball and court sizes for younger participants; television, video tape, and programmed materials.

The supervisory program, by providing expert leadership, can assist in defining instructional programs for research, designing experiments, carrying out studies, and preparing and reporting findings. By conducting research, teachers grow through increased awareness of scientific procedures and through the development of intellectual curiosity and scientific-mindedness in relation to instructional problems, as well as through increased information resulting from their research findings.

INDIVIDUAL TECHNIQUES

Group techniques prove valuable because teachers learn group-action skills through this type of participation, because many teaching problems involve more than one teacher and need group effort for solution, and because through group activities many more teachers can be reached at one time, saving much supervisory effort.

Nevertheless, need still exists for use of individual supervisory techniques, since there are many times when a teacher needs assistance as an individual. One of the advantages of the current emphasis on group supervisory techniques is that it helps a teacher to acquire a favorable attitude toward supervisory activities and to seek further assistance on his uniquely individual problems. Some of the individual supervisory techniques helpful particularly in relation to method are described below.

SUPERVISORY VISIT AND FOLLOW-UP CONFERENCE

The earliest kind of school supervision consisted of the visitation of the classroom teacher by lay board members. As professional supervision was established, first as a duty of the head teacher, then as an obligation of the superintendent or principal, and finally as the work of the professional supervisor, emphasis continued to be placed upon an analysis of a teacher's classroom methods, with a follow-up conference on the findings of the observation. Much of the residual teacher fear and resentment of supervision lay in misuse of this practice.

Current concepts of supervisory function, however, recognize the value of the classroom visit and conference but with modifications in both purpose and technique. Emphasis is placed upon the visiting person as a coworker and assistant. He comes to assist the teacher to analyze strengths and weaknesses. He focuses not only on teacher methods but also on all conditions of the learning environment. He seeks facts beyond those he can ascertain in the classroom visit and tries to identify basic instructional problems. He is unconcerned with minute happenings and has the insight to see the lesson observed as a part of a greater whole. He does not jump to hasty conclusions about single happenings. He seeks reasons for a teacher's method rather than evaluating it at surface value.

Preferably this type of supervisory visit should be made on an on-call basis, in which the teacher requests the assistance of a supervisory officer or consultant. Needless to say, it requires sound personal relationships between teacher and supervisory staff, or else assistance will not be requested when the need is greatest. Also, if proper relationships exist between supervisors or consultants and teachers, they will feel free to drop in on teachers unannounced, and teachers will be equally happy to have them do so.

New teachers particularly need assistance. Under traditional supervisory practices, a new teacher is more likely to dread a supervisor's arrival, which may only add to his insecurity before his classes. A helpful, rather than a critical, attitude on the part of the consultant leads a new teacher to welcome the assistance of a coworker and friend.

Visitation based upon a study-analysis approach obviously requires follow-up conferences. If the sole purpose of a supervisory visit is to rate the teacher for promotion, retention, or salary increment, no need exists to talk to the teacher about the visit. If the visiting is to be a factor in teacher growth, a conference in which teacher and consultant analyze the observed work appears essential.

INTERVISITATION

Intervisitation refers to teachers visiting among themselves to observe others at work. Teaching method can never be stereotyped or exactly prescribed. It remains so much a manifestation of a particular learning environment that one demonstration or one illustration may be of little real value. One of the best ways to have teachers exposed to a variety of workable methods is to encourage visitation among staff members within a school and also in other schools, both within and without the system. The supervisory staff promotes this program by first helping teachers to analyze factors on which they need particular help. It then seeks to locate teachers or schools doing a noteworthy job on the factors with which teachers need assistance. It also helps teachers to free themselves from regular classroom duties for the intervisitations.

In many systems intervisitation grows as a result of group activities of many kinds. Teachers working together on a special problem visit each other in the classroom to see how various individuals among them are resolving problems under discussion. Alert teachers often pick a well-liked coworker for partner evaluation. They visit each other at frequent intervals for mutual self-help and evaluation.

INDIVIDUAL PROFESSIONAL ACTIVITIES

The supervisory program serves an important function in advising and stimulating individual teacher growth. A supervisor or consultant can encourage individual teachers to read professional literature, attend meetings, take an active part in professional associations, and continue academic education. The supervisory staff can provide a good basic professional library easily accessible to teachers, can encourage them to subscribe to professional journals, and can help to organize book clubs and reading circles where each teacher member buys one book a semester and circulates it among a reading group. The supervisory staff can assist teachers to make arrangements to attend professional meetings and can give cooperation in their accepting and carrying out professional-organization assignments. The staff can help teachers discover college courses pertinent to their individual needs and many times can persuade nearby colleges to offer extension courses in the community for the convenience of local teachers.

No amount of supervisory effort will result in teacher growth unless the teacher himself sees the need for continued improvement. Group activities serve the purpose of indicating that need to grow is shared, that others seek for continual improvement. Individual techniques assist to meet particular personal needs. Many times a supervisor can help an individual teacher in analyzing his own problems and directing his efforts into the most fruitful channels.

SUMMARY

The purpose of supervision is to improve the design and process of instruction. Modern supervision is characterized by the provision of democratic professional leadership. It directs its primary efforts toward study of all factors of the teaching-learning environment. It stimulates teacher growth through cooperative study and analysis of all factors in the teaching-learning environment. Teachers and supervisors, often called consultants, have a peer relationship, with leadership shared and supervisory policy and program determined by group action.

Supervision deals with all aspects of the school program, curriculum, instruction, and administration. Supervision relates to method in three basic ways: (1) It strives for the overall professional growth of teachers; (2) it provides direct experiences through which teachers improve specific teaching skills; and (3) pupil participation in supervisory activities serves as one method of teaching certain kinds of learnings.

Supervisory techniques most useful in encouraging teacher improvement in method include both group and individual activities. Group activities, such as cooperative study of curriculum instruction and administrative problems, interest study groups, cooperative community groups, clinics and workshops, supervisory bulletins, and research, serve to provide mutual stimulation, teach skills of group action, and bring realistic solution to problems hindering best teaching efforts. Individual techniques, including supervisory visits and conferences, intervisitations, and individual professional activities, focus upon the uniquely individual personal problems of teachers and assist in both their personal and their professional adjustment.

Questions and problems for discussion

1. Discuss any parallelism between changes in supervisory concepts from an inspectional approach to the present emphasis on democratic leadership and similar changes in the areas of curriculum, instruction, and administration.
2. Discuss some of the advantages of a secondary school physical education teacher serving in a supervisory capacity to elementary school classroom teachers. Indicate possible disadvantages.
3. How may the physical education supervisory program contribute to more effective use of audio-visual and other instructional materials?
4. All-school or all-city physical education demonstrations are often promoted by supervisory personnel for publicity or public relations purposes. Discuss ways in which such events can be made of optimum value to pupils.
5. Pose two supervisory problems in each of the areas of curriculum and instruction. Describe supervisory techniques appropriate to their solution.
6. List some of the problems unique to inexperienced teachers. How can a supervisor best assist with these problems?
7. List types of instructional problems on which experienced teachers might seek supervisory assistance.
8. Discuss ways in which teachers may encourage democratic supervisory procedures in a system where inspectional supervision has been traditional.
9. Discuss ways in which group or individual teacher research can be utilized to improve the supervisory program.
10. Draw up in detail specific operating plans for a workshop or clinic on any physical activity for a group of in-service teachers.

Selected references

Evans, Ruth, and Leo Gans: *Supervision of Physical Education,* McGraw-Hill Book Company, New York, 1950.

Eye, Glen G., and Lenore A. Netzer: *Supervision of Instruction, A Phase of Administration,* Harper & Row, Publishers, Incorporated, New York, 1965.

Franseth, Jane: *Supervision as Leadership,* Harper & Row, Publishers, Incorporated, New York, 1961.

Harris, Ben M.: *Supervisory Behavior in Education,* Prentice-Hall, Inc., Englewood Cliffs, N.J., 1963.

Lucio, William H.: *Supervision: A Synthesis of Thought and Action,* McGraw-Hill Book Company, New York, 1962.

McKean, Robert C., and H. H. Mills: *The Supervisor,* Center for Applied Research in Education, Washington, D.C., 1964.

chapter 16
METHOD AND ADMINISTRATION

INTRODUCTION

The function of administration is to provide a setting for learning which will be conducive to achieving desired goals. Instructional planning indicates the road to be traveled and suggests a structure to facilitate operation. Administration provides the necessary facilities, equipment, and staff personnel and formulates operational policies and procedures which contribute to efficient learning. Chapter 1 clarified distinctions among the three terms curriculum, instruction, and administration. Curriculum involves determining objectives and planning learning experiences; instruction decides upon methods and conducts learning experiences; administration sets policies to provide structure and procedures to implement operation. Although curriculum, instruction, and administration are distinct functions, they do, and should, overlap. It is unreal and unnecessary to attempt to divide the three functions sharply for operational use, although categorizing them does serve to clarify responsibilities.

Teaching physical education involves executive or administrative functions. Supplies and equipment must be requisitioned or purchased and cared for. Carrying out plans requires repeated decisions by teachers. Reports and records must be prepared and made. Contracting of games, employment of officials, and arranging for transportation frequently are responsibilities of coaches. Participation in league and district meetings which consider plans and policies has many administrative implications.

Generally on the classroom level administrative duties performed by teachers are called *organization*. Many of the issues discussed in Part 4 on the conduct of class and extraclass programs concern organizational problems closely related to teaching methods. In addition to teacher-controlled administrative decisions, the head administrative officer of a school must accept responsibility for and carry out many policies relative to the physical education program. Teachers more and more, however, in present-day school practice participate in administration on this level. For example, consider the registration practice in school A. Students are assigned to physical education classes by the common though undesirable practice of selecting all other subjects first. They are scheduled for physical education during whatever free period or periods remain. The physical education teacher will object to such a practice and recommend a better one, very likely assignment according to grade. The principal and other teachers may agree that this would be desirable but point to scheduling difficulties. The physical education teacher may be asked to submit a plan by which such assignment could operate in the school. In preparing such a plan he would be participating in all-school administration. Acceptance or rejection of his proposals would depend largely on their feasibility. Also, it would depend upon administrative and teacher opinion regarding importance which, in turn, would depend upon the merit of the proposals presented. Activities such as this frequently are important parts of the work of a physical education teacher. They represent not autocratic administrative decisions but participation in administration which requires a high degree of cooperation with other school personnel.

The remainder of the chapter explains two basic ways administration interrelates with method. Then scheduling of classes and its subproblems receive explanation, since amount of time, grouping procedures, time of day, class size, and provisions for atypical students set basic conditions which affect the kind of program and the types of method possible. The final portion of the chapter concerns the area of facilities, showing how improvement of facilities aids learning but conversely how planning and apt selection of method can produce better learning with available facilities.

RELATION OF METHOD TO ADMINISTRATION

Administration concerns method in two fundamental ways. (1) Administration provides basic material resources and leadership for conducting learning experiences, the nature of which influences selection of method. (2) Students, who learn from all conditions of the school environment, not just from planned classroom experiences, are affected by the administrative structure which sets the conditions and climate of a program.

EFFECTS OF MATERIAL RESOURCES

The kind and amount of material resources available affect the type and quality of a physical education program and to a large extent the types of method used. Good physical education programs do exist despite the lack of expensive materials of many kinds. Such programs have compensated by maximum use of natural resources, ingenuity in adapting methods to make optimum use of available limited equipment and facilities, and generally sound and creative administrative practices. The fact remains, however, that good educational programs cost money, and, in general, research indicates that the higher the budget, the better the school program. Administration must continually strive to provide the best possible facilities, equipment, and organizational design to assure good learning. A teacher with 60 students in a low-ceilinged gymnasium must use different kinds of teaching procedures and cannot be expected to achieve as good results in basketball, for example, as if he had 30 students in an adequate activity area. An inadequately prepared teacher with competencies in but one or two activities and lack of skill in a variety of different teaching techniques is less likely to accomplish outstanding results than the highly qualified. Equipment, too, affects learning and achievement. Boys running on a sandy track in tennis shoes could not compete with those training on a cinder track with spiked shoes. A teacher with two soccer balls for a class of forty must use different and generally less effective methods than if provided with sufficient equipment to conduct practice drills with maximum student participation.

EFFECTS OF OVERALL ADMINISTRATIVE STRUCTURE

In addition to the general effects of material resources on learning, the administrative structure itself assumes equal importance in respect to learning and teaching procedures. For example, even a competent teacher having a well-equipped gymnasium would be seriously handicapped by and administrative policy which allowed but two 40-minute periods, including dressing time, per week. A short period may require reliance on teacher-centered methods in order that all students have maximum physical participation, but it may thus deny social learnings of various kinds. Such policies obviously interfere with obtaining good results.

Administrative policies also set the social climate of a program. A safe, happy environment in which a high degree of rapport exists between teachers and students contributes to good learning. Policies which deny the basic needs and interests of students often seriously interfere with learning. A story told by a county supervisor visiting the physical education plant of a new central rural junior high school, which boasted every possible material resource and well-qualified teaching personnel, illustrates this point. Despite a well-planned, though routine, skill-drill lesson, the supervisor was amazed to note the marked listlessness and disinterest of the students. A desultory clapping of hands on the completion of a relay constituted the only display of any noise or response during the entire period. On inquiry the supervisor learned that an autocratic principal had arbitrarily ruled that there must be no talking in the halls or gymnasium. This policy stifled response and enthusiasm and resulted in reduced student interest and effort to learn. The distressed teacher, new to the school and fearing to raise the issue with the principal, appealed to the supervisor for assistance in the matter. The supervisor learned in conference with the principal that the policy simply represented an unconsidered carry-over from his previous four-roomed school where physical education was conducted in classrooms and excessive noise disturbed other classes. A change in policy in this regard soon transformed the entire attitude of the school toward the physical education program.

Another example also shows the effect of administrative policy on the social climate of the program. In this instance the entire community looked forward with eagerness to the opening of a new swimming pool in the local school. On its completion elementary school pupils were assigned use of the pool on Mondays, with the remainder of the time allocated to high school boys on Tuesdays and Thursdays and high school girls on Wednesdays and Fridays. All went well the first month, but then the teacher of the Friday girls' classes began to experience increasing problems of excuses and cuts. Developing discipline cases soon threatened to destroy much of the interest of the girls in the swimming program. Two simple administrative adjustments solved this problem. Additional hair driers, enough for an entire class, were installed, and the elementary pupils were rescheduled to use the pool on Fridays, with the high school girls reassigned to Mondays. These adjustments circumvented the girls' distress at wet, unattractive hair for their Friday afternoon dates and activities and showed sound consideration of a reasonable adolescent concern.

It is beyond the scope of this text to deal with the multitude of administrative factors which affect learning both directly and indirectly. The basic principle which governs this problem suggests that each administrative policy and procedure related to the physical education program be examined in light of its effect on the attitudes, habits, and other learning outcomes of students.

SCHEDULING OF CLASSES

Scheduling of physical education classes represents an important administrative function involving the total school program. Consideration must be given to relative needs among the various areas of the school program. On the other hand, such scheduling factors as time available, group structure, time of day, class size, and handling of special students fundamentally affect a physical education teacher's choice of activities and methods and ultimately, of course, the kinds of results achieved.

The school administration must make final decisions concerning the scheduling of classes. Compromises between ideal physical education practices and limitations imposed by difficulties in arranging school schedules usually prove necessary. Ordinarily, scheduling problems are most acute in small high schools which offer a wide variety of subjects and activities. Large high schools having multiple sections of various courses provide more flexibility than do schools with single sections.

TIME ALLOTMENT

Physical educators are almost unanimous in the belief that a daily period is required in both elementary and secondary schools if the developmental, recreational, and skill needs of young people are to be met with reasonable adequacy. Not all the physical activity needed for healthful growth and development can be provided during one school period daily. However, a daily period of liberal length does allow time for considerable healthful activity. Further it permits the teaching of a variety of physical activities that develop skills, abilities, and interests that form a basis for further participation in worthwhile activities.

How long should the daily period be? Since five minutes at the start and ten minutes at the end are needed for dressing and showering, the longer the period the higher the percentage of time available for physical activity. A sixty-minute period allows 75 percent of the total time for activity other than dressing, whereas a forty-minute class permits 62.5 percent. Relatively long periods are advantageous for physical education classes. When school schedules are divided into short periods, the desirability and possibility of double periods for physical education should be considered. Secondary schools are making progress in developing flexible schedules which permit varying allocation of time according to needs. Some schools use units of fifteen minutes, others twenty minutes, and arrange for length of a given period by scheduling one of these short units for some activities such as homeroom meetings, two consecutive units for some classes, and three or four consecutive units for some classes. These flexible schedules make relatively long periods for physical education quite feasible. At least one school using this flexible, short-unit plan arranges physical classes so that some classes are dressing and showering while others are in a gymnasium or other teaching station. This arrangement, of course, stretches peak-load usage by eliminating empty gymnasiums between periods or at least by lessening the amount of time expensive facilities lie idle.

ASSIGNMENT TO CLASSES

A reasonable degree of homogeneity within a class group unquestionably facilitates adjustment of the activities and methods to the needs of individuals. A class made up of a mixture of ninth-, tenth-, eleventh-, and twelfth-graders presents interests and abilities so varied that it is most difficult, if not impossible, for a teacher to give sufficient leadership and guidance to all members of the group. Such a class seriously limits the opportunities for effective group work.

Completely homogeneous groups are neither possible nor desirable. Many physical education teachers do express a belief that classes should be made up of pupils whose physical characteristics are alike. But alike in what physical characteristics? Weight, height, running speed, strength, physical fitness index, basketball-playing ability, tumbling ability, swimming or volleyball or badminton ability, or some other measure or combination of abilities? Obviously, it is not possible to arrange groups that are homogeneous in all the physical abilities likely to be called upon in a given physical education class during the course of a year. If it were possible, there would be serious question concerning the desirability of such groups. Intergroup relationships would be narrowed, peer stimulation probably would be lessened, and attention to individual differences in mental, social, and emotional characteristics probably would suffer.

Generally speaking, it is best to assign students to physical education classes according to single grade level, i.e., seventh, eighth, ninth, tenth, eleventh, and twelfth grades. This permits a progressive program; it permits activities and a course of study for freshmen, sophomores, etc. Such assignment produces groups that have much in common. Chronological ages will be quite alike, past school experiences will be similar, there will be considerable commonality in interests, and acquaintances and friendships will have been formed. Flexibility which permits cutting across grade lines in cases of outstanding deviation in health status, size, or physical ability makes for improved grouping.

Administrative feasibility presents one reason why it is held here that assignment by individual grade level generally is best. It may well be that physical educators can arrange groups more advantageously through use of measures such as height-weight-age coefficients, physical fitness indexes, physical-educability measures, tests of skill in various sports, or social-maturity measures. However, it must be recognized that in almost all schools arrangement of classes on such bases presents serious administrative difficulty.

Subgrouping within a class usually is desirable. When a class is taught by one teacher, subgrouping is facilitated through squad organization. When a group of 100 freshmen, for example, are assigned to a class with several teachers available, further homogeneity can well be achieved through use of anthropometric measures, fitness scores, skill-performance records, teacher and student judgments, and activities to be pursued.

Groups within a class may well be rearranged as different units or activities form a center of attention. A grouping for badminton may not be a good grouping for softball. The activity at hand should determine grouping. A school structure that makes it relatively easy for groups to change readily seems desirable. As soon as a group completes the work for which it was formed, students should be regrouped for the next learning experience.

Regardless of how students are grouped, the most important consideration is the teaching, the handling, of a class. From an instructional standpoint it is the differences within a group which become important, and there always will be differences within any group unless it is "a group of one" or perhaps identical twins. Understanding the composition of a group relative to the focal point of learning or of the activity is the base for the real advantage of various grouping practices.

TIME OF DAY

A period near the middle of the morning or near the middle of the afternoon is favored by some schools for physical education classes. Among reasons given for favoring these mid-half-day times are these: (1) a break from and variation of sedentary classroom activity is needed; (2) before-school and after-school physical activity makes physical education classes near the beginning or near the end of a session unnecessary; (3) early morning hours should be reserved for more difficult subjects; and (4) rigorous physical activity should be avoided after meals.

Although each of the reasons given may have some validity, no one of them, nor the four combined is compelling in the sense that any hour of the day should be eliminated for physical education purposes. Whether or not relief from classroom work is needed depends largely upon the nature of that work. Assuming that before-school and after-school activity makes physical education inappropriate for hours near the beginning or end of sessions implies that physical education is chiefly a relief from sedentary work. Such an assumption fails to give adequate attention to needs for skill development and for social and emotional development through physical activities. The concept of reserving early morning hours for difficult subjects is outmoded. Difficulty depends upon individual aptitude and teaching method much more than upon a subject. Possible interference with digestion has frequently been cited as a reason for avoiding strenuous physical activity shortly after meals. However, almost all medical and physiological scientists agree that exercise after luncheon will produce no harmful effects provided the exercise is not accompanied by emotional strain and provided it is not of an extremely strenuous type such as competition in distance running.

Provision of adequate time for physical education and efficient use of facilities transcend the arguments for limiting physical education to mid-half-day periods. In most schools of large enrollment it becomes necessary to use almost all the school hours for physical education classes in order to provide daily periods for all students. In the event that gymnasiums, swimming pools, outdoor facilities, and teaching personnel are plentiful enough so that only selected hours are needed, there is no objection to limiting physical education to certain hours. But such situations seldom exist. They would be difficult to justify economically. Gymnasiums and swimming pools are expensive; they should hum with activity rather than lie idle a good deal of the time.

SIZE OF CLASS

Generally speaking, classes should be limited to 30 students and 40 should be regarded as a maximum. It is true, of course, that type of program, teaching methods, and available facilities affect the number that can adequately be provided for in one class. An undesirable lock-step program which pays little or no attention to individualization of instruction can accommodate large numbers in small spaces. Command-response teaching, in which all members of a group respond with a definite movement to a teacher command, puts little premium on small classes.

Effective teaching that encourages students to accept responsibility for their own activities frees the teacher from routine direction so that he can guide learning activities rather than function as a didactic issuer of orders. How does this affect class size? A teacher who approaches individual instruction by insisting upon guiding every detail of every student's movement can provide individual instruction for only a very small group. One who guides learning activities by helping class members in subgroups to see what the problem is and how to attack it can guide the learning of 30 to 40 effectively if the groups take responsibility for their own projects.

It is apparent that it is easier to accommodate 40 in volleyball when three courts are available than it is to accommodate 25 with only one court available. Similarly, worthwhile experiences for 12 in volleyball, 14 in badminton, and 14 in tumbling can be arranged when facilities for all these sports at one time are available, whereas it is impossible to do so if any one of the activities requires all usable space. Forty students can make effective use of time devoted to softball skill development and play when there are two diamonds, but if there is only one diamond and no additional practice space, both quantity and quality of development will suffer if softball for 40 is attempted.

ASSIGNMENT OF ATYPICAL STUDENTS

It is a responsibility of the school health service or the family physician to recommend types of activities appropriate for those whose physical condition prevents full participation in a broad program. School administrators and physical education teachers must accept responsibility for determining the best organization of classes for carrying out medical recommendations. Opinions of physical educators differ considerably with respect to the question, "Should boys and girls who require adapted or restricted activities be assigned to special classes?" Necessary considerations in determining the answer to the question include (1) the likely effects of regular class assignment and of a special class upon social and emotional development, (2) ability of the teacher or teachers involved to adapt activities and procedures so that individual needs will be met, (3) seriousness and degree of disability, and (4) fluidity of school schedule.

Good school mental-hygiene practices help boys and girls adjust to their individual problems. Those who have abnormalities such as structural or organic defects, functional disorders, poor body mechanics, or poor nutritional status may suffer feelings of isolation and inferiority. If so, they need to learn to live with their handicaps, to accept their circumstances, adjust, alleviate, or compensate for their particular atypical condition. Young people appreciate attention to their problems. Assignment to regular classes and understanding guidance may help ease and remedy feelings of inferiority whereas assignment to special groups may tend to accentuate them. Assimilation into the school community is likely to be made easier by membership in regular classes.

Atypical students need more individual guidance than do most others. Teachers who have developed effective techniques of adapting instruction to individual differences find it quite possible to serve well the needs of students possessing defects within the framework of a class made up mostly of normal persons. On the other hand, there may be merit to the contention that special classes permit greater attention to individuals.

Seriousness and degree of defect is an important consideration in determining appropriate class assignment. Surely, boys and girls with only minor abnormalities should be permitted class membership along with normals. Gross deviates such as paraplegics and those with very serious heart abnormalities profit by assignment to special groups.

Small schools offering only single sections of the several courses or activities find it difficult to arrange special classes for deviates. Some have solved the problem well by having special classes on Saturdays or before or after class hours in addition to inclusion of atypical students in the regular physical education classes. Schools with readily flexible schedules are more able to arrange classes as deemed desirable.

METHOD AND FACILITIES

Improving the usefulness of available facilities constitutes a problem faced by the majority of physical education teachers. This problem represents a typical overlapping one for curriculum, instruction, and administration. Although administration must make efforts to provide increasingly adequate facilities, good instructional planning and apt selection of methods can do much to compensate for facility deficiencies.

Without question, programs are limited by inadequate equipment and facilities. Schools need more and better gymnasiums, swimming pools, outdoor play areas, locker rooms, shower rooms, activity rooms, health units, equipment, and supplies. However, intelligent planning can improve programs which can be offered with limited facilities. Indeed teachers sometimes use complaints about inadequate facilities as alibis and fail to adapt activities and method to existing facilities as well as they might. An important measure of a teacher's ability is his resourcefulness in planning for optimum use of available facilities.

Comments such as, "I certainly wish we had such facilities back home; then we really would have a program," are made frequently by teachers who are visiting schools during conventions, tournaments, meets, or play days. Teachers from small schools rather frequently marvel at the facilities of large schools without analyzing them in terms of the number of students to be served. Recently several teachers were looking over the field house of a high school whose enrollment is about 2,500. They were talking about the fine field house and the splendid program conducted in it and about what they could do in their schools if they had such a place in which to work. Yet when the director of physical education who headed the program conducted in the field house joined the group and conversation turned to considering the number of students served, it was agreed that every one of the smaller schools represented by the visiting teachers had better facilities in terms of serving their students than did the school with the large field house.

How, then, can a teacher of physical education improve the usefulness of available facilities? After a brief indication of desirable teacher attitude and activity toward the securing of needed improvements which require large capital outlay, the remainder of the chapter offers suggestions for improving the usefulness of existing facilities.

WORKING FOR MAJOR IMPROVEMENTS

A teacher or director of physical education is in a position to suggest needs for building improvements requiring major capital outlay. Such suggestions, based upon needs of boys and girls, may be made to administrators and to other interested persons. Too many physical education teachers decide that it is not within their province or ability to influence new building plans and settle down to complaining that it is impossible to have much of a program.

It is generally recognized that there is a great necessity for major building programs to satisfy the needs of a large number of youngsters, so many that school districts experience considerable difficulty with needed bond issues which increase taxes, especially on real estate. But it also should be recognized that almost all schools can use their present facilities to better advantage. Intelligent planning by resourceful teachers and school administrators can bring about improved use of gymnasiums and playgrounds. Minor investments may significantly enhance the usefulness of property already available.

IMPROVING THE USEFULNESS OF EXISTING FACILITIES

Means of increasing the usefulness of facilities which are discussed below include suggestions for assigning of classes, making more indoor courts and teaching stations available, arrangement of apparatus and mats, better use of outdoor facilities with suggested activities and procedures, and planning for increased usefulness of existing facilities.

Assignment of classes Good scheduling practices must take account of available facilities. Basic scheduling procedures were discussed earlier in this chapter. Some additional considerations relative to assignment of classes where facilities are particularly limited bear mention.

Classes should be assigned so that gymnasium and playground space can be used throughout the day. It is not easy to schedule classes in all schools so that full use may be made of gymnasiums. In large schools where there are multiple sections of classes, the problem is simplified, and usually such schools do use their facilities throughout the day. In small schools, especially those which offer a wide variety of courses, scheduling problems are difficult. Usually, however, in such schools it is possible to schedule so that a given period during the day is available to the ninth grade for classes in the gymnasium, another period for the tenth grade, and so on. In schools having only one gymnasium and no other physical education teaching station, it sometimes becomes necessary to schedule boys and girls of a given grade to physical education classes at the same hour. Although this presents a difficult problem it is possible to provide a daily program by, for example, arranging for boys and girls to meet together one day a week for coeducational activities such as square dancing, social dancing, archery, or volley ball. This would leave two days per week during which the gymnasium would be available for girls only, and two for boys only. During the two days a class cannot use the gymnasium it can engage in activities such as:

1. Physical education activities out of doors.
2. Classroom instruction in physical education skills, techniques, and rules.
3. Studying physiological, psychological, and sociological effects of exercise.
4. Planning units or projects.
5. Paper and pencil tests.
6. Helping each boy or girl to develop his or her own plans for a physical education program, both in and out of school, plans that are adequate for the individual and will contribute toward the development of an intelligent program of work, play, recreation, and rest for each person.
7. Studying health and safety as they relate to physical education.
8. Viewing appropriate films.
9. Studying public, commercial, and private recreational opportunities provided in the community.
10. Taking field trips.

Another approach to the problem of assigning classes in schools having insufficient gymnasium space is to divide a gymnasium so that half of it may be used by girls while the other half is used by boys. Such division accomplished by installation of a movable curtain has been used with considerable success in some schools to accommodate concurrent classes and intramural activities for boys and girls. The success of this arrangement depends upon the size of classes, amount of floor space available, and activities scheduled, as well as upon cooperative planning by the men and women teachers involved.

Making more indoor courts and teaching stations available One of the ways in which a gymnasium may be made to serve more people during any given activity period is to make more courts available. Examples of this may be taken from such sports as basketball, volleyball, handball, and badminton. One-basket basketball of the half-court or circle type can double the number of active participants without stripping the activity of its appeal or beneficial results. It is true that full-court play, i.e., playing the regulation game without modification, is more desirable than play under modifications necessary for half-court or circle play in which both teams shoot at the same basket. However, these variations have been found very appealing to students when the class organization provides stimulation which comes from competition in games and in gamelike situations. Secondary school boys, eager and keen to play full-court basketball, have been found to be very much satisfied with half-court play which provides competition among constituted teams.

Volleyball participation may be doubled in many situations without impoverishing the game. Many schools have gymnasiums varying in size from 75 feet by 40 feet to 90 feet by 50 feet. Such gymnasiums will accommodate only one regulation-size volleyball court. But at very moderate expense, two cross courts may be laid out in a 75 feet by 40 feet gymnasium, and three may be installed in a gymnasium 90 feet in length. Although such courts are not regulation in size, they permit quite satisfactory play. Indeed, it may well be that such courts are superior for boys and girls who are learning to play and for those who do not play expertly. Although such facilities are not satisfactory for highly organized competition such as is found in interscholastic play, they not only double or triple the number who may participate at one time, but also provide quite satisfactory playing and learning conditions for physical education–class and intramural use.

One-wall handball courts frequently can be placed in a gymnasium simply by painting lines on the floor and walls. This, of course, depends upon the type of wall. Although not all wall spaces are appropriate for the ball bouncing of handball, many may be so utilized. Quite frequently four one-wall handball courts may be installed in a small gymnasium Since four courts will accommodate a maximum of only 16 players at one time for competitive games, it usually is desirable to plan handball so that some of the class members are playing on the courts while others are practicing strokes at a wall away from the playing courts, or else to plan handball and some other activity or activities simultaneously so that there is activity for all. The addition of handball to a program adds a desirable and popular game of the dual type, highly regarded as an activity possessing strong carry-over values.

Badminton courts, like handball courts, may be lined on gymnasium floors with little expense, and the game may be a part of the physical education–class program as well as an intramural and recreational activity. As with handball, small gymnasiums will not accommodate large numbers of players; so classes usually should be organized so that some of the members are playing badminton while others are engaging in some other activity such as tumbling, wrestling, apparatus, rope jumping, weight lifting, or high or broad jumping.

In addition to optimum use of gymnasium areas, location of other available space warrants consideration. An extra classroom may be converted to a wrestling or adapted-activities room. The lunchroom or auditorium stage may accommodate dance or other activities. A dead-end corridor may provide space for table tennis. An extra-wide corridor or breezeway may prove suitable for fencing instruction. Not all physical education activities require the commodious, high-ceilinged space of a gymnasium.

Arrangement of apparatus and mats Maximum use of available apparatus depends upon arrangement and placing as well as upon class organization. In some instances space and time may be conserved by placing apparatus and mats on stages or in nearby activity rooms. The several pieces of apparatus should be placed so that all can be used at the same time if the lesson calls for all class members to perform on apparatus. Some teachers want only one apparatus performance at a time. Except during the introduction of a new stunt or during the performance of one that requires exceptional care to prevent injuries, this procedure is wrong and wasteful. If sufficient apparatus—horizontal bars, parallel bars, horses, bucks, and rings—to provide activity for all without waste of time by waiting turns is not available, then apparatus should be combined with other activities such as tumbling, free throwing, testing, standing high and broad jump, and stunts so that there is appealing activity for all.

Arrangement of tumbling mats affects their usability. Multiple mat stations short in length provide for more activity than does one long station. When multiple stations are used, one may be used for stunts requiring movement over a length of mats such as rolls and handsprings; another may be used for more stationary stunts such as headstands, handstands, and ground kips; and still another may be used for double stunts such as balances, stands, and flips.

Better use of outdoor facilities The touch of resourceful persons is apparent on some playgrounds though regretfully absent on most. In many instances inexpensive installations such as lines and standards for nets make possible the addition of new activities or add new life and vigor to games already sponsored.

Hard surfacing of outdoor areas greatly increases usability. It has been estimated that hard surfacing, such as blacktop or cement, doubles the amount of time during the school year for which outdoor play areas may be used in north temperate climates. Although surfacing requires expenditure, the outlay is small in comparison to that required for building.

Some games and other activities require hard surfaces such as blacktop or cement or difficult and expensive maintenance of clay or grass surfaces, whereas others may be conducted very satisfactorily on any firm surface.

Volleyball, badminton, aerial tennis, and deck tennis typify games which may well be added to the physical education program for out-of-doors play. Since it is not necessary to provide a surface from which balls may bound, the surface needs only to be firm and smooth enough to permit movements such as running, stopping, starting, changing direction, and jumping.

Some schools have found the several games considered here to be popular with and appealing to students, as well as rich contributors to physical development, improvement of skills in the use of the body, recreation, and socializing play. None of them requires expensive installations. A teacher, faced with a problem of enriching a program within limited facilities, may find considerable opportunity for program expansion by considering the several possibilities described below

Frequently thought of as an indoor game, volleyball is a splendid outdoor game. Volleyball-court installation can be inexpensive. Lines may be made with lime markers which most schools already have. Movable standards, which will not interfere with use of the area for such games as touch football, soccer, speedball, baseball, or softball, may be installed at small cost by using four-by-four wood posts or two two-by-fours nailed or bolted together. To make such standards easily movable, it is necessary that postholes be fitted with encasements so that the standards can be easily put into place. Covers for the postholes should be provided so that holes may be covered when the standards are not in use. If this is done, the area may safely be used for other activities. Two-inch material has been found satisfactory both for encasement of holes and for covers. If courts adjacent at the sidelines are employed, four standards will accommodate three nets and, of course, three courts. An area 80 feet by 110 feet provides sufficient space for three courts with a reasonable amount of space at the sidelines and endlines.

Some teachers shy away from installations such as the standards described because of the work, time, and nuisance involved in getting the courts ready for play and removing the standards and nets when the space is to be used for other activities. Two things should be considered here. One is the amount of enrichment of play opportunities for students which can be accomplished. The other is class organization which provides student help in preparing the courts for play and in removing the equipment when it needs removal. If students develop the attitude that helping to prepare for play is labor that should be performed by a janitor or caretaker, they will dislike doing it; on the other hand, if they develop the attitude that they are helping to organize a worthwhile activity, they will regard it as a privilege.

Badminton played out of doors can enrich most physical education programs. Although expert performers generally frown upon competitive badminton play out of doors because of wind interference, use of the heavier outdoor shuttlecock makes for quite satisfactory outdoor play for persons learning the game or for competition at levels that do not involve highly developed championship play. Both class and intramural badminton are appropriate out of doors on reasonably quiet days.

Since the nets are light and only a small amount of support is needed, satisfactory standards can be made by using a two-by-two wood piece for an upright and building a base about 18 inches square of 1- or 2-inch material. These standards do not require hole installations; they may stand on the ground supported only by their own base. If courts are adjacent at the sidelines, standards may be conserved by attaching two nets to one standard. In this way four standards may support three nets for three courts, five standards may support four nets, or six standards may be used for five courts.

Since one court can accommodate a maximum of four players, it frequently proves desirable to combine badminton with some other activity because of the limitations in the number of courts. Track and field events usually combine well with badminton. Softball, football, soccer, or speedball combine well if there is sufficient space. Activities such as archery, casting, rope jumping, obstacle-course running, combative contests, horseshoes, quoits, and stunts go well with badminton in many outdoor play areas.

Although not widely popular, aerial tennis finds favor in some localities. Played with a birdie or shuttlecock which is struck with the hand rather than a racket, it is an active and interesting game, one that is likely to become popular wherever an enthusiastic teacher introduces it, teaches enough so that reasonable skill is developed, and provides for competition. The shuttlecock is similar to the badminton bird but heavier. It may be purchased from most large sporting-goods stores. Hand badminton would seem like a good name for the game because it is essentially badminton without a racket. Recommended size for an outdoor singles court is 20 feet by 65 feet; for an outdoor doubles court, 26 feet by 65 feet. Ideal indoor-court sizes are 20 feet by 50 feet for singles and 26 feet by 50 feet for doubles. The recommended net height is 7½ feet, and the service line is 10 feet in front of the backline. However, it is reasonably satisfactory to play either singles or doubles on a doubles badminton court (20 feet by 44 feet) and over the 5-foot-high badminton net.

Outdoor hard-surfaced areas (cement, blacktop, clay, and the like) provide for games such as basketball, handball, paddle tennis, and sidewalk tennis. Although these games may be played in the gymnasium, outdoor play offers healthful and invigorating advantages as well as much less expensive provision of opportunity to learn skills and to play.

Basketball played on outdoor courts can increase the opportunities to play and improve the quality of the physical education student's experiences in this very popular game. Because the game is so appealing to boys and girls, particularly to boys, and because of limited facilities, it is all too common to find it conducted in classes with considerable inefficiency in use of student time. For instance, one teacher who has large classes and only one basketball court available devotes a good deal of time each year to basketball classes in which each boy gets to play five minutes during a class period. The rest of the time is spent in watching and waiting for the precious five minutes of play. This teacher's reasoning is that it is better for a boy to play five minutes of full-court basketball than it is for him to engage in other less attractive, less meaningful, and less beneficial activities for thirty or forty minutes. Is there any alternative?

Adjacent to this gymnasium in which boys spend many periods playing basketball for five minutes and awaiting their turns the rest of the time are six cement tennis courts. During a substantial number of days when these indoor basketball periods are in progress, the weather is appropriate for outdoor play. Backboards which would not interfere with the use of the courts for tennis could be installed on the tennis courts with comparatively little expense. If this were done and the classes were organized into squads or teams with student leaders and student officials, the boys could play basketball for a full period, instead of for five minutes, on many days.

Handball, an excellent dual or doubles games which requires only about half as much space as tennis, can become a much more widely played outdoor game. Outdoor courts have proved particularly popular in many city-playground programs. Although one-wall courts are generally used, corner shots can be provided by adding low and narrow side walls attached to the corners of the wall. This game develops balance, speed, timing, agility, ability to start, ability to stop, and endurance. It demands self-control as well as aggressiveness, decisiveness, and self-confidence. It is safe to say that any secondary school would enrich its program of physical education by providing handball courts or adding to its present supply.

Four-wall handball courts are expensive. They exist in only a small minority of schools. Although four-wall courts are most desirable, the one-wall game becomes satisfactory for class, recreational, and intramural play. As pointed out earlier, one-wall courts can be installed in many gymnasiums at small cost. However, through making more outdoor courts available, schools could promote this game immeasurably.

One-wall courts, with short and narrow side pieces that make corner shots possible, can be installed on outdoor hard surfaces by building a wall 20 feet wide and 10 to 16 feet high (the standard height is 16 feet) and painting boundary lines. One wall that has playable surfaces on both sides can serve two courts. Thus one wall and an area 20 feet by 68 feet can accommodate two courts. As is the case with all dual or doubles games, considerable space is required to permit large numbers to play at one time. It should be remembered, however, that handball requires only about half as much space as does tennis.

When given an opportunity, boys and girls enjoy paddle tennis. Originally popularized as a pretennis or tennis-leadup game for children, paddle tennis likewise appeals to older youngsters. Also, in some communities, it finds favor among adult players.

Schools, particularly junior high schools, would perform significant service by providing outdoor courts. This can be done by making boundary lines on any hard surface and supplying nets and standards. Four courts may be laid out on one tennis court. Standard size of the court is 39 feet by 18 feet. The net is 28 inches high at the standards and 26 inches at the center. Paddles and balls are inexpensive and durable. They may be purchased from most sporting-goods outlets. Badminton courts double satisfactorily as paddle-tennis courts, although the standard sizes of the playing areas for the two games are not exactly the same. However, for paddle tennis the surface must be hard and smooth so that the ball will bounce accurately.

Sidewalk tennis enjoys exceptional popularity in some localities. It is appealing to junior high school youngsters, both boys and girls. An outstanding advantage is that it can be and is played as a recreational game on home sidewalks and driveways, thus serving as an excellent leisure activity. In communities where schools sponsor and popularize sidewalk tennis there is a good deal of out-of-school play. Serving and volleying is with the hand rather than with a racket or paddle. Play and scoring follow the table-tennis pattern.

The game can be played satisfactorily on a wide sidewalk. An area 9 feet by 24 feet makes an excellent court; however, adaptation to courts of varying size can be made successfully. A seam in a sidewalk or driveway serves as a center line and as a substitute for a net. The 6-foot sections of sidewalk on each side of the center seam provide an excellent court with natural boundary lines. The ball can be a volleyball, an inflated playball, a paddle-tennis ball, or a tennis ball. Larger and less lively balls are appropriate for young and inexperienced players; similar balls which bounce rapidly are satisfactory for excellent players.

It is true, of course, that providing for many of the outdoor activities suggested here requires effort and inconvenience. Better facilities which are easier to use certainly are desirable and worth the money a community spends for them. It has been argued that resourceful, dedicated, and energetic physical education teachers who provide many opportunities for youngsters at little cost discourage community expenditures for better and more satisfactory facilities. The exact opposite is more likely. Citizens who become aware that youngsters have valuable experiences in physical education, recreation, and sports increase their appreciation for the youngsters' opportunities and will want better facilities.

SUMMARY

Administration relates to the provision and operation of a setting for learning which will be conducive to achieving desired educational goals.

Teaching physical education involves executive or administrative functions. Generally, on the classroom level, administrative duties performed by teachers are called organization, but in addition, in democratically administered schools, teachers increasingly participate in all-school administration.

Administration relates to method in two fundamental ways. It provides basic material resources and leadership for conducting learning experiences, the nature of which influences selection of method. Pupils who learn from all conditions of the school environment, not just from planned classroom experiences, are affected by the administrative structure which sets the conditions and climate for learning.

Scheduling of classes represents an important administrative function involving the total school program. Such scheduling factors as time available, group structure, time of day, class size, and disposition of special pupils fundamentally affects a physical education teacher's choice of methods, and ultimately the kinds of results achieved.

Good physical education programs exist despite the lack of extensive and expensive material resources. The fact remains, however, that good educational programs cost money, and the quality of educational programs is usually commensurate with expenditures. Existing facilities should be progressively improved, but immediate means of increasing the usefulness of available facilities include apt procedures for assigning classes; making more indoor and outdoor courts and teaching stations available through good organization; more extensive year-round use of outdoor facilities; and selection of methods which provide for optimum use of available facilities.

Questions and problems for discussion

1. Examine assignment-to-class practices in a high school which assigns students to physical education classes during whatever free periods remain after other classes are selected. Propose a plan for improving assignment practices used by this school. State reasons for your proposal, and support their feasibility.

2. Assume that the principal of a high school known to you which allots two 40-minute periods weekly to physical education has asked you to evaluate that time allotment and make suggestions for needed changes in the time devoted to physical education. Do so, and support your suggestions.

3. Do you favor special classes for atypical students? Why or why not, and under what conditions?
4. What basis do you prefer for assigning pupils to physical education classes? Why?
5. Select a junior high school or a high school with which you are acquainted, and indicate ways in which the usefulness of the gymnasium facilities might be improved.
6. Select a school as in question 5 above, and suggest procedures for improving the usefulness of outdoor physical education facilities.

Selected references

Chamberlain, Leo M., and Leslie W. Kindred: *The Teacher and School Organization,* 4th ed., Prentice-Hall, Inc., Englewood Cliffs, N.J., 1966.

Forsythe, Charles E., and Ray O. Duncan: *Administration of Physical Education,* 4th ed., Prentice-Hall, Inc., Englewood Cliffs, N.J., 1962.

Howard, Glenn Willard, and Edward Masonbrink: *Administration of Physical Education,* Harper & Row, Publishers, Incorporated, New York, 1963.

Miller, Van, and Willard B. Spalding: *The Public Administration of American Schools,* The Macmillan Company, New York, 1965.

Nash, Jay B., Francis J. Moench, and Jeannette S. Saurborn: *Physical Education: Organization and Administration,* A. S. Barnes and Co., Inc., New York, 1951.

Sachs, Benjamin M.: *Educational Administration,* Houghton Mifflin Company, Boston, 1966.

Vernier, Elmon L. (ed.): *Administration of High School Athletics,* American Association for Health, Physical Education, and Recreation, Washington, D.C., 1963.

Voltmer, E. F., and A. A. Esslinger: *The Organization and Administration of Physical Education,* Appleton-Century-Crofts, Inc., New York, 1958.

Williams, Jesse Feiring, Clifford Lee Brownell, and Elmon L. Vernier: *The Administration of Health Education and Physical Education,* 6th ed., W. B. Saunders Company, Philadelphia, 1964.

Zeigler, Earle F.: *Administration of Physical Education and Athletics, The Case Method Approach,* Prentice-Hall, Inc., Englewood Cliffs, N.J., 1959.

chapter 17

METHOD AND EVALUATION

INTRODUCTION

Earlier chapters have stated that learning represents change in behavior as the result of experience and that teaching consists of conducting planned experiences to promote learning. The worth of any teaching-learning experience, then, must be appraised in relation to the extent the learner's behavior has changed in the desired direction. Thus, simply stated, *evaluation is the process of appraising the extent to which educational objectives are achieved.* Evaluation is recognized as an integral part of educational programs. That is, an education program, to be termed adequate, must attempt to appraise the degree to which desired goals are approximated.

NEED TO EVALUATE ALL OBJECTIVES

Adequate evaluation implies appraisal of progress toward *all* objectives and is used herein in its broadest connotation. It includes use of all devices and judgments employable to measure or estimate status. The term *measurement* implies objective (quantitative) procedures which produce precise answers usually in numerical form. Measurement proves useful to the extent that it contributes to evaluation which considers all the stated educational objectives. Since, however, measurement tools are not yet available to appraise many aspects of educational structure and individual student growth, education, as an art, must employ qualitative judgment to appraise many outcomes. Reliance must be placed upon other forms of appraisal in addition to measurement, such as simple ratings, observation, interviews, and other judgment (qualitative) techniques.

For example, measurement tools exist to appraise, with some degree of accuracy, such factors as body size, physical-growth rates, effects of stated periods of exercise, and achievement in single-skill activities. Factors such as effects of games on character and personality, actual carry-over value of a given activity, attitudes toward physical-fitness factors, leadership and group membership ability, and achievement in complex activities consisting of variable skills and attitudinal learnings lend themselves less aptly to precise measurement. For the present time and until considerably more scientific measurement tools become available, measurement can represent only a portion of the evaluative techniques used by the alert teacher who accepts the importance of appraising all objectives sought by physical education.

SHOULD WE TEACH ONLY WHAT WE CAN ACCURATELY EVALUATE?

The need to evaluate all objectives of teaching is quite apparent. Equally obvious is the fact that present ability to appraise certain kinds of learning varies greatly. It must be noted that one current school of thought holds that what cannot be accurately and precisely appraised should not be included in a curriculum. That is, if one cannot define and accurately evaluate such traits as carry-over value (permanence), good sportsmanship, appreciation of sports as a spectator, worthy team membership, and other such philosophical goals which have long been a part of the educational vernacular, curricular efforts should be directed elsewhere, that is, toward more precise goals. In terms of the behavioral objectives described in Chapter 4, The Objectives of Physical Education, it is permissible to make assumptions regarding possible effects of current learnings on future behavior. For example, one can assume that if a student has acquired certain specific measurable skills, understandings, and favorable attitudes, he is likely to achieve remote goals. However, some educators are advocating that if a teacher cannot be sure he is teaching what he hopes to teach, he would do better to concentrate on what he can clearly define and accurately evaluate. Exponents of programmed learning and operant conditioning theories base most of their practices on this point of view. Logical and cogent reasons can be advanced for this concept. It does have certain weaknesses, however.

One weakness in limiting teaching to measurable goals is that any specific goal is a part of a greater whole. Achievement of an immediate goal cannot be evaluated solely in relation to its own realization since the act of achievement inevitably has an effect on progress toward other and perhaps more important goals. This also has particular reference to the methods used. A teacher may use methods which achieve immediate goals of a limited nature but which create, in the process, fears and dislikes which negate the true value of the original achievement. Similarly, one must consider the "sin of omission," the achievement of one goal at the expense of another. If one taught, let us say, only the skill of basketball shooting, since it is easily measured, and omitted teaching team play and strategy, since it is difficult to appraise accurately, he would be unlikely to achieve logical, although as yet accurately unmeasurable goals.

Too vague objectives and lack of systematic efforts to evaluate do mark an area which needs consistent professional improvement. The inability to agree on the relative worth of selected specific objectives, as well as the primitiveness of available evaluation tools, suggests that the alternative is not to restrictively narrow curricular efforts to fit present scientific development in this area. The ultimate resolution of this controversy lies in the profession's continuous efforts to perfect evaluation tools and to increase understanding of the personal and social needs of learners.

STEPS IN THE EVALUATION PROCESS

The evaluative process consists of three steps: first, delineating and ascertaining the worth of educational objectives; second, collecting data concerning the status of the factors being appraised; third, interpreting the data collected in light of desired goals.

Steps one and three in the evaluative process involve philosophical analysis using inductive and deductive reasoning. The better qualified the educator and the more he understands all factors concerned, the more valid his judgments and interpretations are likely to be. Step two, the collection of data, includes use of measurement (quantitative) tools and subjective (qualitative) appraisals of various kinds. The adeptness and ability of the evaluator determine the worth of the data collected, and as more data are collected, provided they are accurate, sounder judgments can be made from them.

Merely undertaking evaluation does not assure that worthwhile results will accrue. One must understand the evaluation process, have skill in collecting accurate and meaningful data, and have the ability to make scientific and common-sense interpretations of data. Ability to interpret data includes knowing when evidence is insufficient to make valid judgments as well as knowing when conclusions can be drawn. Ability to carry on evaluation is a necessary competency for every teacher.

BASIC TYPES OF EVALUATIVE PROCEDURES

Since progress toward all objectives should be evaluated, it is necessary to use different techniques for gathering data about various factors in teaching-learning situations. Techniques may be classified into two basic types: *quantitative evaluative procedure*—tests and measurement; and *qualitative evaluative procedures*—judgment and observational techniques.

Each of these types has a place in the evaluation of progress in physical education. Although neither of them can sustain a claim to complete objectivity as instruments for total evaluation, each of them, when used by skilled persons, approach objectivity. Since teaching is both an art and a science, evaluation also is both. Because evaluation requires artistic, subjective judgments, it cannot qualify as a complete science. However, it can and should make use of scientific methods.

QUANTITATIVE EVALUATIVE PROCEDURES—TESTS AND MEASUREMENTS

Tools of measurement in physical education include standardized and teacher-made tests, achievement scales, score cards, rating scales and other measuring instruments, the findings of which are precise, objective, quantitative, and capable of statistical treatment. Measurement characteristically reports its findings in terms of time, distance, number, or amount. Available measurement tools give precise and objective information about many aspects of concern to physical education.

Student teachers and young teachers frequently comment regarding the discrepancies between concepts of the proper use of tests and measurements which they have learned in college courses, on the one hand, and school practices in the use of tests, on the other. The area represents an aspect in which physical educators tend to be extremists. Some like testing, feel that it merits a large place in the program because of its objectivity and exactness, and use it liberally. Others believe that tests produce little worthwhile information, feel that they can secure by observation all the information which tests might produce, and think that the expenditure of time and energy required for testing is not justified. Neither extreme proves sound.

Tests contribute significantly to total evaluation. They provide diagnostic evidence for guidance in further work and furnish data for administrative purposes such as classification, keeping cumulative records, and making reports. In addition, they provide information which helps teachers and administrators judge the effectiveness of programs and teaching methods.

Tests contribute evaluative information as they supply evidence of performance abilities (psychomotor learnings) and of knowledge and understanding (cognitive learnings). A limited number of tests and inventories are available to measure attitudes and appreciations (affective learnings). Well-constructed tests supply objective information. It must be recognized that they cannot objectively measure progress toward all the objectives because items to be included must be selected subjectively and because there do not exist instruments or tests adequate for the measurement of many important objectives. However, a teacher should not reject tests because of their limitations. Rather, he will use judgment in selecting and interpreting imperfect instruments and seek to improve them.

Tests can provide a valuable means of motivating students to learn. For instance, a boy who discovers that he can do fewer pull-ups than 75 percent of a random sampling of his age group may be motivated by a helpful teacher to try to improve his ability to do pull-ups. And the boy who discovers that he can do more pull-ups than can 75 percent of the same random sampling is likely to desire to improve further his already superior ability in this particular event.

It may prove helpful to examine the above illustration from the standpoint of diagnosis and guidance for further work. Although the boy who performs pull-ups poorly may desire to work for improvement, he may also be discouraged. He needs teacher help in interpreting the meaning and consequences of such poor performance, and he is likely to need help in planning to improve his ability if it is decided that such improvement is desirable. The boy whose pull-up performance is superior may aspire to achieve further satisfaction and recognition by increasing his ability. But in his case guidance might direct efforts toward improvements in other types of physical activity since his ability in pull-ups already shows adequate development.

Results of physical-fitness tests, for instance, may be used administratively to classify students for types of physical education activities. Students who make low scores might be assigned to a program designed primarily to develop strength and endurance, whereas those making high scores might be assigned to a program which emphasizes the development of recreational skills, or they might be given a choice from among several types of activities. Records of test results kept in cumulative files help to give an overall picture of the development of the individual. Also, progress or lack of it as shown by tests helps administrators and teachers to judge the effectiveness of their programs and methods.

Types of physical education tests Test and measurement specialists in physical education vary considerably in their classification of tests. However, the differences are in bases of classification and in terminology rather than in markedly different concepts of tests and their use. A composite of various lists of test classification would include all the following headings: circulatory-respiratory function, anthropometry and body mechanics, muscular strength, power and endurance, flexibility, motor-fitness and (or) physical-fitness tests, general motor tests, sports skills, dance skills, knowledge and understanding, and attitudes and appreciations.

Selection of abilities to be tested Appropriate selection of abilities to be tested depends upon the objectives and emphases sought. Since tests tend to motivate, they would be used liberally (if adequate instruments are available or can be devised) in areas where emphasis is desired. Selection also depends upon decisions concerning what diagnostic evidence is needed, what information concerning progress is desired, what classification devices are to be used, and what information is needed for reports and records and for judging the effectiveness of the program. A desire to conduct research is also a substantial and laudable reason for the selection of abilities to be tested.

Securing aid in the selection of tests The selection of tests which will best measure abilities which are desirable to measure requires considerably more knowledge of tests than can be presented here. Courses dealing with testing, measuring, and evaluating are desirable; standard texts in the field are most helpful. Several of these are listed in the selected references at the end of the chapter. Local school resources including libraries, supervisors, and curriculum consultants may be available to the teacher; state departments of public instruction may supply help upon request; and consultants from colleges and universities may be called upon. Like any other scientific endeavor, testing requires study and careful application of scientific principles.

Standardized and teacher-made tests Standardized tests are likely to have the advantage of being refined, precise, and tested instruments. Since they usually provide norms, it is possible to compare an individual or a group with the norms. Standardized tests require less teacher time because they are already prepared, have standard directions, and frequently provide an easy means of translating performance into scale scores. Good standardized tests satisfy the criteria of objectivity (various examiners obtain the same results) and reliability (consistency). Satisfaction of the criterion of validity (measuring what the test purports to measure) varies a good deal among standardized physical education tests depending upon what they purport to measure and upon the criterion selected.

Some of the standardized tests intend to measure only ability to perform each of the events included in the test. Many of the tests of physical fitness or condition fall into this category. So, too, do the achievement tests in various physical education activities and some of the sports-skills tests. Thus, less question concerning their validity and fewer questions of interpretation of the significance of performance are left with users of the tests. A physical-condition or physical-fitness test may include items such as pull-ups and sit-ups designed to sample strength and endurance of various muscle groups and items designed to sample speed, coordination, balance, flexibility, and agility, but it may purport to measure only the ability to perform each of the events rather than overall condition or fitness. Empirically selected, the items are thought to represent aspects of condition or fitness, but makers of the tests may make no claim other than that they measure ability to perform the several selected events.

Similarly, achievement tests and tests of isolated sports skills may purport to measure only ability to perform each item; hence their validity lies in the simple fact that they do not claim correlation with any general criterion. Ability to jump a certain height from a standing position, ability to bounce a ball against a wall a certain number of times in a certain length of time, and the like may show that the performer's ability lies at a certain location in comparison with the group used to develop the norms; but, so far as intention of the test goes, there may be no further claims.

One of the abuses of standardized tests lies in a tendency among teachers and students to read more into them than they were intended to mean. This is a cause for much of the present controversy concerning the desirability of using the physical-fitness tests in schools. Teachers and students may overemphasize the importance of the tests, may regard them as more or less complete indications of fitness when there is no basis for so doing. Because of the preciseness, the recorded results, and the dramatic appeal of the tests, there may be an unwise tendency to regard ability to perform them as almost total evaluation of progress in physical education. Such practice leads to overemphasis upon development of certain abilities. In the case of most such physical-condition or -fitness tests, it leads to overemphasis upon development of certain aspects of strength and endurance and general overemphasis upon the physical objectives of physical education with resultant underemphasis upon sport and recreational skills and social objectives.

The teacher should not, however, reject tests because they cause overemphasis when improperly interpreted. Rather, he should use tests as an aid to achieving an appropriate balance in his program by interpreting them properly and helping students to do the same. It seems undeniably true that school physical education in the United States has tended to overemphasize physical objectives during war periods and to overemphasize recreational and social objectives during times of peace and comparatively easy living. Widespread use of physical-fitness (motor-fitness) tests during the World War II period probably contributed to overemphasis upon the physical. But use of them in the period since, partially spurred by national attention to fitness encouraged both by professional and by lay persons including several of our Presidents, has had a salutory effect on physical education programs. It has served to help programs achieve balance by maintaining interest in and attention to standards of condition, thus avoiding underemphasis upon important objectives in the area of physical development.

Teacher-made or locally constructed tests can be made to measure or appraise objectives which it is desired to appraise in the local situation. They can be made to fit the groups involved and the ends sought. There is less likelihood of improper interpretation of locally constructed tests, particularly so if students have a part in selecting and making them, because there is assurance that they will be designed to meet a felt need rather than be selected because they are readily available and because the teacher feels that there should be some testing in the program, as may be the case with standardized tests.

Tests made to fit the situation may fit better into evaluation as an inherent part of the teaching-learning process and as a continuous process than will standardized tests. It is not possible to compare the performance of local students with that of those in other areas when only local teacher-made tests are used. Another probable disadvantage is that the instruments are likely to be less adequately prepared from the standpoints of refinement in objectivity, reliability, and validity. Preparation of them requires teacher time and energy. However, they may be easier to administer as well as more meaningful because they are made to serve the particular program involved.

QUALITATIVE EVALUATIVE PROCEDURES—JUDGMENT TECHNIQUES

Qualitative evaluative procedures include such techniques as observation, ratings, logs, interviews, case histories (which may also include quantitative data), anecdotal records, checklists, self-appraisals, general surveys, inventories, and diaries through which observations are made or subjective data recorded. Whereas measurement records its findings in numerical form, the qualitative evaluative procedures report findings in verbal descriptions. The following description of observation and interview as basic techniques illustrates the importance and use of the many variations in this category.

Observation Observation is an important and much used method of evaluation in everyday teaching. It may be incidental, systematic, or directed. All teachers engage in incidental observation. It may range from a meager and biased observation of the unusual to a piercing study of an individual's behavior. The anecdotal record, which records the observation of a specific behavior or an episode, represents a technique which tends to give objectivity and exactness to incidental observation. Use of it is likely to cause the teacher to observe more closely as well as to improve memory, provide written records which may be reviewed, and improve inferences from and interpretation of observed behavior.

Using incidental observation the teacher observes behavior which seems significant wherever and whenever it happens to occur. Using systematic observation, the teacher selects types of behavior and (or) types of situations in which he wishes to observe action. A physical education teacher might systematically observe social behavior of individual girls during a dancing unit by watching a particular girl for a five-minute period each day, another girl for another period of time, and recording the responses made. A basketball coach might systematically observe tendencies toward team or individualistic play by observing a specific player for a specific time and recording results. Coaches frequently employ scouts, spotters, or checkers to observe and chart individual and team play during a practice or game.

Directed observation predetermines the items of behavior to be observed. It frequently takes the form of a rating scale. During observation a teacher may make and record judgments concerning a number of items determined and defined prior to the observation and may record instances which support the judgment. Behavior descriptions or performance standards, prepared and defined beforehand, with gradations of degree of conformance are used to direct the observation.

Trustworthiness of observation depends upon the skill of the observer. All of us tend to form judgments concerning our friends and associates as we watch and listen. Teachers should use caution and preparation because the results of observation may be untrustworthy. There may be sampling errors which cause failure to observe in a sufficient variety of circumstances and in which causes may be overlooked. There may be observer errors in which the observer notes some behavior but fails to note others. Both types of errors can be reduced by training.

Interview As an evaluative device the interview helps the teacher to understand the whole child. It may reveal information concerning the student's knowledge, attitudes, interests, motives, drives, and background. Short of the case study, the interview probably is the most useful single device for helping the teacher understand the individual as a whole. However, its value may be great or small depending upon the ability of users. The quite common response of students when asked to see a teacher, "What's wrong now?" indicates that many teachers use the interview largely for disciplinary purposes. Such use contributes little to evaluation or to help for the student.

Young people usually are anxious to visit with understanding adults upon occasion. When rapport and confidence are established, the teacher will learn about the individual he is interviewing or visiting with, provided he refrains from overdirection of the interview. Exchange of information helps the teacher to evaluate, and it helps the student to evaluate himself. Although ambitious programs of interviewing are time-consuming, it seems evident that physical education teachers can improve their understanding of, and services to, students by developing and using interviewing abilities. Judgments made during interviews or as a result of them may be untrustworthy. They are limited by the skill of the interviewer, as the results of observation are limited by the skill of the observer. Errors reduce as skill increases.

THE RELATION OF EVALUATION TO INSTRUCTION

Since evaluation is concerned with the extent to which educational goals are achieved, evaluators must consider all parts of the educational structure—curriculum, instruction, administration, and supervision—as each affects learning. The objectives, processes, and outcomes of each area should be appraised in relationship both to their own internal structure and to the effectiveness of their interrelationships with other areas in achieving stated goals. If it were possible to appraise student growth accurately, all evaluative efforts could properly be directed to evaluating the effects of any educational procedure solely on student growth. Actually, however, we have seen that educational growth not only often evades precise evaluation but many times is sporadic and remote. This means, then, that a teacher selects and uses subject matter, methods, and administrative procedures which he believes will logically lead to desired results. He evaluates his administrative structure, curricular materials, and teaching methods rather than relying solely on inadequate appraisal of student growth.

Important as evaluation of all parts of the educational program is, in keeping with the stated scope of the text, this chapter considers evaluation primarily in relation to instruction or method.

EVALUATING TEACHING METHODS

The forgoing discussion suggests that teaching methods can be evaluated in two basic ways: (1) by directly appraising student growth resulting from exposure to a method used, and (2) by analyzing the logical or expected effects of a method used on growth which is not immediately observable or measurable. In preliminary instructional planning, on the basis of all known facts about the nature of the educational goals, the kind of subject matter, and the status of the learner, a teacher selects methods which appear appropriate to achieving desired goals. This text has previously explained this process in relation to instructional planning. A corollary suggests that sometime during or after a learning experience, a similar analytical diagnosis of method should be made, particularly in areas where student growth is not readily observable. Insofar as evaluation of student growth proves impossible because of the remoteness and evasiveness of some educational outcomes, evaluation of method on a logical basis becomes necessary. Obviously, however, the most desirable way to appraise aptness of method remains to evaluate the effect of method on student growth.

EVALUATION AS AN ESSENTIAL PART OF TEACHING

Evaluation is inherent in the teaching-learning process. As learning progresses, evaluation proves both desirable and inevitable. Knowledge of progress provides a basic motivating force; thus teachers should help students see their progress. Evaluation brings major goal and subgoal attainments to light. It has been emphasized repeatedly that teacher and student analysis of performance comprises one of the steps in the teaching and learning of motor skills. Such analysis requires evaluative judgments and is a part of the total evaluation process. As a teacher analyzes performance, he evaluates it. His evaluation both appraises progress and indicates needs for further development. As a student, with the help of a teacher, analyzes his performance, he makes evaluative judgments which bring satisfaction or dissatisfaction and which move him toward further action or inaction. Even if they wish to do so, neither teacher nor student could avoid day-by-day evaluative judgments concerning progress. It is a function of the teacher to make such evaluation as accurate as possible and to help students make it as accurate and meaningful as possible.

CONTINUOUS VERSUS PERIODIC EVALUATION

Evaluation is actually a continuous process even though tests, examinations, and periodic formal reports by teachers usually highlight it. Since tests and reports frequently form a large part of, and sometimes the only, written record of evaluation, often a tendency exists to overemphasize their importance. This forms the basis of one source of dissatisfaction with school marking systems. It suggests a reason for the development of school record and reporting systems which attempt to evaluate growth toward *all* the objectives. This requires presenting an overall picture of the development of the individual through use of devices such as rating of trait characteristics, preparation of a paragraph or letter-style description of the student's progress, and holding teacher-student and teacher-parent conferences. Lack of confidence in school evaluation records as they reflect or fail to reflect a total picture of the ability and development of an individual is a reason why many employers seek information concerning the extracurricular and out-of-school activities of prospective employees.

Although tests, examinations, and periodic written reports do highlight evaluation, there can be no escaping the fact that continuous evaluative judgments occur during almost all teacher-student relationships. Recitations, performances, questions, and answers to them are judged; every behavioral detail which the teacher observes produces evaluative material. Teacher suggestions are based upon aspects of evaluation. Teacher-student conversation can hardly avoid producing two-way evaluative judgments; and teacher-parent and teacher-teacher conferences concerning students represent forms of evaluation. This is another way of saying that continuous evaluation is an integral part of teaching-learning experiences: students evaluate as they learn, teachers evaluate as they teach, and the day-by-day teacher-student activities are the quintessence of the educational process.

TEACHER–STUDENT COOPERATION IN EVALUATION

Although students do evaluate themselves and can improve their self-rating abilities through practice and training, they cannot evaluate themselves without teacher help any more than they can direct and guide their learning without teacher help. As an integral part of the whole teaching-learning process, evaluation involves continuous teacher-student cooperation. High-quality teaching strives to help students accept expanding amounts of responsibility for self-direction, and evaluation is a part of self-direction.

The extent to which students can accept responsibility for evaluation of themselves depends upon their abilities, which in turn depend to a large extent upon opportunities for practice provided by the whole school and by individual teachers. It also, of course, depends upon concept of evaluation. If it erroneously is considered as synonymous with marking, the advantages of student participation are at a minimum; when evaluation is broadly and realistically viewed with emphasis upon its diagnostic and directive functions, the value of student involvement increases as the student grows in the ability to direct himself. The section on procedures for using evaluative tools (page 414) gives several examples of how students can be used in giving and scoring tests. Of major importance, of course, is the role of student self-evaluation in learning.

SELF–EVALUATION BY STUDENTS

Perhaps the most important function of student participation in evaluation is the development of ability in self-evaluation. In a very real sense final evaluation of physical education rests upon the extent to which it becomes a meaningful part of adult living of former students. Self-evaluation is basic to the use of physical education activities and concepts by adults. Student practice in self-evaluation increases the chances that physical education may become a part of one's balanced living over a long period of years.

Students do engage in self-evaluation whether or not teachers encourage and consciously help them to do so. When summarized results of teacher evaluation appear on reports to students and parents, it is customary for many students to express feelings of agreement or disagreement; this is evidence of self-evaluation. Coaches know that not all players agree with their evaluation of playing ability as is reflected by the selection of players for various positions on a team.

The ability of students to evaluate themselves realistically depends upon their guided experiences in self-evaluation and upon their understanding of the objectives which are to be evaluated. When teachers do not permit students to share in approved evaluative procedures and do not help them to determine sound bases for making judgments concerning themselves, students may be expected to evaluate themselves less accurately than when they have practice and understanding which clarifies their thinking. Not all people will rate themselves realistically. Some, lacking confidence, will rate themselves too low; others, not recognizing some of their limitations, will rate themselves too high. However, a majority of students can be taught to evaluate themselves fairly realistically.

Teachers can help students to rate themselves by encouraging them to do so, by helping them to see themselves as others see them, and by helping them to analyze bases upon which judgments should be made. Procedures which tend to accomplish these ends include class discussion which clarifies group goals; discussion between teacher and individual student which helps to identify individual goals; tests; checklists; rating scales; and questionnaires.

With considerable frequency writers have presented arguments favoring the encouragement of self-evaluation by students. When evaluation is conceived as an integral part of the teaching-learning process and when responsibility for learning is placed upon the shoulders of the student, an element of self-evaluation necessarily must exist. The student is a part of the appraisal process just as he is a part of other aspects of the learning situation. Teacher encouragement and guidance of self-evaluation are believed to help the student to better understand himself and direct his efforts, to become more purposefully involved in the work, and to develop initiative and responsibility. In order to achieve self-direction there must be an element of self-evaluation.

THE IMPORTANCE OF FEEDBACK TO STUDENTS

Since a student must know what he is doing in order to learn and often knows better than anyone else what he actually tries to do, he should participate in determining the extent to which he reaches desired ends; in the case of a teacher-administered test, he should be advised of his achievement so test results will be an integral part of the teaching-learning process.

Knowledge of success serves as motivation for the further pursuit of goals. Knowledge that a desired goal has not been reached can serve to redirect learning efforts. The principle of *immediate feedback,* that is, letting the student know at once if he has achieved the goal, is inherent in the concept of programmed learning. It is a principle that should be applied whenever possible to other types of teaching methods.

EVALUATION AND GUIDANCE

Evaluation is basic to guidance. Schools and teachers serve their purpose of helping students achieve toward the upper limits of their potentialities as they secure information about individual students and use it in their work with them. All information about an individual provides material for the continual evaluation process. Whether one conceives of guidance as the whole teaching process of guiding young people toward achievement of *all* the objectives of education or as a specialized function of helping students with their problems, the conclusion is inescapable that information about individuals forms a necessary base for guidance. Basically evaluation consists of securing information about students and validly interpreting it in order to teach or counsel the individual student according to his needs.

PROCEDURES FOR USING EVALUATIVE TOOLS IN TEACHING

Appropriate class organization and other procedures for using evaluative tools depend, of course, upon the amount and kinds of appraisal contemplated. General practice in regard to time spent on evaluation varies from no formal class time in some programs to overemphasis in others, resulting in devotion of as much as 25 percent of the total time available for physical education. Neither of these extremes seems desirable. It has been suggested that not more than 10 percent of the instructional time be used for appraising the results of teaching. An adept use of appraisal tools helps to save time.

PHYSICAL-PERFORMANCE TESTS

Three general methods are suggested for administering tests: (1) partner method, (2) student-leader and squad-organization methods, and (3) teacher administration to individual students. The partner method is economical of time. It is recommended for use in tests such as push-ups, sit-ups, squat-thrusts, and stunt-type tests. Class members are paired, usually by counting off, and one of the pair serves as judge, counter, and recorder while the other performs the test. At a given signal, one-half of the class members start performing a test while the other half judge and count. When all performers have completed the test and scores have been noted, the class members exchange responsibilities, and those who took the test become judges, counters, and recorders while those who served as judges become performers of the test.

Economy of time through use of the partner or pair method is shown by the fact that as many as 50 students may be tested in several activities in a thirty-minute period. An objection to this method is that there may be inaccuracies when all class members serve as judges, counters, and recorders. Whether or not this objection is valid in specific cases depends upon rapport between teacher and students and upon whether or not students wholeheartedly accept the tests as worthwhile. Experience has shown that accuracy is sufficient for most purposes when teachers have presented the program well, when clear standardized directions have been given, and when practice has been provided prior to testing for the record. In cases where unfailing accuracy is important, such as in the creation of data for basic research, only well-trained individuals should participate in the administration of tests.

Student-leader and squad-organization methods are effective for tests such as jumps, runs, and throws. Four or five test activities may be in progress simultaneously. One group may be taking a high-jump test, another group a broad-jump test, another a 100-yard-dash test, another a weight-throwing test, and another an accuracy-throwing test. Student leaders manage, judge, and record while the teacher oversees the progress of all groups. Groups move from one station to another in predetermined sequence after they have completed a test.

Teacher administration of tests to individual students is likely to produce greater accuracy of results than does either of the other two methods. Although this method is appropriate for clinical and research-laboratory testing, wide use of it is impractical in most school situations because of the time required. In most testing programs individual administration by teachers finds its most useful application in rechecks of questionable cases and in makeups for students who may have been absent or incapacitated at the time of group tests.

Record forms for performance tests Individual record cards should be used for filing data which is to be kept for a period of years. Because of probable mutilation, it is not wise to distribute permanent cards among students for use during testing. Rather, temporary records which may be transferred later to permanent forms should be employed. Temporary records may be written on individual cards or on group cards or sheets. Although some teachers prefer individual cards, most experienced persons find the group method more convenient. Names of students to be tested are listed with spaces provided for the scores of the various tests. Scores are recorded either by the teacher or by dependable student leaders. If recording is done by the teacher, he may call roll after the completion of one, two, or three tests and record scores as students respond to the calling of their name by giving their score or scores. It has been found that secondary school students respond accurately with as many as three scores. Thus, a teacher may record three test scores with one calling of the roll.

WRITTEN TESTS, RATING SCALES, CHECKLISTS

Procedures which require writing by students present difficulties. The best physical education plants provide a room that is convenient for the projection of pictures, for lectures and discussions, and for writing. However, since convenient availability of such rooms is not common, the teacher who uses instruments requiring students to write during a class period must make arrangements that permit writing in gymnasiums or playgrounds. Two questions arise: Should procedures requiring all students to write during class periods be used in physical education classes? If writing is to be done, what arrangements should be made?

It surely is true that the essence of physical education is physical activity. Yet knowledge and understanding are important, and written tests may serve to stimulate learning as well as to measure both the quantity and the quality of learning and the effectiveness of teaching. Some teachers feel that such stimulation of learning is not necessary and that adequate evaluation of both learning and teaching can take place through observation and discussion during the ongoing process of learning and teaching. Others believe that written knowledge tests motivate significantly and provide information not otherwise available. Each teacher must answer the question in the light of his own situation. One factor to be considered is the amount of time available. If ninety minutes a day, five days a week is allotted, there is more reason to take time for writing than is the case if there are only two or three 45-minute periods per week. The availability of convenient facilities for writing is another factor.

So far as is feasible, writing in connection with physical education should be done outside of class periods. Rating scales, checklists, workbooks, and programmed learning materials can be distributed for return at a later time. Outside assignments designed to promote study and measure learning may deal with such matters as rules, techniques, health, and physical fitness.

If tests or other instruments requiring writing are to be used in gymnasiums or on playgrounds, the amount of writing necessary should be held to a minimum, and supplies should be as easy to handle as possible. Essay-type tests seem out of order. Short tests requiring only checking or short completion answers which students can make while in sitting or prone positions on a floor or on the ground may be worthwhile. Because supplies such as pencils and paper brought to a gymnasium or playground by students prove to be a nuisance, these things should be distributed from central storage places. Short pencils, such as used for golf, and heavy paper or cards are appropriate.

Any rating of form, whether done by teacher or student, should always be done as the performance takes place or immediately after. If swimming form is to be rated, the rating should be given as the swimmer performs; diving should be rated immediately after the dive. A teacher who attempts to remember how well each student performs may retain a good generalized opinion, but more likely he will lose sight of specific strengths and weaknesses and be influenced by outside factors, even conduct and behavior. The effectiveness of ratings and observations rests upon a close analysis of individual items, then consideration of the whole problem. For example, in evaluating a student's progress in beginning swimming, a teacher should rate separately on form on each basic stroke, attitudes toward the water, adherence to pool safety regulations, and any other factors pertinent to the course of instruction. Such an analysis gives a better indication of where strengths and weaknesses lie. A student with excellent basic skills may need special guidance relative to his overestimation of his prowess, which has accompanying elements of danger to himself. Another student with equal skill may be overly timid and need assistance in developing greater confidence. A single overall rating of a student's entire classwork, made hastily and in retrospect at marking time, may result in an unreliable judgment.

Teachers should make use of checklists, rating scales, and other evaluative procedures which are an integral part of the teaching method. The use of achievement progressions represents one example of such a technique. In swimming the skills to be taught and practiced can be listed on a full-sized bulletin board with a simplified class record form available to either teacher or student. As each skill is mastered, the student is checked off and in some cases may be given a score or rating on the skill. This system precludes using a period solely for checking progress. Similar checking techniques can be used in such activities as tumbling, stunts, and dance where activity is based upon a progression or series of skills.

Many activities in physical education are of a self-testing nature.

Bowling, archery, golf, and some of the track and field events are typical examples. In these activities students can keep daily or regular practice-period records of their own progress, rather than having their progress judged solely on one performance during a testing period. In using this system, care must be exercised that sufficient attention is given to form and that students do not direct their sole energies to considering scores, particularly in beginning classes.

INTERPRETING ACHIEVEMENT—RELATIVE VERSUS ABSOLUTE STANDARDS

Should evaluation indicate the extent to which an individual achieves in relation to a group, a standard, or a norm, or should it represent the extent to which he achieves ends which are valuable to him without regard to his standing in comparison with others or with a fixed standard? Should it be relative to individual capacity or relative to standards expected of all? If one accepts the concept that objectives should be individualized, and one must if the student is to be accepted as he is and helped to develop at his own rate, then evaluation must have an individualized aspect in order to serve its purpose of appraising progress toward objectives. But total individualization is neither possible nor desirable. Individuals should understand their abilities and capacities in relation to others in society as well as their progress in relation to their own capacities.

Evaluation in physical education, based entirely upon fixed standards, overlooks the individual. On the other hand, evaluation which does not portray status in relation to others may overlook reality and cause young people to direct their energies into unrewarding channels. Evaluation in baseball, for instance, should give considerable indication concerning the advisability of an attempt to pursue a career in professional baseball by helping the student to see his abilities in relation to those of others. But it also should be individualized. Experience in baseball may help even the student of little playing aptitude to enjoy playing the game with and against others of similar ability and to experience concomitant developmental exercise as well as social, emotional, and ethical development. Realistic evaluation in baseball calls upon comparison with standards of skilled performance to guide those of mediocre aptitude away from setting goals of varsity team membership or professional pursuit. It also individualizes evaluation as it helps students of mediocre ability to see that they might enjoy recreational play with concomitants of healthful exercise, friendship, and release of tensions.

Using fixed standards, such as ability to make thirty hits in 100 turns at bat, as a yardstick, the physical education teacher and (or) student might evaluate ability to play baseball at a high level of skill as unsatisfactory for a given boy. Using individualized evaluation, however, the same boy might be rated lightly in a baseball unit with regard to other important objectives of physical education.

Another illustration of evaluation in terms of individualized objectives is found in running speed. One boy may be able to run 100 yards in 10.5 seconds. Another, because of innate-capacity limitation, may never be able to run 100 yards in less than 12 seconds regardless of effort and instruction. How should each be evaluated? The answer, of course, is in terms of objectives. If the sole objective were to run 100 yards in 11.5 seconds or less, one of the boys obviously would satisfy the objective easily, whereas the other never would be able to attain it. But the boy who runs slowly might, while engaging in running, satisfy an objective of development of strength and endurance to a greater extent than might the one whose innate capacities permit him to run fast. Again, the slow runner might satisfy an objective of emotional adjustment through self-satisfaction by lowering his time from 13 to 12.5 seconds to a greater extent than would the fast runner by lowering his time from 10.5 to 10.4 seconds.

School practices in evaluation give attention to individualization of objectives and their evaluation. Evidence is found in increasing tendencies among teachers to use evaluation as a basis for guidance. It also is found in the growth of schemes of reports to parents which attempt to evaluate progress other than achievement in subject matter.

When progress in physical education is evaluated almost wholly in terms of strength, endurance, and ability to perform physical feats according to some predetermined standard, student emphasis is quite different from when social, emotional, ethical, and life-balancing objectives are given a prominent place in evaluation. Evaluation practices tend to direct student energies, to motivate. A physical education teacher who evaluates very largely upon bases of physical development directs attention and effort of students to objectives in that area. There may be overemphasis with concomitant slighting of social, emotional, ethical, and life-balancing ends. On the other hand, a teacher who directs almost all evaluation toward objectives which emphasize social ends may cause students to slight important objectives in physical development.

Since teacher evaluation or student evaluation guided by a teacher tends to set the stage for relative emphasis, it is important that the evaluating procedures give attention to all the desired objectives. Excessive use of any one particular type of evaluation medium lessens desirable balance in a physical education program.

RECORDING AND USING THE FINDINGS OF EVALUATION

Evaluation serves its best purposes when data collected are properly recorded and made available for use. A good system of record keeping enhances the effectiveness of interpretation and use of the findings of evaluation. The physical education teacher retains some of the information he collects about students for his own use in working with them and reports some of it to other officers or persons. A teacher, of course, must conform to the system of records and reports used in the school which employs him. However, record and reporting practices change as experience indicates need, and physical education teachers have many opportunities to suggest improvements as they see better ways of recording and reporting student progress.

TYPES OF SCHOOL RECORDS

The teacher's school register or class book, additional records kept by the teacher, the principal's office record, the student's cumulative record, and records concerning students who need special attention constitute major types of records with which the teacher deals.

Cumulative records, which present a picture of the growth and development of a student over a period of years, are essential to understanding and guiding individual students. The cumulative record almost always contains information about the student's age, sex, parents or guardians, scholastic aptitude, scholastic achievement, attendance and withdrawal, and the results of psychological examinations, if any, and (or) conferences with guidance personnel. It usually records information about health and physical conditions, various tests taken, extraclass activities, vocational experiences, vocational and educational aspirations, and ratings on various characteristics or traits. There is a great deal of difference among school records, however, in both the type and the amount of information about students.

Such records serve the functions of providing information for reports to students and parents; providing information to help school personnel better understand and guide the individual student; and providing transferable information which may be used by other individuals or school systems. They stimulate teachers to see the child as an individual, to consider the quality of his own teaching, and to view education as a long-range plan in terms of the life of an individual student.

REPORTS TO STUDENTS AND PARENTS

The customary reports at six- or nine-week intervals may not be necessary for students. When cooperative teacher-student evaluation operates realistically and fully, the student knows where he stands throughout the school year. He does not need to wait for periodic formal reports to learn the results of his teacher's evaluation of him. However, few schools have arrived at such a point. In almost all cases periodic reports by teachers serve as a basis for the student to take stock of himself to redirect his energies as he interprets the report.

Parents, in general, are interested in the progress of their children, and they have a right to know the results of the school's evaluations. Good reports provide not only summaries of scholarship and attendance but also pertinent information regarding school and social adjustment, physical and mental health, strengths and weaknesses, and the extent to which the student is working up to his capacity.

Although reports to parents most frequently take the form of report cards, some schools, and their number seems to be increasing, employ letters written by the teacher and (or) student and personal interviews. In some schools forms prepared by each teacher or department, rather than standard forms for the whole school, are in use. Also, report cards frequently include descriptions of reasons for the marks given. These descriptions sometimes take the form of checking listed items or statements; sometimes they are phrase-, sentence-, or paragraph-style descriptions written by the teacher.

REPORTS CONCERNING STUDENTS WHO NEED SPECIAL ATTENTION

Some schools call, at specified intervals, for reports about students who teachers believe are in need of special attention. Some require reports on students who are failing to meet subject matter standards. Usually these reports go to the adviser of the student concerned. Sometimes parents receive them. They are diagnostic and remedial in nature, designed for the purpose of locating students who need help early enough so that help may be given when it is most likely to produce results.

Whether or not school administrations require special reports on students who need help, teachers should make such reports when there is good reason to believe they will serve useful purposes. Elementary school physical education teachers frequently help children to adjust better by reporting significant behavior or incidents observed in playgrounds, gymnasiums, and playrooms to classroom teachers. Such reports help the classroom teacher understand and guide the child. Secondary school physical education teachers may help troubled students to get on the right track by reporting to other teachers who work with the individual involved, to advisers, or to guidance specialists. Better than a one-way written report, however, is discussion between two or more staff members who have occasion to work with a student who is having serious difficulty, followed by a general staffing arranged by the guidance service. Discussions or conferences lead to clarification and interpretation of facts and opinions, to mutual understandings, and to the mapping of plans for remedial action.

SUMMARY

The term evaluation applies to the appraisal of the extent to which educational objectives are achieved. Adequate evaluation implies attention to all objectives of an educational program and includes use of both quantitative and qualitative appraisal devices. Measurement refers to objective procedures whose findings are reported in numerical form. Since sufficient measurement tools are not yet available to appraise all outcomes of education programs, reliance must be placed on qualitative-judgment procedures such as observation and simple ratings, interviews, and other similar techniques.

Evaluation is inherent in the teaching-learning process. As learning progresses, both teachers and students must make judgments concerning the degree and direction of progress. In addition, knowledge of progress provides a basic motivating force by bringing major goal and subgoal attainments to light and giving understanding of success levels. Evaluation, while necessarily a continuous process, may also be done periodically. Tests, examinations, and others periodic formal reports by teachers highlight evaluation.

Teaching methods can be evaluated directly by appraising student progress and indirectly by analyzing the logical or expected effects of a given method on student growth. The latter kind of evaluation is essential because very often this growth is not immediately measurable or observable and, in addition, many aspects of it evade precise evaluation.

Tests and other evaluative devices can be used as teaching aids or materials apart from their use to appraise growth.

Individuals should understand their abilities and capacities in relation to others as well as their progress in relation to their own capacities, but in physical education, evaluation based entirely on fixed normative standards overlooks important individual needs.

Extensive efforts in collecting evaluative data serve little purpose unless findings are used to improve instruction. Proper recording practices are essential to best use of data. Records form a basis for understanding individuals, furnish transferable information for use by others, provide information for reports to the home, and stimulate teachers to evaluate their own methods and objectives.

While periodic reports to parents prove useful and essential continuous day-by-day evaluation is the core of good teaching. Students must evaluate as they learn; teachers must evaluate as they teach; and these day-by-day teacher-student activities are the quintessence of the educational process.

Questions and problems for discussion

1. Formulate a list of evaluative criteria for appraising a teacher's aptness with selection and use of methods.

2. Reread the discussion of the directed-study method (pages 128–129). Devise a list of study questions and two open-book examinations for study and

completion outside of class. Base them on any physical education–activity unit, such as basketball or dance.

3. Discuss the merits of relative- as contrasted with absolute-marking systems. What kinds of reporting systems enhance the value of relative-marking plans?

4. Are available standardized tests in physical education more or less valid than tests in other subject matter fields? How do you account for less emphasis on testing in physical education classes than in other school subjects?

5. Prepare a series of form-diagnosis sheets for student use in self-checking for any individual or dual sport.

6. What changes in educational philosophy gave rise to the shift from emphasis on "measurement" to use of "evaluation" as the inclusive term?

7. Draw up an achievement-progression chart for basic skills for a class in either swimming or stunts and tumbling.

8. Would you be willing to pick a varsity team from a squad of boys whose abilities were unknown to you solely on the basis of results from available skill tests? Explain your answer.

9. Describe the specific provisions which should be made for evaluation in educational planning on each of the following levels: vertical plan, yearly plan, unit plan, and daily plan.

Selected references

Barrow, Harold, and Rosemary McGee: *Practical Application of Measurement to Physical Education,* Lea and Febiger, Philadelphia, 1965.

Clarke, H. Harrison: *Application of Measurement to Health and Physical Education,* 4th ed., Prentice-Hall, Inc., Englewood Cliffs, N.J., 1967.

Gronlund, Norman E.: *Measurement and Evaluation in Teaching,* The Macmillan Company, New York, 1965.

Mathews, Donald K.: *Measurement in Physical Education,* W. B. Saunders Company, Philadelphia, 1963.

Meyers, Carlton R., and T. Edwin Blesh: *Measurement in Physical Education,* The Ronald Press Company, New York, 1962.

Scott, Myrtle G., and Esther French: *Measurement and Evaluation in Physical Education,* Wm. C. Brown Company, Publishers, Dubuque, Iowa, 1959.

Smithells, Phillip A., and Peter E. Cameron: *Principles of Evaluation in Physical Education,* Harper & Row, Publishers, Incorporated, New York, 1962.

INDEX